This is the park where I often played as a child.
I took this photo on a (literal) trip down memory
lane. About once a year, I think back on the places
where I grew up and get all sentimental. I picture
the three Cortlaw children daydreaming like this...
which led to this volume's cover. Hope you like it.

— Yoshiyuki Nishi

Yoshiyuki Nishi was born in Tokyo. Two of
his favorite manga series are *Dragon Ball* and
the robot-cat comedy *Doraemon*. His latest
series, *Muhyo & Roji's Bureau of Supernatural
Investigation*, debuted in Japan's *Akamaru
Jump* magazine in 2004 and went on to be
serialized in *Weekly Shonen Jump*.

MUHYO & ROJI'S
BUREAU OF SUPERNATURAL INVESTIGATION

VOL. 14
SHONEN JUMP Manga Edition

STORY AND ART BY
YOSHIYUKI NISHI

Translation & Adaptation/Alexander O. Smith
Touch-up Art & Lettering/Brian Bilter
Design/Yukiko Whitley
Editor/Amy Yu

VP, Production/Alvin Lu
VP, Publishing Licensing/Rika Inouye
VP, Sales & Product Marketing/Gonzalo Ferreyra
VP, Creative/Linda Espinosa
Publisher/Hyoe Narita

Printed in the U.S.A.

Published by VIZ Media, LLC
P.O. Box 77010
San Francisco, CA 94107

10 9 8 7 6 5 4 3 2 1
First printing, December 2009

www.viz.com   www.shonenjump.com

SHONEN JUMP MANGA EDITION

Muhyo & Roji's Bureau of Supernatural Investigation BSI

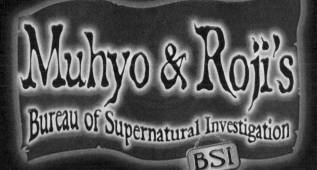

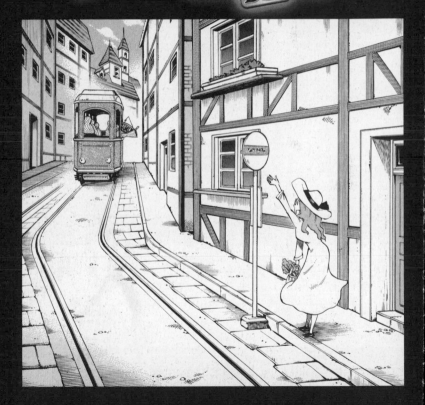

Vol. 14 Umbrella

Story & Art by **Yoshiyuki Nishi**

Dramatis Personae

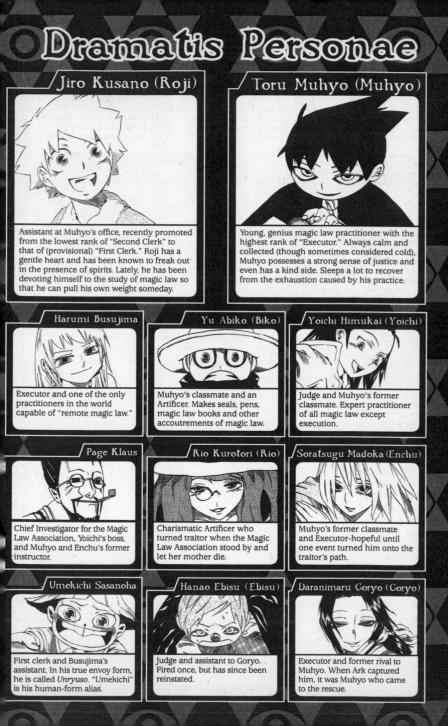

Jiro Kusano (Roji)

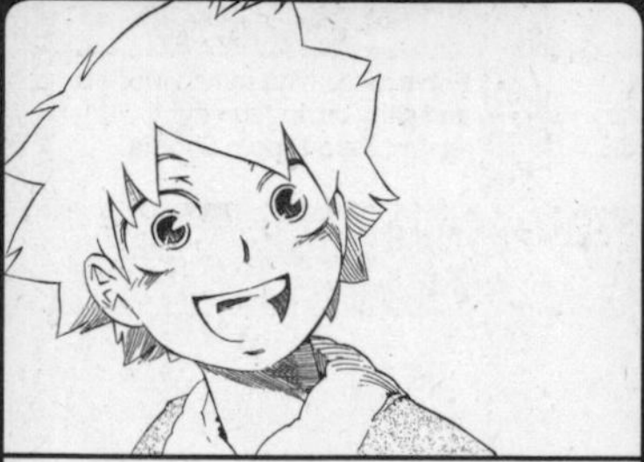

Assistant at Muhyo's office, recently promoted from the lowest rank of "Second Clerk" to that of (provisional) "First Clerk." Roji has a gentle heart and has been known to freak out in the presence of spirits. Lately, he has been devoting himself to the study of magic law so that he can pull his own weight someday.

Toru Muhyo (Muhyo)

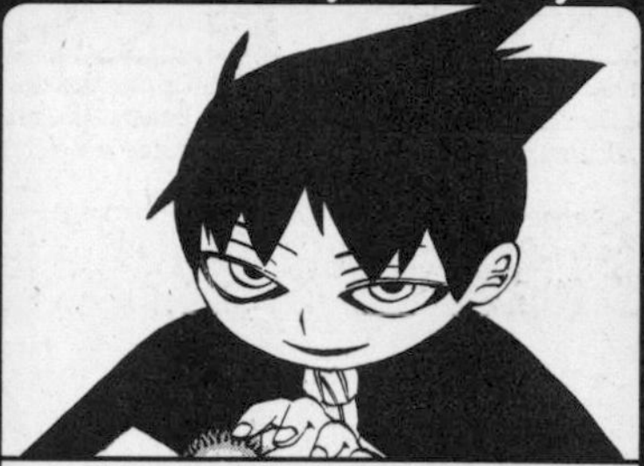

Young, genius magic law practitioner with the highest rank of "Executor." Always calm and collected (though sometimes considered cold), Muhyo possesses a strong sense of justice and even has a kind side. Sleeps a lot to recover from the exhaustion caused by his practice.

Harumi Busujima

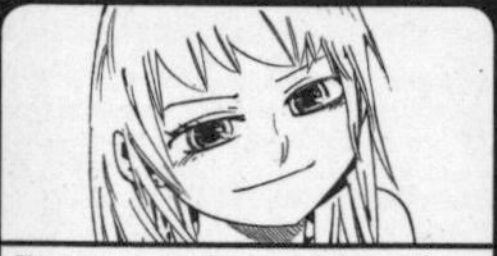

Executor and one of the only practitioners in the world capable of "remote magic law."

Yu Abiko (Biko)

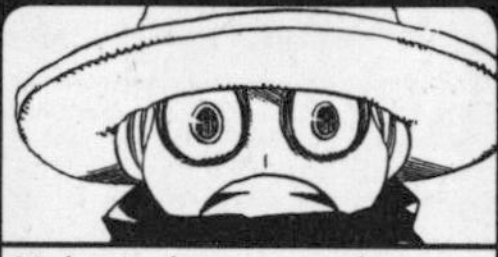

Muhyo's classmate and an Artificer. Makes seals, pens, magic law books and other accoutrements of magic law.

Yoichi Himukai (Yoichi)

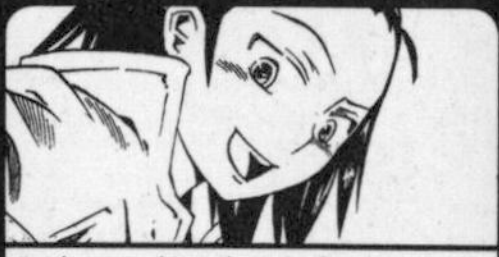

Judge and Muhyo's former classmate. Expert practitioner of all magic law except execution.

Page Klaus

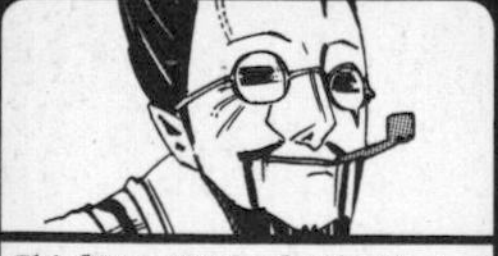

Chief Investigator for the Magic Law Association, Yoichi's boss, and Muhyo and Enchu's former instructor.

Rio Kurotori (Rio)

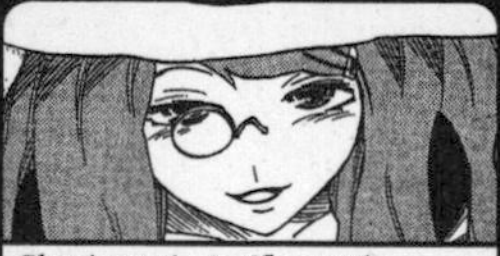

Charismatic Artificer who turned traitor when the Magic Law Association stood by and let her mother die.

Soratsugu Madoka (Enchu)

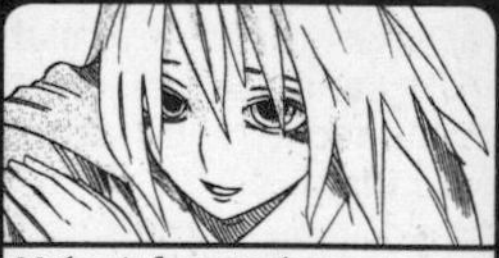

Muhyo's former classmate and Executor-hopeful until one event turned him onto the traitor's path.

Umekichi Sasanoha

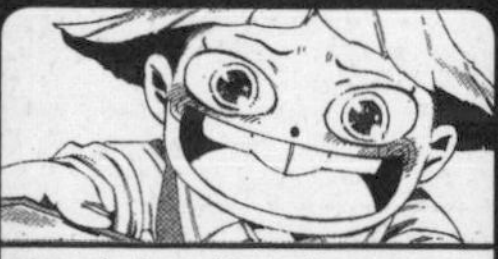

First clerk and Busujima's assistant. In his true envoy form, he is called *Unryuso*. "Umekichi" is his human-form alias.

Hanao Ebisu (Ebisu)

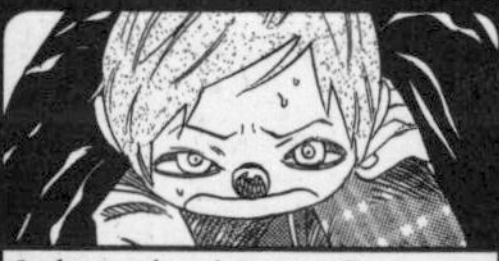

Judge and assistant to Goryo. Fired once, but has since been reinstated.

Daranimaru Goryo (Goryo)

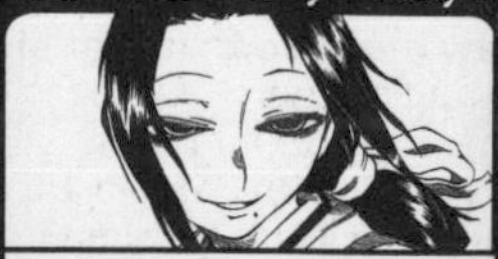

Executor and former rival to Muhyo. When Ark captured him, it was Muhyo who came to the rescue.

Seven-Faced Dog

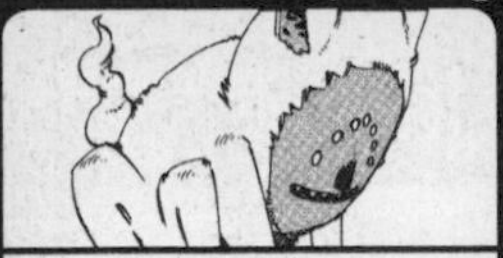

An envoy with the ability to change shape. Specialist at uncovering spectral crimes.

Ginji Sugakiya

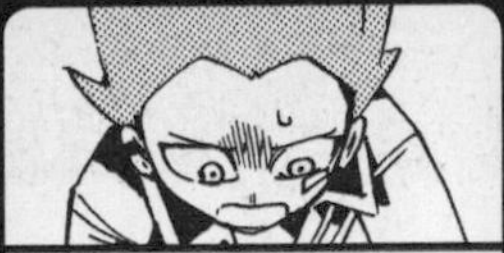

Upperclassman at M.L.S. Boasts the rank of Assistant Judge even though he is still enrolled in school.

Reiko Imai

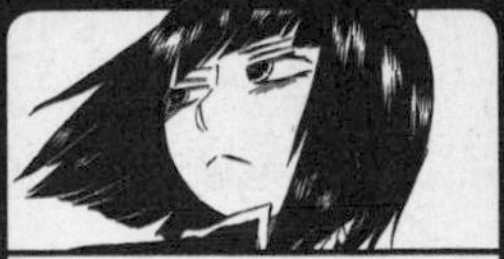

Brave Judge who joined Muhyo and gang during the fight against Face-Ripper Sophie.

Ivy Cortlaw

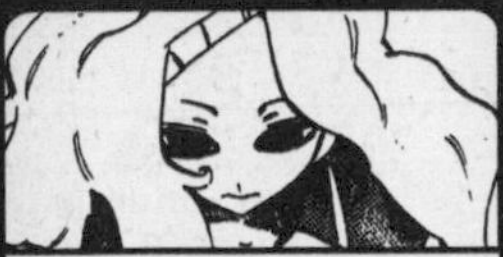

Member of the forbidden magic law group known as Ark. A powerful Ghostmaster, she has the ability to create and control ghosts.

Nana Takenouchi (Nana)

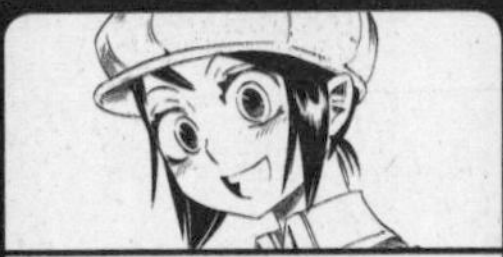

High school student, spirit medium and amateur photographer. Working as an assistant photographic investigator.

Lili & Maril Mathias

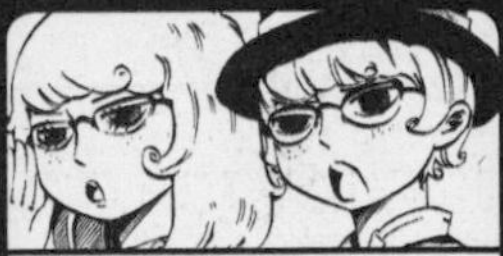

Twin siblings world-renowned for their research in magic law.

Pakero

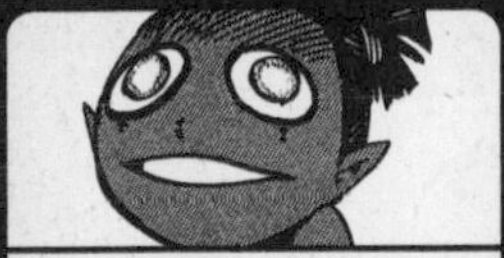

Prince of the Plutonian Sea and an envoy, summoned forth by Goryo. Seems a bit detached at times but follows through in the end.

Buhpu

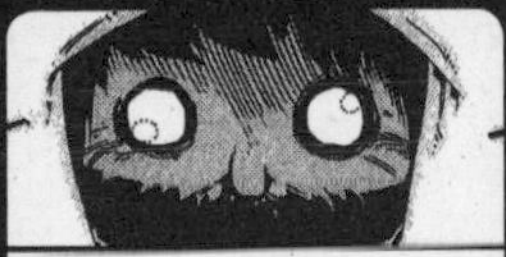

Member of Ark and Ivy's mentor.

Michael Cortlaw (Mick)

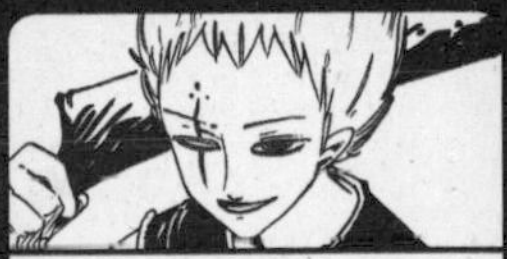

Member of Ark and Ivy's younger brother. Defeated by Busujima & Co.

The Story

Magic law is a newly established practice for judging and punishing the increasing crimes committed by spirits; those who use it are called "practitioners."
Muhyo and gang successfully deal with Gingko Hag—Ivy Cortlaw's "gift" to the M.L.S.—and obtain the Writ of Passage to the Endless Abyss. An ancient, powerful envoy lies sleeping in the abyss, but the practitioners won't be able to contact it just yet. First they have to fuse the Writ of Passage with the new Book of Magic Law that Biko made for Muhyo. While they are trying to figure out how to do that, Ivy attacks them! Goryo and Ebisu show up in the nick of time, allowing Muhyo and gang a swift retreat. Meanwhile, Goryo's envoy Pakero triumphs over Ivy's wrathwyrm Roxi, and Ivy is spent…or is she?

Teeki

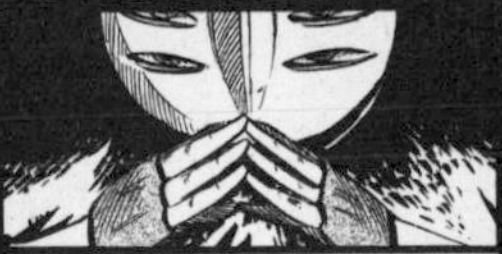

Dangerous entity marked as a traitor to the Magic Law Association for 800 years.

Kiriko

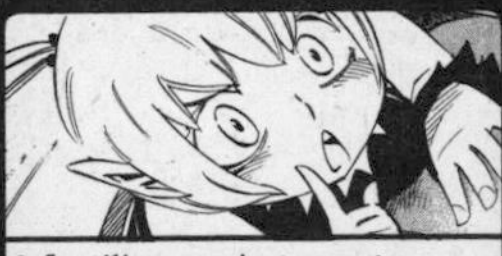

A familiar, serving as a go-between for practitioners and their envoys. Fond of Nana, whom she calls "Sis."

Muhyo & Roji's Bureau of Supernatural Investigation

BSI

CONTENTS

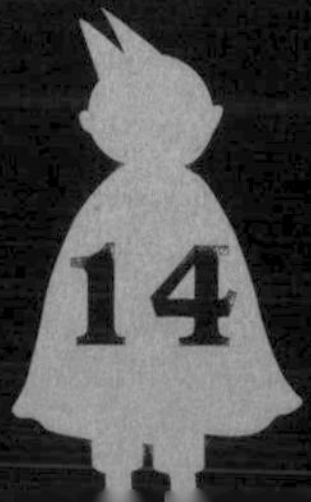

14

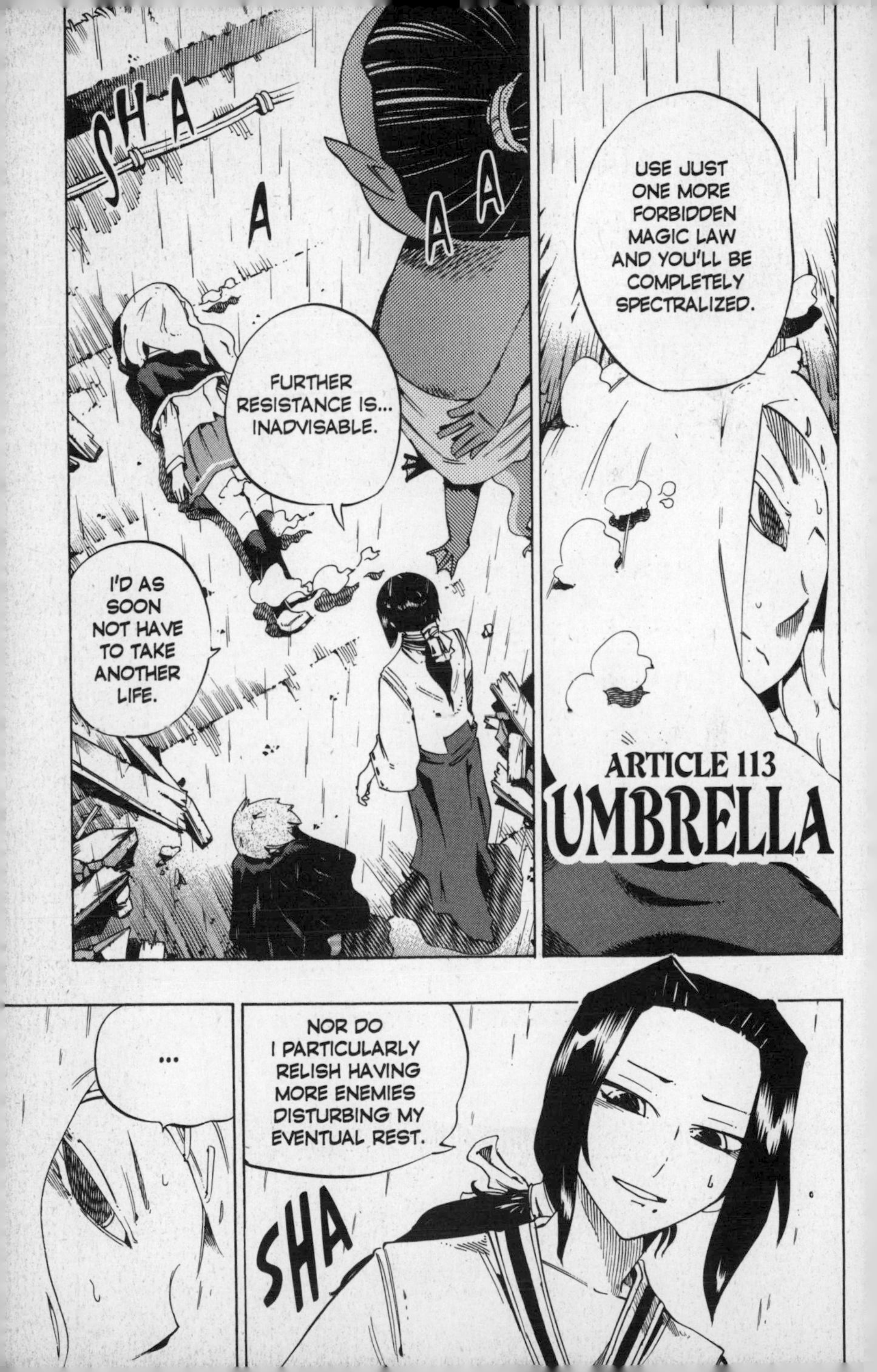
USE JUST ONE MORE FORBIDDEN MAGIC LAW AND YOU'LL BE COMPLETELY SPECTRALIZED.
ARTICLE 113
UMBRELLA
SHA
A
A A
FURTHER RESISTANCE IS... INADVISABLE.
I'D AS SOON NOT HAVE TO TAKE ANOTHER LIFE.
NOR DO I PARTICULARLY RELISH HAVING MORE ENEMIES DISTURBING MY EVENTUAL REST.
SHA
...

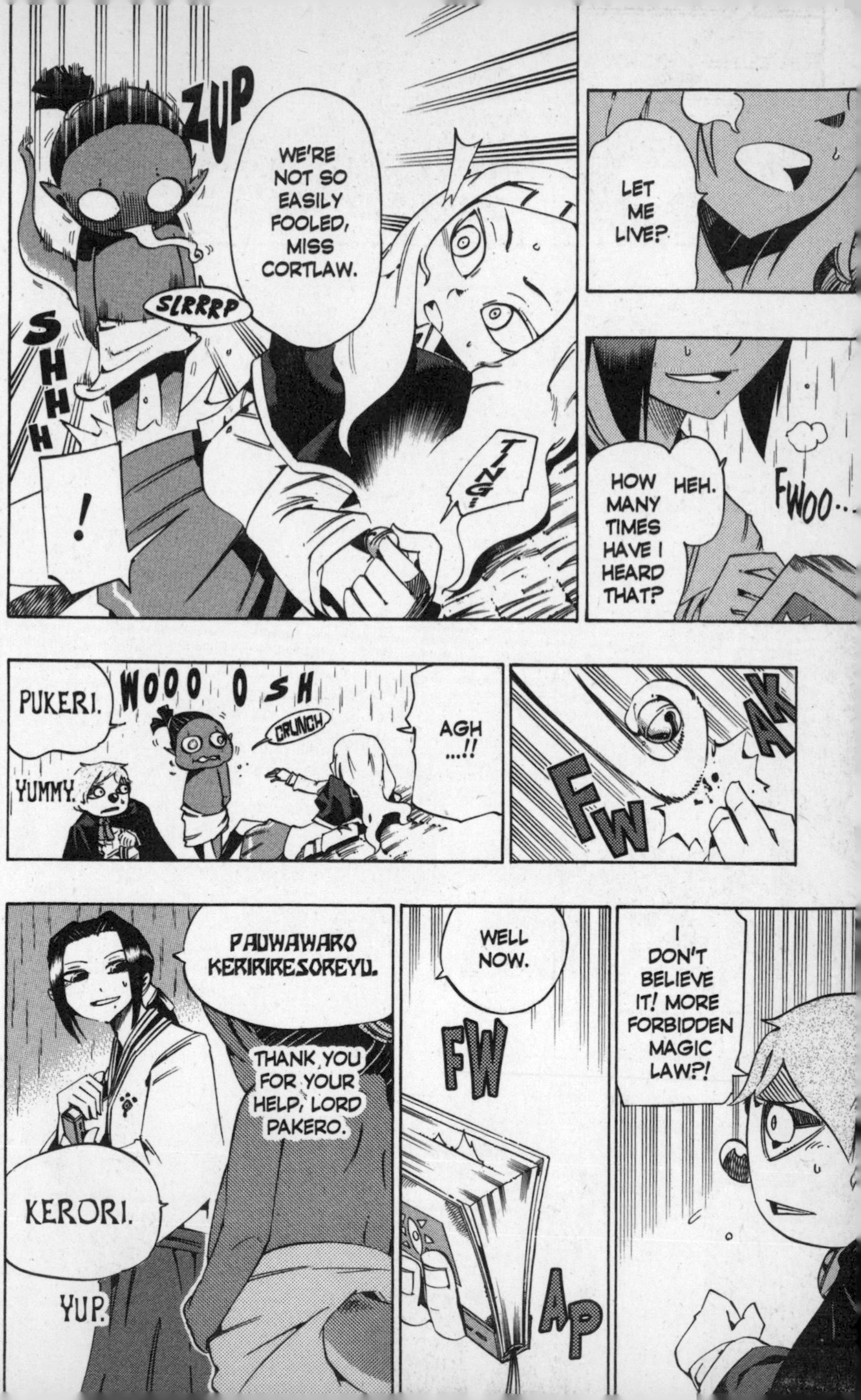
LET ME LIVE?
HEH.
HOW MANY TIMES HAVE I HEARD THAT?
FWOO...
ZUP
WE'RE NOT SO EASILY FOOLED, MISS CORTLAW.
TING!
SLRRRP
SHHHH
!
FW AK
AGH ...!!
CRUNCH
WOOOOSH
PUKERI.
YUMMY.
I DON'T BELIEVE IT! MORE FORBIDDEN MAGIC LAW?!
WELL NOW.
FWAP
PAUWAWARO KERIRIRESOREYU.
THANK YOU FOR YOUR HELP, LORD PAKERO.
KERORI.
YUP.

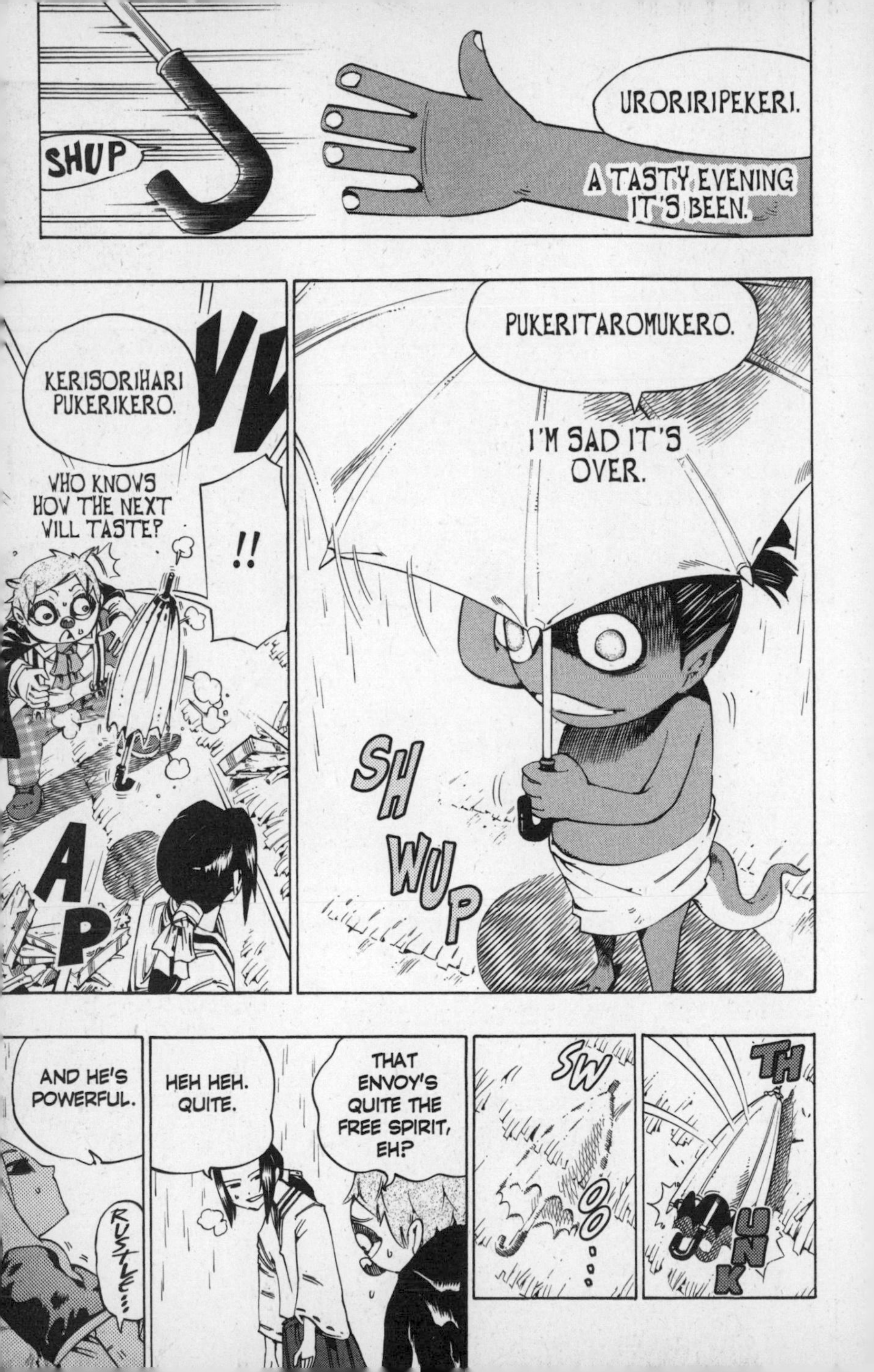
URORIRIPEKERI.
A TASTY EVENING IT'S BEEN.
SHUP
PUKERITAROMUKERO.
I'M SAD IT'S OVER.
SH WUP
KERISORIHARI PUKERIKERO.
WHO KNOWS HOW THE NEXT WILL TASTE?
!!
AP
THUNK
SWOOOO...
THAT ENVOY'S QUITE THE FREE SPIRIT, EH?
HEH HEH. QUITE.
AND HE'S POWERFUL.
RUSTLE...

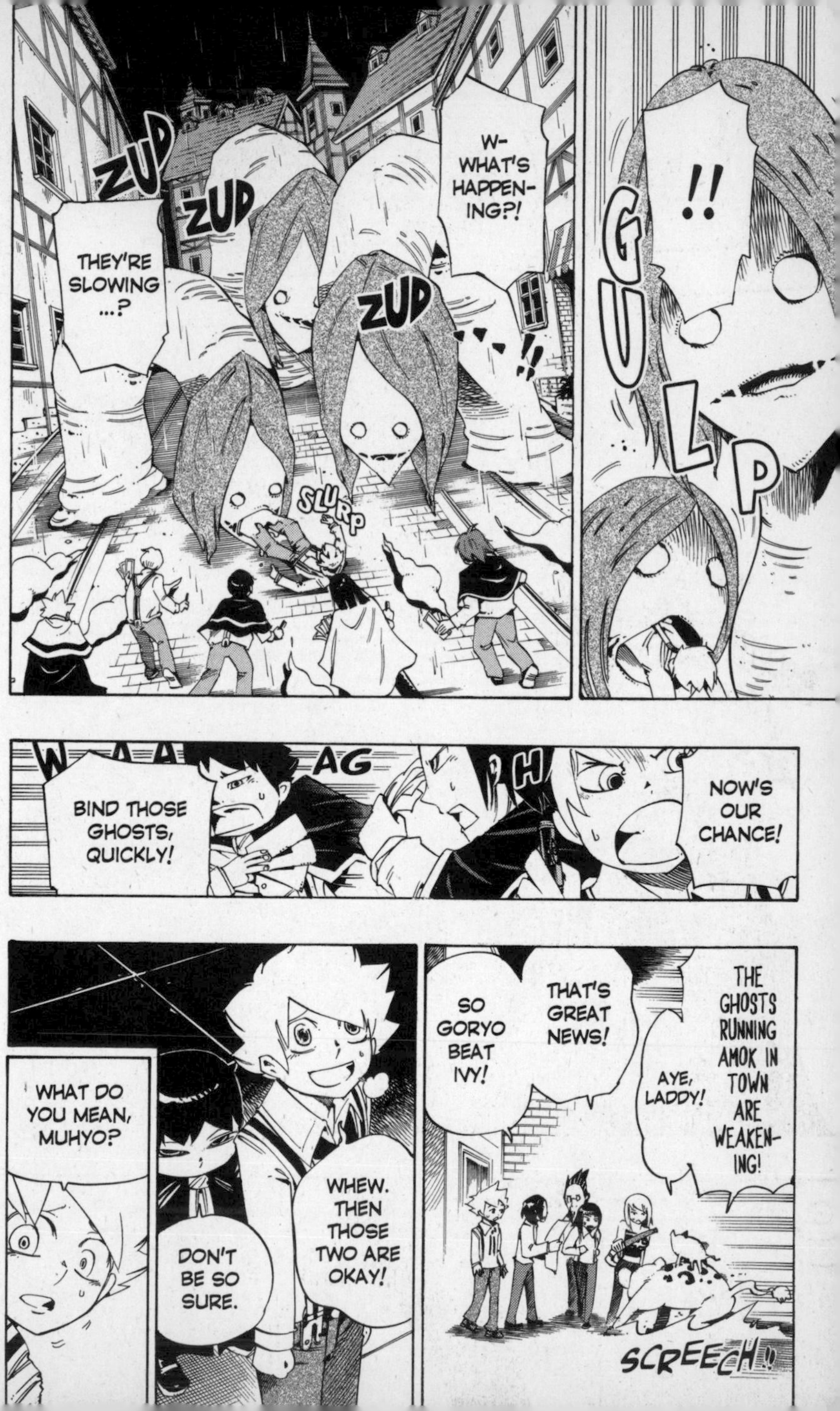
!!
GULP
W-WHAT'S HAPPENING?!
ZUD
ZUD
THEY'RE SLOWING ...?
ZUD
...!!
SLURP
NOW'S OUR CHANCE!
WAAAGH
BIND THOSE GHOSTS, QUICKLY!
THE GHOSTS RUNNING AMOK IN TOWN ARE WEAKENING!
AYE, LADDY!
THAT'S GREAT NEWS!
SO GORYO BEAT IVY!
SCREECH!!
WHEW. THEN THOSE TWO ARE OKAY!
DON'T BE SO SURE.
WHAT DO YOU MEAN, MUHYO?

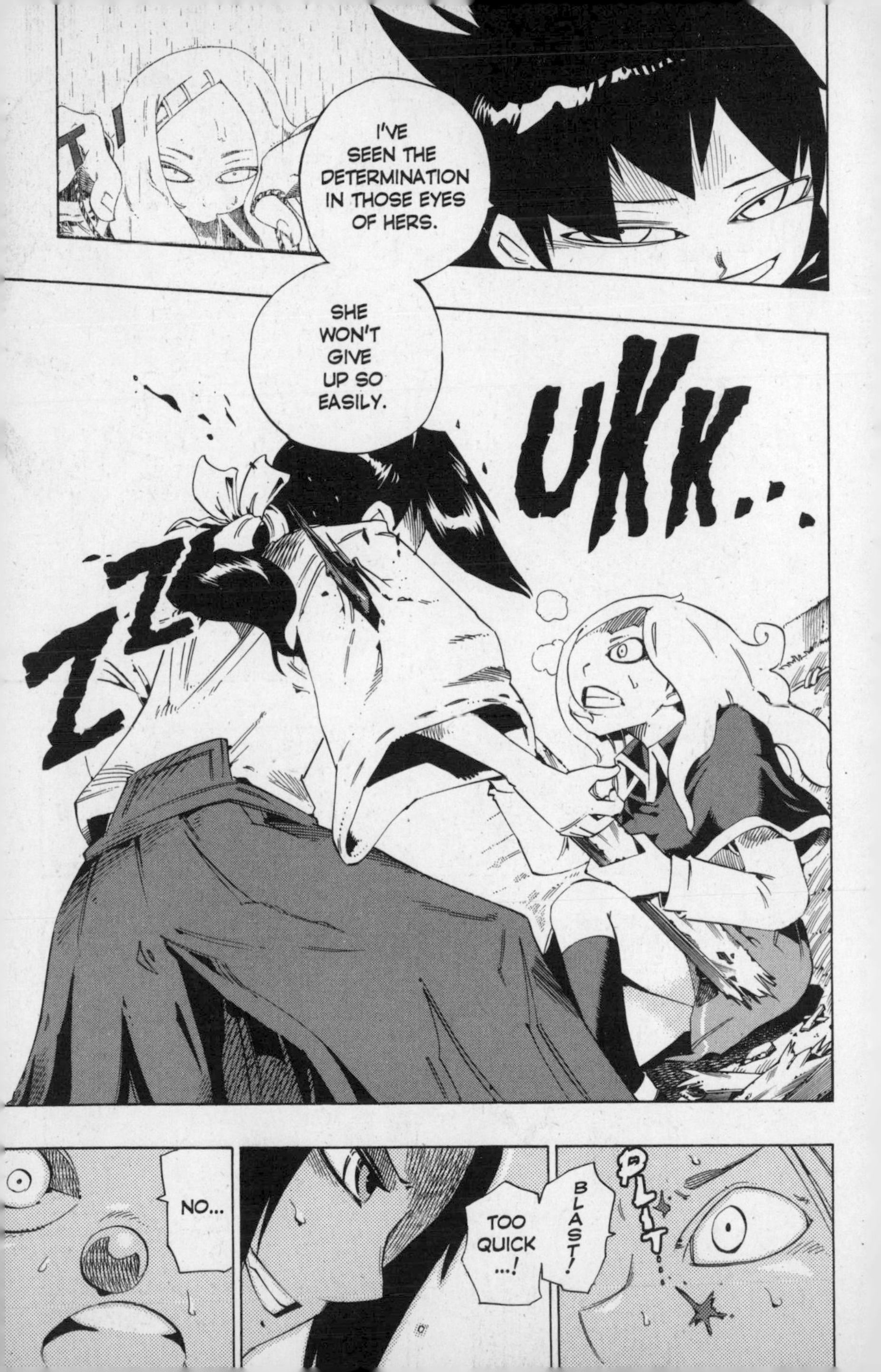
I'VE SEEN THE DETERMINATION IN THOSE EYES OF HERS.
SHE WON'T GIVE UP SO EASILY.
UKK...
ZZ
PLIT...
BLAST!
TOO QUICK ...!
NO...

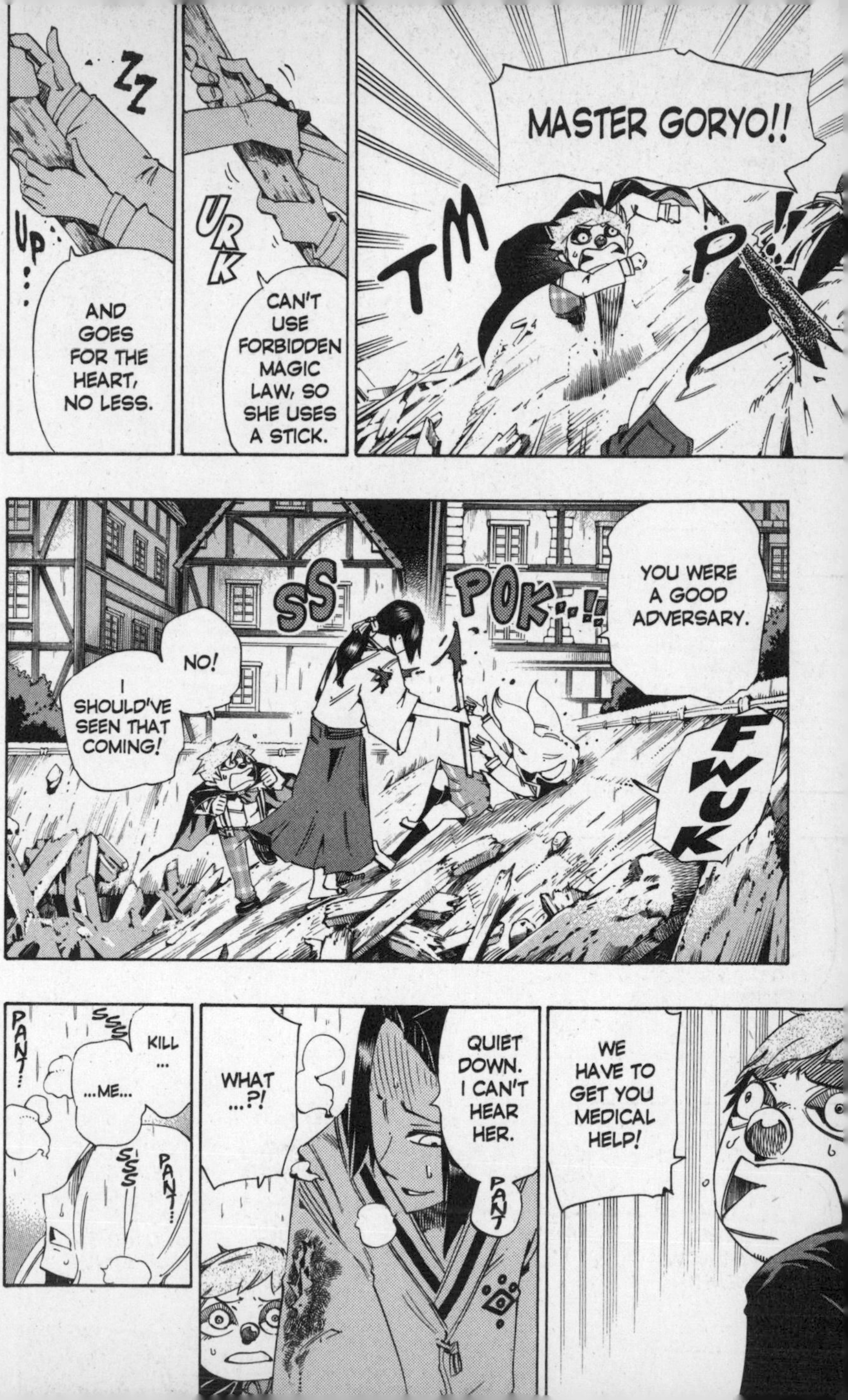
MASTER GORYO!!
TMP!!
URK
CAN'T USE FORBIDDEN MAGIC LAW, SO SHE USES A STICK.
ZZ
UP...
AND GOES FOR THE HEART, NO LESS.
YOU WERE A GOOD ADVERSARY.
FWUK
POK..!!
SS
NO!
I SHOULD'VE SEEN THAT COMING!
WE HAVE TO GET YOU MEDICAL HELP!
QUIET DOWN. I CAN'T HEAR HER.
PANT
WHAT ...?!
SSS
KILL ...
...ME...
SSS
PANT...
PANT...

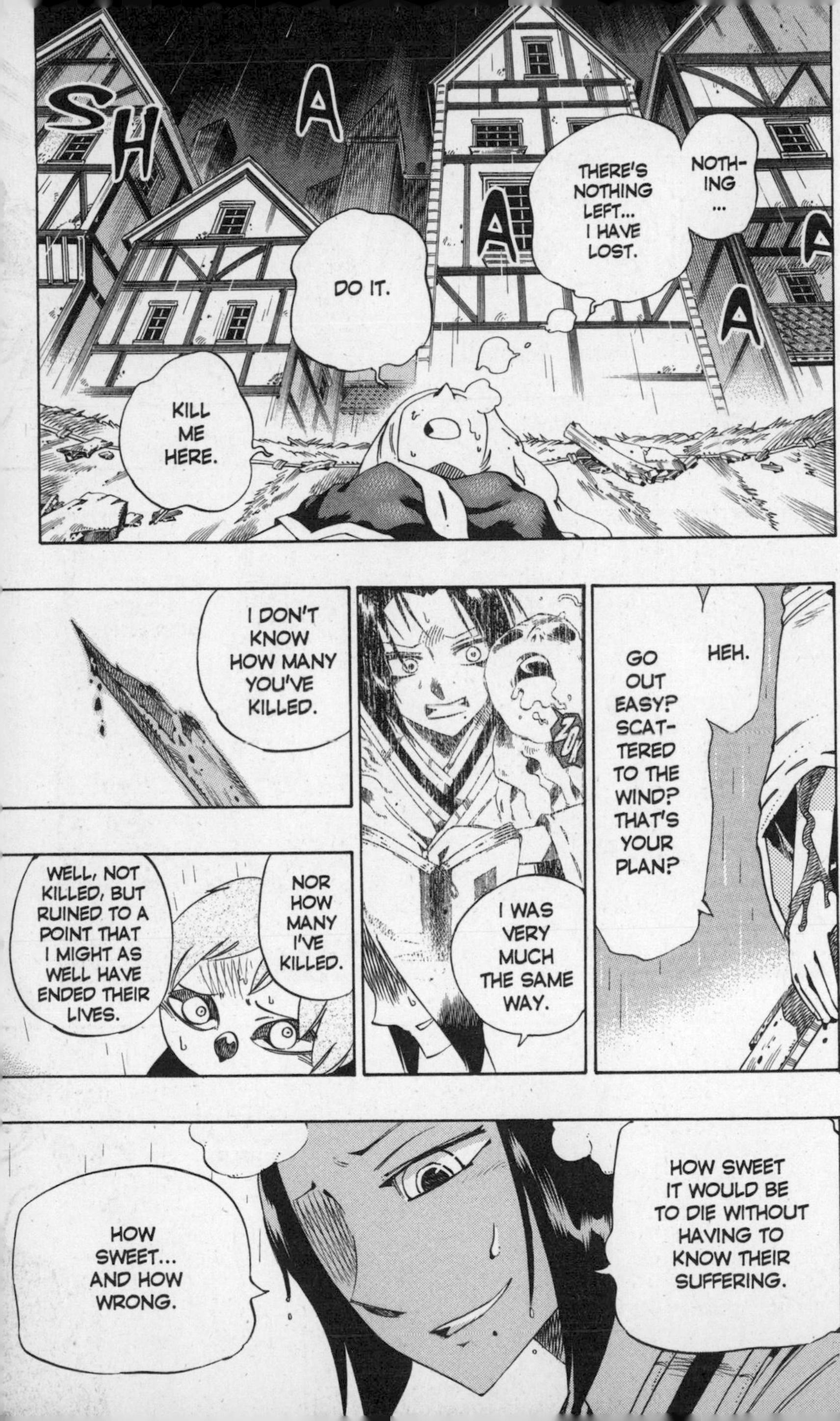
SHAAAA
NOTHING...
THERE'S NOTHING LEFT... I HAVE LOST.
DO IT.
KILL ME HERE.
HEH.
GO OUT EASY? SCATTERED TO THE WIND? THAT'S YOUR PLAN?
I WAS VERY MUCH THE SAME WAY.
I DON'T KNOW HOW MANY YOU'VE KILLED.
NOR HOW MANY I'VE KILLED.
WELL, NOT KILLED, BUT RUINED TO A POINT THAT I MIGHT AS WELL HAVE ENDED THEIR LIVES.
HOW SWEET IT WOULD BE TO DIE WITHOUT HAVING TO KNOW THEIR SUFFERING.
HOW SWEET... AND HOW WRONG.

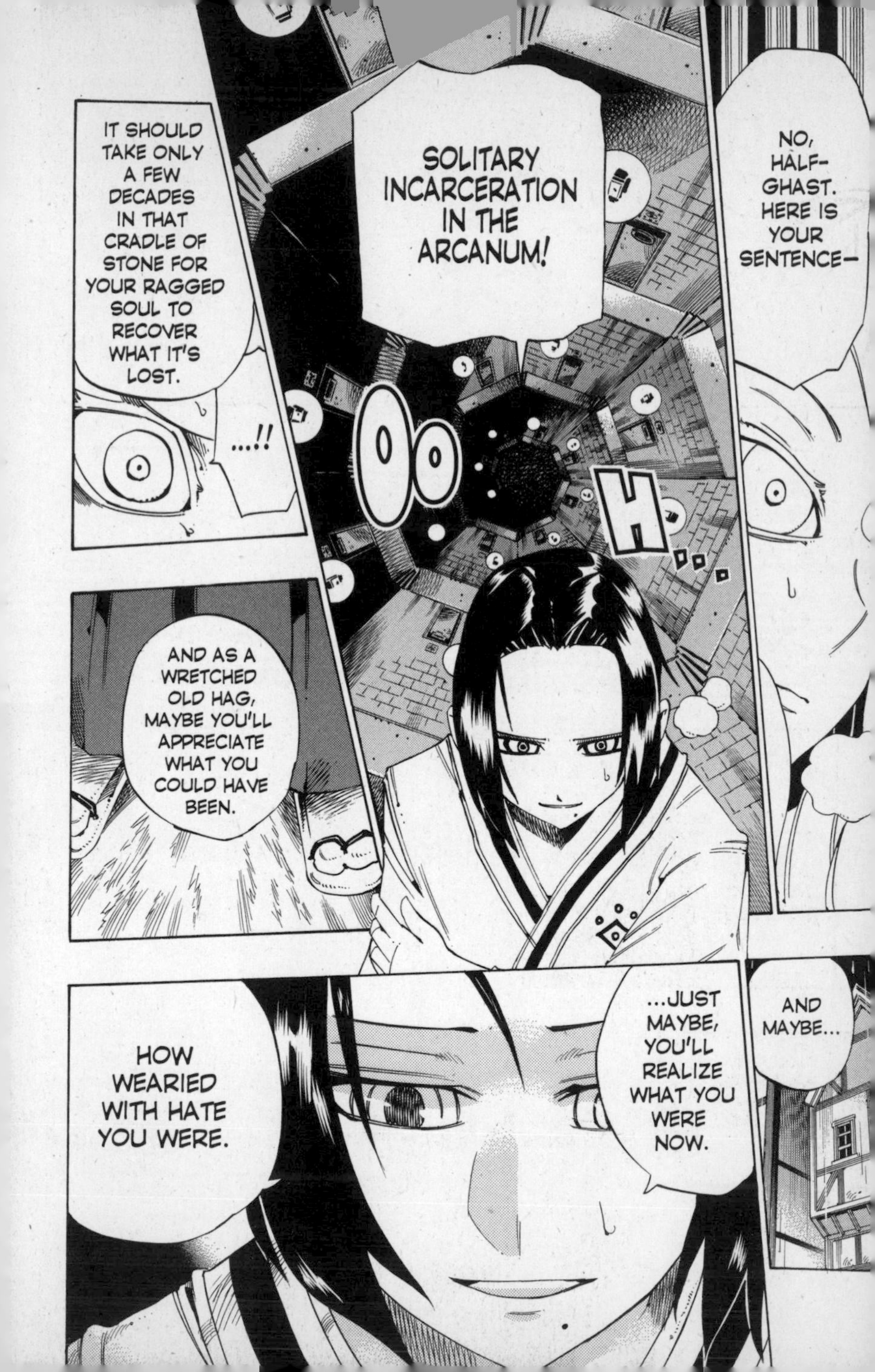
NO, HALF-GHAST. HERE IS YOUR SENTENCE—
SOLITARY INCARCERATION IN THE ARCANUM!
OOH
IT SHOULD TAKE ONLY A FEW DECADES IN THAT CRADLE OF STONE FOR YOUR RAGGED SOUL TO RECOVER WHAT IT'S LOST.
...!!
AND AS A WRETCHED OLD HAG, MAYBE YOU'LL APPRECIATE WHAT YOU COULD HAVE BEEN.
AND MAYBE...
...JUST MAYBE, YOU'LL REALIZE WHAT YOU WERE NOW.
HOW WEARIED WITH HATE YOU WERE.

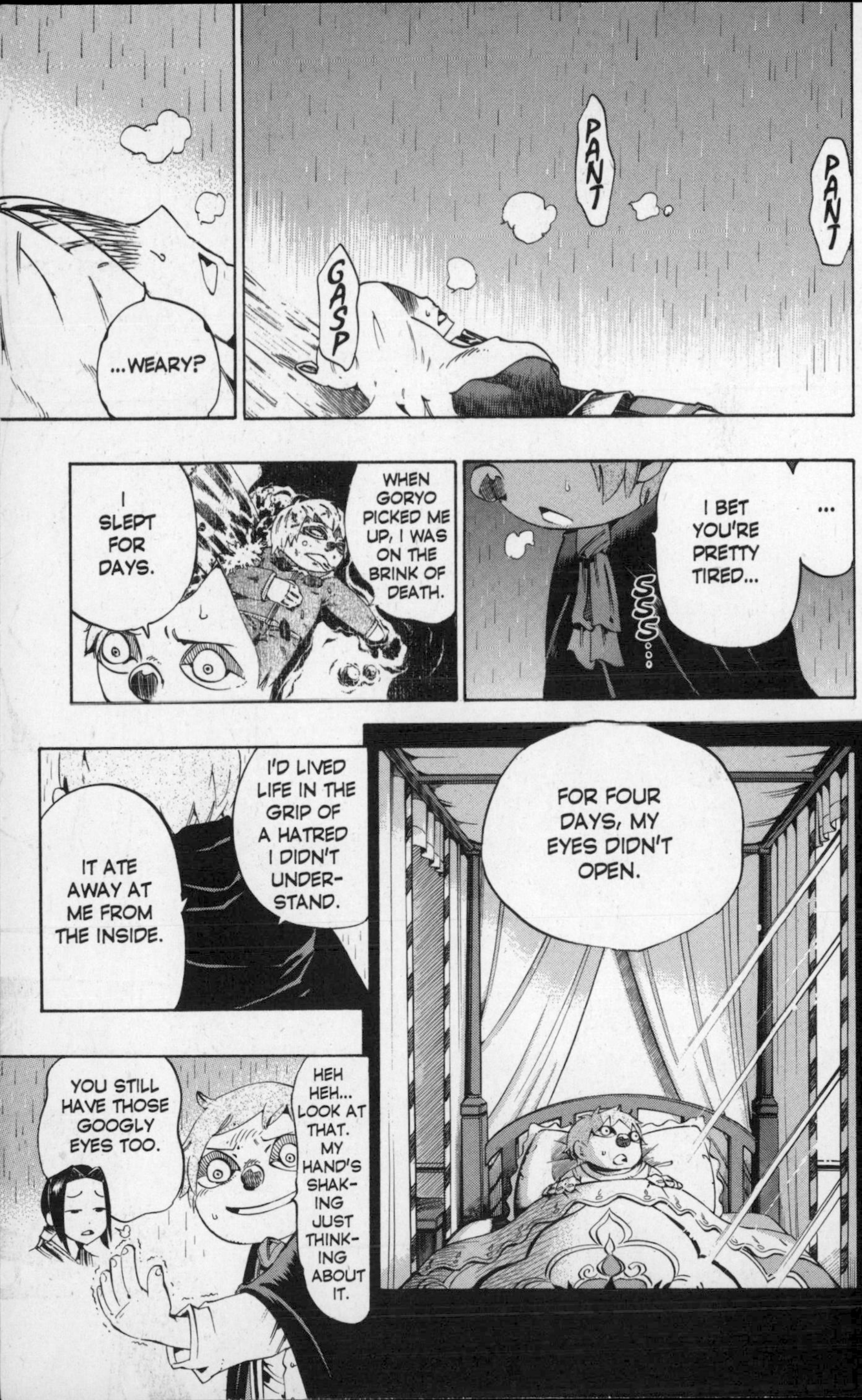
PANT
PANT
GASP
...WEARY?
...
I BET YOU'RE PRETTY TIRED...
SSS...
WHEN GORYO PICKED ME UP, I WAS ON THE BRINK OF DEATH.
I SLEPT FOR DAYS.
FOR FOUR DAYS, MY EYES DIDN'T OPEN.
I'D LIVED LIFE IN THE GRIP OF A HATRED I DIDN'T UNDER-STAND.
IT ATE AWAY AT ME FROM THE INSIDE.
HEH HEH... LOOK AT THAT. MY HAND'S SHAK-ING JUST THINK-ING ABOUT IT.
YOU STILL HAVE THOSE GOOGLY EYES TOO.

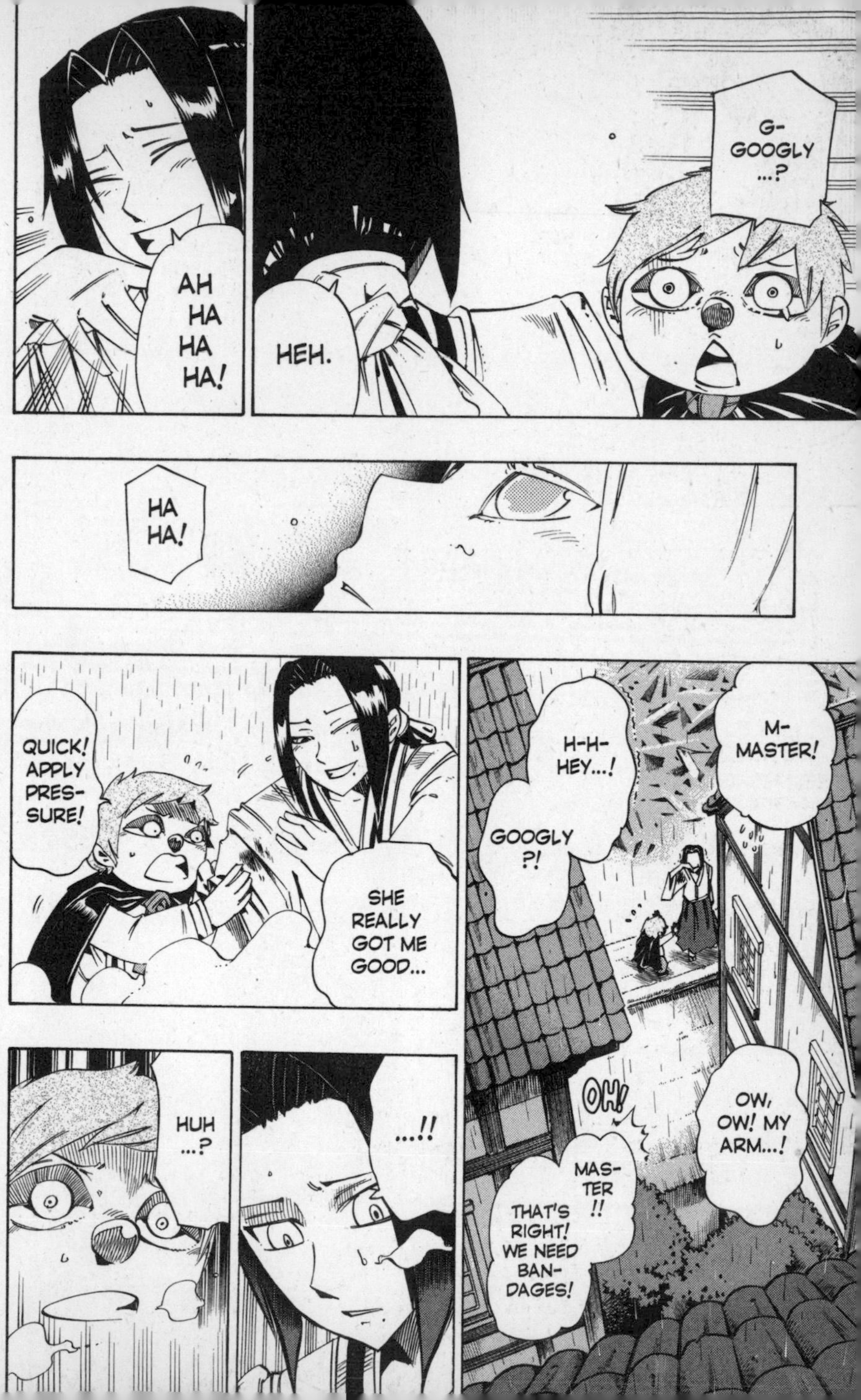
G-GOOGLY...?
HEH.
AH HA HA HA!
HA HA!
M-MASTER!
H-H-HEY...!
GOOGLY?!
OW, OW! MY ARM...!
OH!
MASTER!!
THAT'S RIGHT! WE NEED BANDAGES!
SHE REALLY GOT ME GOOD...
QUICK! APPLY PRESSURE!
...!!
HUH...?

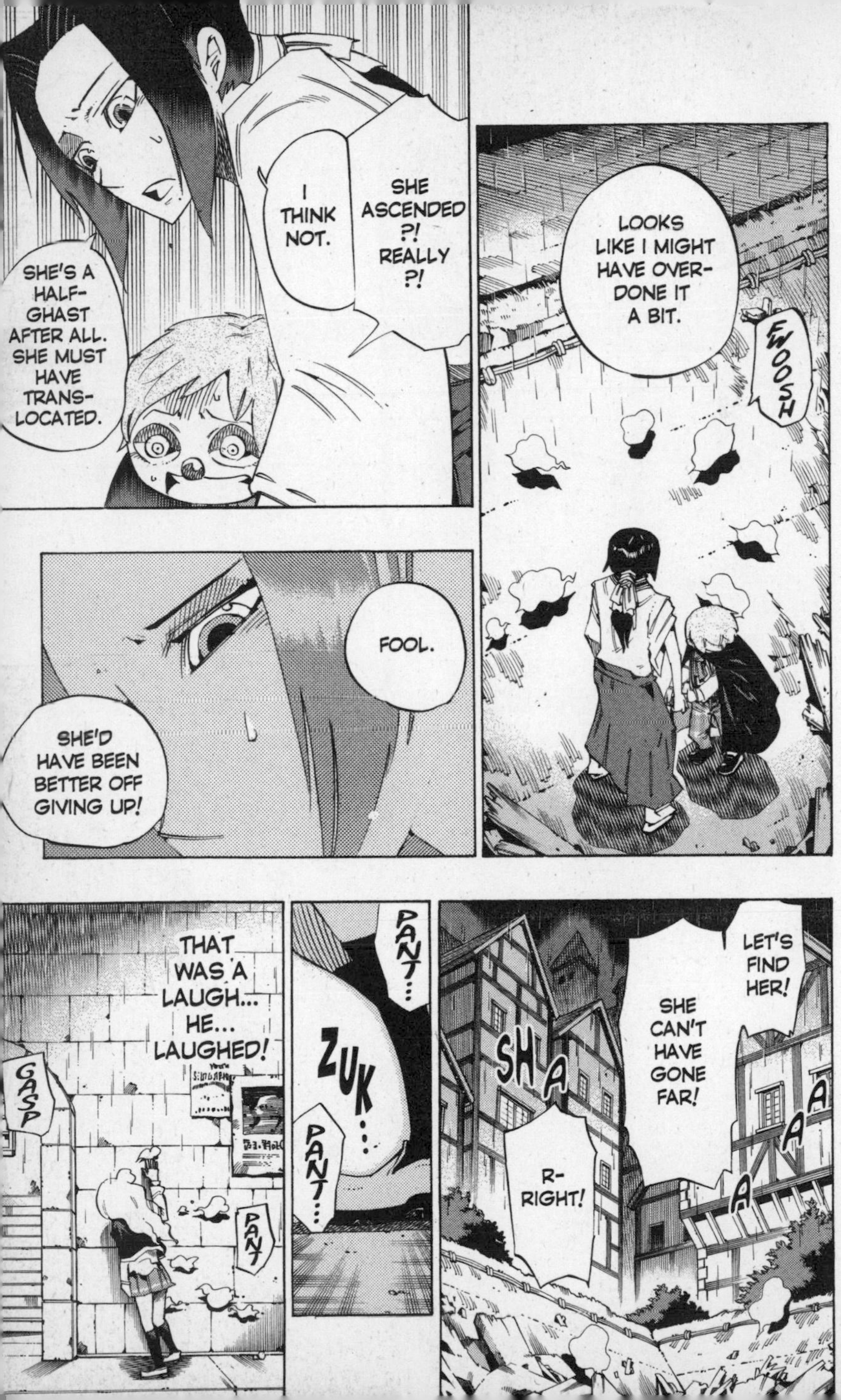
LOOKS LIKE I MIGHT HAVE OVER-DONE IT A BIT.
FWOOSH
SHE ASCENDED?! REALLY?!
I THINK NOT.
SHE'S A HALF-GHAST AFTER ALL. SHE MUST HAVE TRANS-LOCATED.
FOOL.
SHE'D HAVE BEEN BETTER OFF GIVING UP!
LET'S FIND HER!
SHE CAN'T HAVE GONE FAR!
SHAAAA
R-RIGHT!
PANT...
ZUK...
PANT...
THAT WAS A LAUGH... HE... LAUGHED!
GASP
PANT

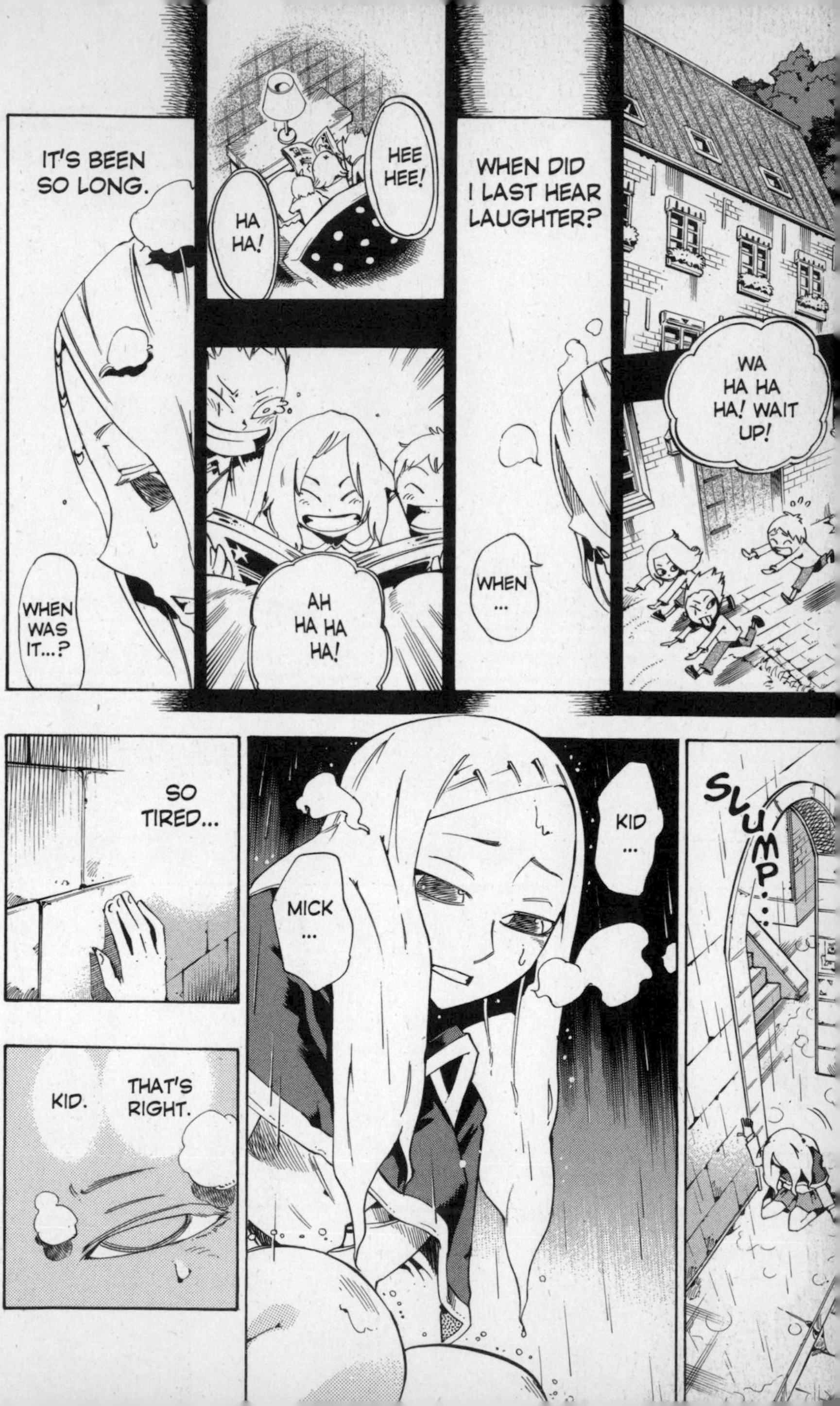
WA HA HA HA! WAIT UP!
WHEN DID I LAST HEAR LAUGHTER?
WHEN ...
HEE HEE!
HA HA!
AH HA HA HA!
IT'S BEEN SO LONG.
WHEN WAS IT...?
SLUMP...
KID ...
MICK ...
SO TIRED...
THAT'S RIGHT.
KID.

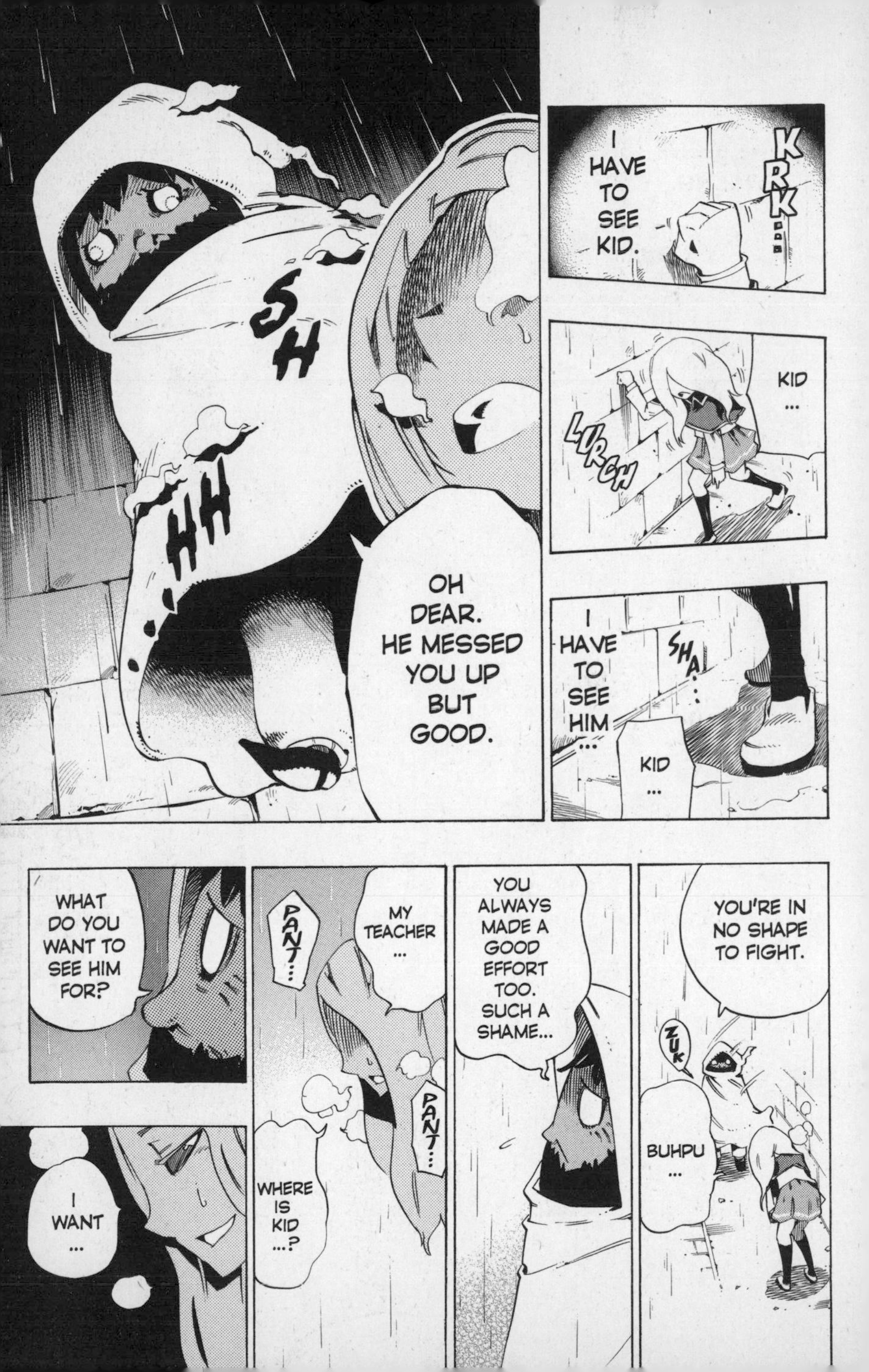
I HAVE TO SEE KID.
KRK...
KID ...
LURCH
I HAVE TO SEE HIM ...
SHA...
KID ...
SH
HH
OH DEAR. HE MESSED YOU UP BUT GOOD.
YOU'RE IN NO SHAPE TO FIGHT.
ZUK
BUHPU ...
YOU ALWAYS MADE A GOOD EFFORT TOO. SUCH A SHAME...
PANT...
MY TEACHER ...
PANT...
WHERE IS KID ...?
WHAT DO YOU WANT TO SEE HIM FOR?
I WANT ...

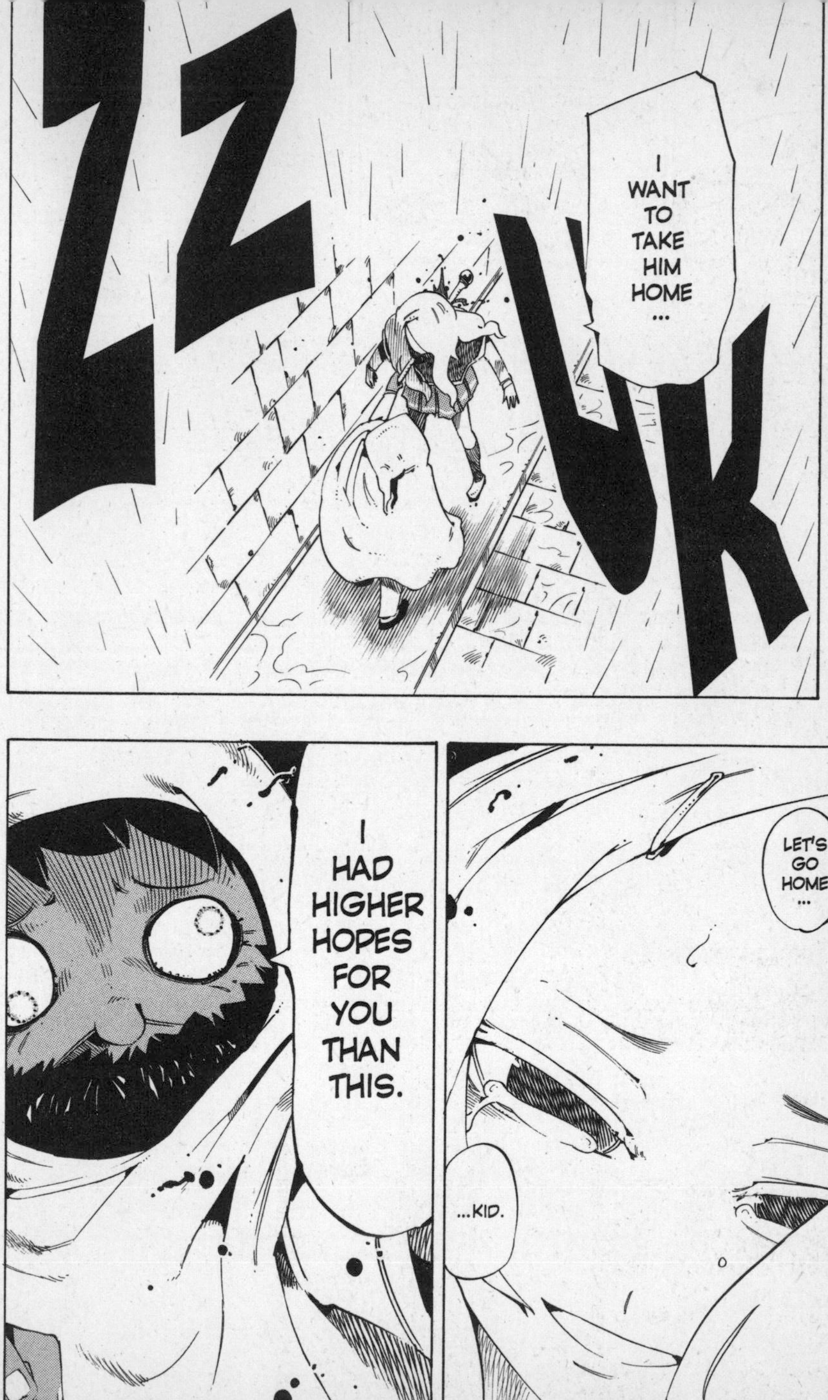
I WANT TO TAKE HIM HOME...
ZZUK
LET'S GO HOME...
...KID.
I HAD HIGHER HOPES FOR YOU THAN THIS.

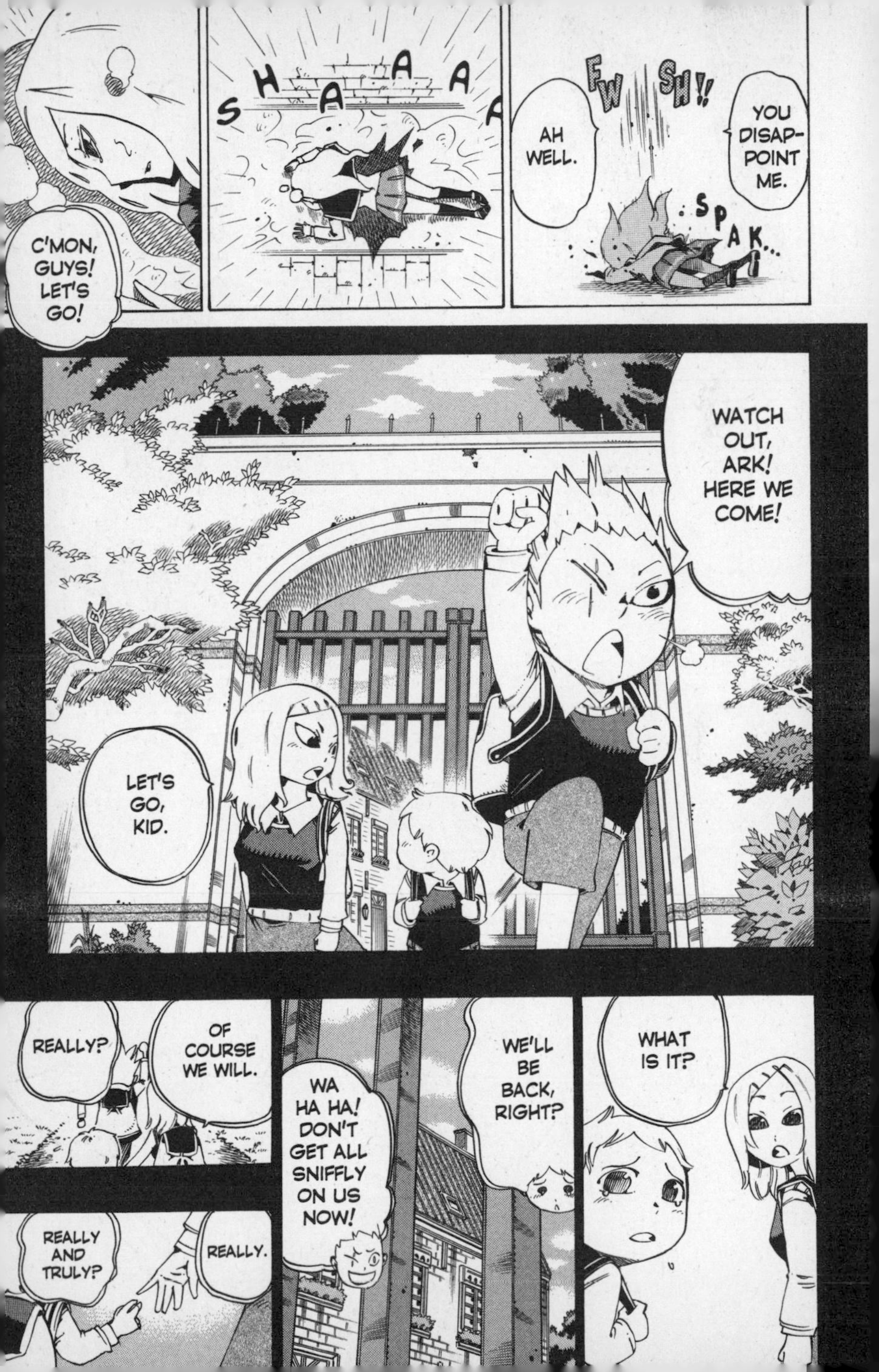
YOU DISAP-POINT ME.
FWSH!!
AH WELL.
SPAK...
SHAAAAA
C'MON, GUYS! LET'S GO!
WATCH OUT, ARK! HERE WE COME!
LET'S GO, KID.
WHAT IS IT?
WE'LL BE BACK, RIGHT?
WA HA HA! DON'T GET ALL SNIFFLY ON US NOW!
OF COURSE WE WILL.
REALLY?
REALLY.
REALLY AND TRULY?

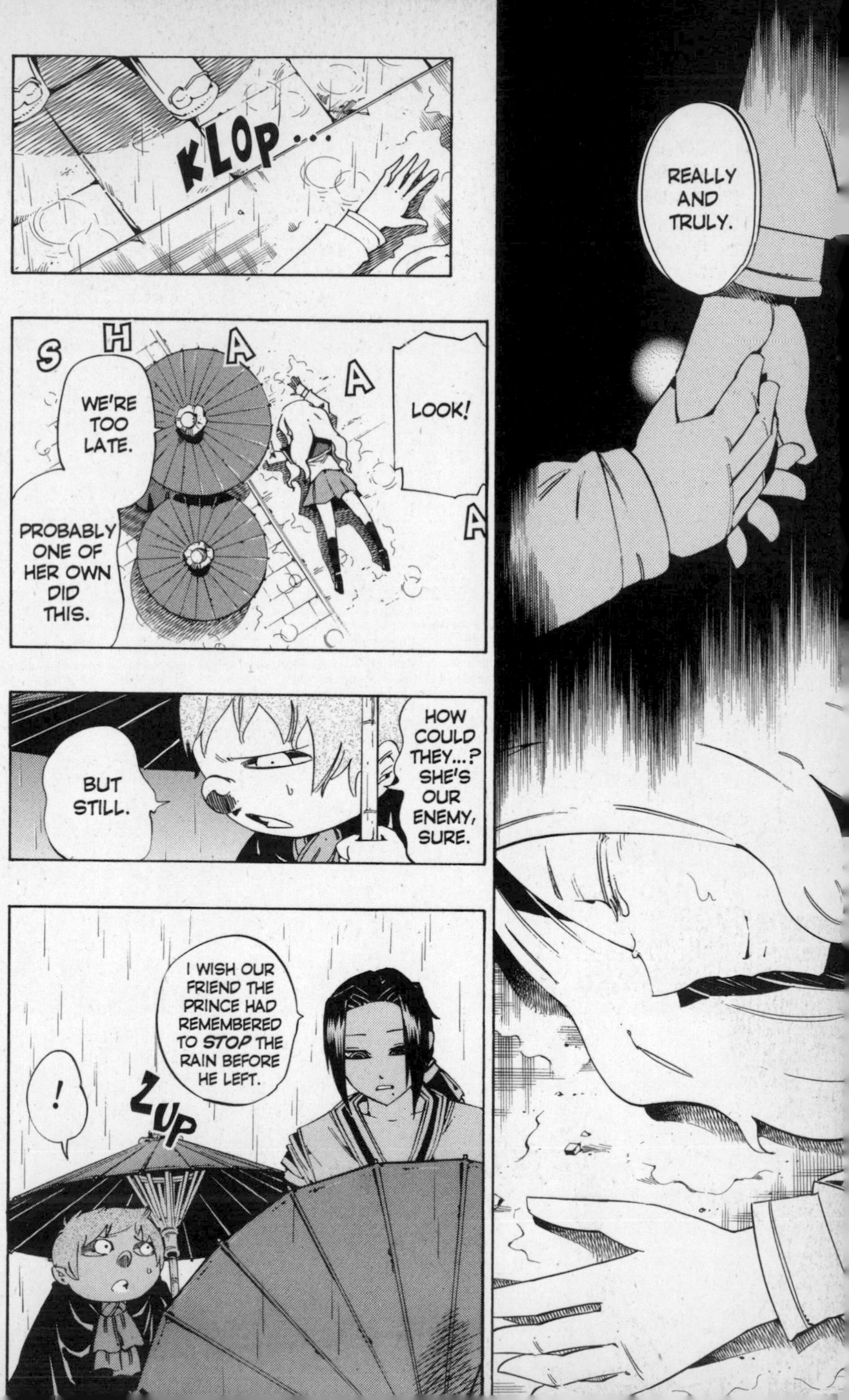
REALLY AND TRULY.
KLOP...
SHAAA
LOOK!
WE'RE TOO LATE.
PROBABLY ONE OF HER OWN DID THIS.
HOW COULD THEY...? SHE'S OUR ENEMY, SURE.
BUT STILL.
I WISH OUR FRIEND THE PRINCE HAD REMEMBERED TO *STOP* THE RAIN BEFORE HE LEFT.
ZUP
!

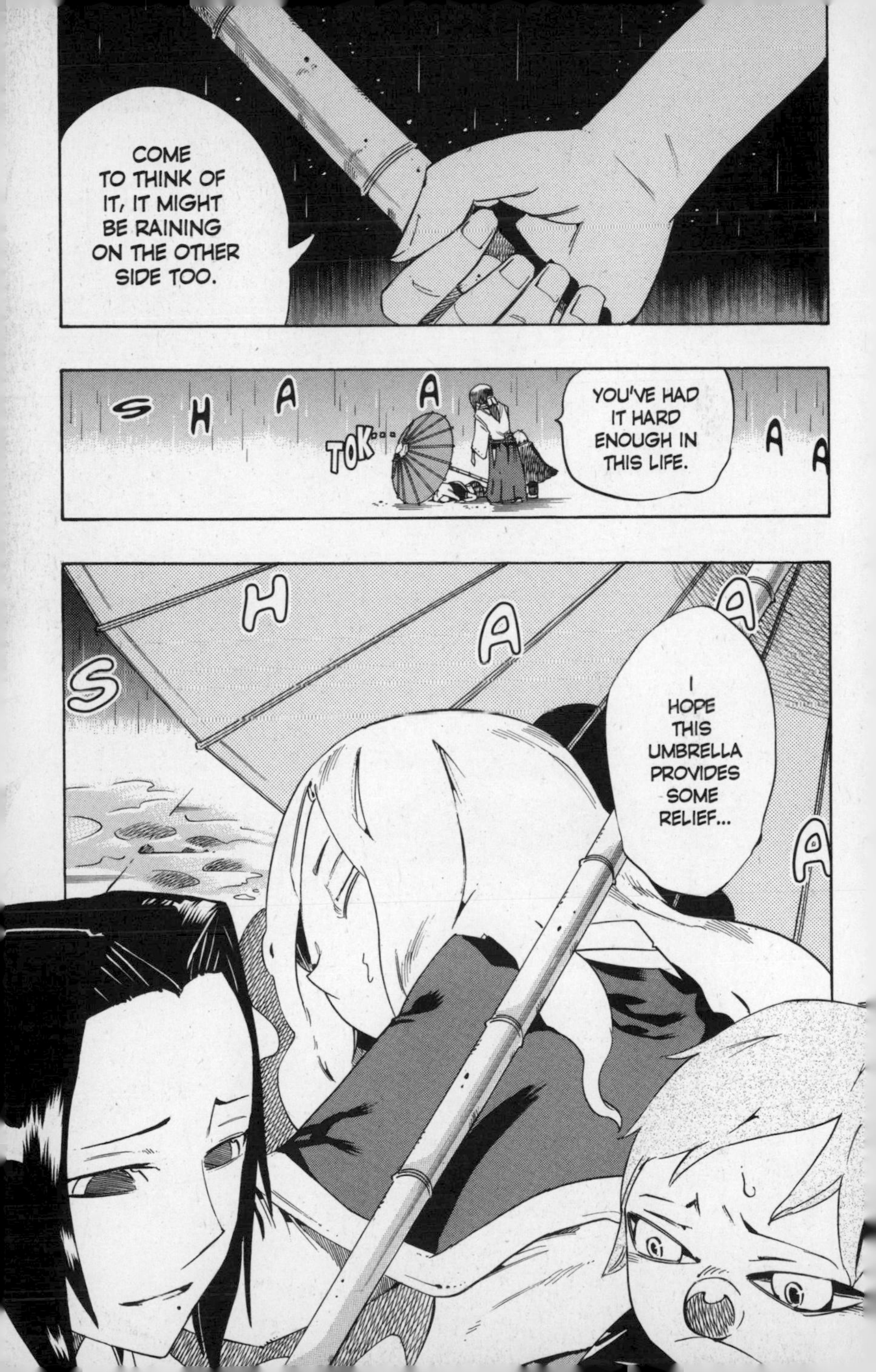
COME TO THINK OF IT, IT MIGHT BE RAINING ON THE OTHER SIDE TOO.
YOU'VE HAD IT HARD ENOUGH IN THIS LIFE.
TOK...
SHAAAA
SHAAA
I HOPE THIS UMBRELLA PROVIDES SOME RELIEF...

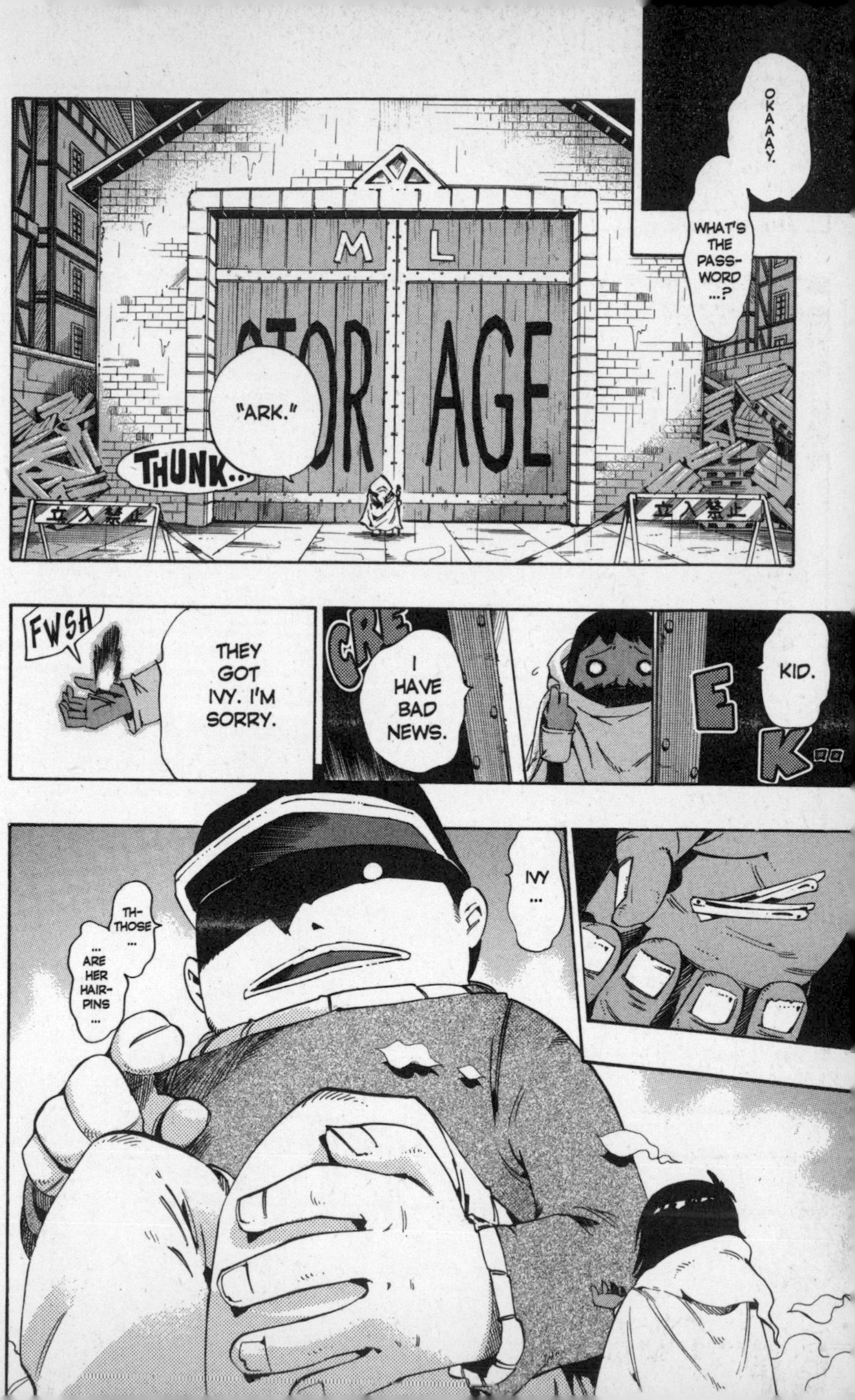
OKAAAY.
WHAT'S THE PASS-WORD ...?
M L
STORAGE
"ARK."
THUNK...
立入禁止
立入禁止
KID.
EK..
I HAVE BAD NEWS.
CRE
THEY GOT IVY. I'M SORRY.
FWSH
IVY ...
TH-THOSE ...
... ARE HER HAIR-PINS ...

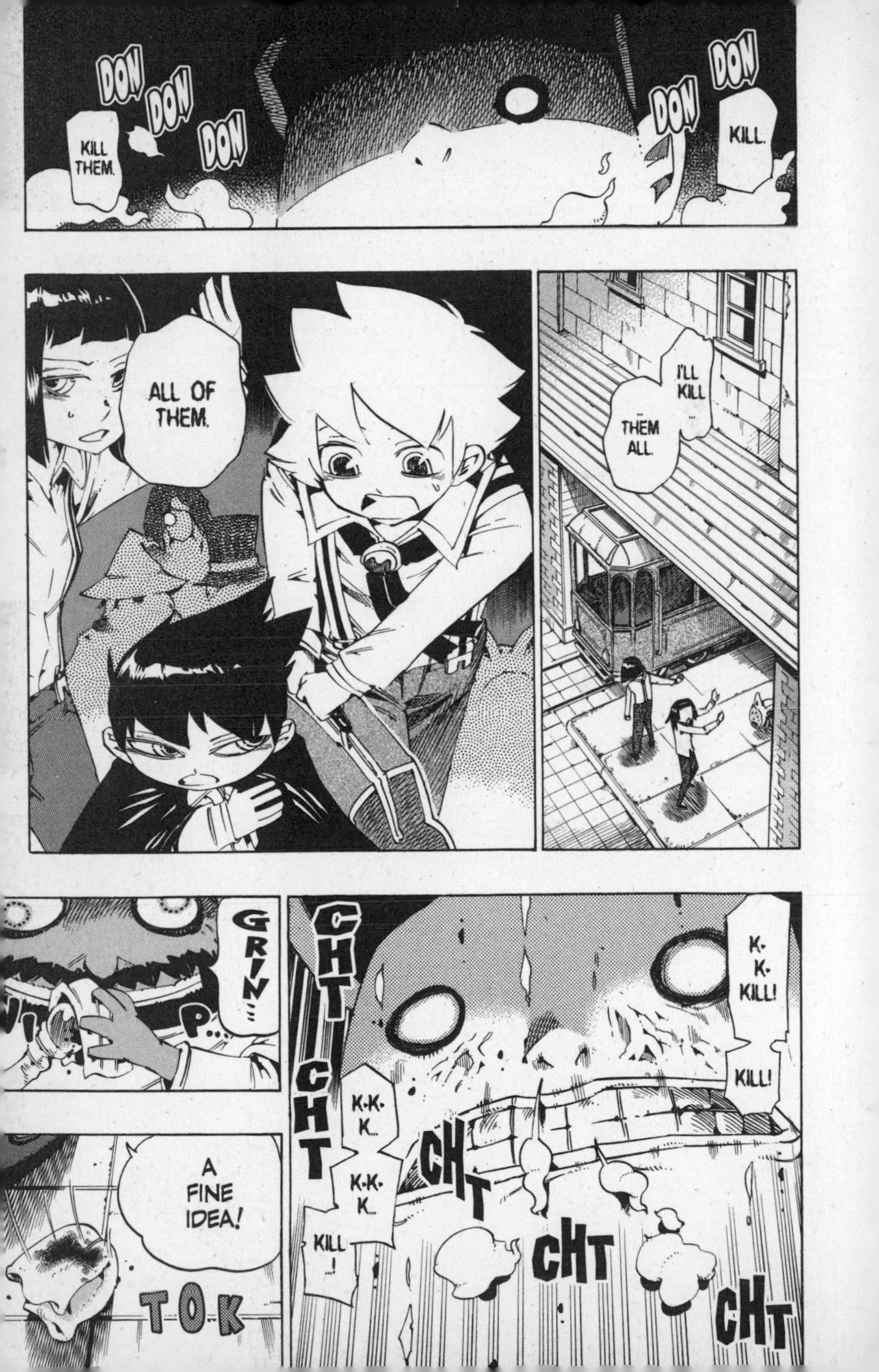
DON
DON
KILL.
DON
DON
DON
KILL THEM.
I'LL KILL ... ... THEM ALL.
ALL OF THEM.
K-K-KILL!
KILL!
CHT
K-K-K...
K-K-K...
KILL...!
CHT
CHT
CHT
CHT
CHT
GRIN...
P...
A FINE IDEA!
TOK

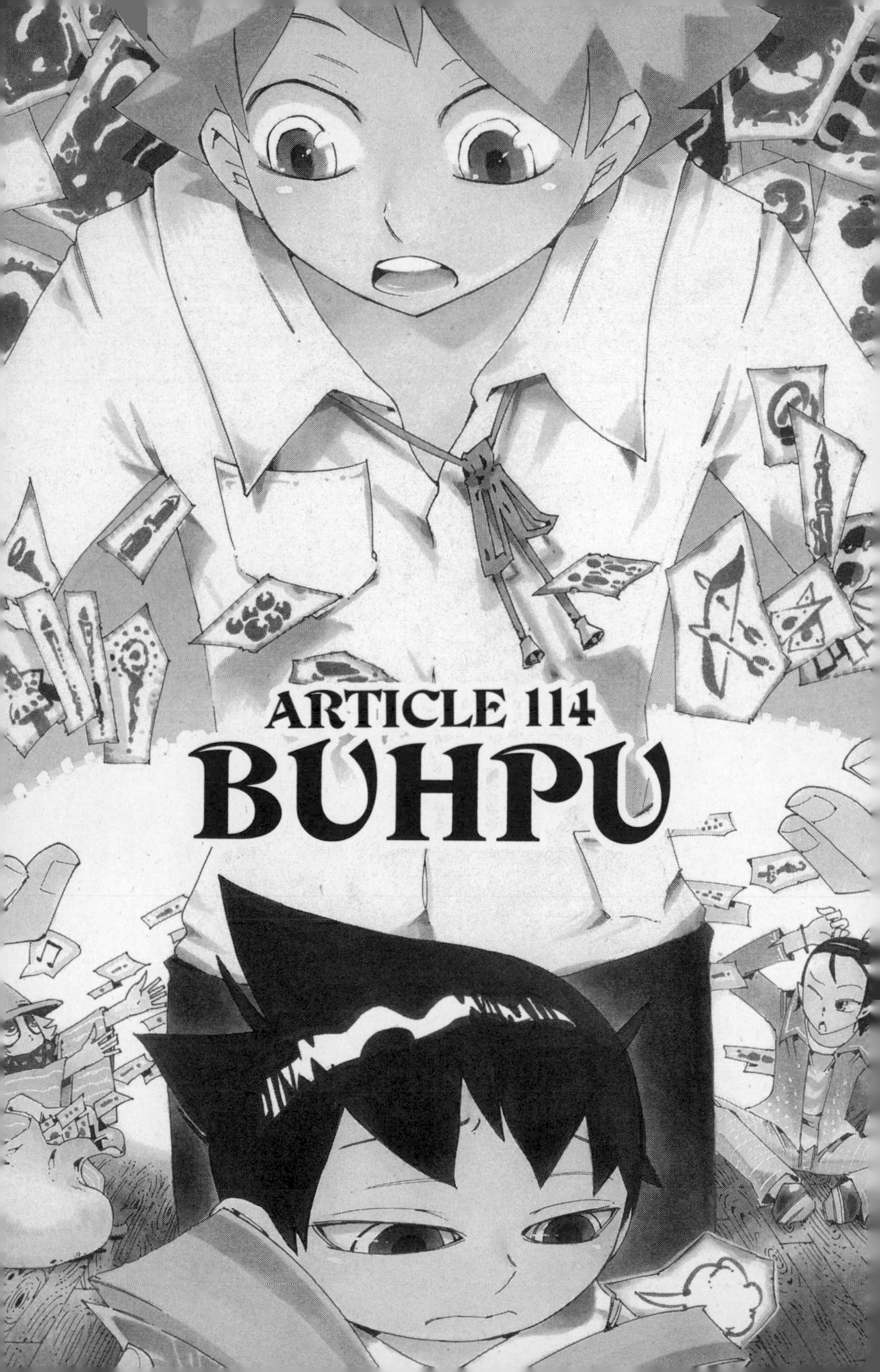
ARTICLE 114
BUHPU

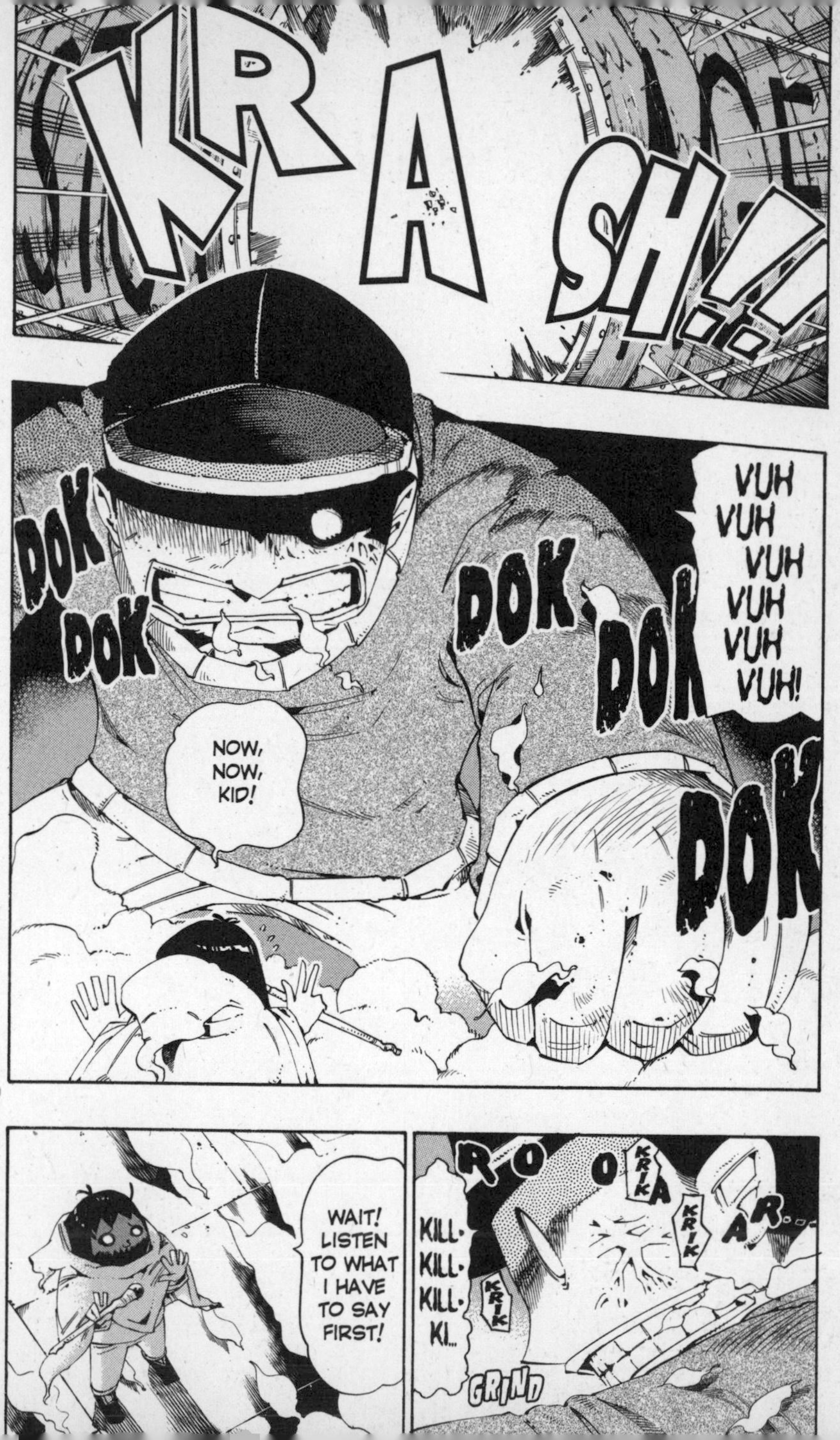
KRASH!!
VUH VUH VUH VUH VUH VUH!
DOK DOK
DOK
NOW, NOW, KID!
DOK DOK
ROOAAR...
KRIK KRIK
KILL. KILL. KILL. KI...
KRIK
GRIND
WAIT! LISTEN TO WHAT I HAVE TO SAY FIRST!

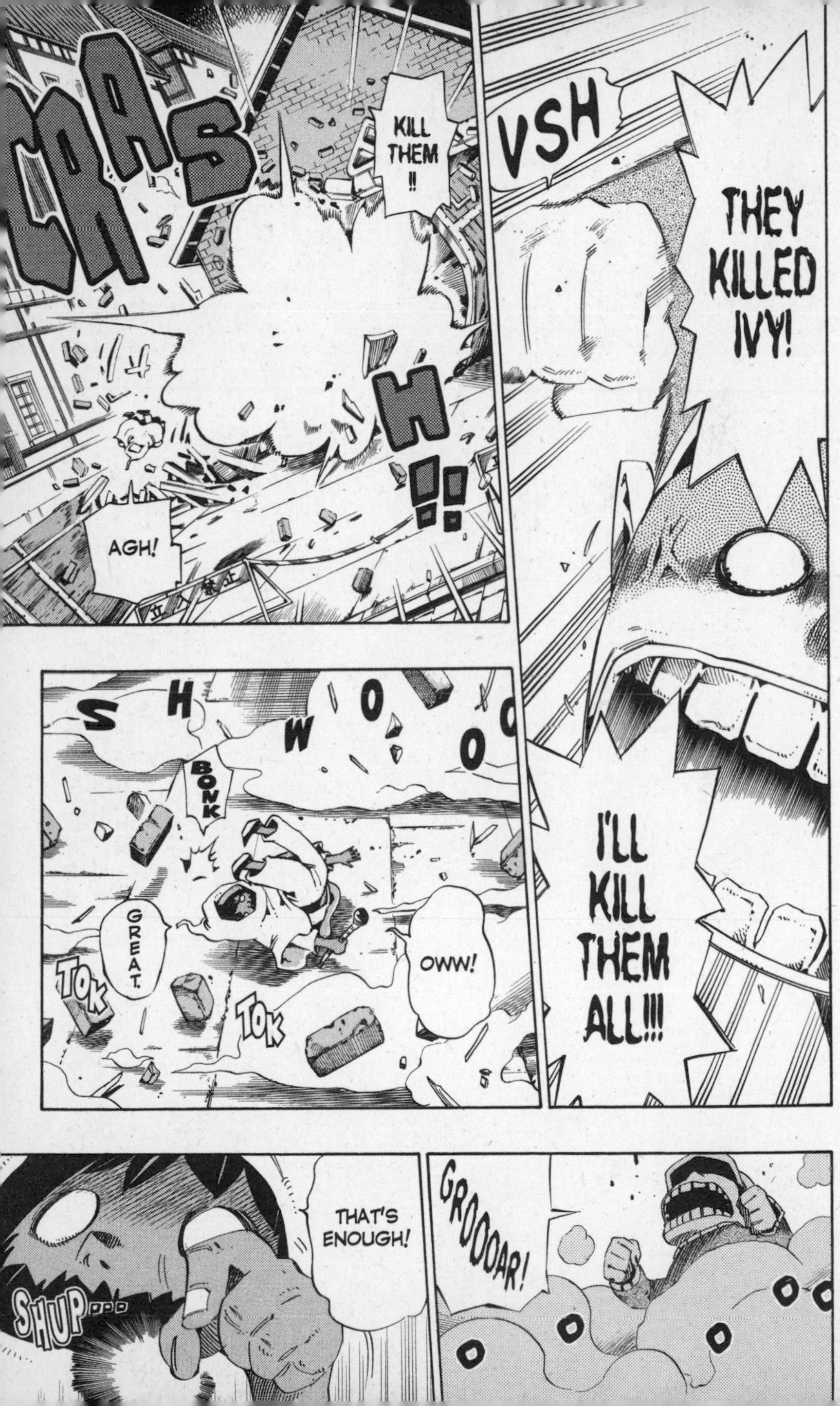
VSH
THEY KILLED IVY!
I'LL KILL THEM ALL!!!
KILL THEM !!
CRASH!!
AGH!
SHWOOO
BONK
OWW!
GREAT.
TOK
TOK
GROOOAR!
THAT'S ENOUGH!
SHUP...

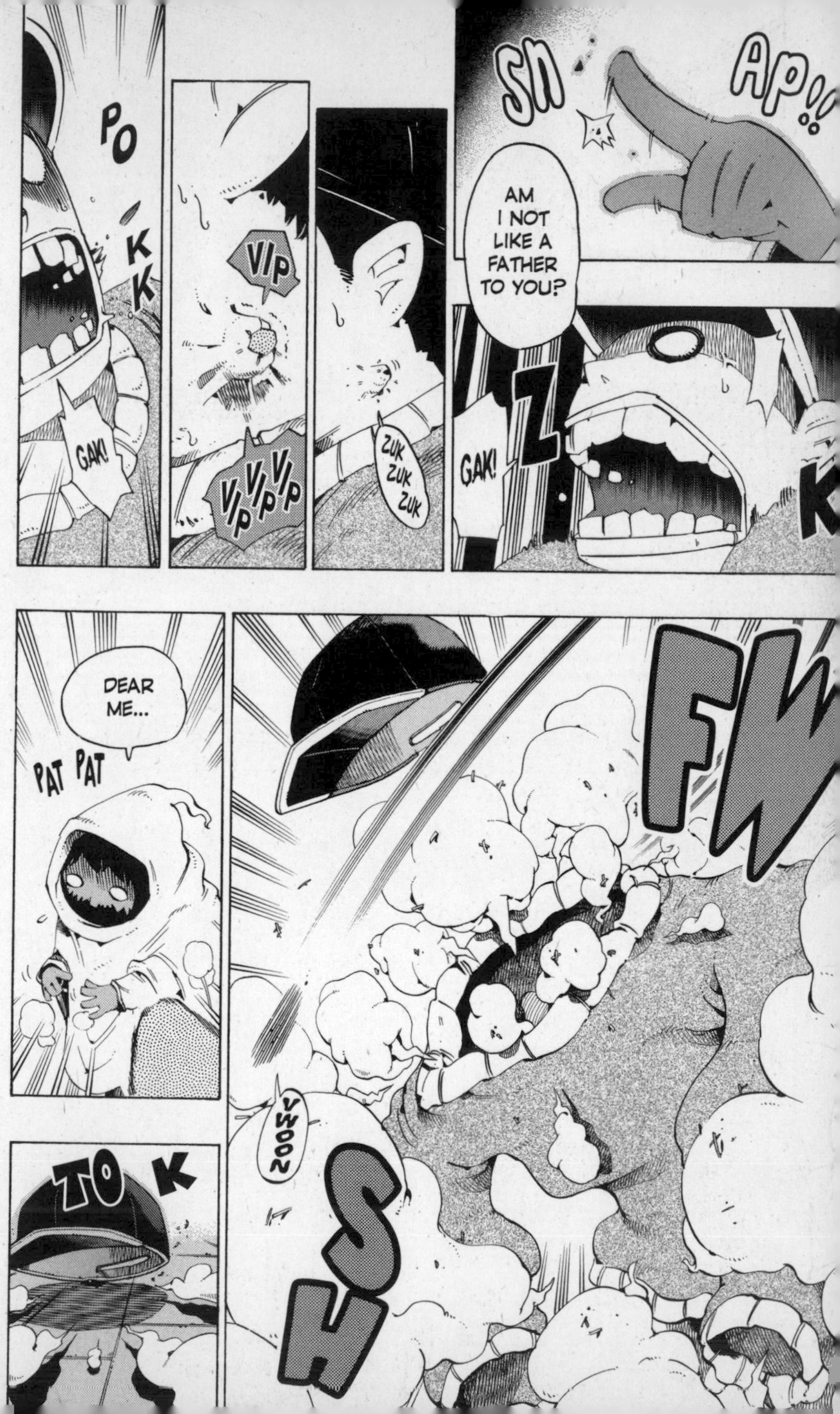

SN
AP!!
AM I NOT LIKE A FATHER TO YOU?
GAK!
Z
K
ZUK ZUK ZUK
VIP
VIP VIP VIP VIP
POKK
GAK!
FW
VWOON
SH
DEAR ME...
PAT PAT
TOK

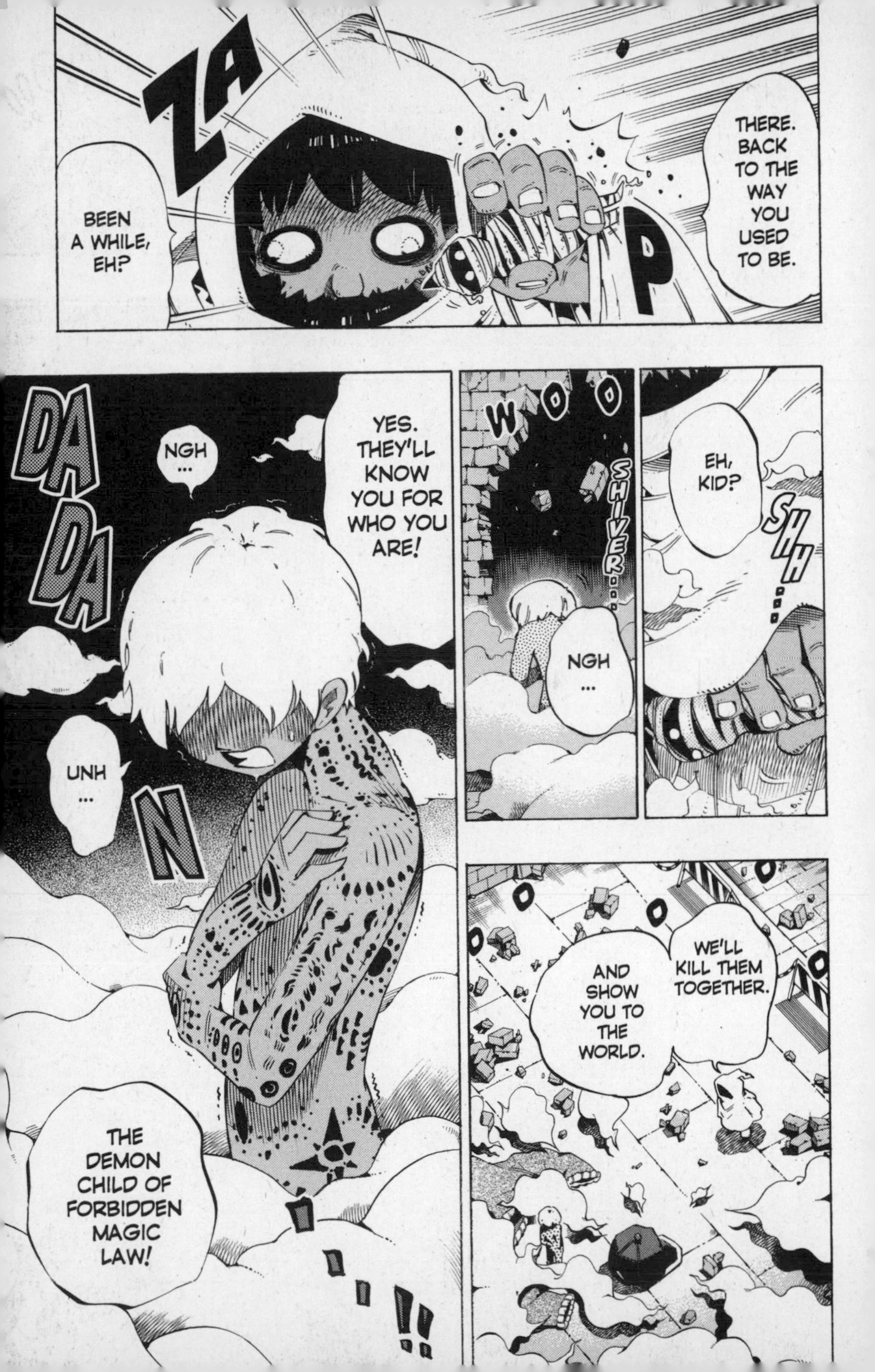
THERE. BACK TO THE WAY YOU USED TO BE.
ZAP
BEEN A WHILE, EH?
EH, KID?
SHH...
WOOO
SHIVER...
NGH...
WE'LL KILL THEM TOGETHER.
AND SHOW YOU TO THE WORLD.
YES. THEY'LL KNOW YOU FOR WHO YOU ARE!
NGH...
DA DA DA
N
UNH...
THE DEMON CHILD OF FORBIDDEN MAGIC LAW!
!!!

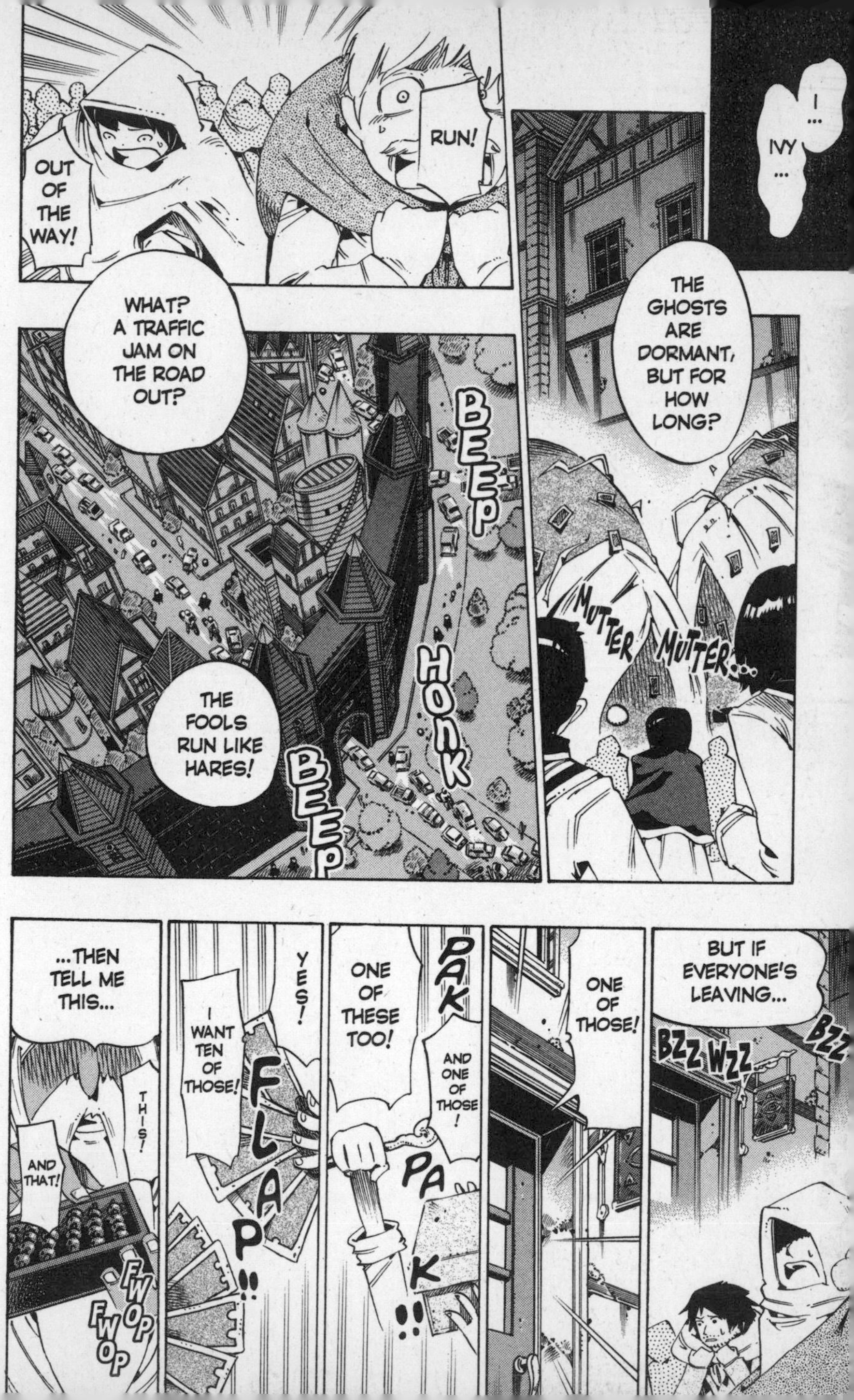
I ... IVY ...
THE GHOSTS ARE DORMANT, BUT FOR HOW LONG?
MUTTER MUTTER
RUN!
OUT OF THE WAY!
WHAT? A TRAFFIC JAM ON THE ROAD OUT?
BEEP
HONK
BEEP
THE FOOLS RUN LIKE HARES!
BUT IF EVERYONE'S LEAVING...
BZZ WZZ
BZZ
ONE OF THOSE!
AND ONE OF THOSE!
PAK
PAK
K!!
ONE OF THESE TOO!
YES!
I WANT TEN OF THOSE!
FLAP!!
...THEN TELL ME THIS...
THIS!
AND THAT!
FWOP
FWOP

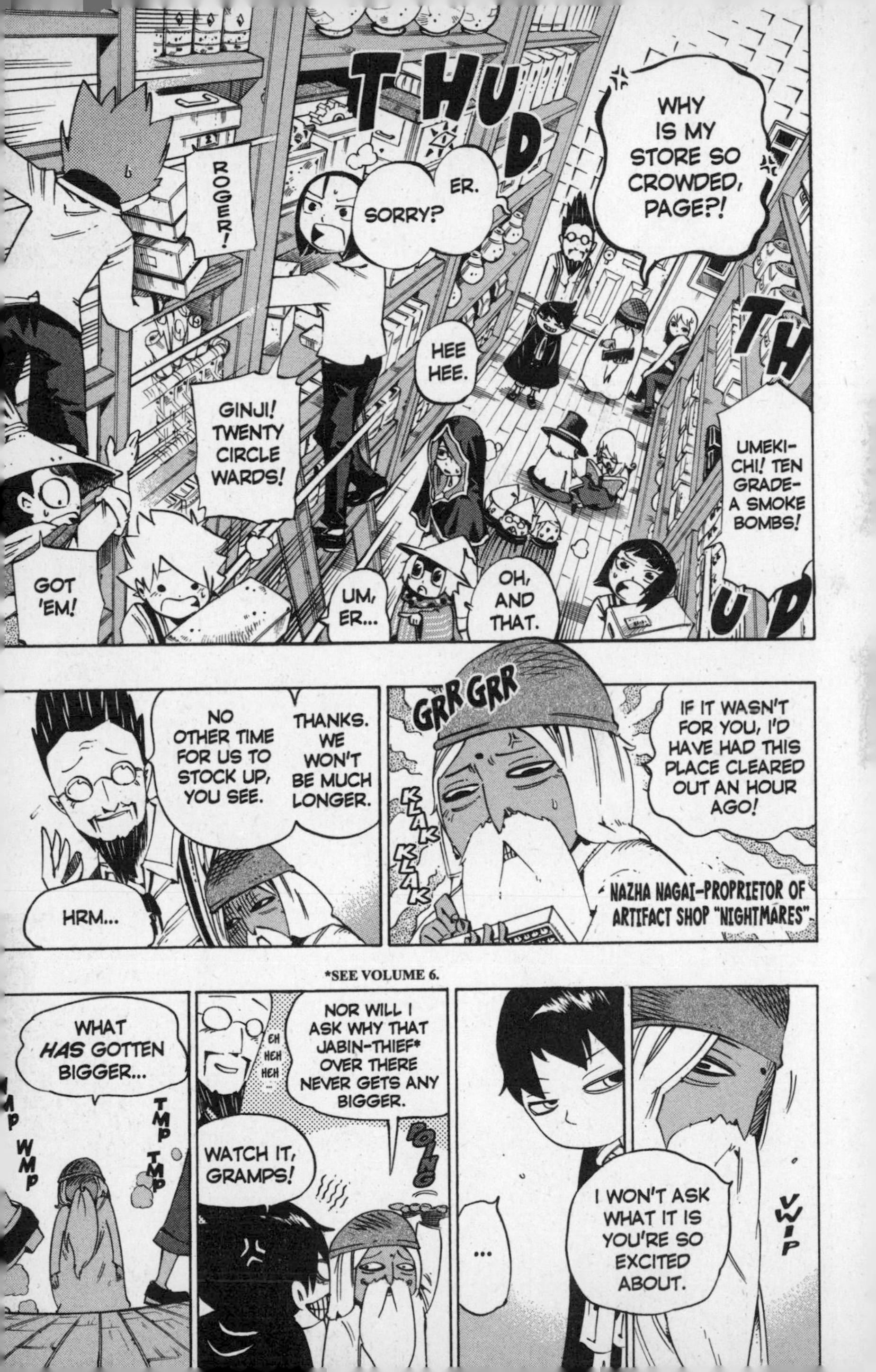
WHY IS MY STORE SO CROWDED, PAGE?!
THUD
ER. SORRY?
ROGER!
TH
HEE HEE.
GINJI! TWENTY CIRCLE WARDS!
UMEKI-CHI! TEN GRADE-A SMOKE BOMBS!
UD
OH, AND THAT.
UM, ER...
GOT 'EM!
GRR GRR
IF IT WASN'T FOR YOU, I'D HAVE HAD THIS PLACE CLEARED OUT AN HOUR AGO!
KLAK KLAK KLAK
NAZHA NAGAI–PROPRIETOR OF ARTIFACT SHOP "NIGHTMARES".
THANKS. WE WON'T BE MUCH LONGER.
NO OTHER TIME FOR US TO STOCK UP, YOU SEE.
HRM...
*SEE VOLUME 6.
VWIP
I WON'T ASK WHAT IT IS YOU'RE SO EXCITED ABOUT.
...
NOR WILL I ASK WHY THAT JABIN-THIEF* OVER THERE NEVER GETS ANY BIGGER.
EH HEH HEH...
POING
WATCH IT, GRAMPS!
WHAT *HAS* GOTTEN BIGGER...
TMP TMP
WMP

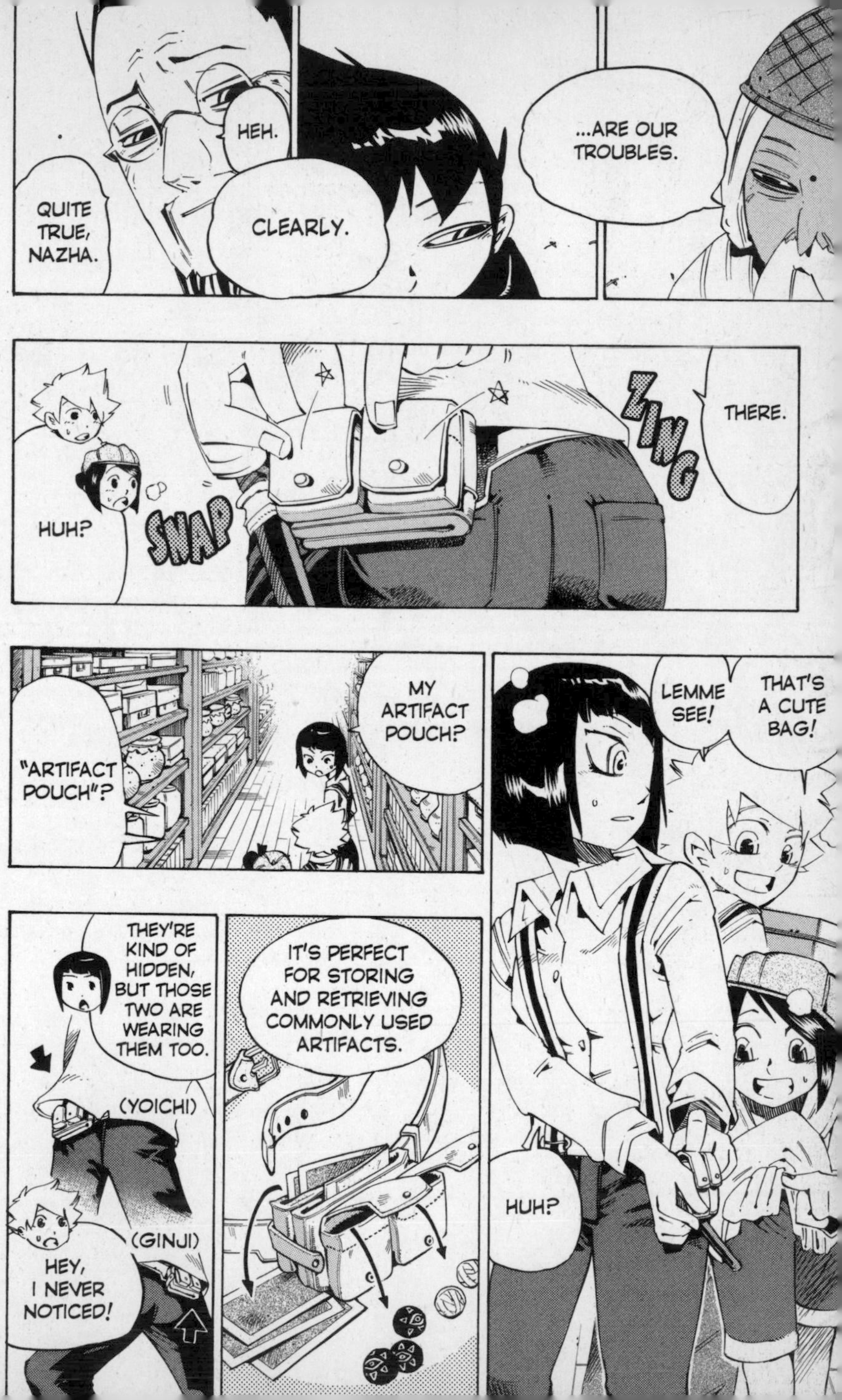
...ARE OUR TROUBLES.
CLEARLY.
HEH.
QUITE TRUE, NAZHA.
THERE.
ZING
SNAP
HUH?
THAT'S A CUTE BAG!
LEMME SEE!
HUH?
MY ARTIFACT POUCH?
"ARTIFACT POUCH"?
IT'S PERFECT FOR STORING AND RETRIEVING COMMONLY USED ARTIFACTS.
THEY'RE KIND OF HIDDEN, BUT THOSE TWO ARE WEARING THEM TOO.
(YOICHI)
(GINJI)
HEY, I NEVER NOTICED!

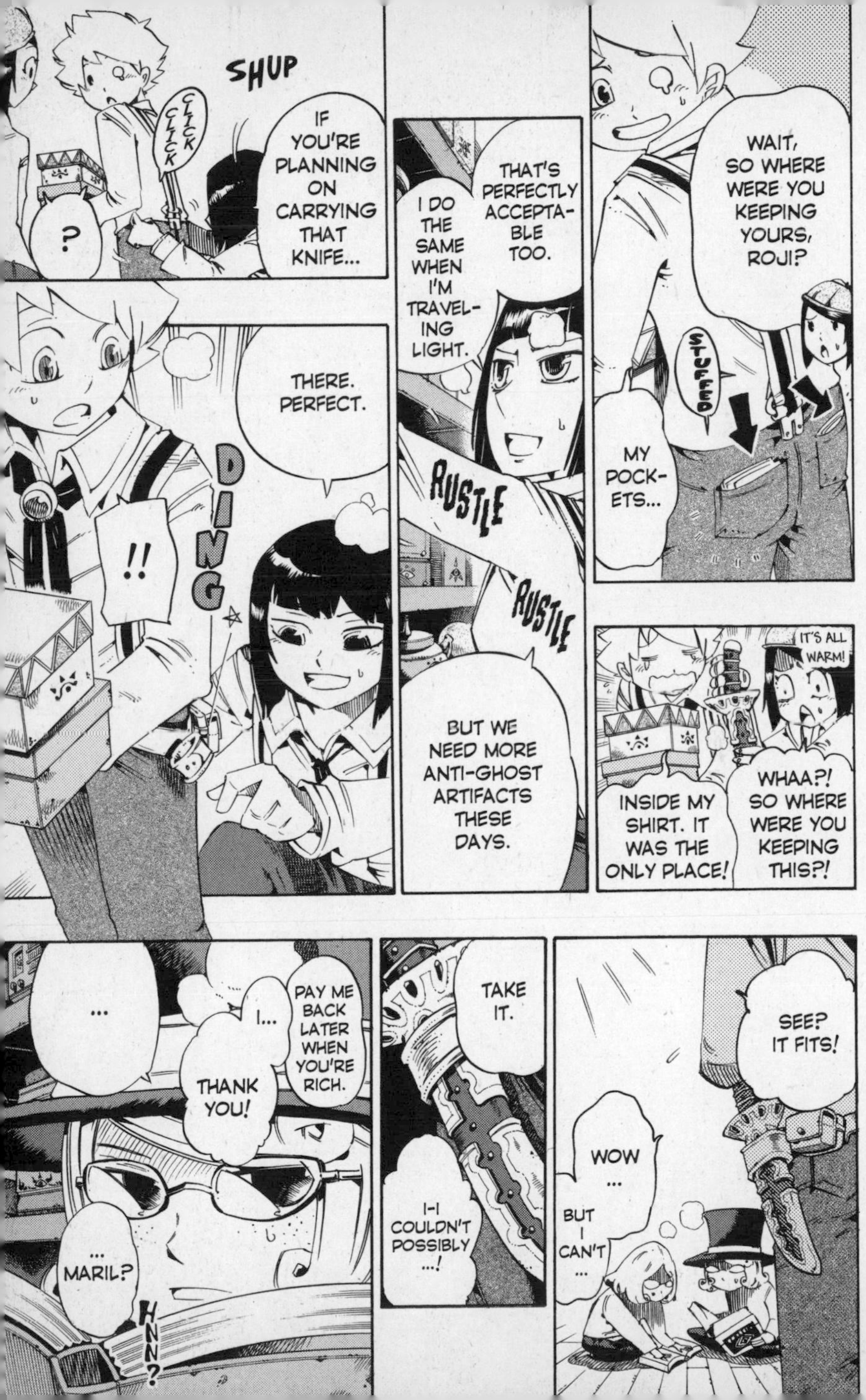

WAIT, SO WHERE WERE YOU KEEPING YOURS, ROJI?
STUFFED
MY POCKETS...
IT'S ALL WARM!
WHAA?! SO WHERE WERE YOU KEEPING THIS?!
INSIDE MY SHIRT. IT WAS THE ONLY PLACE!
THAT'S PERFECTLY ACCEPTABLE TOO.
I DO THE SAME WHEN I'M TRAVELING LIGHT.
RUSTLE
RUSTLE
BUT WE NEED MORE ANTI-GHOST ARTIFACTS THESE DAYS.
SHUP
CLICK CLICK
IF YOU'RE PLANNING ON CARRYING THAT KNIFE...
?
THERE. PERFECT.
DING
!!
SEE? IT FITS!
WOW... BUT I CAN'T...
TAKE IT.
I-I COULDN'T POSSIBLY...!
PAY ME BACK LATER WHEN YOU'RE RICH.
I...
...
THANK YOU!
...MARIL?
HNN?

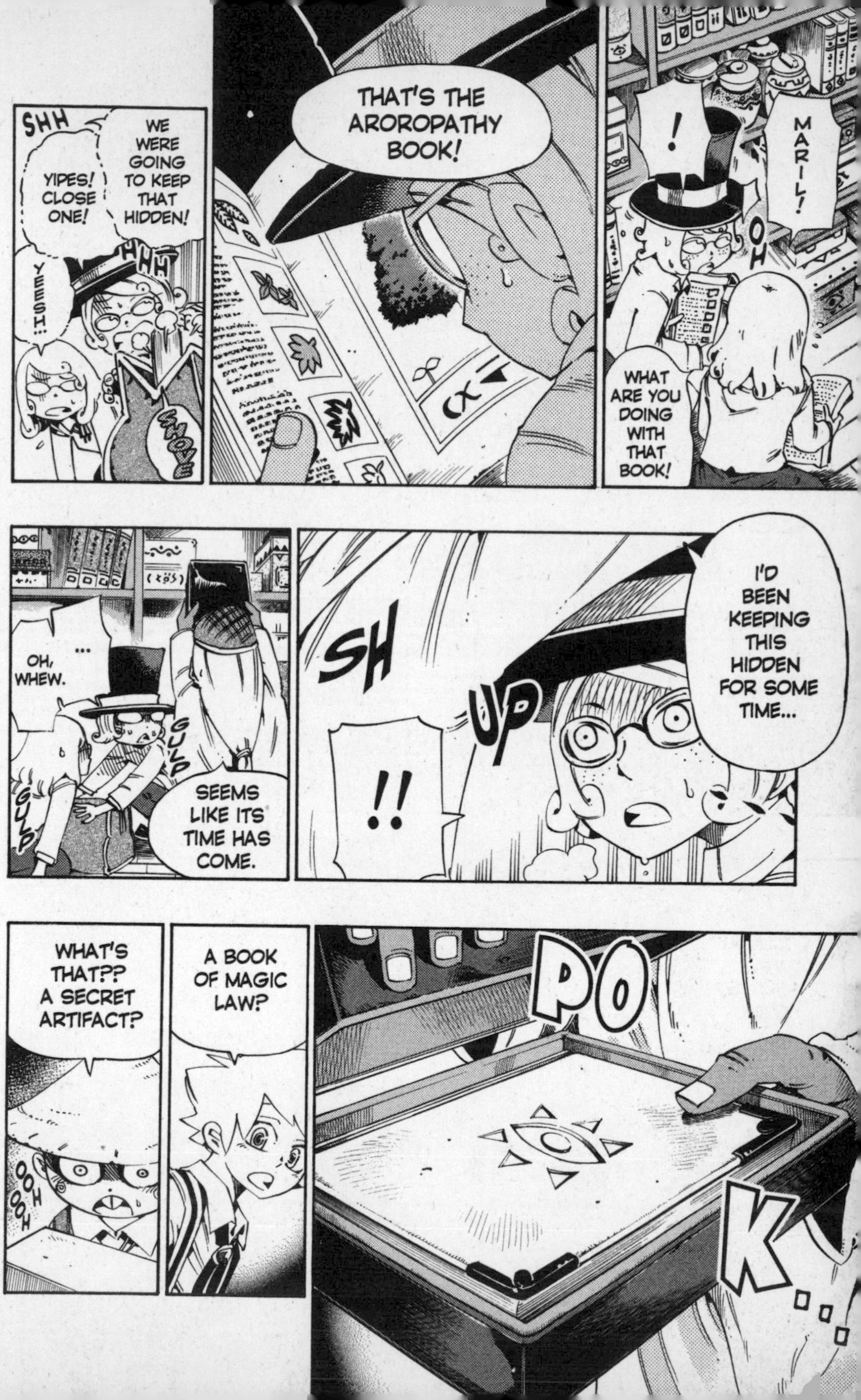
!
MARIL!
OH
WHAT ARE YOU DOING WITH THAT BOOK!
THAT'S THE AROROPATHY BOOK!
SHH
WE WERE GOING TO KEEP THAT HIDDEN!
YIPES! CLOSE ONE!
HHH
YEESH!!
SHOVE
I'D BEEN KEEPING THIS HIDDEN FOR SOME TIME...
SH
UP
!!
...
OH, WHEW.
GULP
GULP
SEEMS LIKE ITS TIME HAS COME.
PO
K...
A BOOK OF MAGIC LAW?
WHAT'S THAT?? A SECRET ARTIFACT?
OOH
OOH

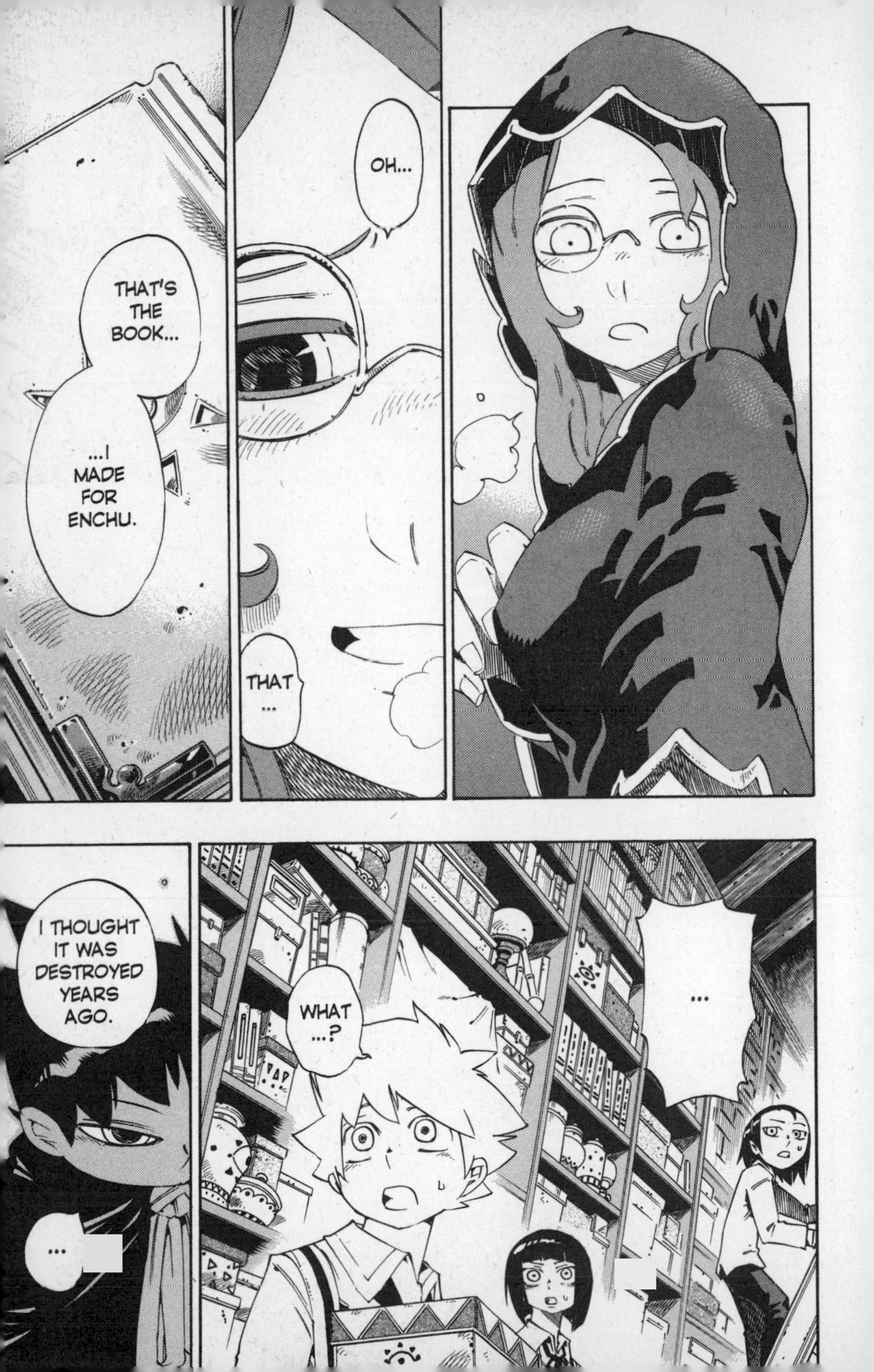
OH...
THAT...
THAT'S THE BOOK...
...I MADE FOR ENCHU.
...
WHAT...?
I THOUGHT IT WAS DESTROYED YEARS AGO.
...

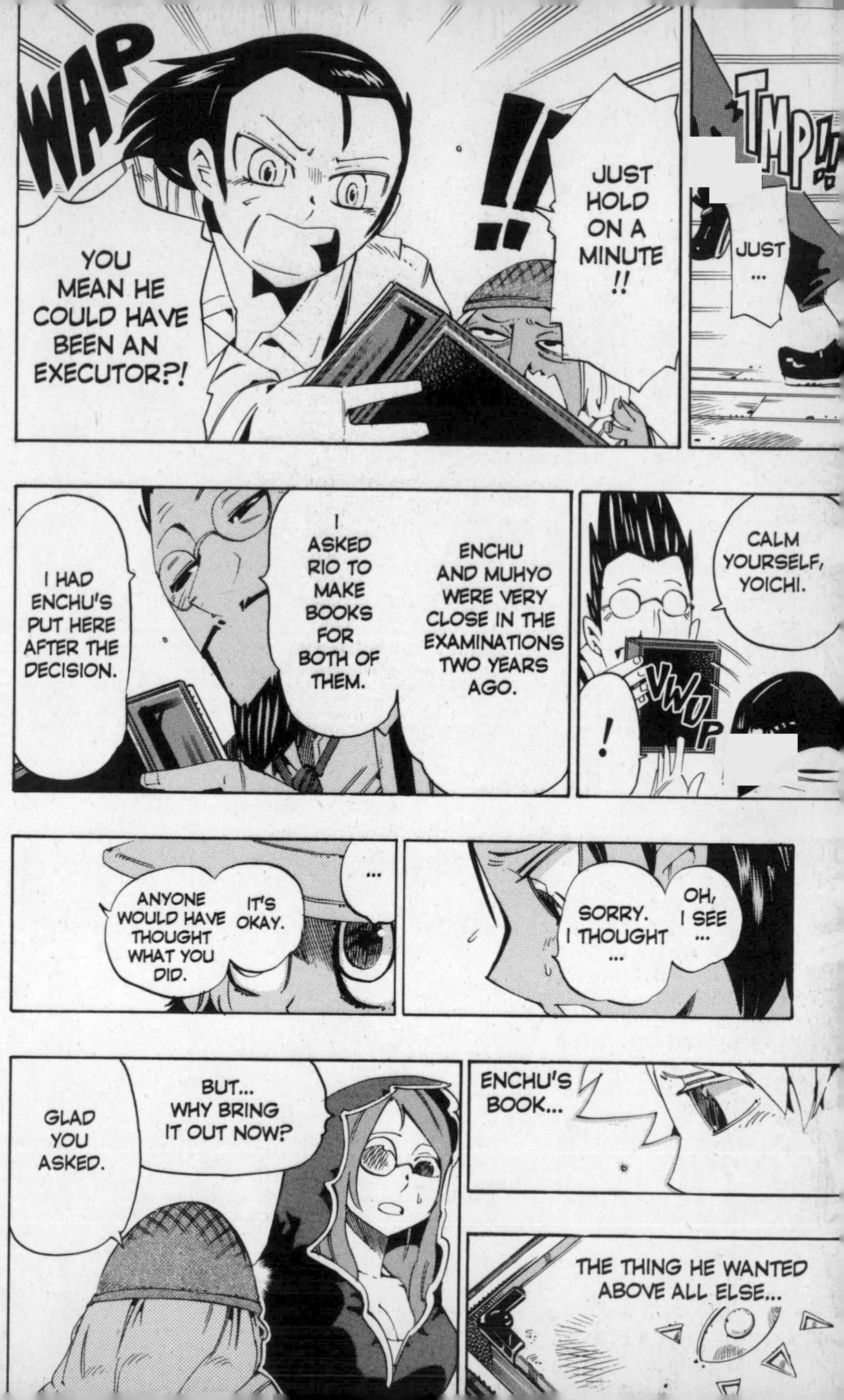
TMP!!
JUST...
!!
JUST HOLD ON A MINUTE!!
WAP
YOU MEAN HE COULD HAVE BEEN AN EXECUTOR?!
CALM YOURSELF, YOICHI.
VWUP
!
ENCHU AND MUHYO WERE VERY CLOSE IN THE EXAMINATIONS TWO YEARS AGO.
I ASKED RIO TO MAKE BOOKS FOR BOTH OF THEM.
I HAD ENCHU'S PUT HERE AFTER THE DECISION.
OH, I SEE...
SORRY. I THOUGHT...
...
IT'S OKAY.
ANYONE WOULD HAVE THOUGHT WHAT YOU DID.
ENCHU'S BOOK...
THE THING HE WANTED ABOVE ALL ELSE...
BUT... WHY BRING IT OUT NOW?
GLAD YOU ASKED.

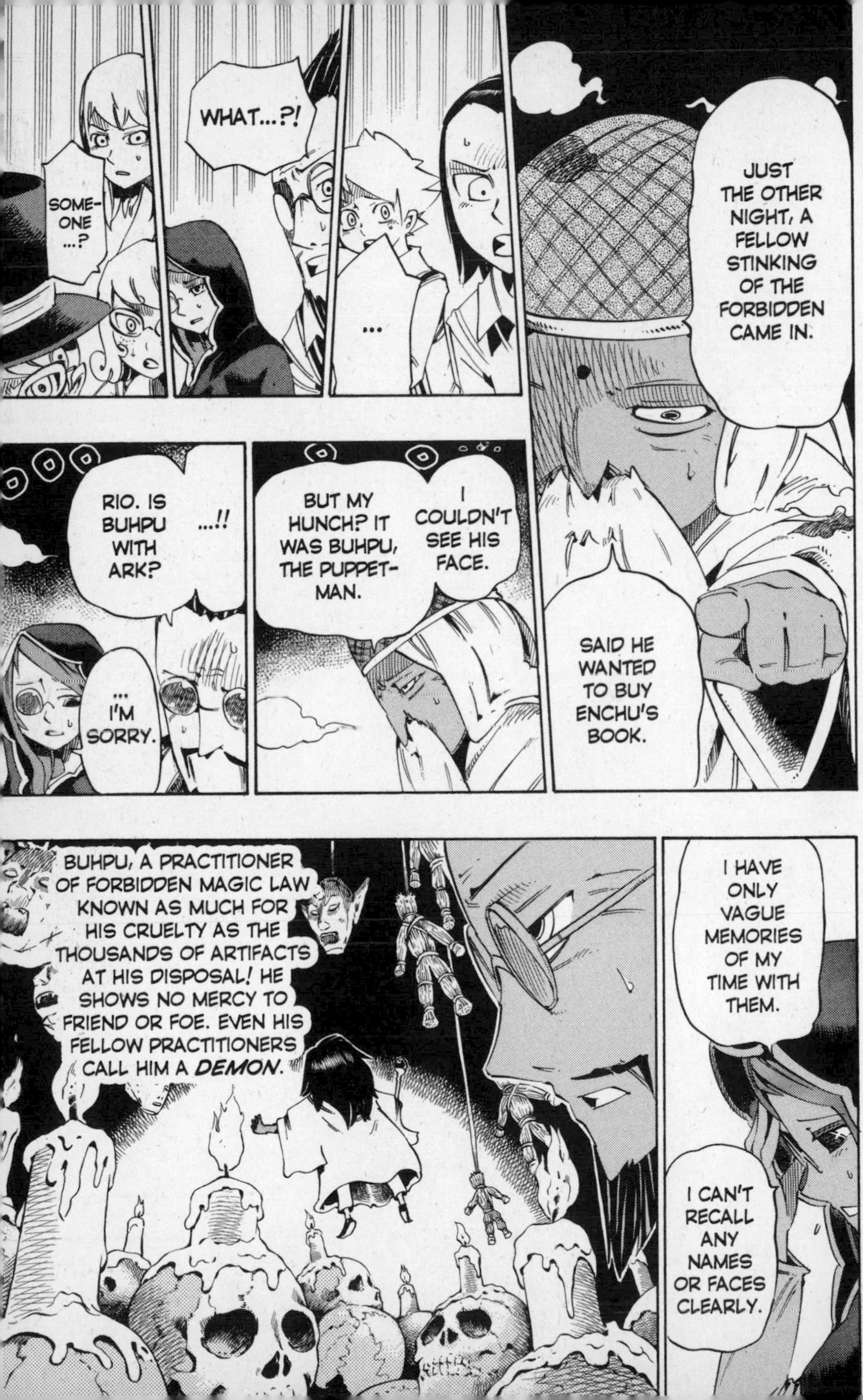
JUST THE OTHER NIGHT, A FELLOW STINKING OF THE FORBIDDEN CAME IN.
SAID HE WANTED TO BUY ENCHU'S BOOK.
WHAT...?!
...
SOME-ONE ...?
I COULDN'T SEE HIS FACE.
BUT MY HUNCH? IT WAS BUHPU, THE PUPPET-MAN.
...!!
RIO. IS BUHPU WITH ARK?
... I'M SORRY.
I HAVE ONLY VAGUE MEMORIES OF MY TIME WITH THEM.
I CAN'T RECALL ANY NAMES OR FACES CLEARLY.
BUHPU, A PRACTITIONER OF FORBIDDEN MAGIC LAW KNOWN AS MUCH FOR HIS CRUELTY AS THE THOUSANDS OF ARTIFACTS AT HIS DISPOSAL! HE SHOWS NO MERCY TO FRIEND OR FOE. EVEN HIS FELLOW PRACTITIONERS CALL HIM A *DEMON*.

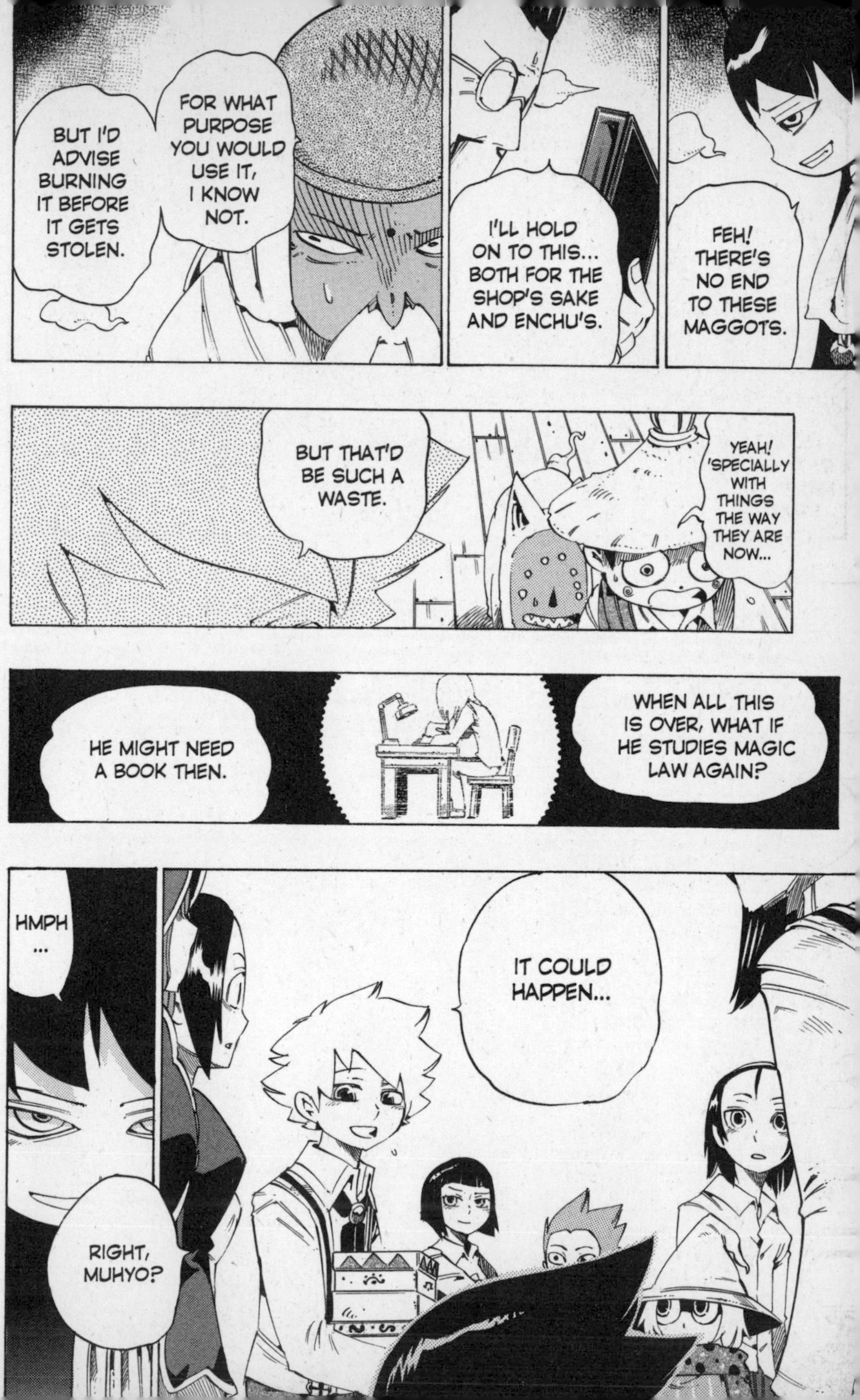
FEH! THERE'S NO END TO THESE MAGGOTS.
I'LL HOLD ON TO THIS... BOTH FOR THE SHOP'S SAKE AND ENCHU'S.
FOR WHAT PURPOSE YOU WOULD USE IT, I KNOW NOT.
BUT I'D ADVISE BURNING IT BEFORE IT GETS STOLEN.
YEAH! 'SPECIALLY WITH THINGS THE WAY THEY ARE NOW...
BUT THAT'D BE SUCH A WASTE.
WHEN ALL THIS IS OVER, WHAT IF HE STUDIES MAGIC LAW AGAIN?
HE MIGHT NEED A BOOK THEN.
IT COULD HAPPEN...
RIGHT, MUHYO?
HMPH ...

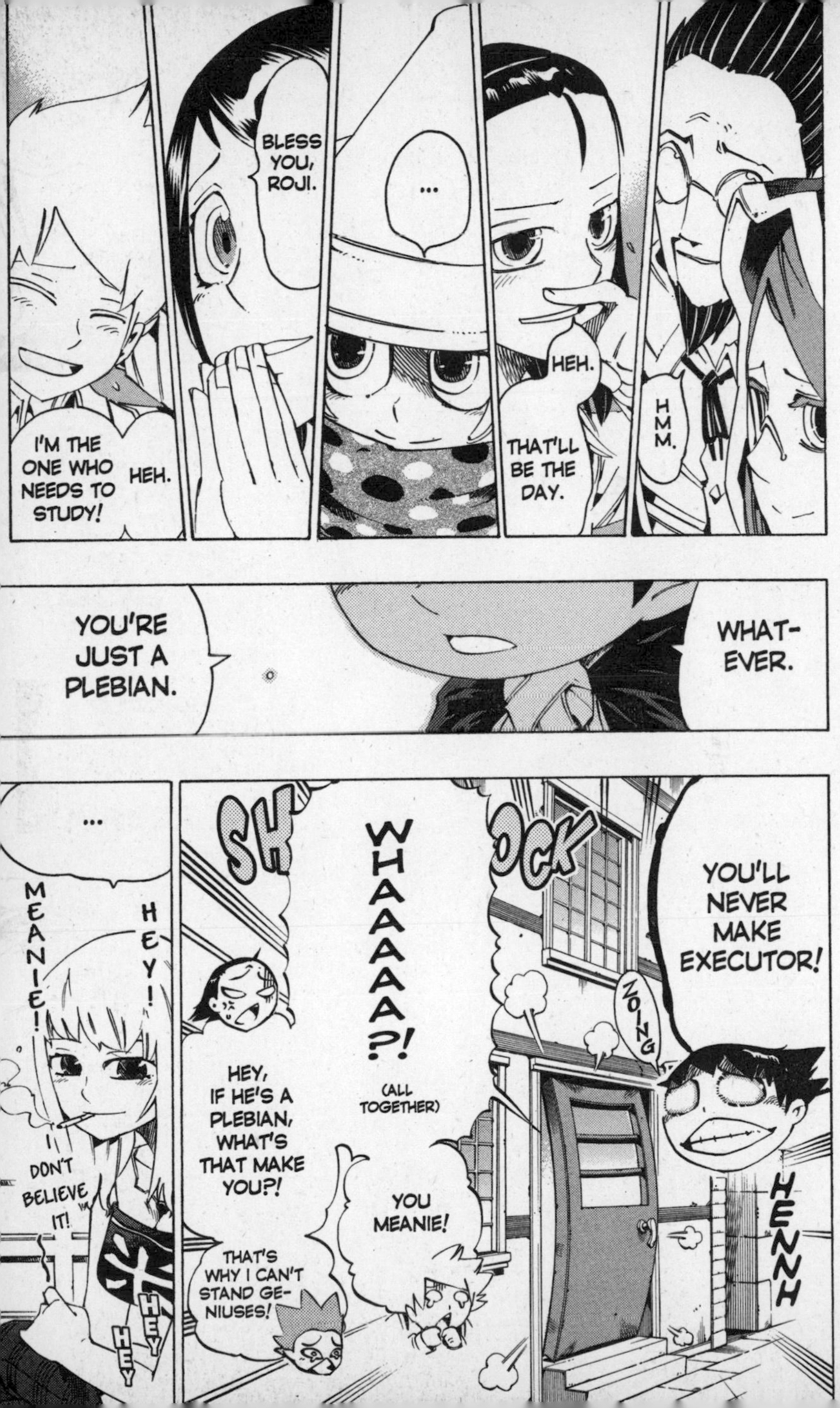
HMM.
HEH.
THAT'LL BE THE DAY.
...
BLESS YOU, ROJI.
HEH.
I'M THE ONE WHO NEEDS TO STUDY!
WHAT-EVER.
YOU'RE JUST A PLEBIAN.
YOU'LL NEVER MAKE EXECUTOR!
ZOING
HENNH
SHOCK
WHAAAAAA?!
(ALL TOGETHER)
HEY, IF HE'S A PLEBIAN, WHAT'S THAT MAKE YOU?!
YOU MEANIE!
THAT'S WHY I CAN'T STAND GENIUSES!
...
HEY!
MEANIE!
I DON'T BELIEVE IT!
HEY
HEY

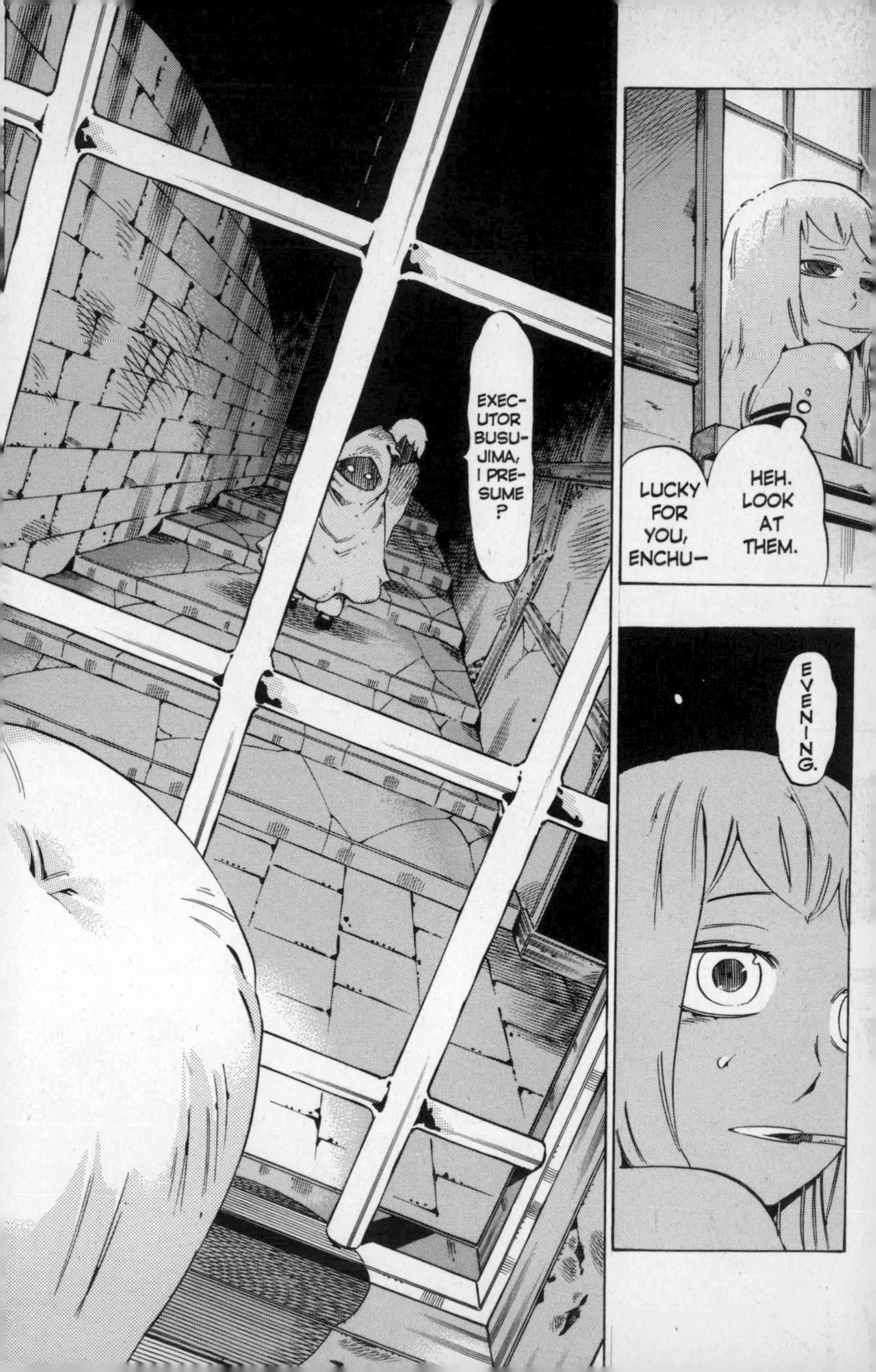
HEH. LOOK AT THEM.
LUCKY FOR YOU, ENCHU—
EVENING.
EXECUTOR BUSUJIMA, I PRESUME?

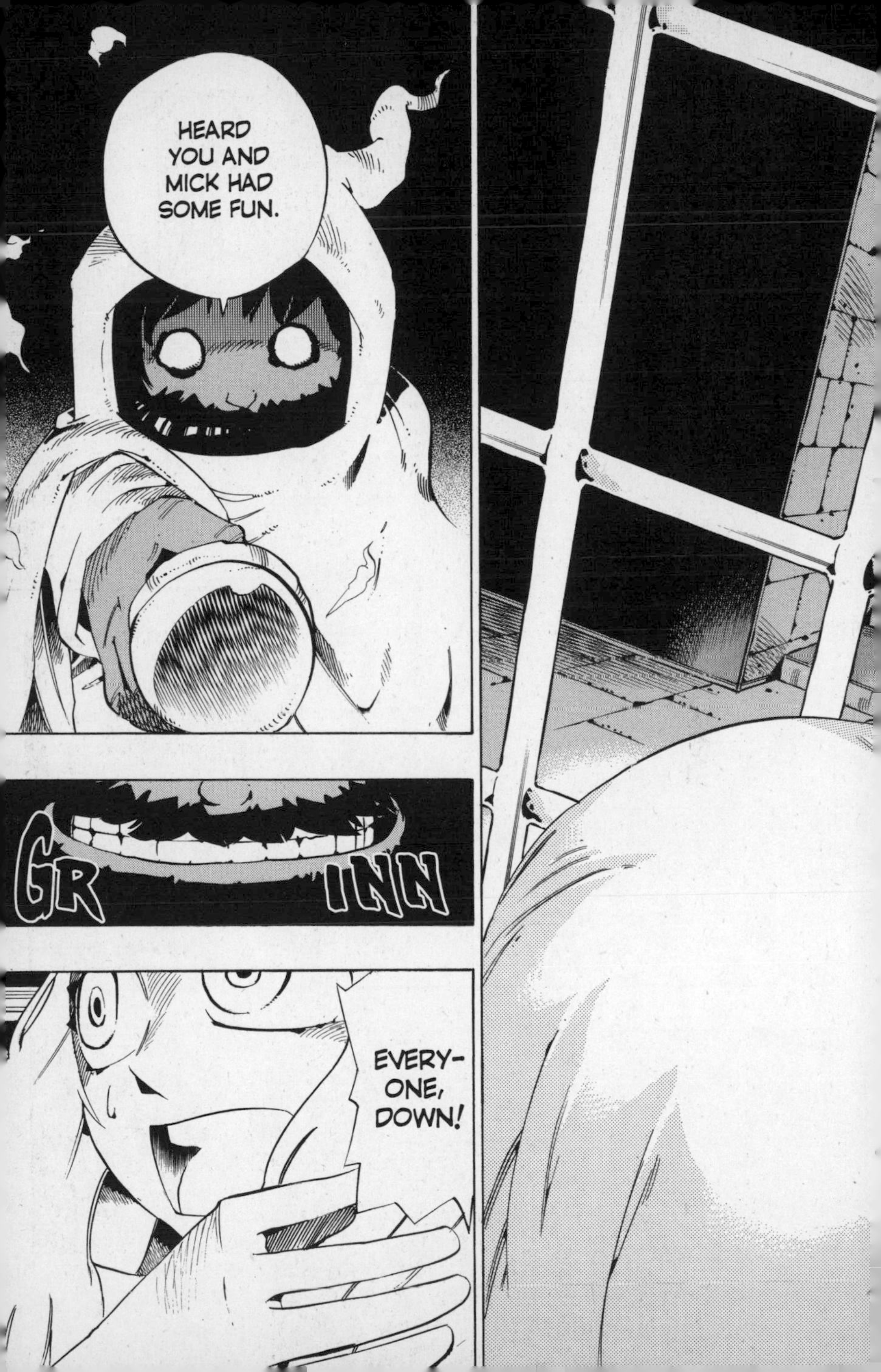
HEARD YOU AND MICK HAD SOME FUN.
GR INN
EVERY-ONE, DOWN!

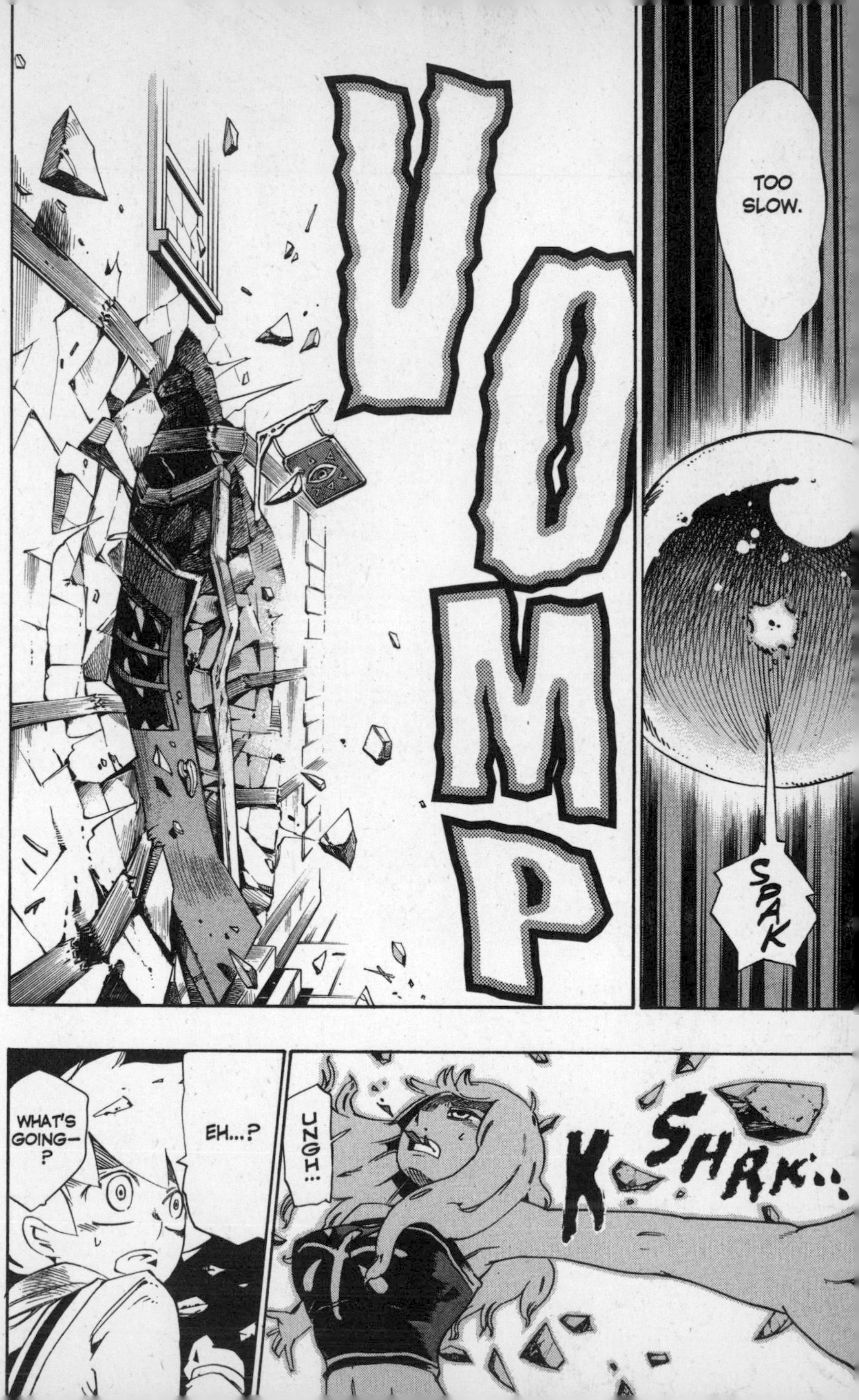
TOO SLOW.
SPAK
VOOMP
KSHRK..
UNGH...
EH...?
WHAT'S GOING—?

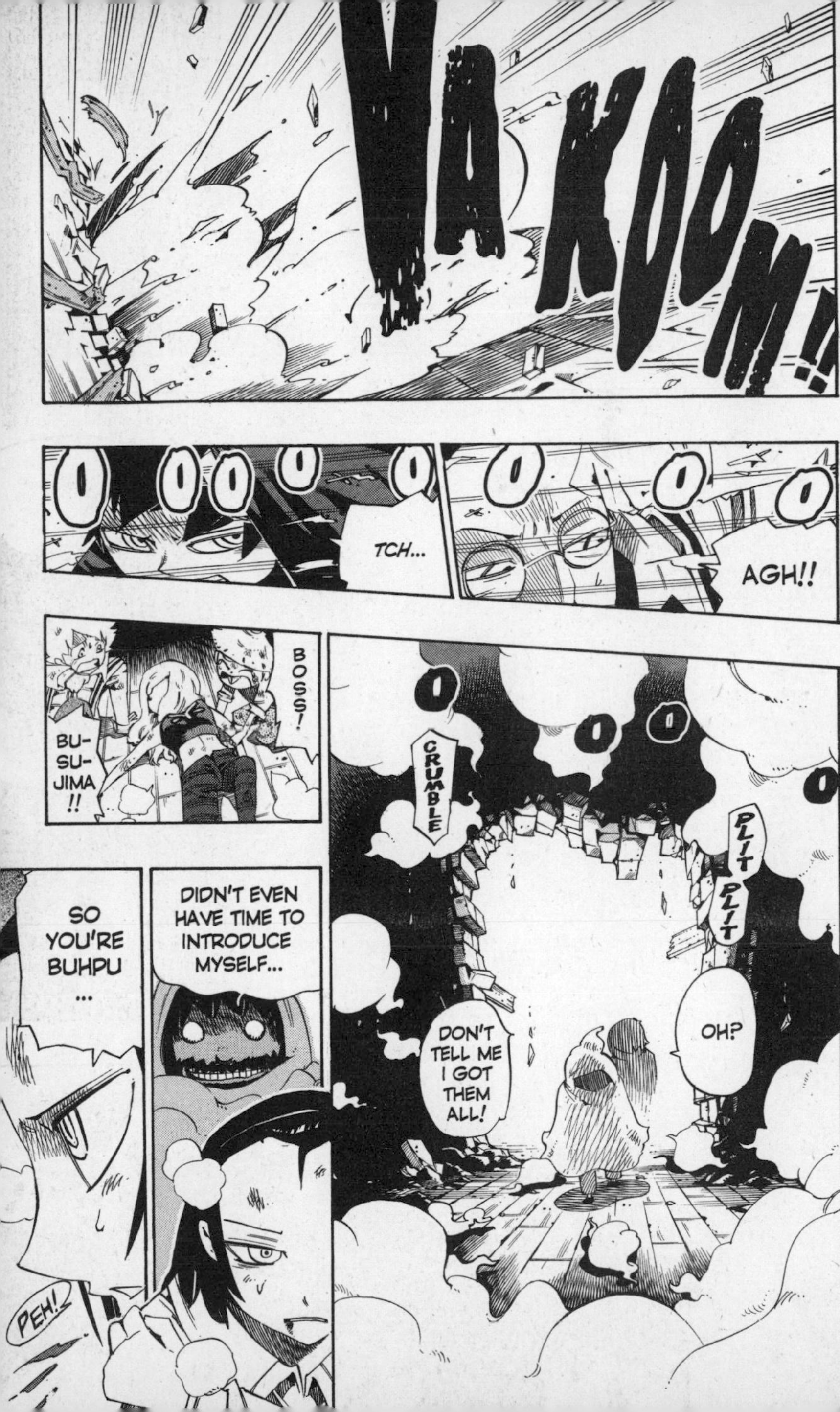
VA KOOM!!
AGH!!
TCH...
CRUMBLE
PLIT PLIT PLIT
OH?
DON'T TELL ME I GOT THEM ALL!
BOSS!
BU-SU-JIMA!!
DIDN'T EVEN HAVE TIME TO INTRODUCE MYSELF...
SO YOU'RE BUHPU ...
PEH!

Q1: HAS GORYO EVER SEEN A PENNY?

Q2: HOW DID YOICHI BECOME THE STRONGEST JUDGE THERE IS EVEN THOUGH HE WAS PRACTICALLY FAILING IN SCHOOL AS A YOUTH? DID HIS "GENIUS" AWAKEN LIKE IT DID WITH MUHYO? OR DID HE JUST APPLY HIMSELF MORE AFTER WHAT HAPPENED WITH ENCHU?

-S.T., SHIZUOKA PREFECTURE

A1: "WHAT'S A PENNY?"

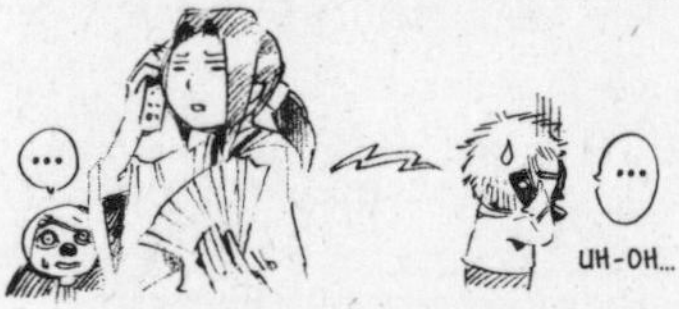
...
UH-OH...
...

NOT ONLY HAS GORYO NEVER SEEN A PENNY BEFORE, BUT HE DIDN'T EVEN SEEM TO KNOW WHAT IT IS! I GUESS THESE MUNDANE MATTERS COME SLOW TO THE OVER-PRIVILEGED...

A2: I THINK HE STARTED APPLYING HIMSELF NOT AFTER WHAT HAPPENED TO ENCHU, BUT AFTER MUHYO DISCOVERED HIS OWN GENIUS... BUT LET'S ASK, SHALL WE?

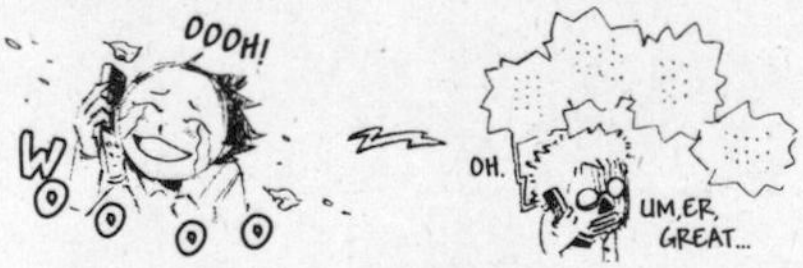
OH.
UM, ER, GREAT...
OOOH!
WOOOOO

YEESH! "GEE! THANKS FOR ASKING!" HE SAYS... THEN HE GOES ON FOR THREE LONG HOURS ABOUT HIS LIFE STORY... I'M EXHAUSTED! AS FOR YOUR QUESTION, YEAH, IT WAS WHAT I SAID—WHEN MUHYO'S GENIUS AWAKENED, YOICHI KICKED INTO HIGH GEAR.

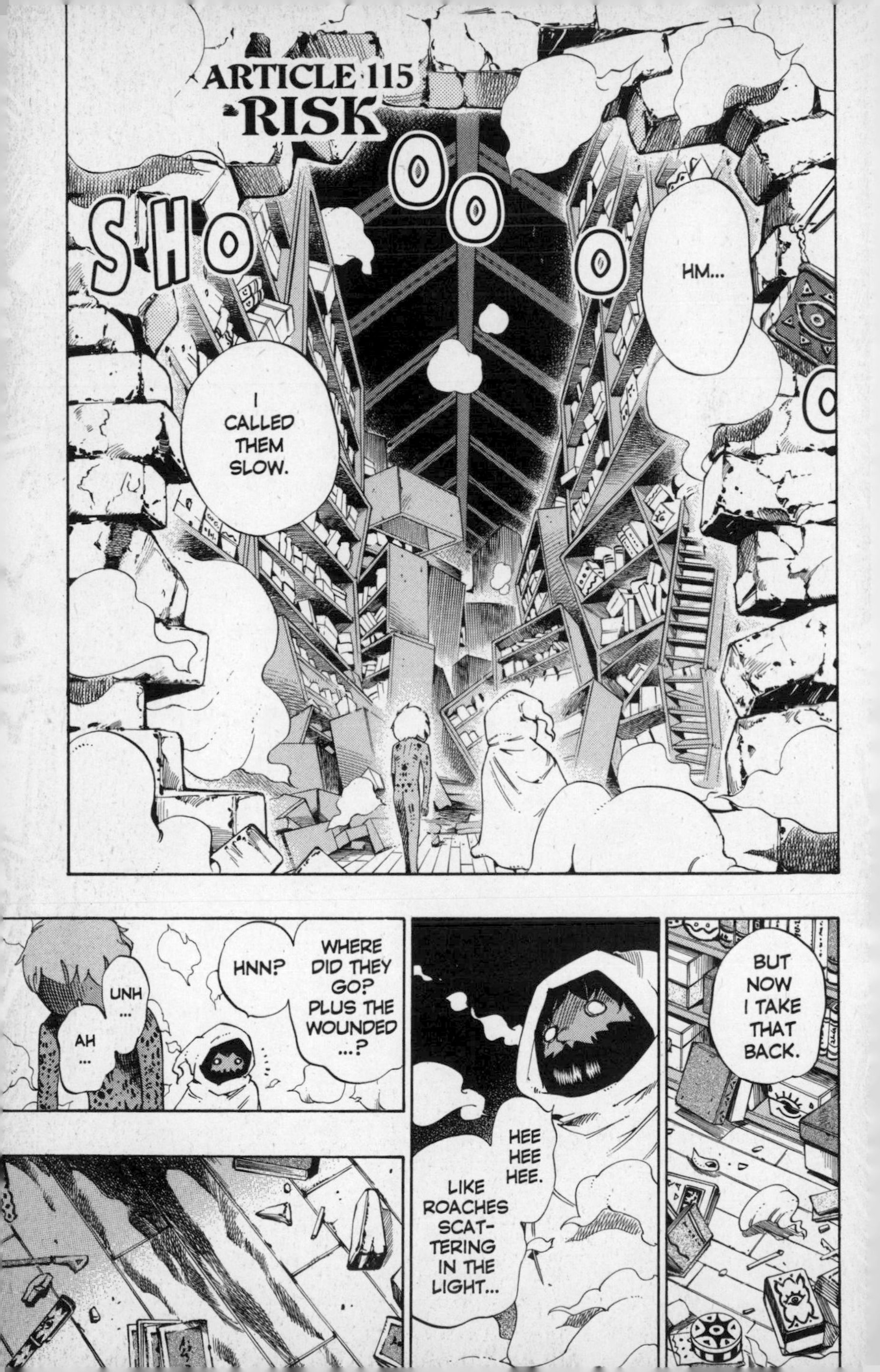
ARTICLE 115 RISK
SHOOOOOO
HM...
I CALLED THEM SLOW.
BUT NOW I TAKE THAT BACK.
HEE HEE HEE.
LIKE ROACHES SCAT-TERING IN THE LIGHT...
WHERE DID THEY GO? PLUS THE WOUNDED ...?
HNN?
UNH ...
AH ...

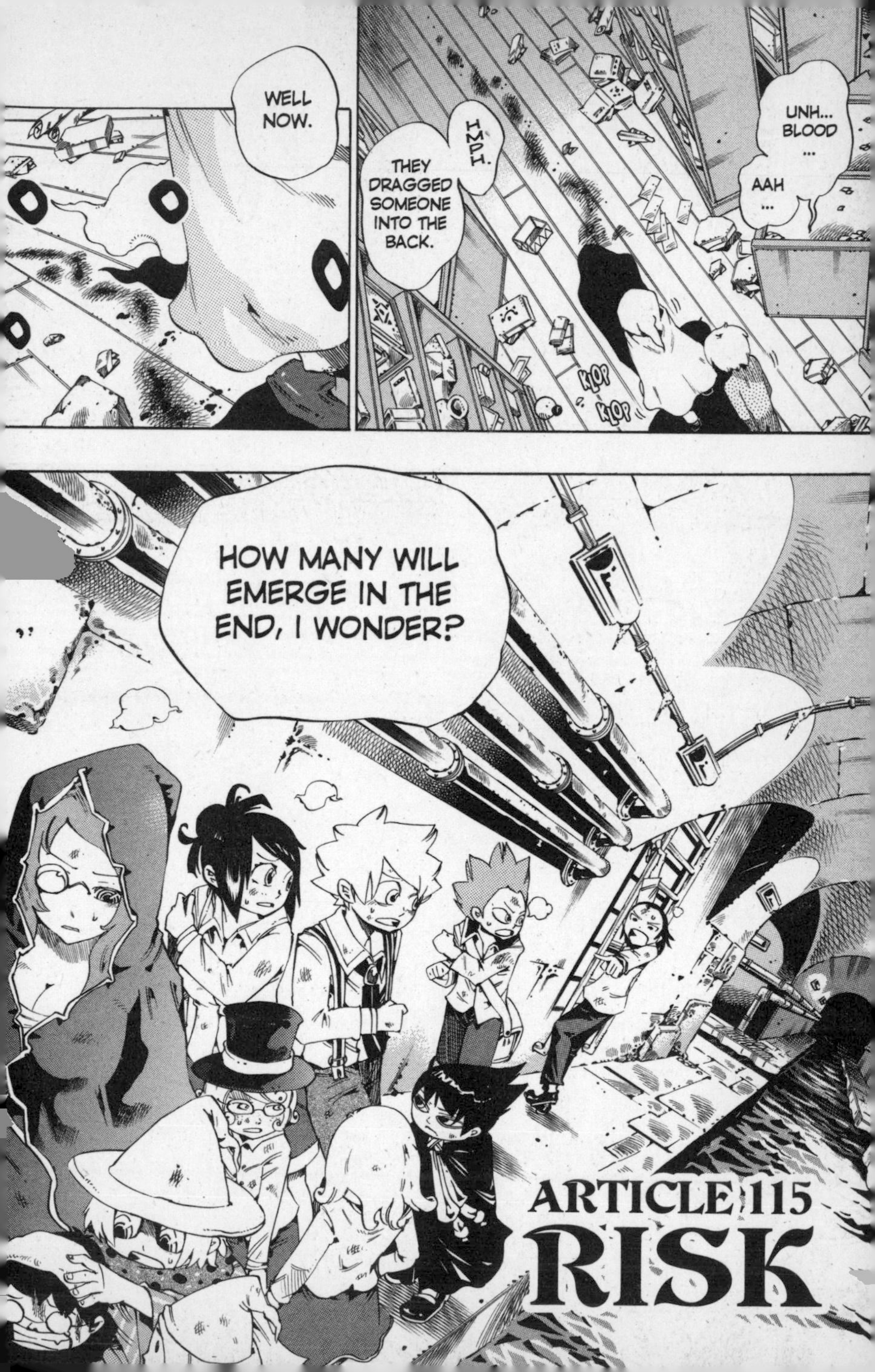
UNH... BLOOD ...
AAH ...
HMPH.
THEY DRAGGED SOMEONE INTO THE BACK.
KLOP
KLOP
WELL NOW.
HOW MANY WILL EMERGE IN THE END, I WONDER?
ARTICLE 115
RISK

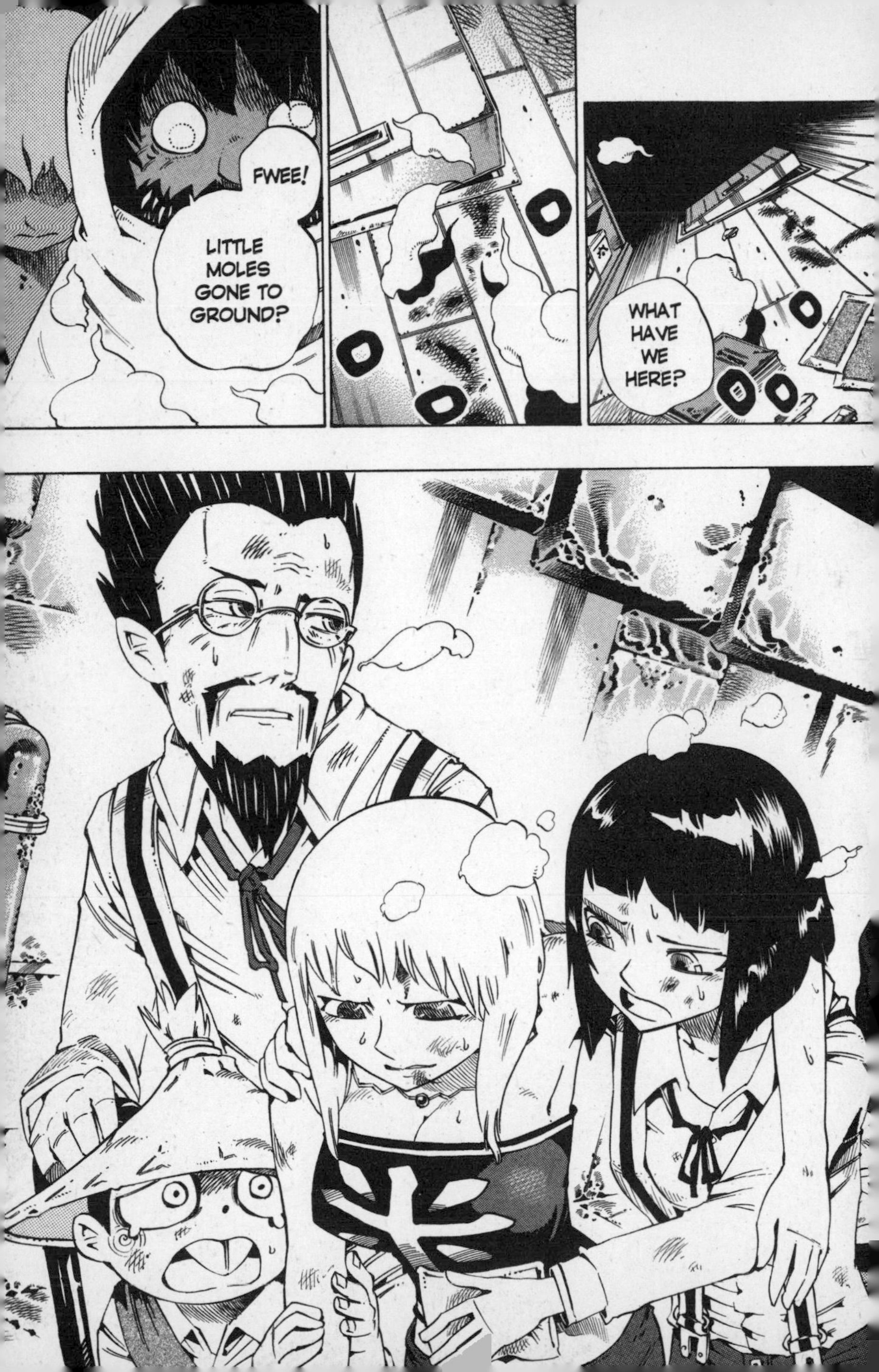
WHAT HAVE WE HERE?
FWEE!
LITTLE MOLES GONE TO GROUND?

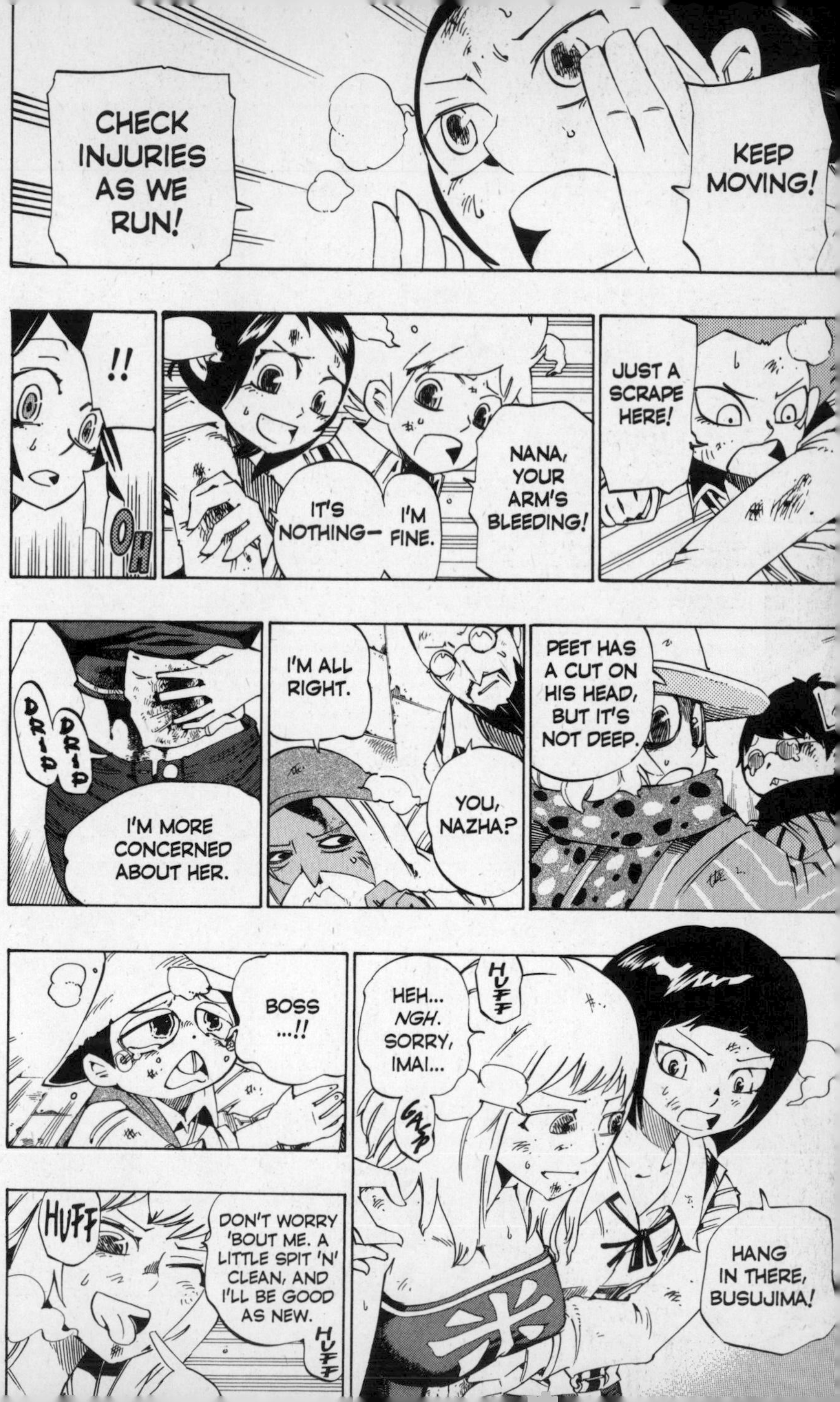
KEEP MOVING!
CHECK INJURIES AS WE RUN!
JUST A SCRAPE HERE!
NANA, YOUR ARM'S BLEEDING!
I'M FINE.
IT'S NOTHING—
!!
OH
PEET HAS A CUT ON HIS HEAD, BUT IT'S NOT DEEP.
YOU, NAZHA?
I'M ALL RIGHT.
DRIP DRIP
I'M MORE CONCERNED ABOUT HER.
HUFF
HEH... *NGH*. SORRY, IMAI...
GASP
HANG IN THERE, BUSUJIMA!
BOSS ...!!
DON'T WORRY 'BOUT ME. A LITTLE SPIT 'N' CLEAN, AND I'LL BE GOOD AS NEW.
HUFF
HUFF

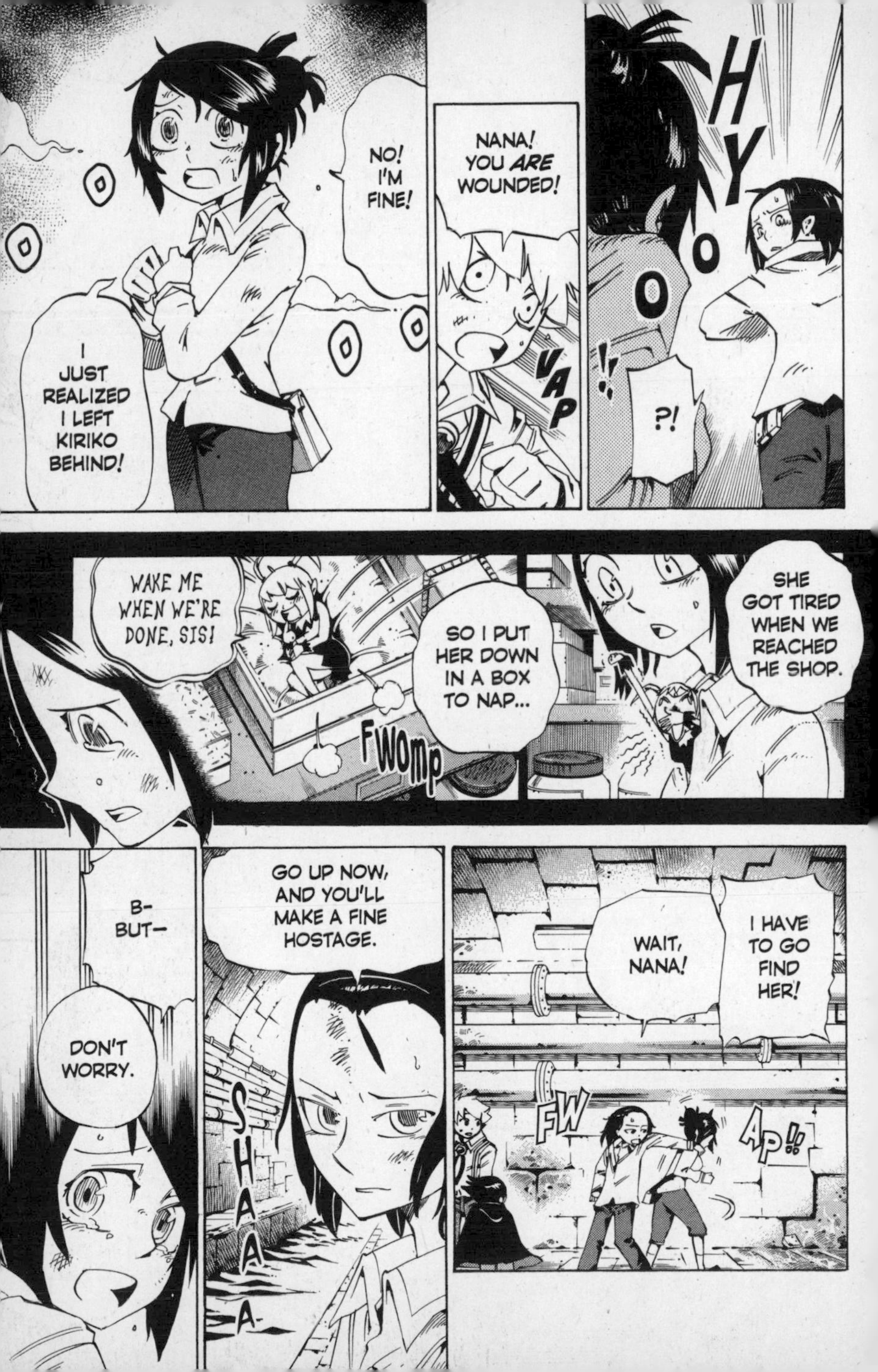
HYOO
!!
?!
NANA! YOU ARE WOUNDED!
VAP
NO! I'M FINE!
I JUST REALIZED I LEFT KIRIKO BEHIND!
SHE GOT TIRED WHEN WE REACHED THE SHOP.
SO I PUT HER DOWN IN A BOX TO NAP...
WAKE ME WHEN WE'RE DONE, SIS!
FWOMP
I HAVE TO GO FIND HER!
WAIT, NANA!
FW
AP!!
GO UP NOW, AND YOU'LL MAKE A FINE HOSTAGE.
SHAAAA
B-BUT—
DON'T WORRY.

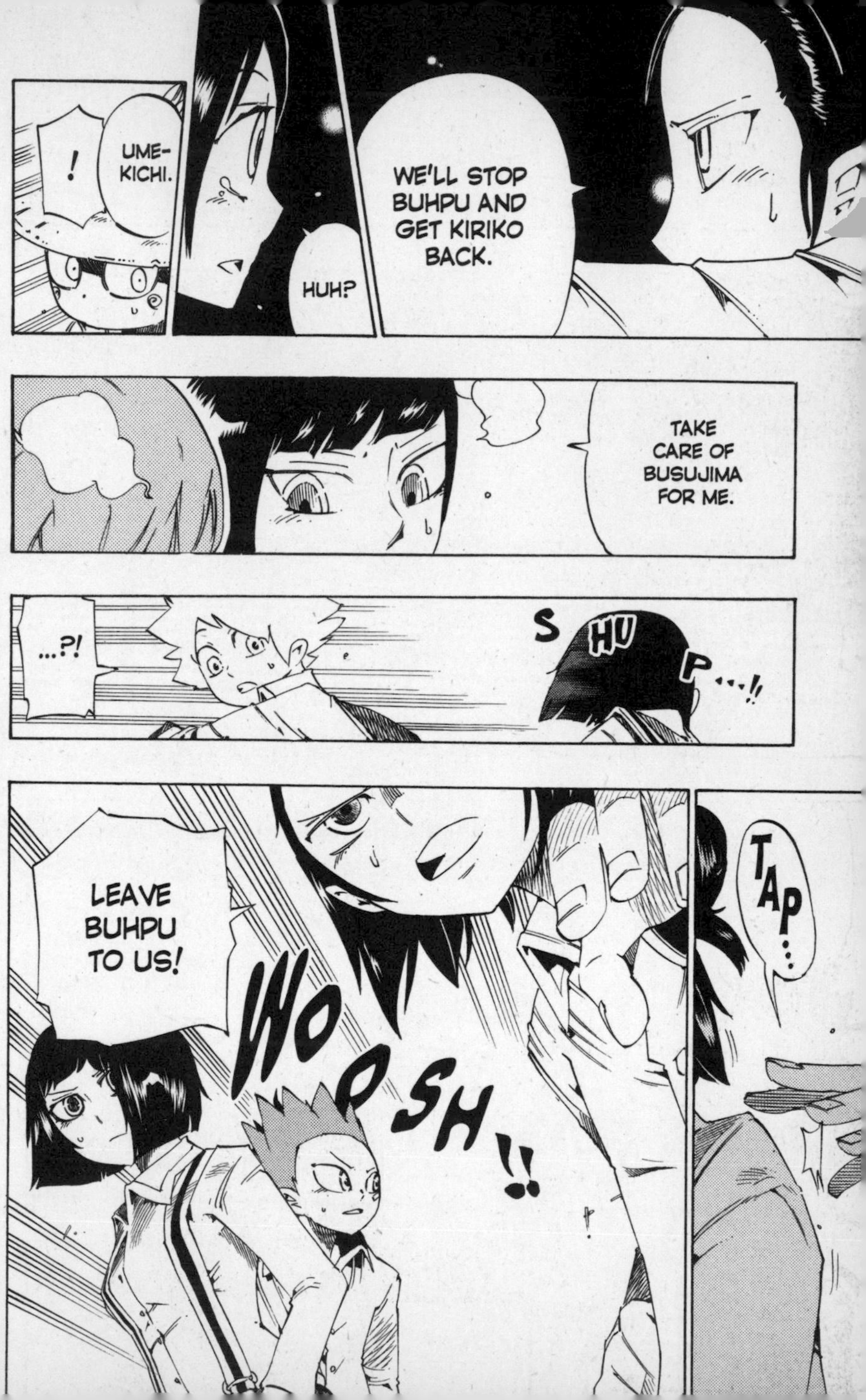
WE'LL STOP BUHPU AND GET KIRIKO BACK.
HUH?
UME-KICHI.
!
TAKE CARE OF BUSUJIMA FOR ME.
SHUP...!!
...?!
TAP...
LEAVE BUHPU TO US!
WOOSH!!

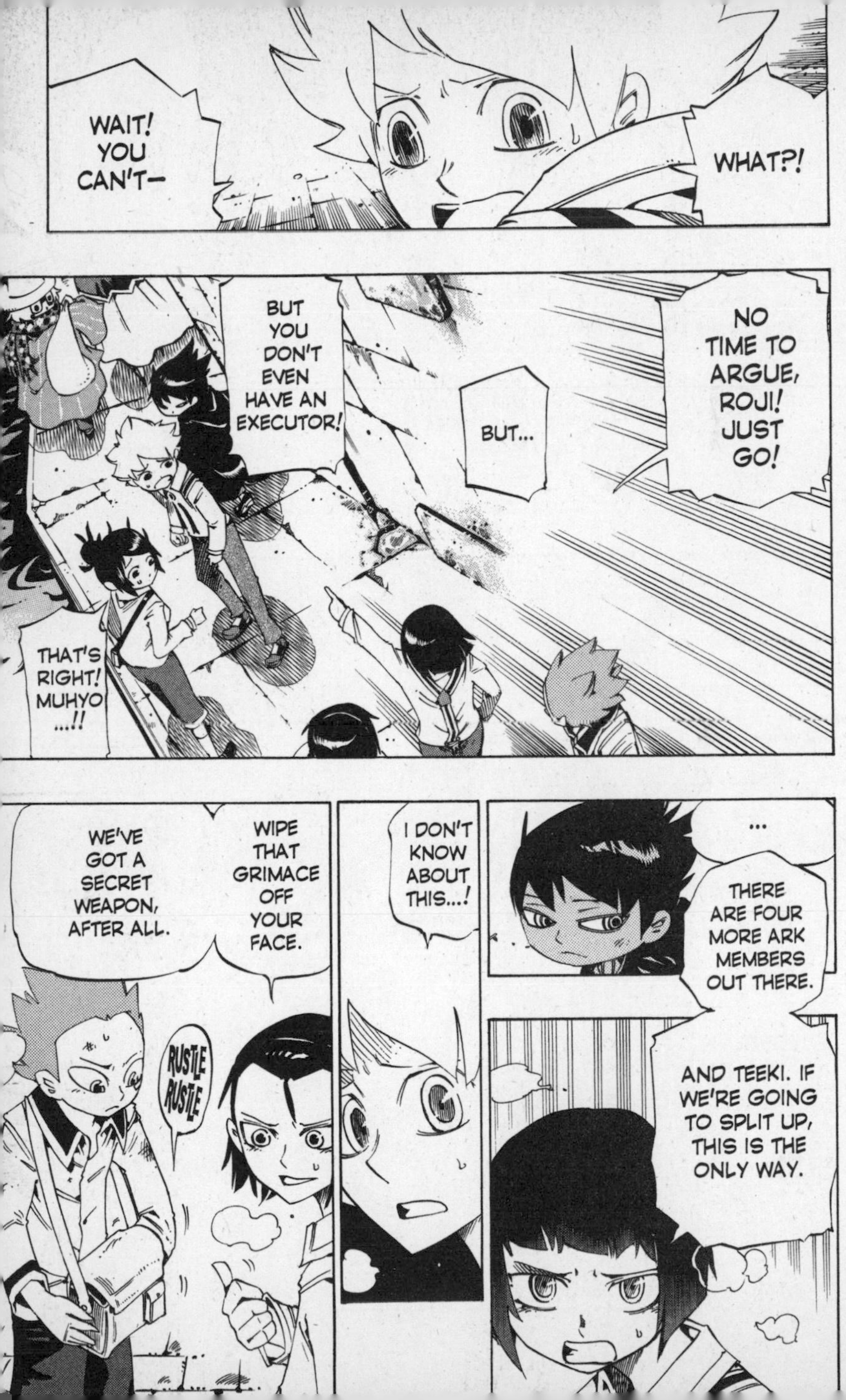
WHAT?!
WAIT! YOU CAN'T—
NO TIME TO ARGUE, ROJI! JUST GO!
BUT...
BUT YOU DON'T EVEN HAVE AN EXECUTOR!
THAT'S RIGHT! MUHYO ...!!
...
THERE ARE FOUR MORE ARK MEMBERS OUT THERE.
AND TEEKI. IF WE'RE GOING TO SPLIT UP, THIS IS THE ONLY WAY.
I DON'T KNOW ABOUT THIS...!
WIPE THAT GRIMACE OFF YOUR FACE.
WE'VE GOT A SECRET WEAPON, AFTER ALL.
RUSTLE RUSTLE

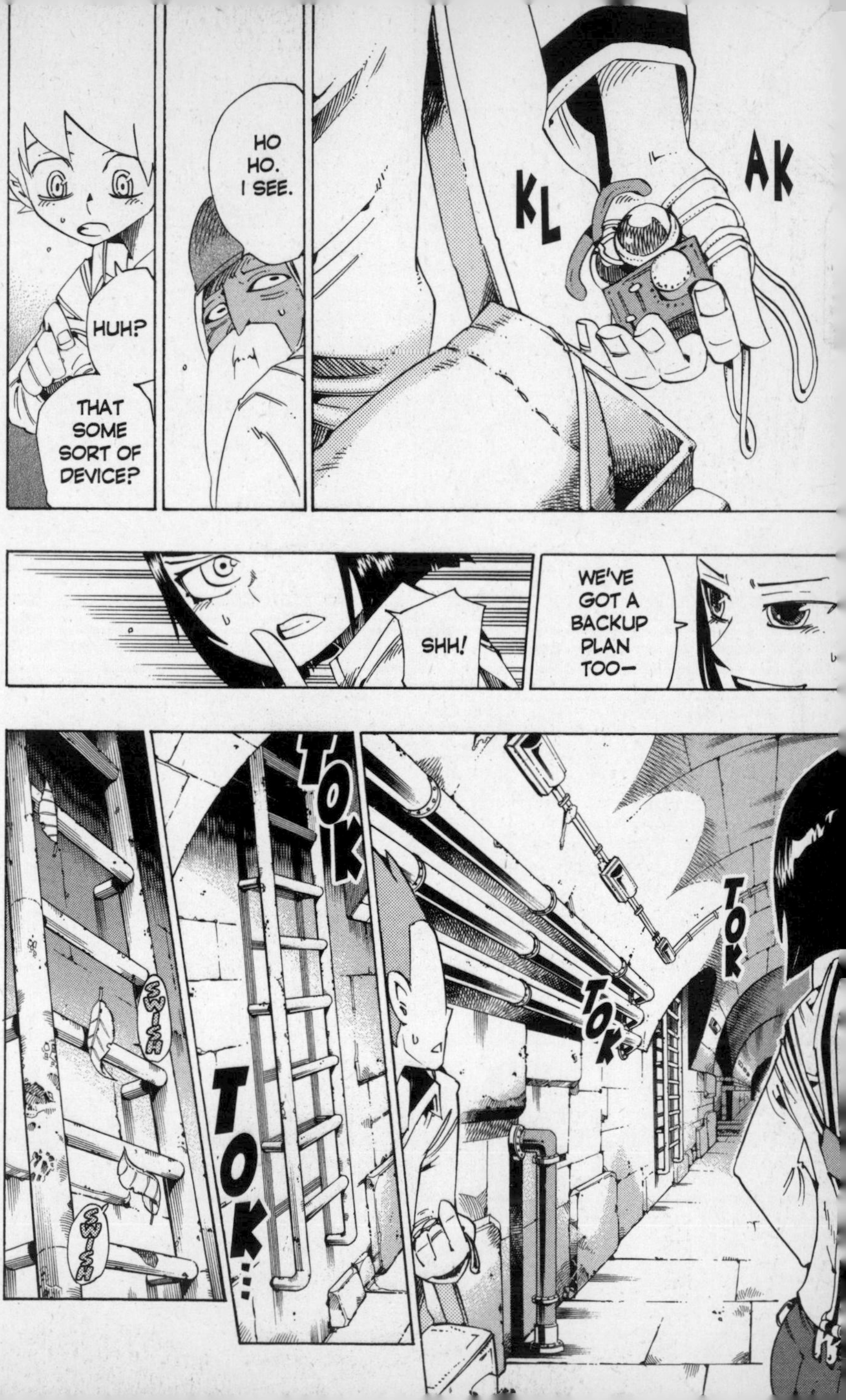
KL
AK
HO HO. I SEE.
HUH?
THAT SOME SORT OF DEVICE?
WE'VE GOT A BACKUP PLAN TOO—
SHH!
TOK
TOK
TOK
TOK
TOK
TOK...
SWISH
SWISH

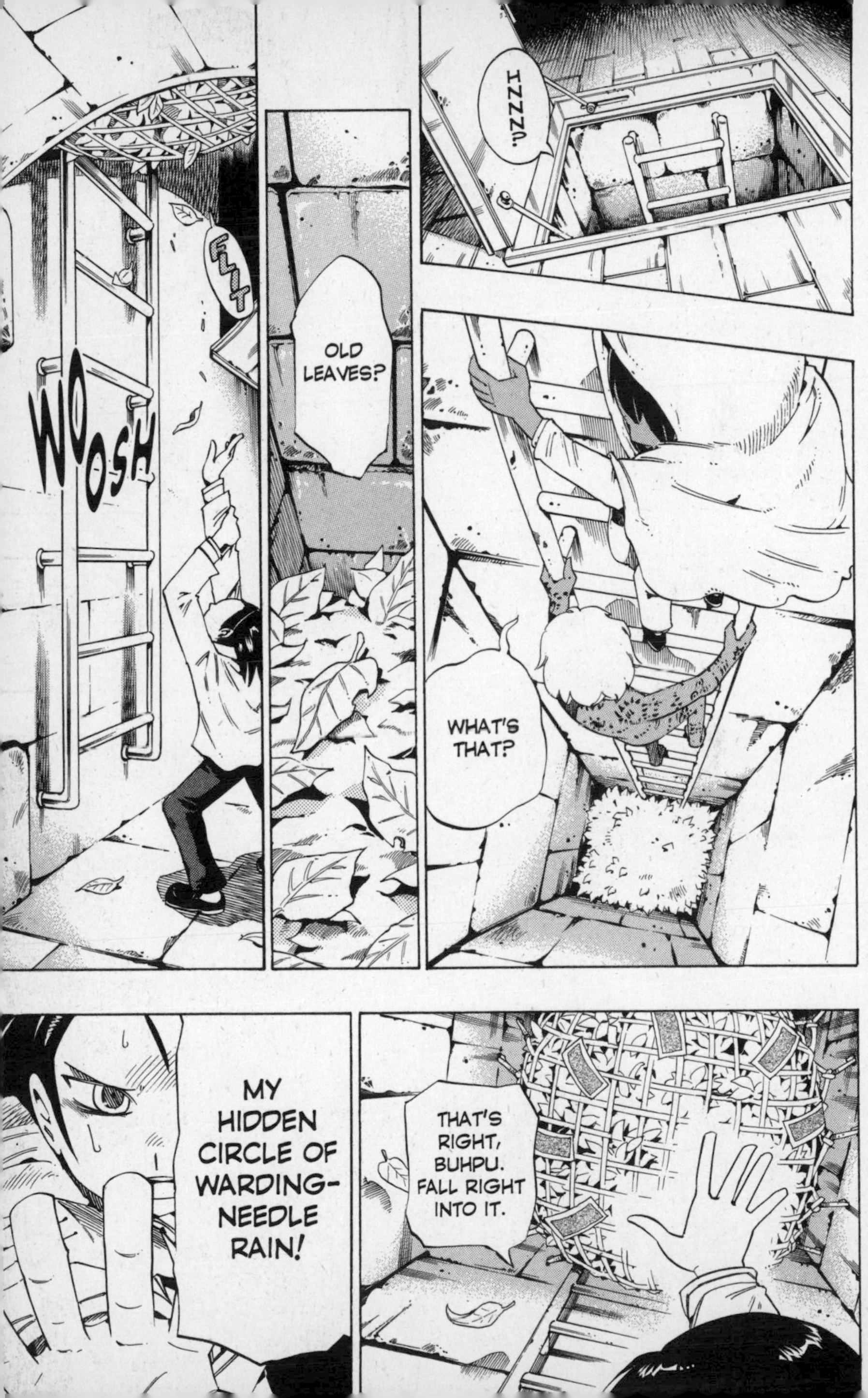
HNNN?
WHAT'S THAT?
OLD LEAVES?
FLIT
WOOSH
THAT'S RIGHT, BUHPU. FALL RIGHT INTO IT.
MY HIDDEN CIRCLE OF WARDING-NEEDLE RAIN!

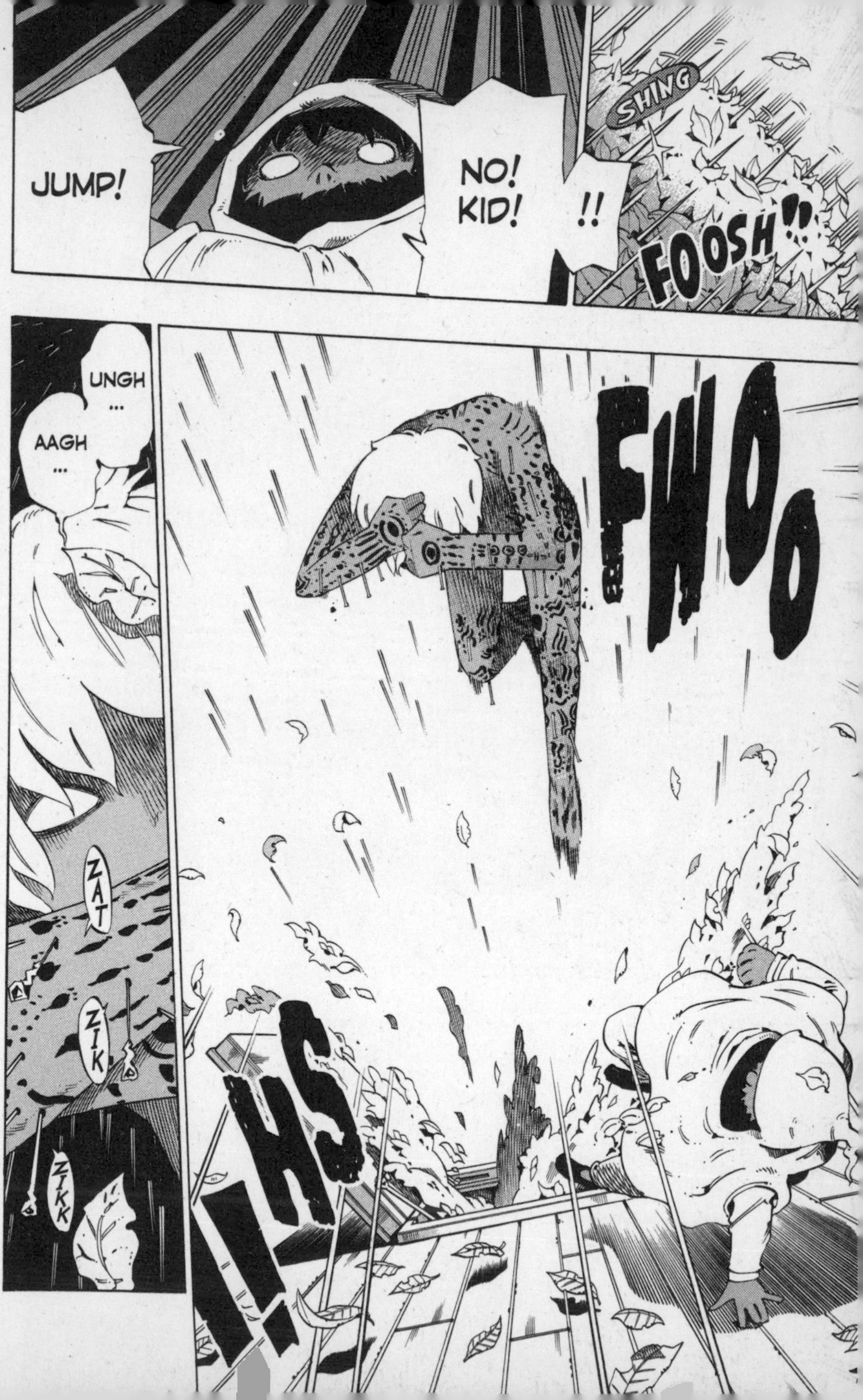
SHING
FOOSH!!
!!
NO! KID!
JUMP!
FWOOO
SHH
UNGH ...
AAGH ...
ZAT
ZIK
ZIKK

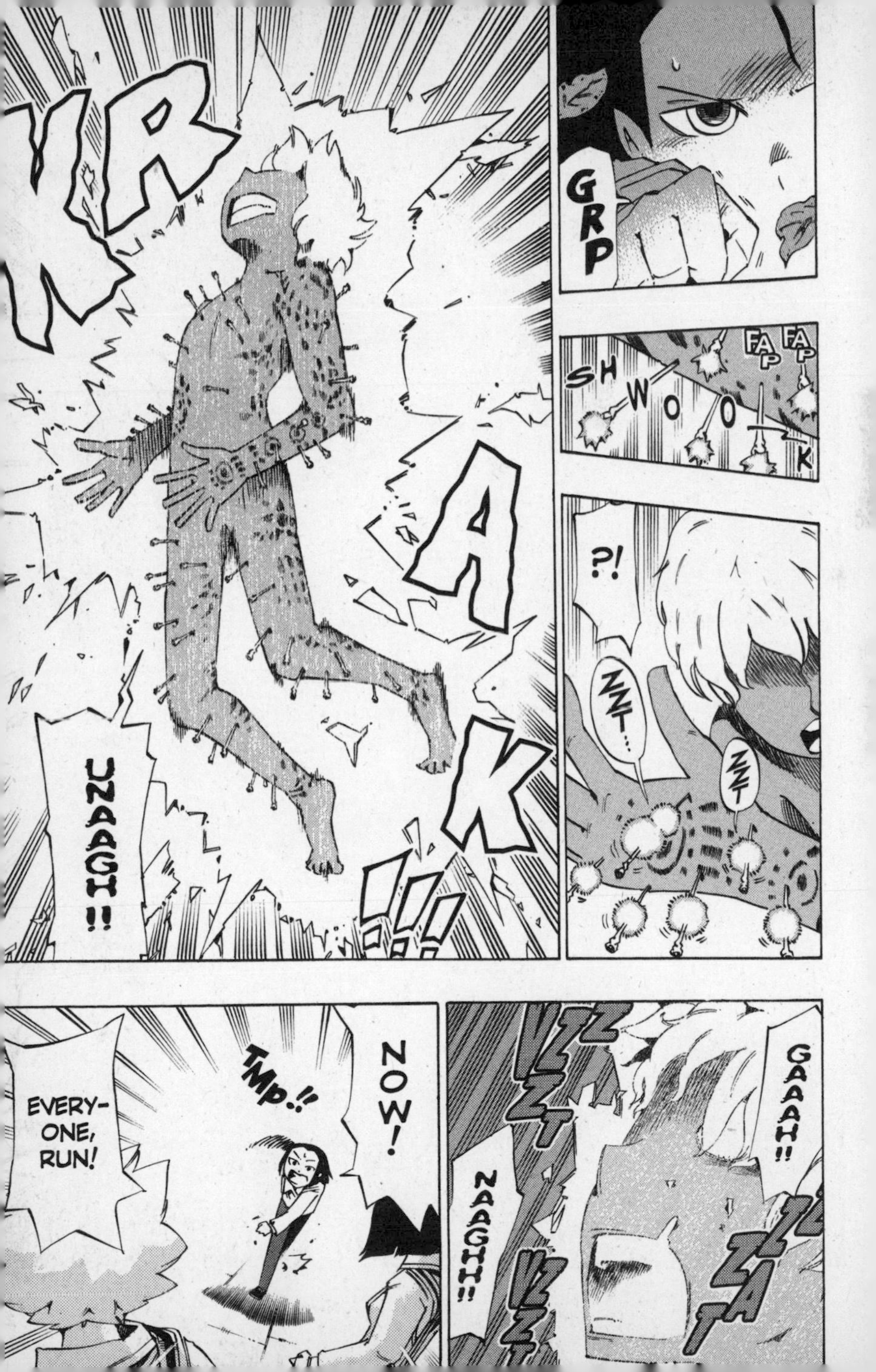
GRP
SHWOOOK
FAP FAP
?!
ZZZT...
ZZZT
KRAK!!!
UNAAAGH!!
GAAAAH!!
VZZT
ZZZAT
NAAAGHH!!
VZZT
NOW!
TMP!!
EVERY-ONE, RUN!

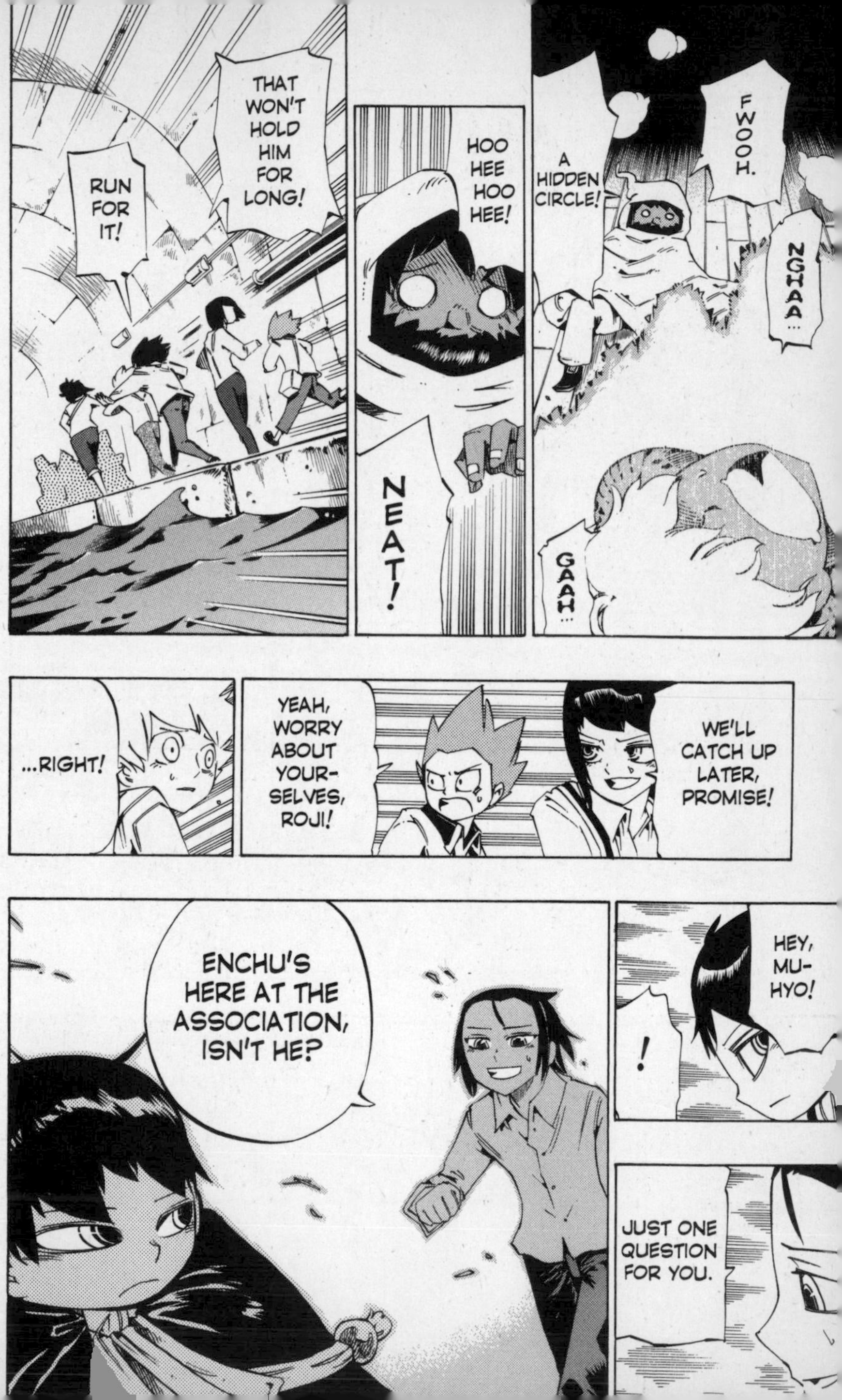
FWOOH.
NGHAA...
A HIDDEN CIRCLE!
GAAH...
HOO HEE HOO HEE!
NEAT!
THAT WON'T HOLD HIM FOR LONG!
RUN FOR IT!
WE'LL CATCH UP LATER, PROMISE!
YEAH, WORRY ABOUT YOUR-SELVES, ROJI!
...RIGHT!
HEY, MU-HYO!
!
JUST ONE QUESTION FOR YOU.
ENCHU'S HERE AT THE ASSOCIATION, ISN'T HE?

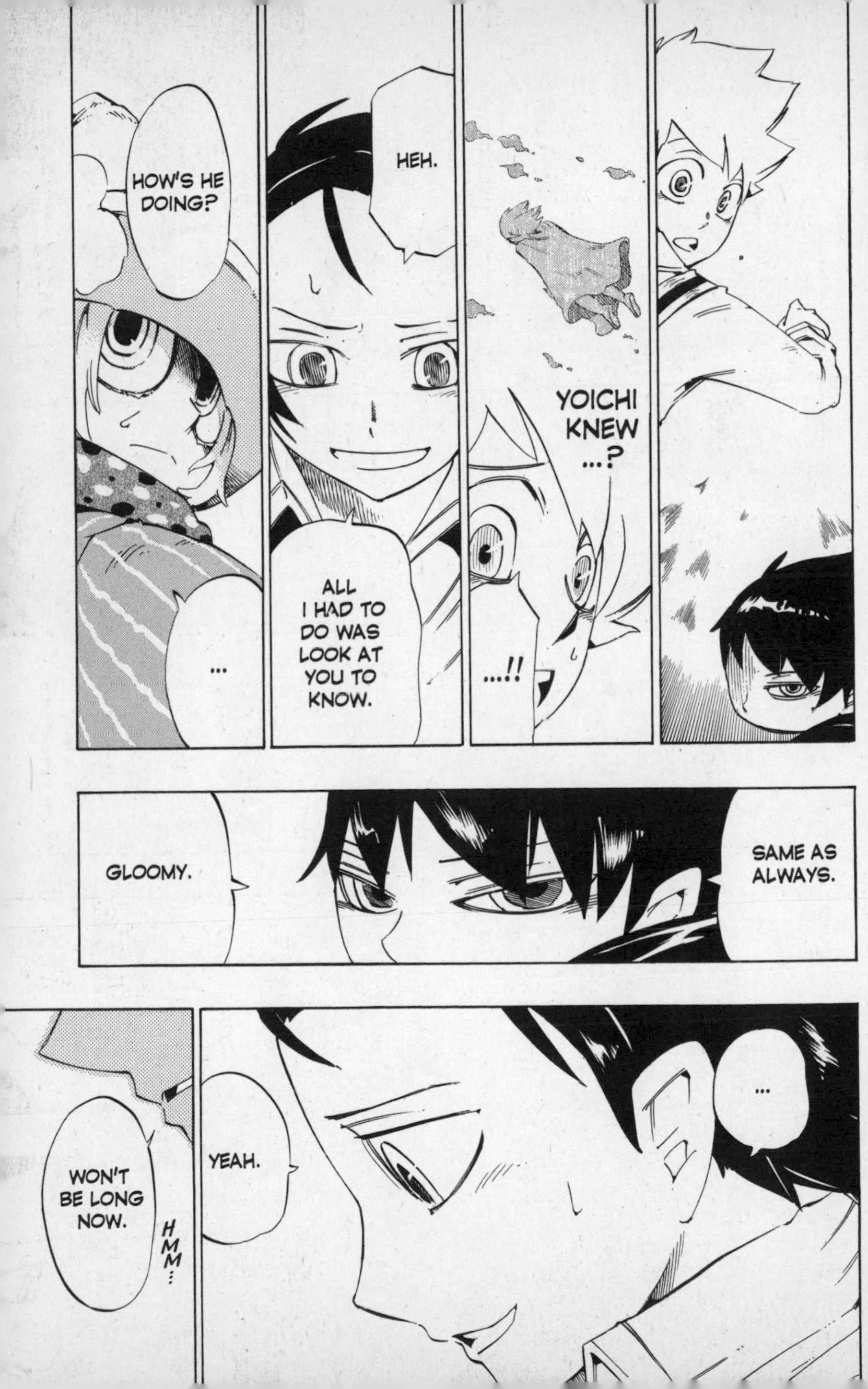
YOICHI KNEW ...?
...!!
HEH.
ALL I HAD TO DO WAS LOOK AT YOU TO KNOW.
HOW'S HE DOING?
...
SAME AS ALWAYS.
GLOOMY.
...
YEAH.
HMM...
WON'T BE LONG NOW.

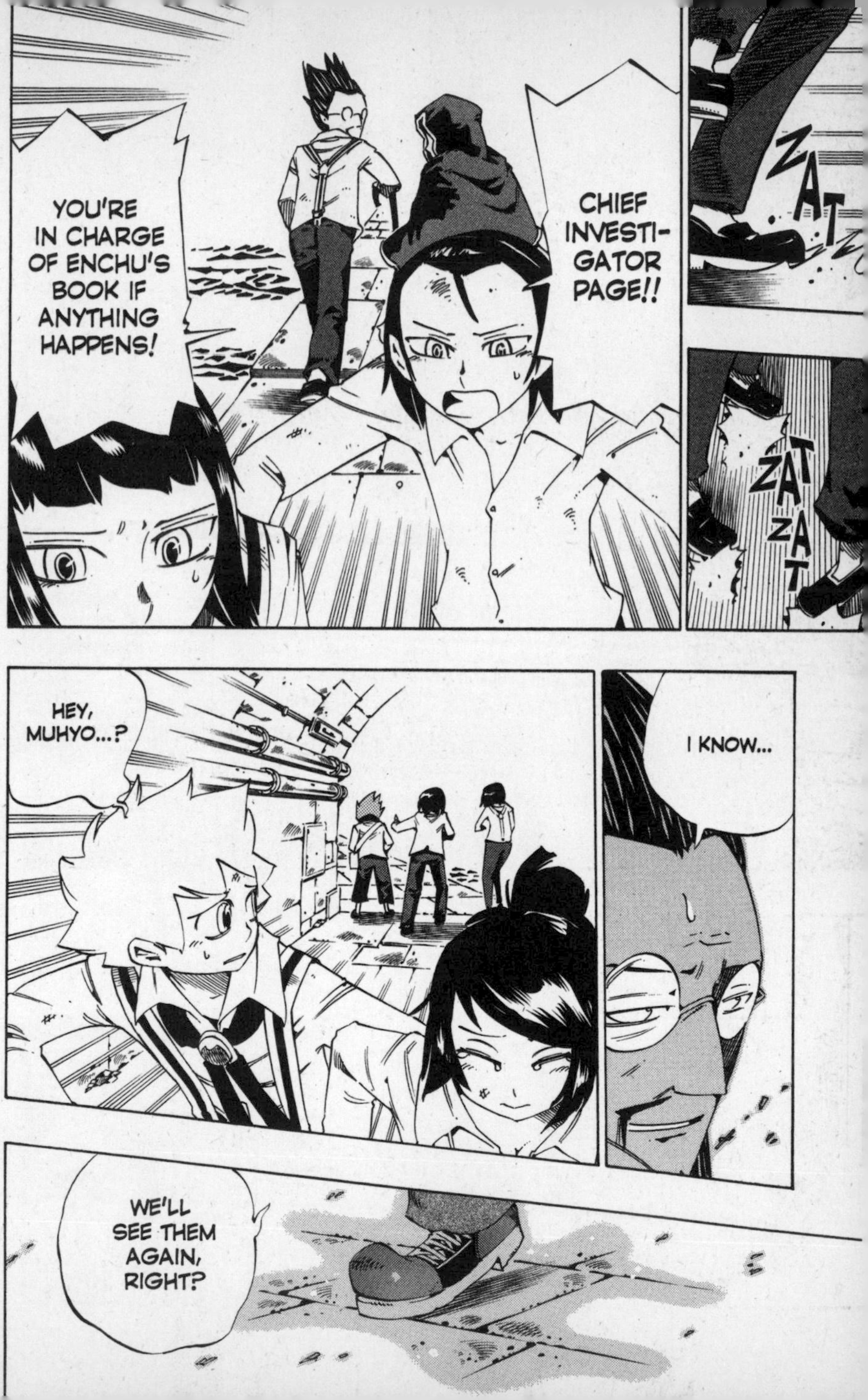
ZAT
ZAT ZAT ZAT
CHIEF INVESTIGATOR PAGE!!
YOU'RE IN CHARGE OF ENCHU'S BOOK IF ANYTHING HAPPENS!
I KNOW...
HEY, MUHYO...?
WE'LL SEE THEM AGAIN, RIGHT?

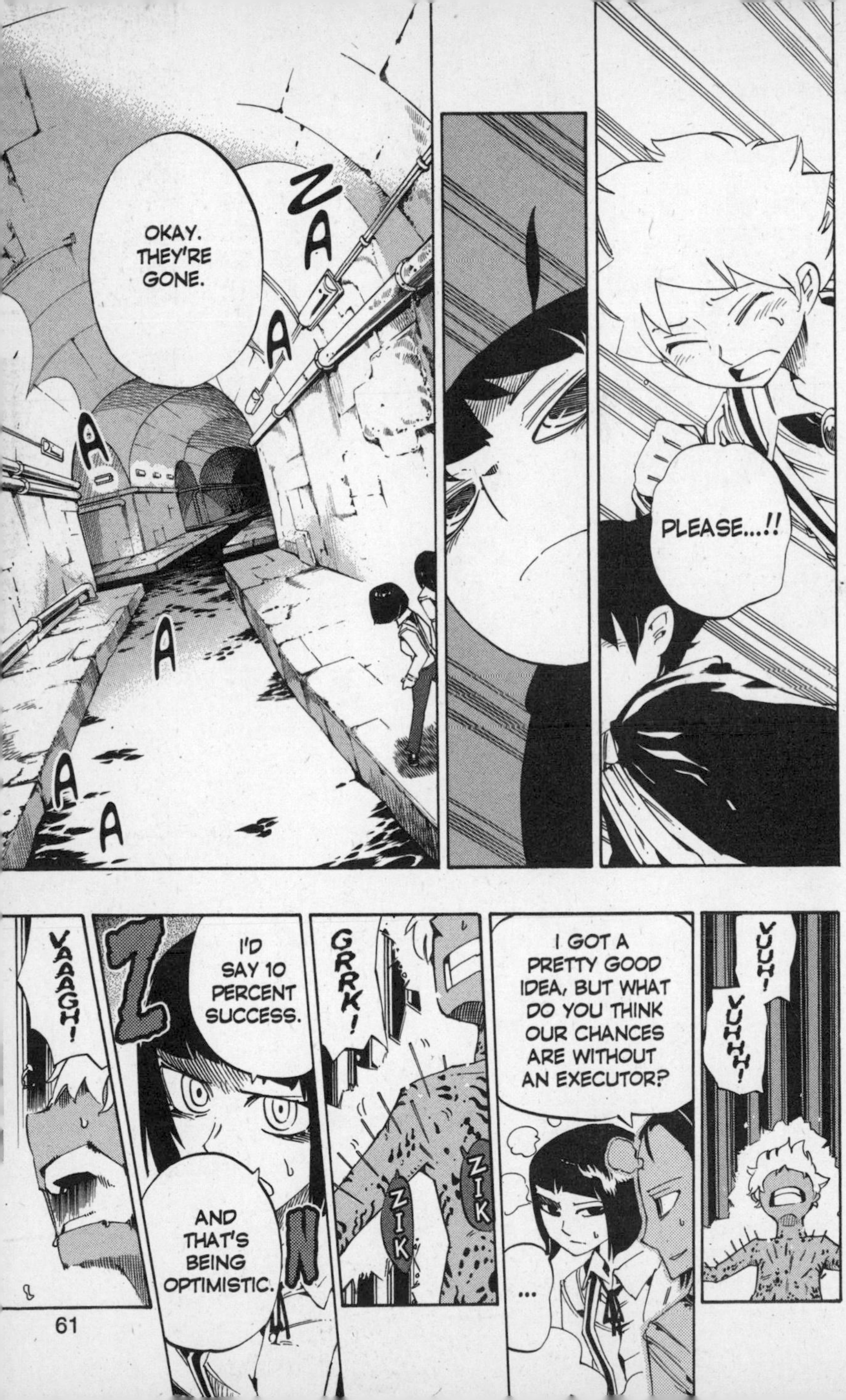
PLEASE...!!
OKAY. THEY'RE GONE.
ZAAAAAA
VUUH!
VUHHH!
I GOT A PRETTY GOOD IDEA, BUT WHAT DO YOU THINK OUR CHANCES ARE WITHOUT AN EXECUTOR?
...
GRRK!
ZIK
ZIK
I'D SAY 10 PERCENT SUCCESS.
AND THAT'S BEING OPTIMISTIC.
VAAAGH!

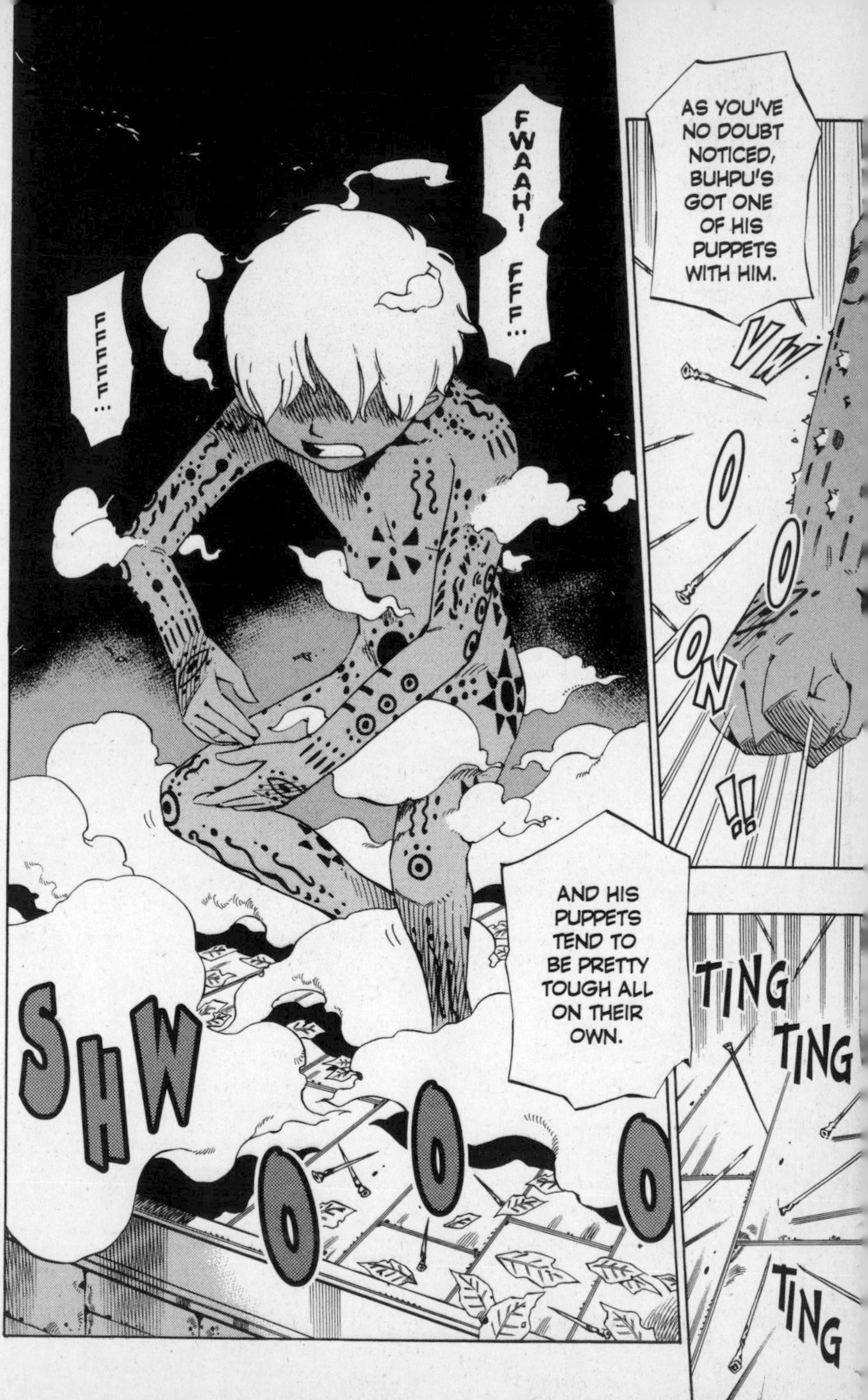
AS YOU'VE NO DOUBT NOTICED, BUHPU'S GOT ONE OF HIS PUPPETS WITH HIM.
VWOOOON!!
TING
TING
TING
FWAAH! FFF...
FFFFF...
AND HIS PUPPETS TEND TO BE PRETTY TOUGH ALL ON THEIR OWN.
SHWOOOO

READ THIS WAY

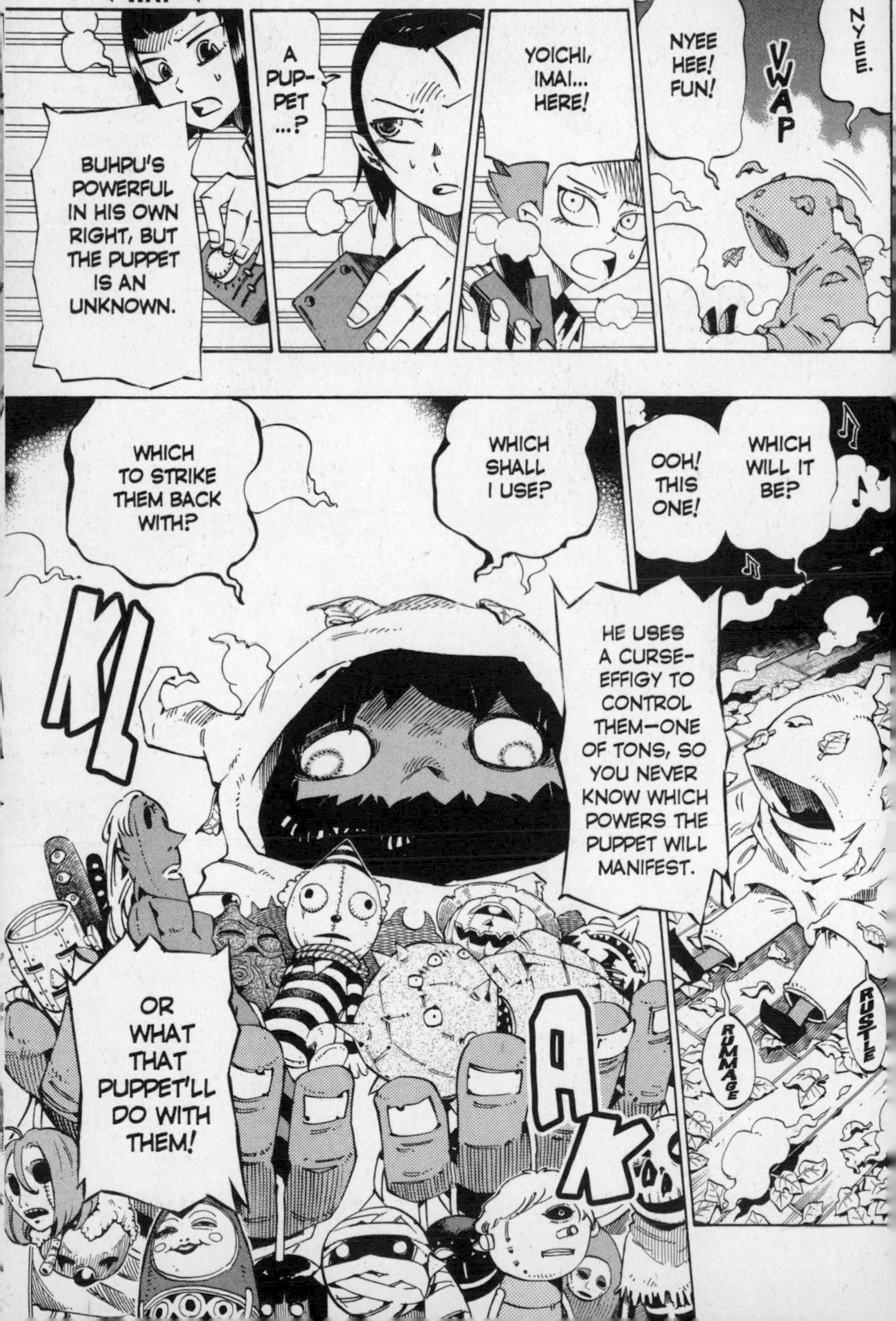
NYEE.
VWAP
NYEE HEE! FUN!
YOICHI, IMAI... HERE!
A PUP-PET ...?
BUHPU'S POWERFUL IN HIS OWN RIGHT, BUT THE PUPPET IS AN UNKNOWN.
WHICH WILL IT BE?
OOH! THIS ONE!
RUSTLE
RUMMAGE
WHICH SHALL I USE?
HE USES A CURSE-EFFIGY TO CONTROL THEM—ONE OF TONS, SO YOU NEVER KNOW WHICH POWERS THE PUPPET WILL MANIFEST.
WHICH TO STRIKE THEM BACK WITH?
OR WHAT THAT PUPPET'LL DO WITH THEM!

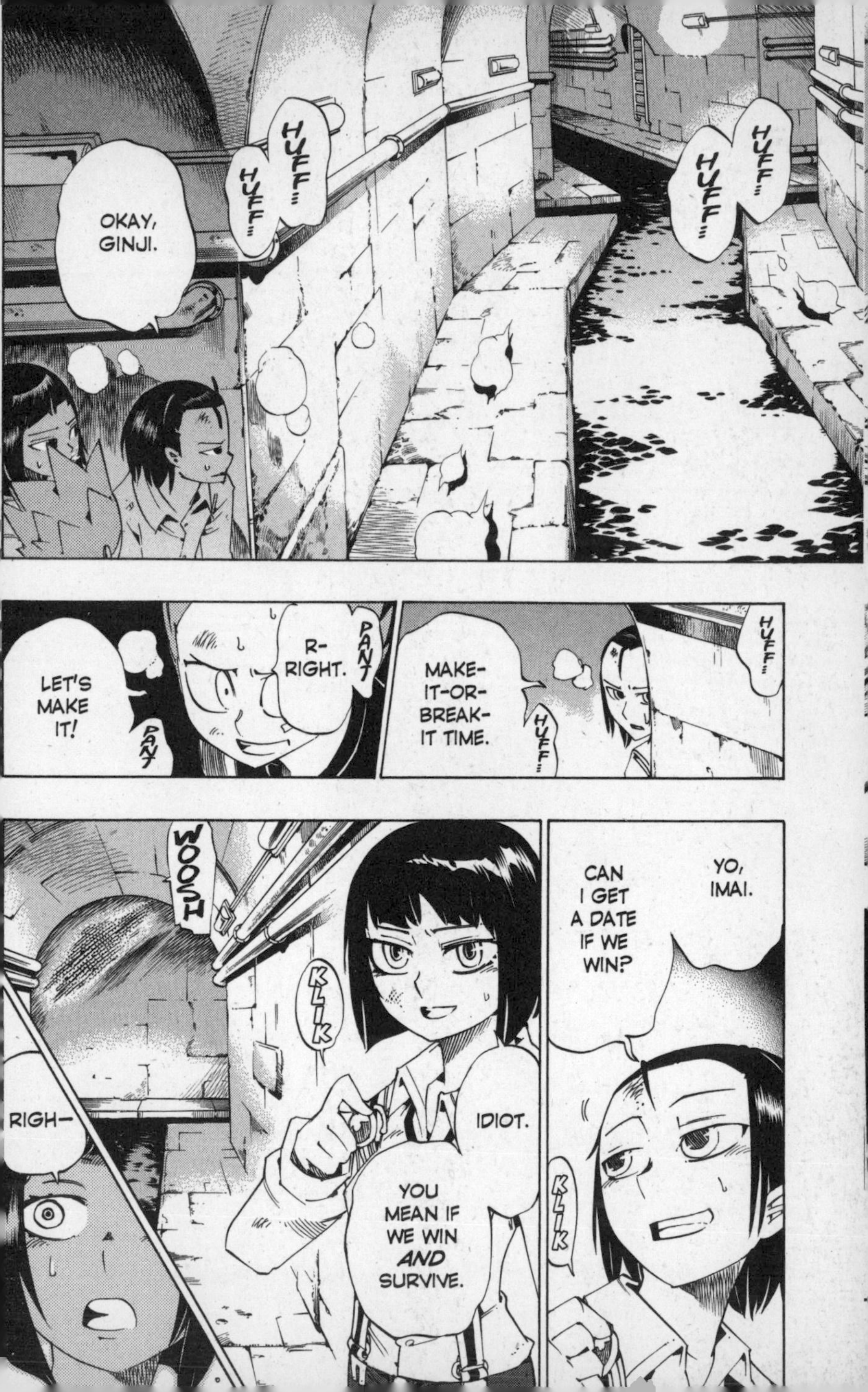
HUFF... HUFF...
HUFF... HUFF...
OKAY, GINJI.
HUFF...
MAKE-IT-OR-BREAK-IT TIME.
HUFF...
PANT
R-RIGHT.
LET'S MAKE IT!
PANT
YO, IMAI.
CAN I GET A DATE IF WE WIN?
KLIK
WOOSH
KLIK
IDIOT.
YOU MEAN IF WE WIN ***AND*** SURVIVE.
RIGH—

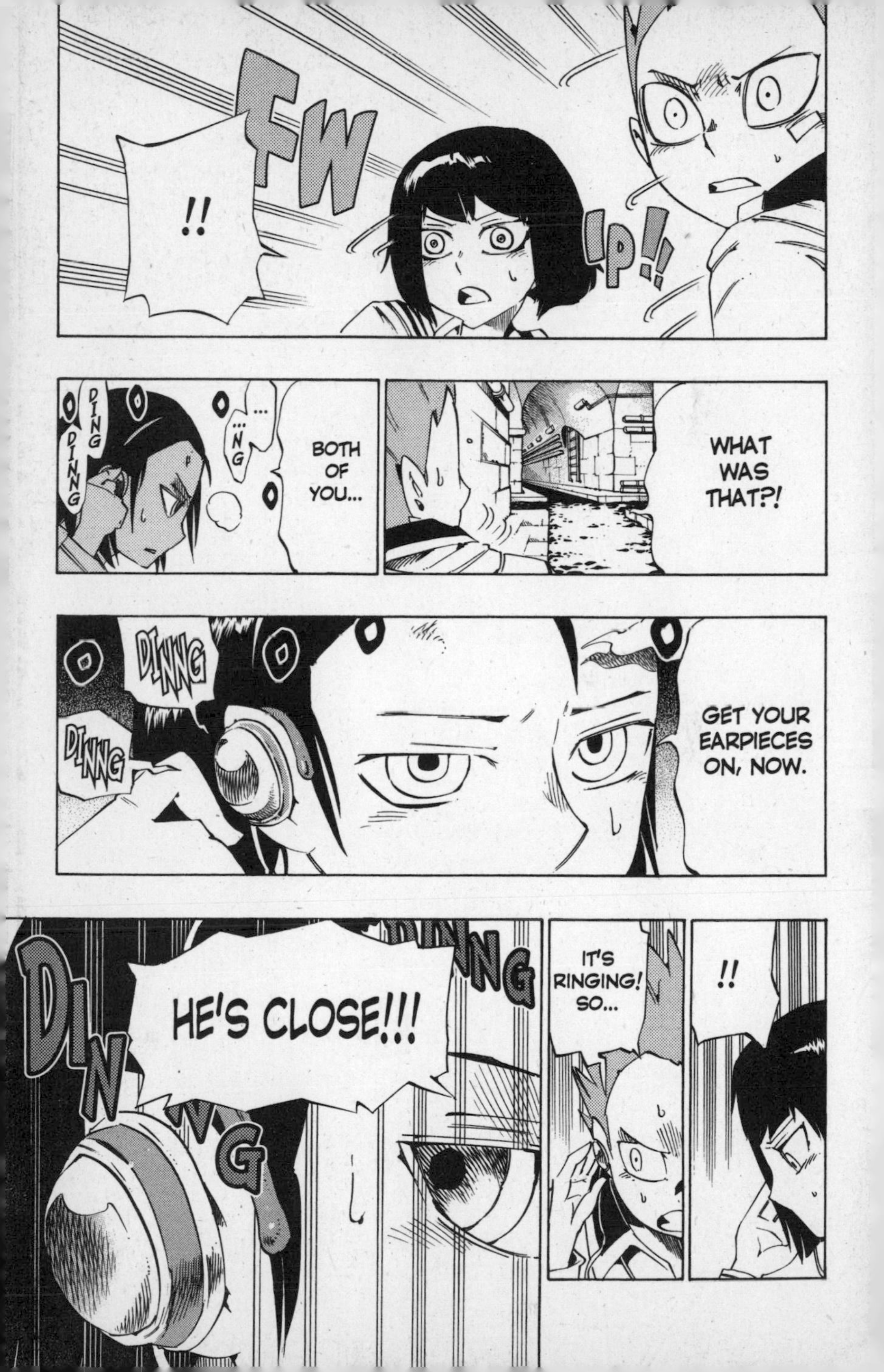
FWIP!!
!!
WHAT WAS THAT?!
BOTH OF YOU...
... ...NG
DING DINNG
GET YOUR EARPIECES ON, NOW.
DINNG
DINNG
!!
IT'S RINGING! SO...
DINNG
HE'S CLOSE!!!
DINNNG

A PLEASANT SURPRISE!

THIS IS SOMETHING I RECEIVED FROM A READER SOME TIME AGO. LOOKS LIKE JUST A CUTE PICTURE, BUT GET THIS! THERE WAS A PIECE OF RUBBER IN THE SAME ENVELOPE—IT WAS ALL BUMPY, WITH WHAT LOOKED LIKE SCULPTING-KNIFE MARKS IN IT... HUH? IT'S A STAMP?

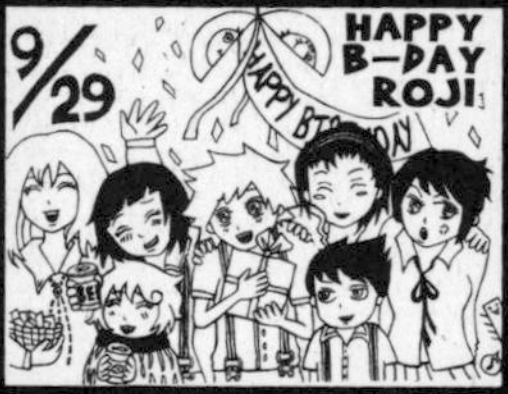
9/29
HAPPY B-DAY ROJI!

THE SECOND PRINTING!

"WHOA!!"

"IT'S A STAMP! THIS POSTCARD'S A STAMP!!! WOW!"

IT WAS SUCH A SURPRISE, I HAD TO PUT IT IN HERE. THANKS, "NOTSU-SAN," FOR GIVING ME THE ORIGINAL STAMP AND PERMISSION TO PRINT THE IMAGE.

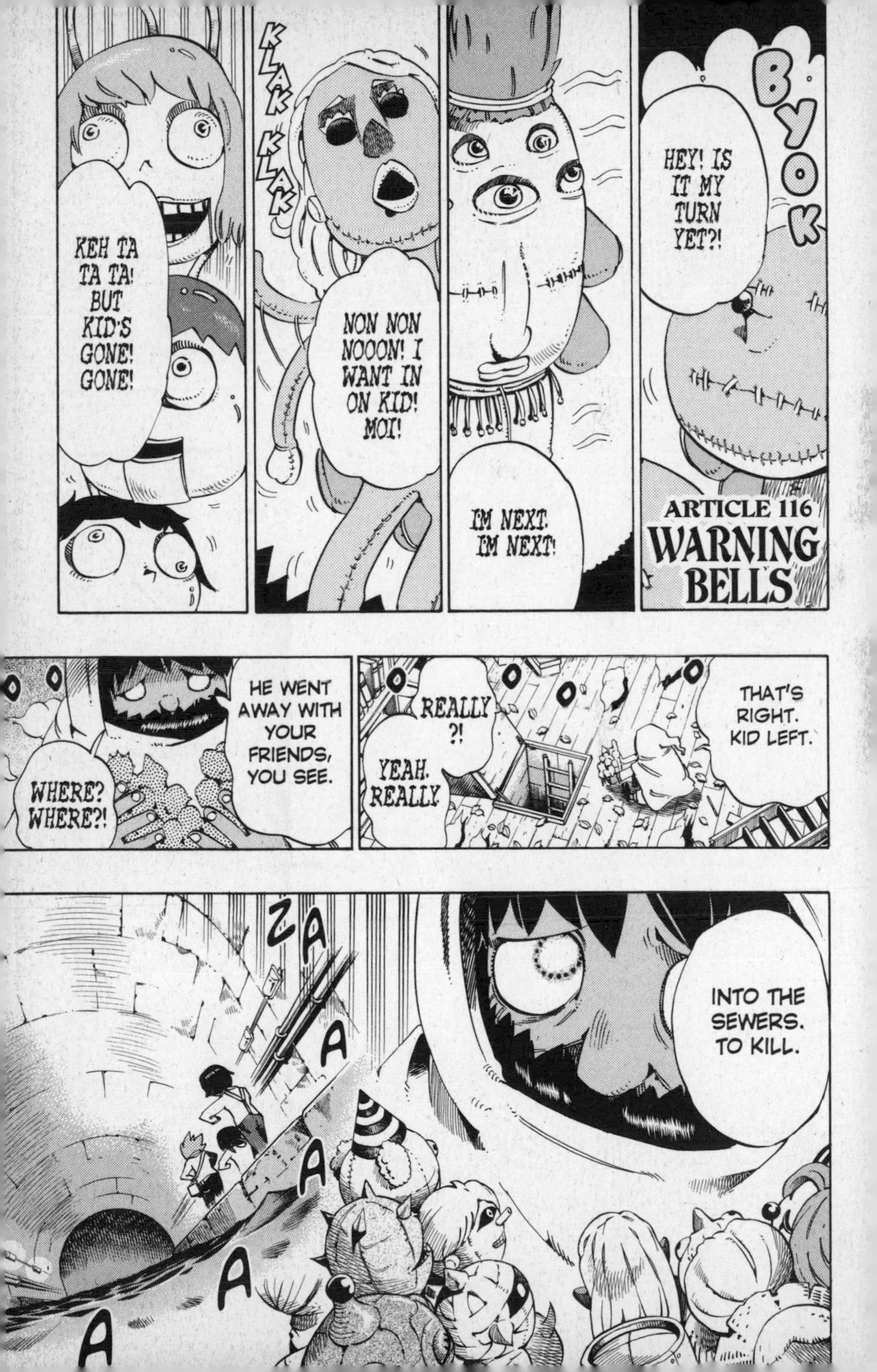
BYOK
HEY! IS IT MY TURN YET?!
ARTICLE 116
WARNING BELLS
I'M NEXT. I'M NEXT!
KLAK KLAK KLAK
NON NON NOOOON! I WANT IN ON KID! MOI!
KEH TA TA TA! BUT KID'S GONE! GONE!
THAT'S RIGHT. KID LEFT.
REALLY ?!
YEAH. REALLY.
HE WENT AWAY WITH YOUR FRIENDS, YOU SEE.
WHERE? WHERE?!
INTO THE SEWERS. TO KILL.
ZAAAAAA

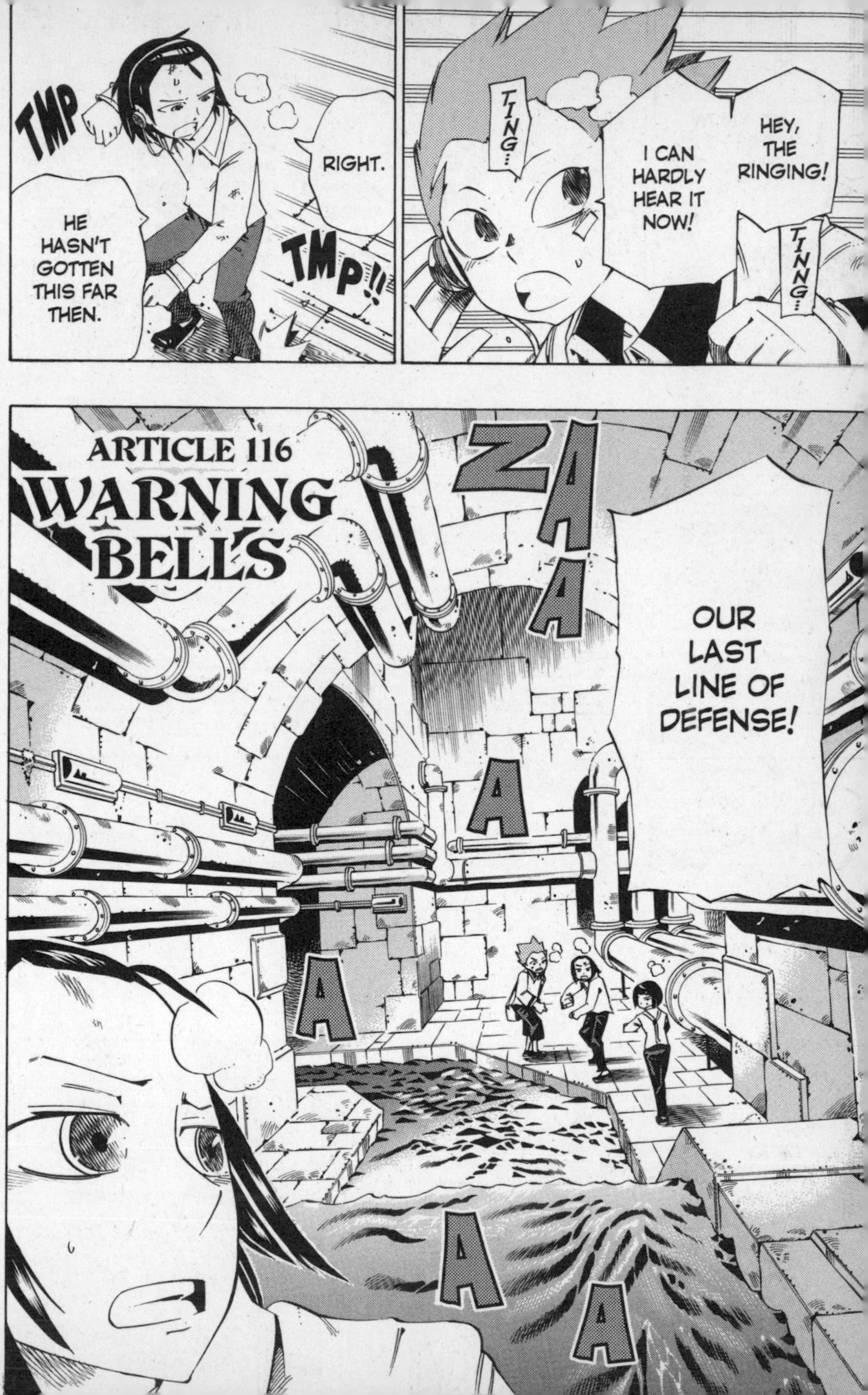
TING...
HEY, THE RINGING!
I CAN HARDLY HEAR IT NOW!
TINNG...
TMP
RIGHT.
HE HASN'T GOTTEN THIS FAR THEN.
TMP!!
ARTICLE 116
WARNING BELLS
ZAAAAAAA
OUR LAST LINE OF DEFENSE!

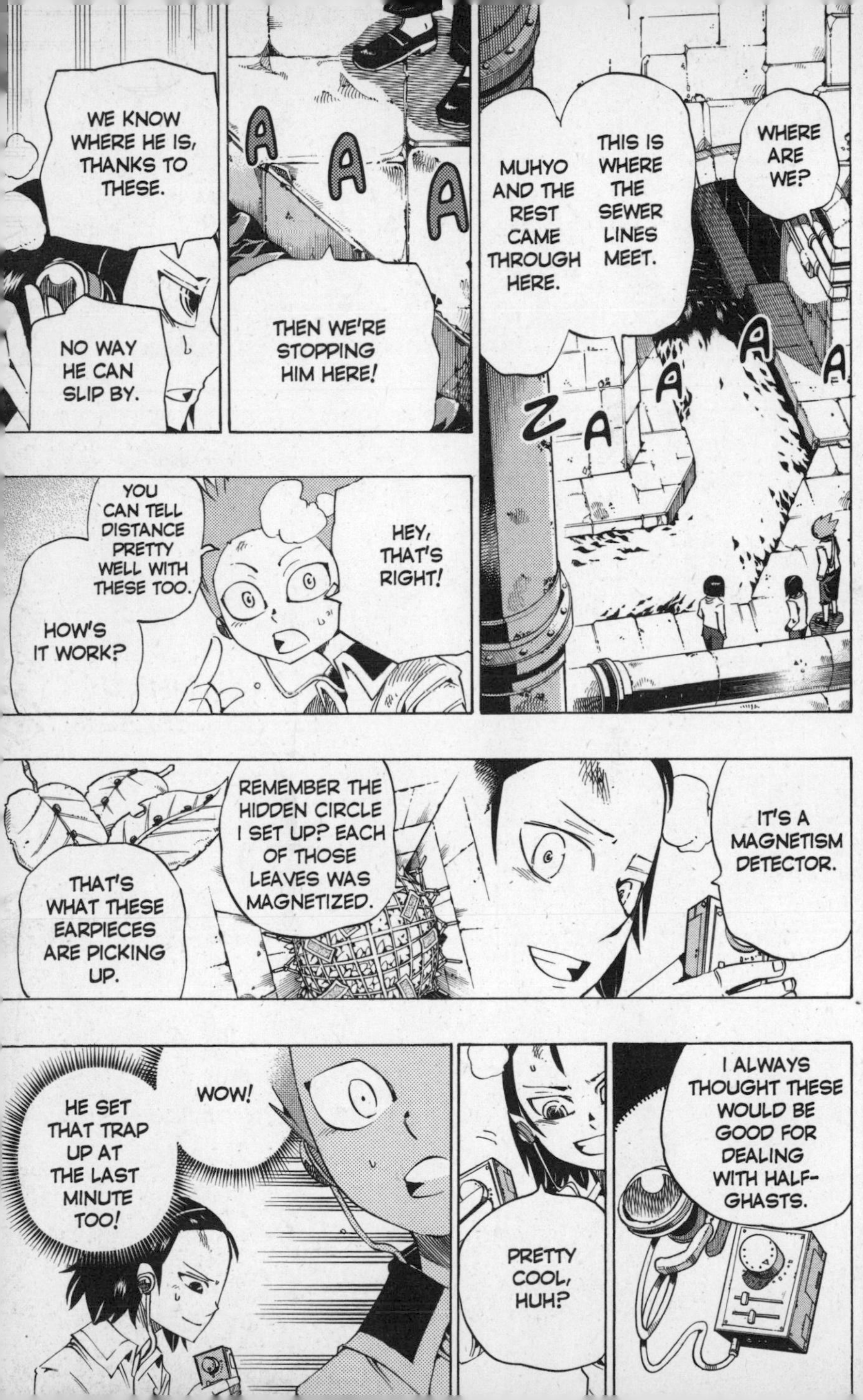
WHERE ARE WE?
THIS IS WHERE THE SEWER LINES MEET.
MUHYO AND THE REST CAME THROUGH HERE.
ZAAAAA
AAA
THEN WE'RE STOPPING HIM HERE!
WE KNOW WHERE HE IS, THANKS TO THESE.
NO WAY HE CAN SLIP BY.
HEY, THAT'S RIGHT!
YOU CAN TELL DISTANCE PRETTY WELL WITH THESE TOO.
HOW'S IT WORK?
IT'S A MAGNETISM DETECTOR.
REMEMBER THE HIDDEN CIRCLE I SET UP? EACH OF THOSE LEAVES WAS MAGNETIZED.
THAT'S WHAT THESE EARPIECES ARE PICKING UP.
I ALWAYS THOUGHT THESE WOULD BE GOOD FOR DEALING WITH HALF-GHASTS.
PRETTY COOL, HUH?
WOW!
HE SET THAT TRAP UP AT THE LAST MINUTE TOO!

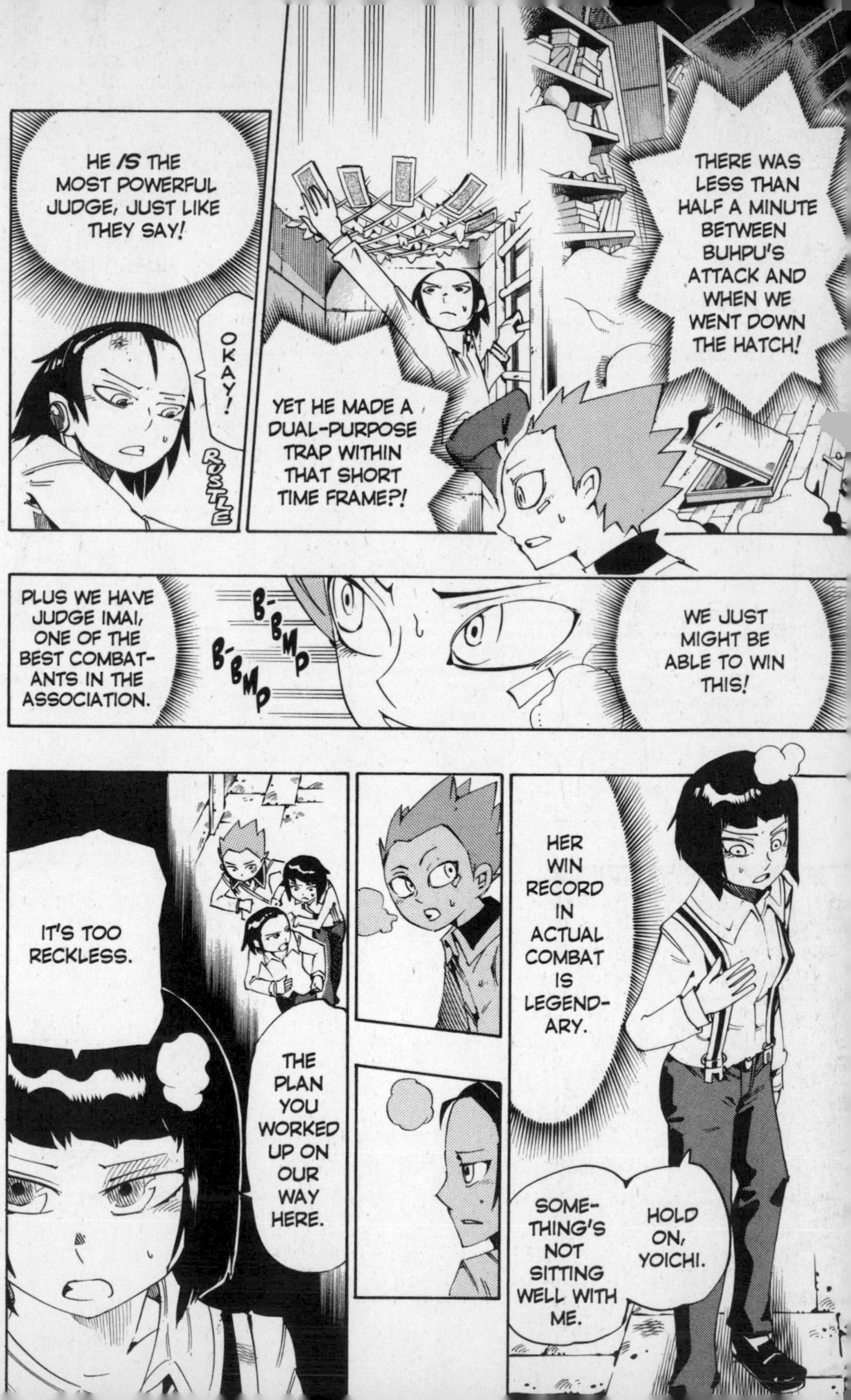
THERE WAS LESS THAN HALF A MINUTE BETWEEN BUHPU'S ATTACK AND WHEN WE WENT DOWN THE HATCH!
YET HE MADE A DUAL-PURPOSE TRAP WITHIN THAT SHORT TIME FRAME?!
HE IS THE MOST POWERFUL JUDGE, JUST LIKE THEY SAY!
OKAY!
RUSTLE
WE JUST MIGHT BE ABLE TO WIN THIS!
B-BMP
B-BMP
PLUS WE HAVE JUDGE IMAI, ONE OF THE BEST COMBATANTS IN THE ASSOCIATION.
HER WIN RECORD IN ACTUAL COMBAT IS LEGENDARY.
HOLD ON, YOICHI.
SOMETHING'S NOT SITTING WELL WITH ME.
IT'S TOO RECKLESS.
THE PLAN YOU WORKED UP ON OUR WAY HERE.

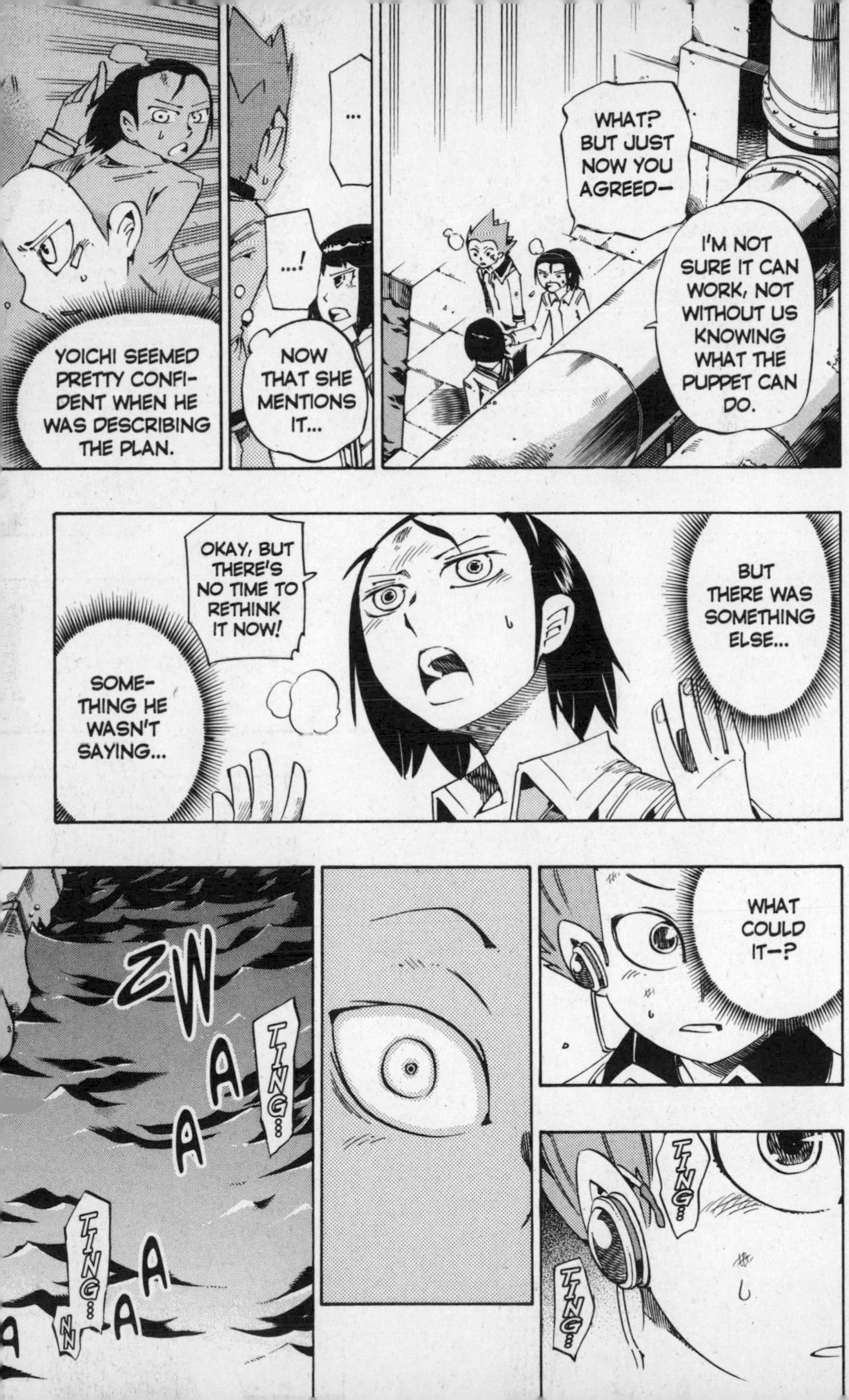
WHAT? BUT JUST NOW YOU AGREED—
I'M NOT SURE IT CAN WORK, NOT WITHOUT US KNOWING WHAT THE PUPPET CAN DO.
...
...!
NOW THAT SHE MENTIONS IT...
YOICHI SEEMED PRETTY CONFIDENT WHEN HE WAS DESCRIBING THE PLAN.
BUT THERE WAS SOMETHING ELSE...
OKAY, BUT THERE'S NO TIME TO RETHINK IT NOW!
SOMETHING HE WASN'T SAYING...
WHAT COULD IT—?
TING...
TING...
ZWAAAAAA
TING...
TING...NN

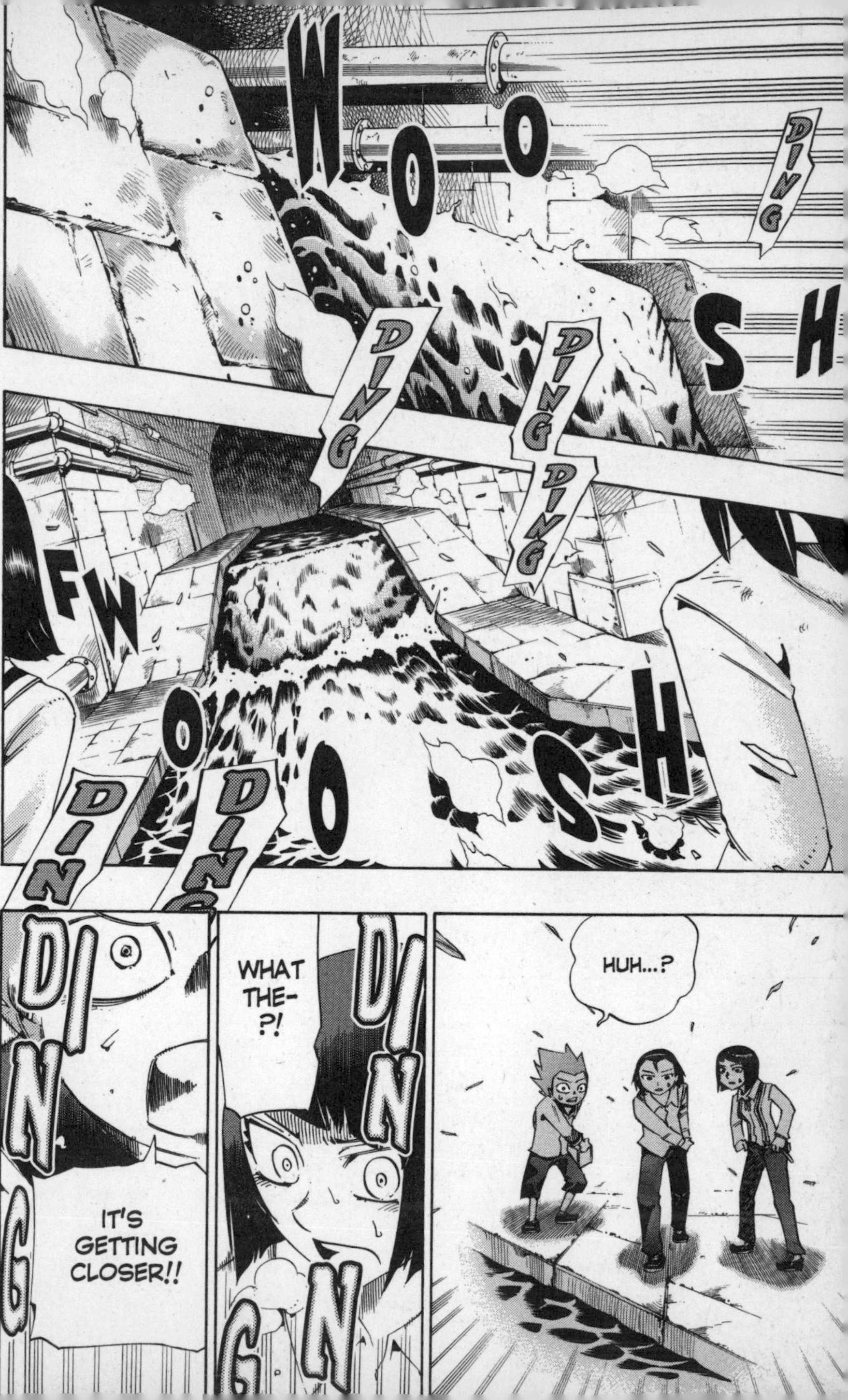
DING
WOOSH
DING
DING
DING
DING
FWOOSH
DING
DING
HUH...?
DING
WHAT THE-?!
DING
IT'S GETTING CLOSER!!

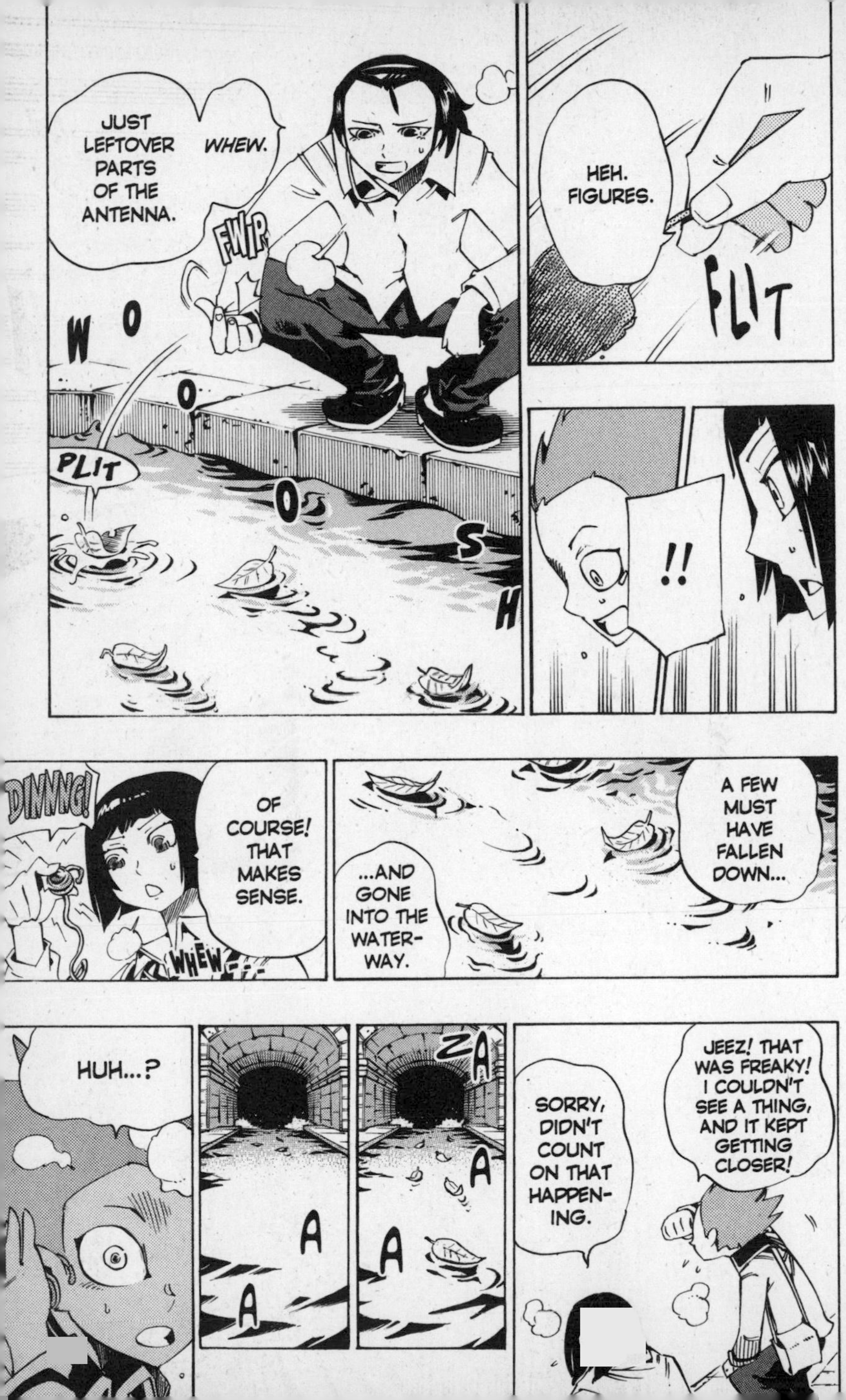
HEH. FIGURES.
FLIT
!!
WHEW.
JUST LEFTOVER PARTS OF THE ANTENNA.
FWIP
WOOSH
PLIT
A FEW MUST HAVE FALLEN DOWN...
...AND GONE INTO THE WATER-WAY.
OF COURSE! THAT MAKES SENSE.
DINNNG!
WHEW...
JEEZ! THAT WAS FREAKY! I COULDN'T SEE A THING, AND IT KEPT GETTING CLOSER!
SORRY, DIDN'T COUNT ON THAT HAPPEN-ING.
ZAAA
AA
HUH...?

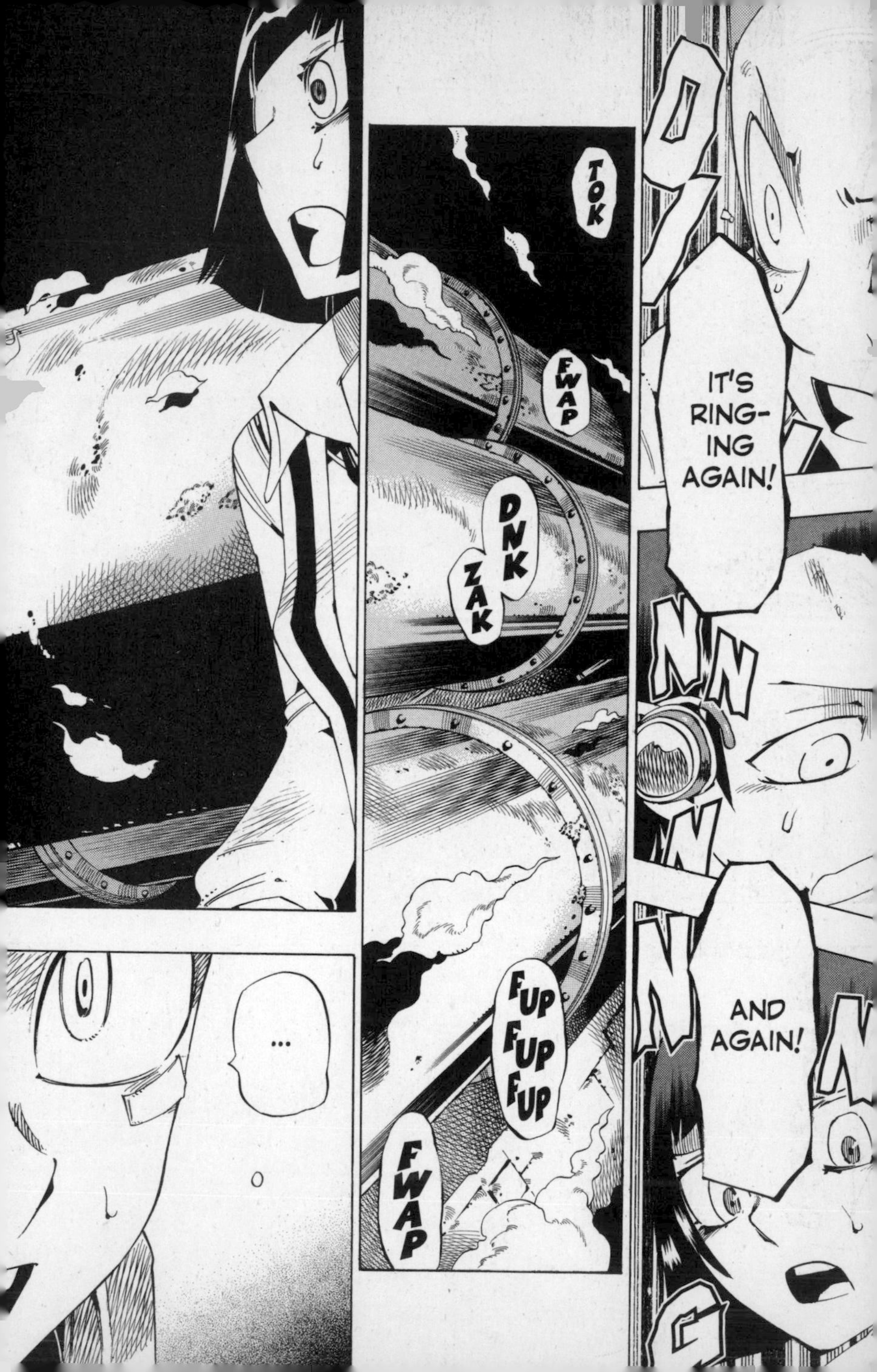
IT'S RING-ING AGAIN!
AND AGAIN!
TOK
FWAP
DNK
ZAK
FUP FUP FUP
FWAP
...

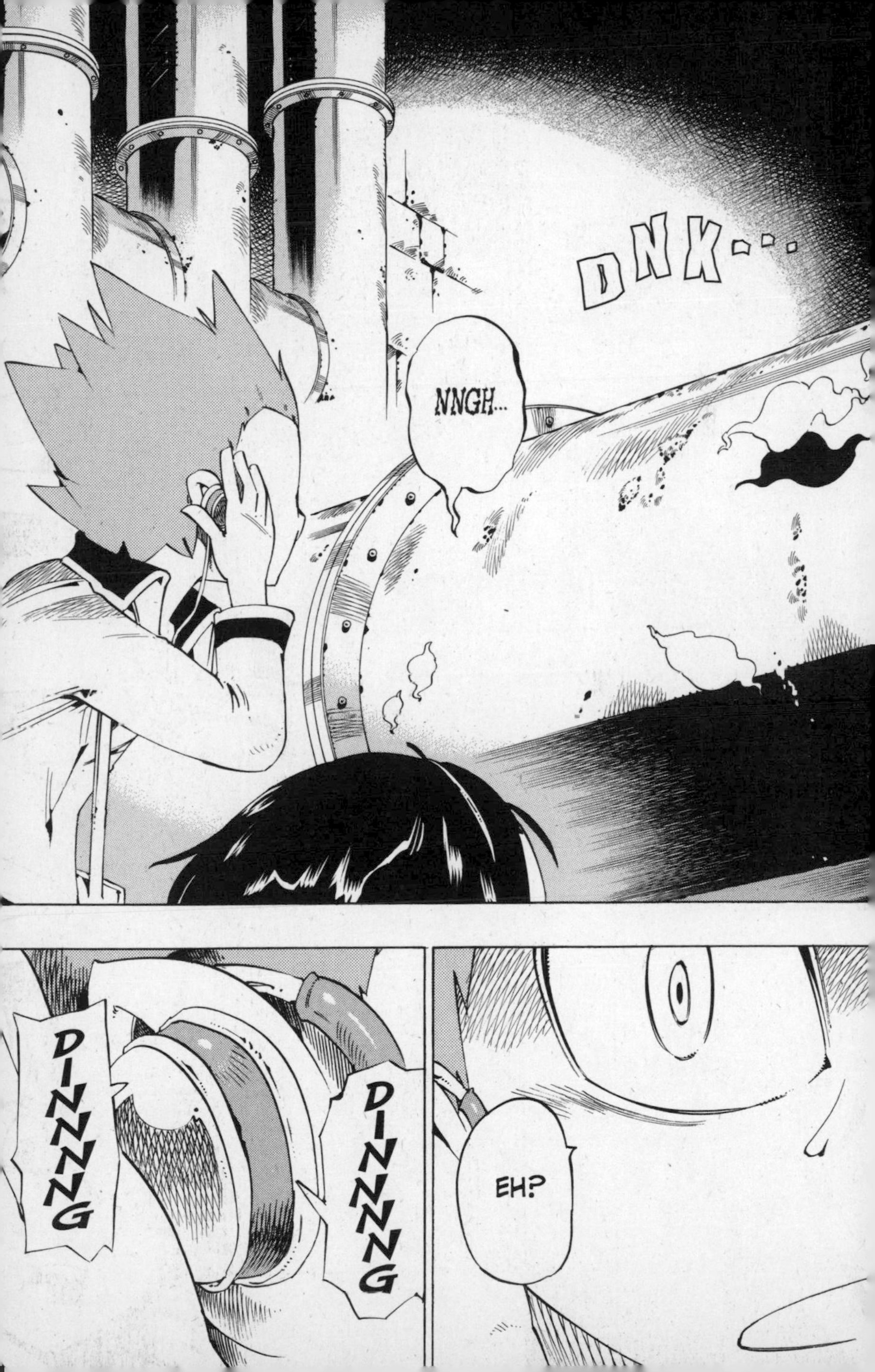
DNK...
NNGH...
EH?
DINNNG
DINNNG

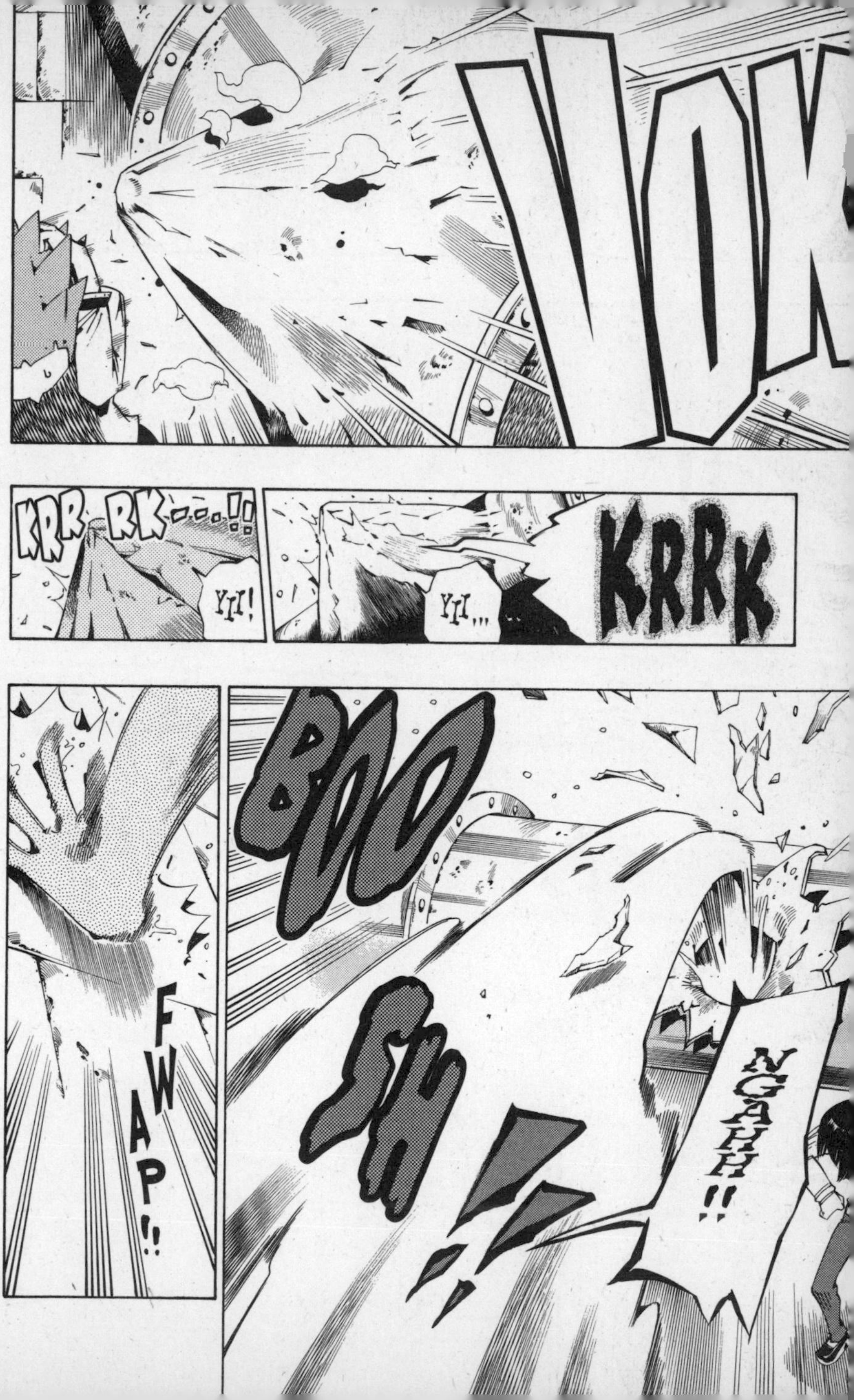
VOK
KRRK
YII...
KRR RK...!!
YII!
BOOSH
NGAHH!!
FWAP!!

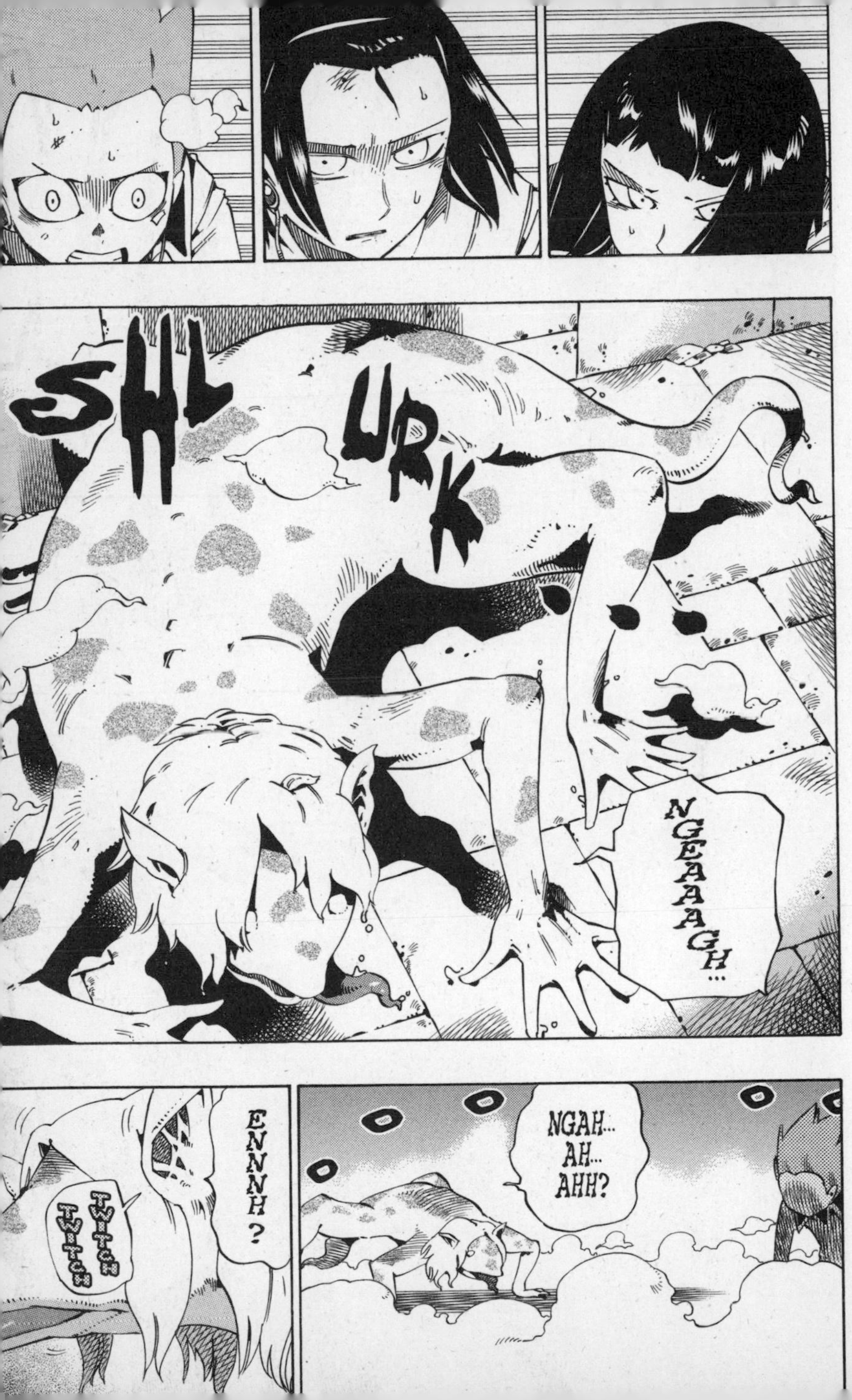
SHLURK
NGEAAAGH...
NGAH... AH... AHH?
ENNNH?
TWITCH TWITCH

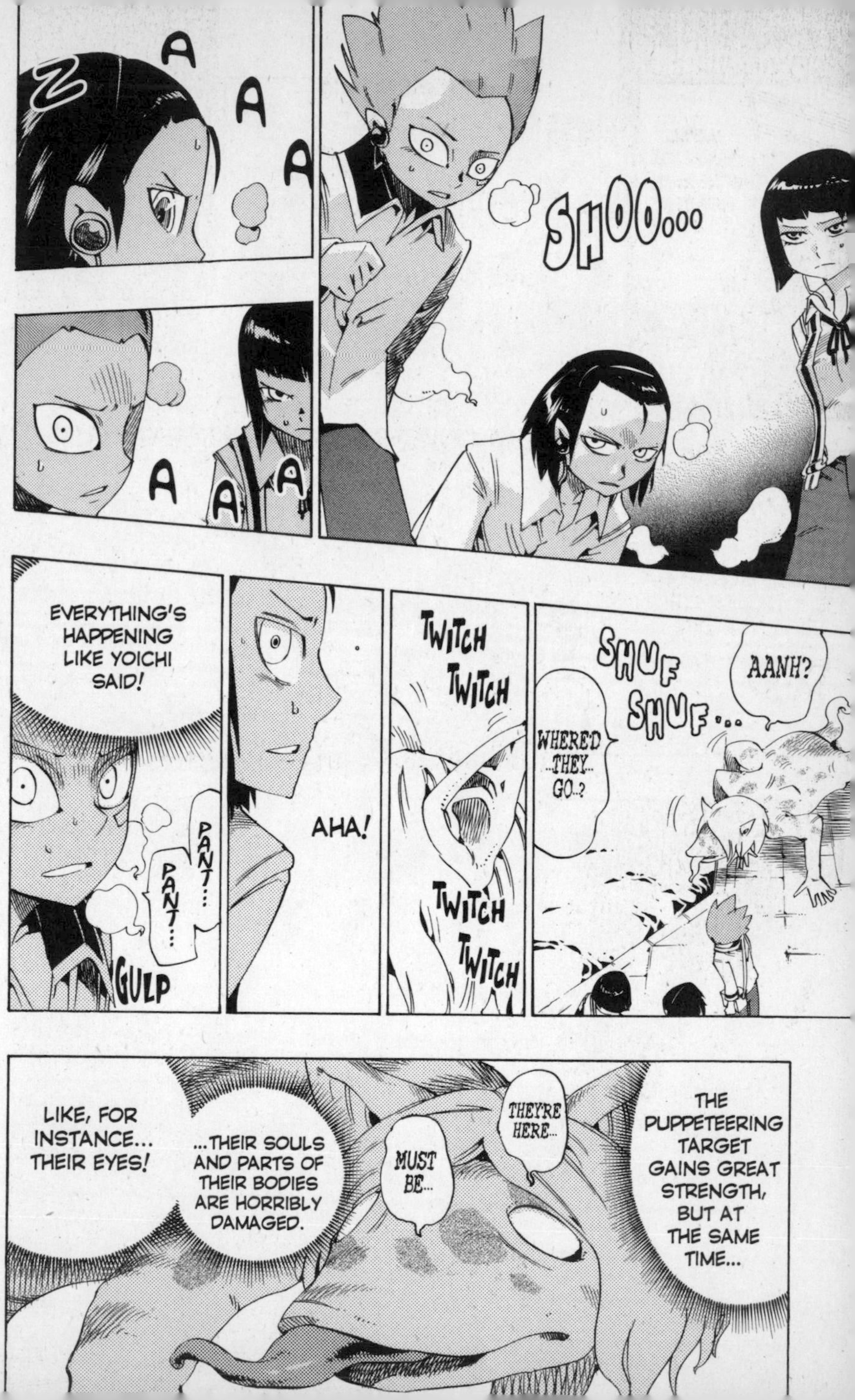
SHOO...
ZAAA
AAAA
SHUF SHUF...
AANH?
WHERED ...THEY... GO..?
TWITCH TWITCH
TWITCH TWITCH
AHA!
EVERYTHING'S HAPPENING LIKE YOICHI SAID!
PANT... PANT...
GULP
THE PUPPETEERING TARGET GAINS GREAT STRENGTH, BUT AT THE SAME TIME...
THEY'RE HERE...
MUST BE...
...THEIR SOULS AND PARTS OF THEIR BODIES ARE HORRIBLY DAMAGED.
LIKE, FOR INSTANCE... THEIR EYES!

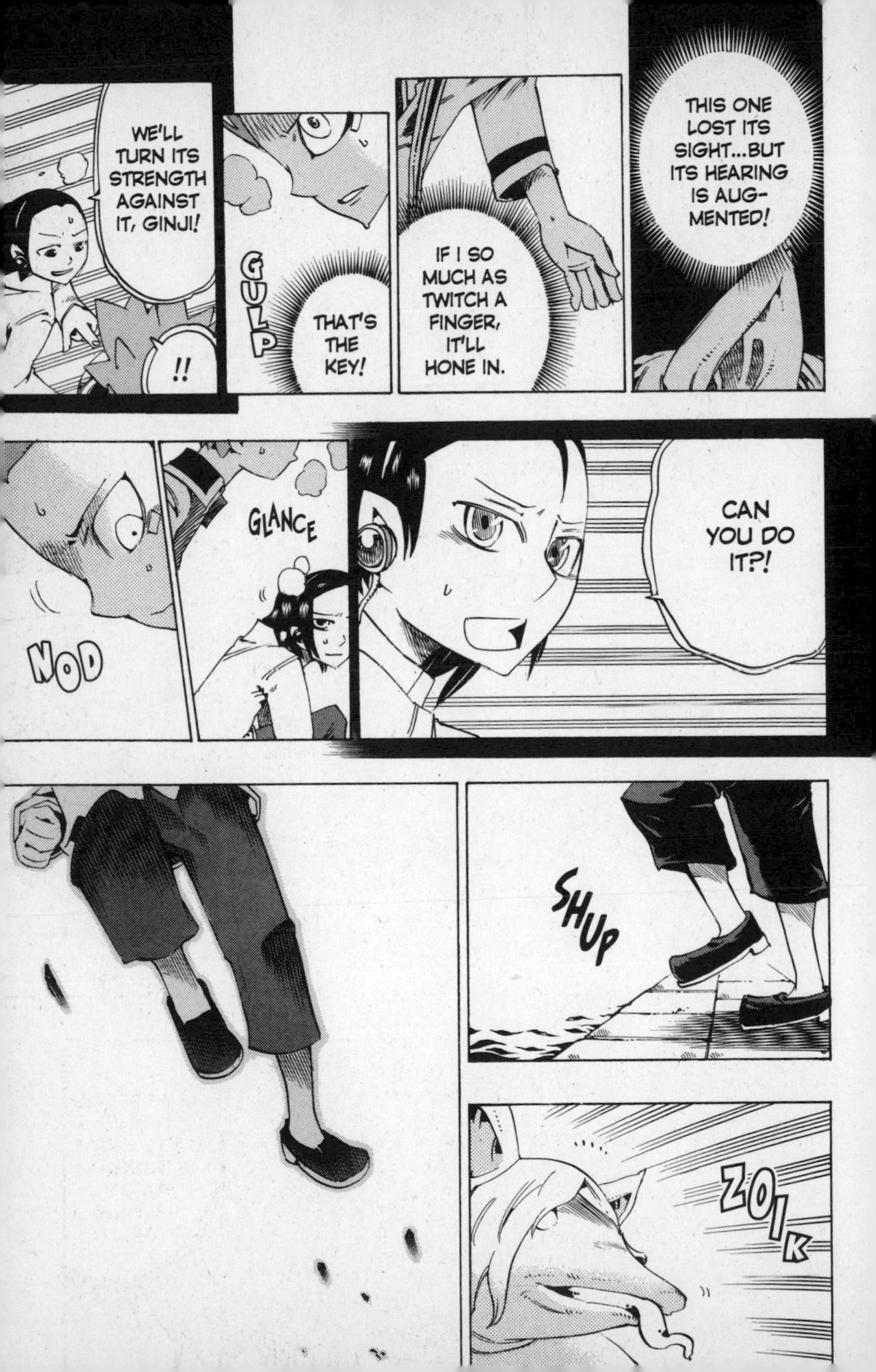
THIS ONE LOST ITS SIGHT...BUT ITS HEARING IS AUG-MENTED!
IF I SO MUCH AS TWITCH A FINGER, IT'LL HONE IN.
GULP
THAT'S THE KEY!
WE'LL TURN ITS STRENGTH AGAINST IT, GINJI!
!!
CAN YOU DO IT?!
GLANCE
NOD
SHUP
ZOIK

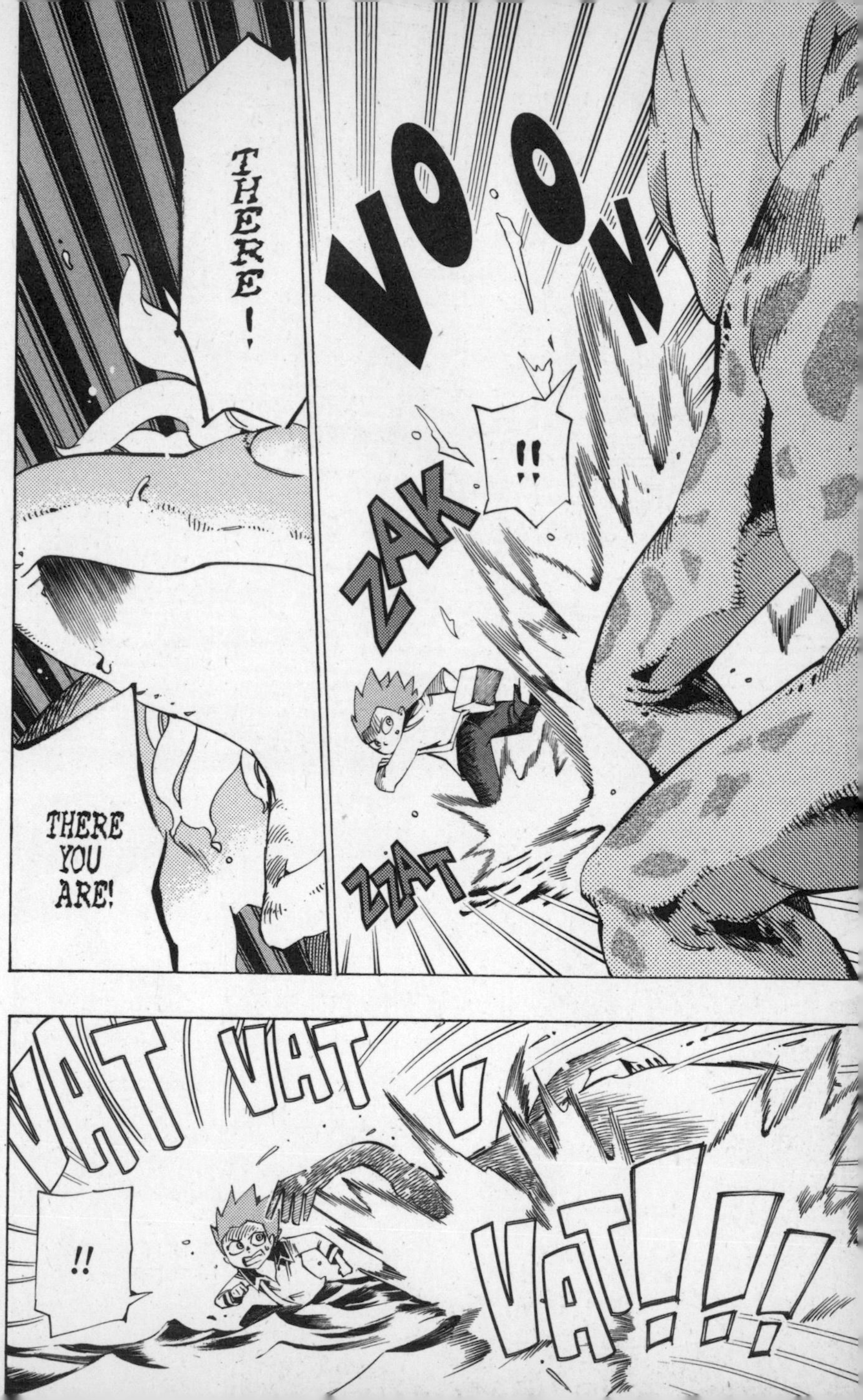
VOOON
!!
ZAK
ZZAT
THERE!
THERE YOU ARE!
V
VAT
VAT
VAT!!!
!!

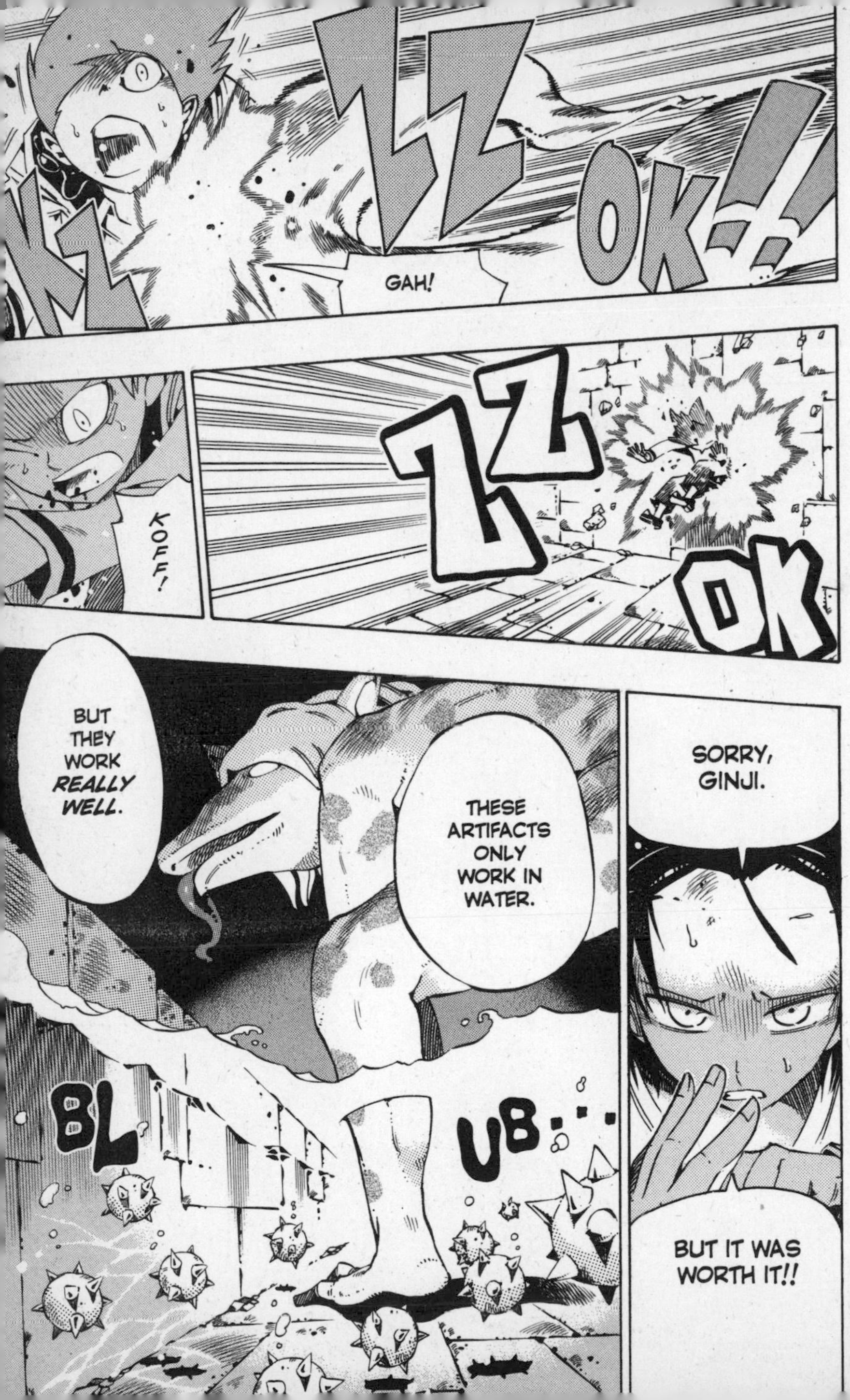
ZZOK!!
GAH!
ZZOK
KOFF!
SORRY, GINJI.
BUT IT WAS WORTH IT!!
THESE ARTIFACTS ONLY WORK IN WATER.
BUT THEY WORK REALLY WELL.
BLUB..

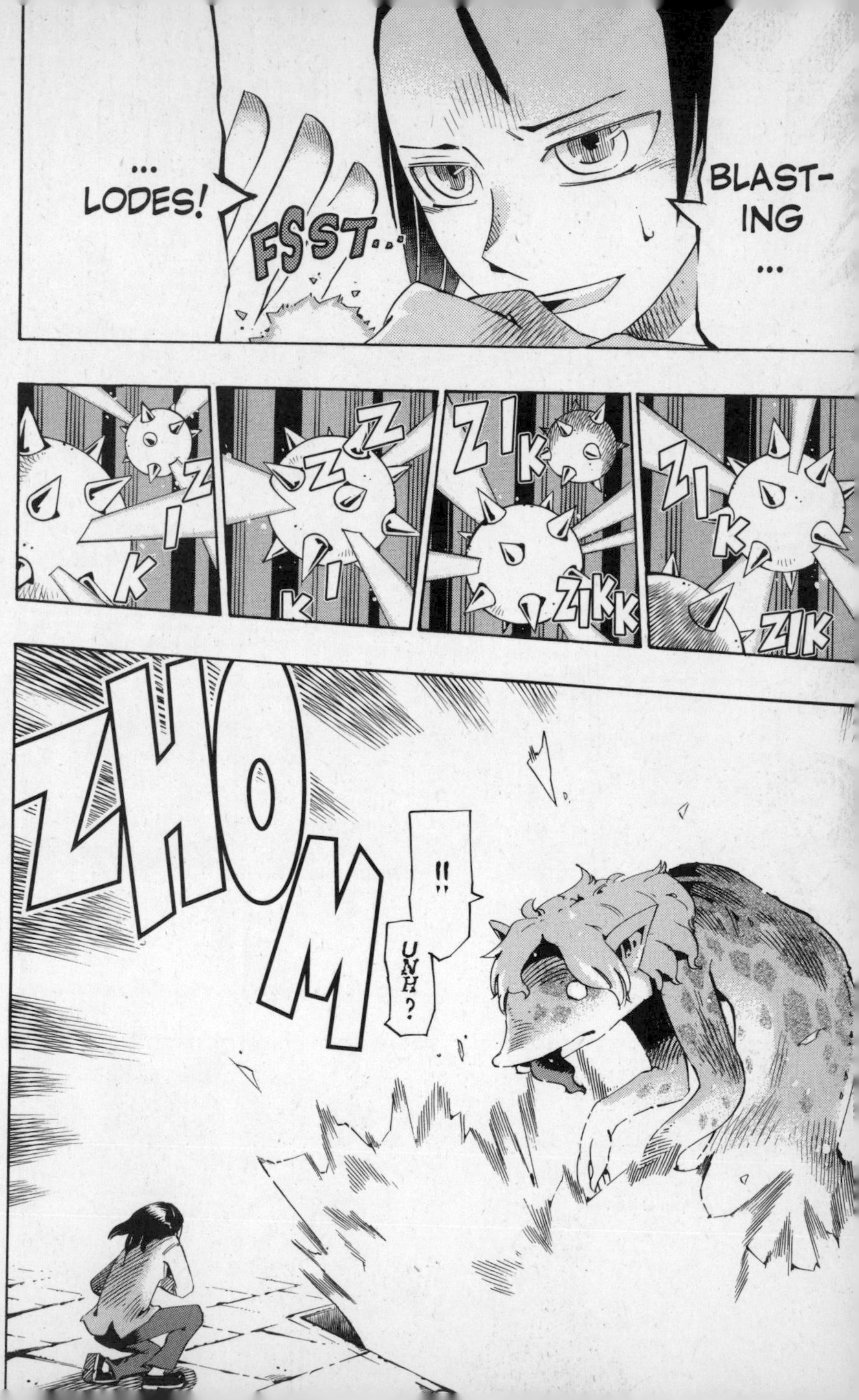
BLAST-ING ...
FSST...
... LODES!
ZIK
ZIK
ZIK
ZIKK
ZZZ
KIK
ZZIK
ZHOM
!!
UNH?

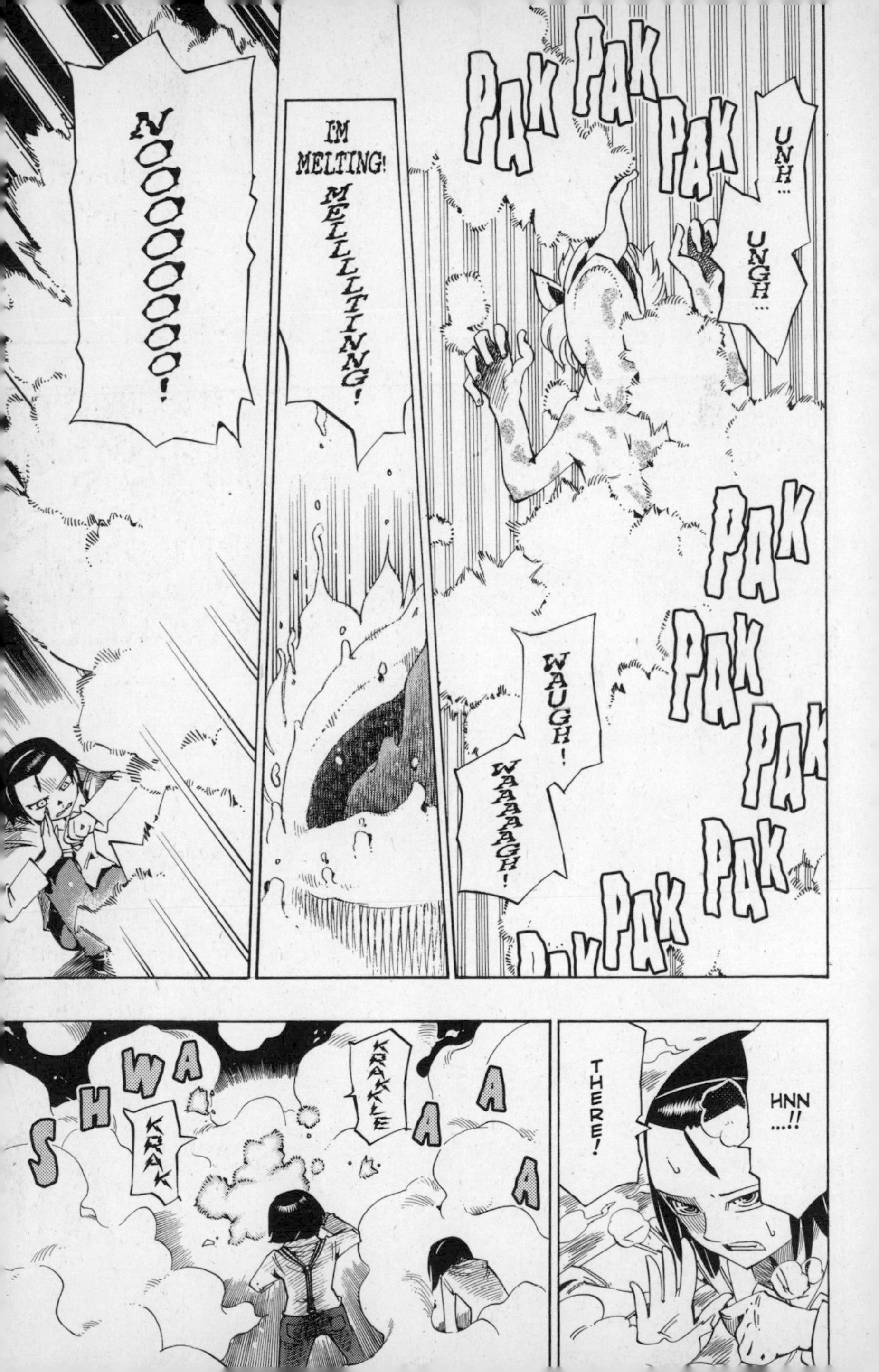
PAK PAK PAK
UNH... UNGH...
PAK PAK PAK PAK PAK PAK
WAUGH! WAAAAAAGH!
I'M MELTING! MELLLLTINNG!
NOOOOOOOOOO!
HNN ...!!
THERE!
KRAKKLE
KRAK
SHWAAAAA

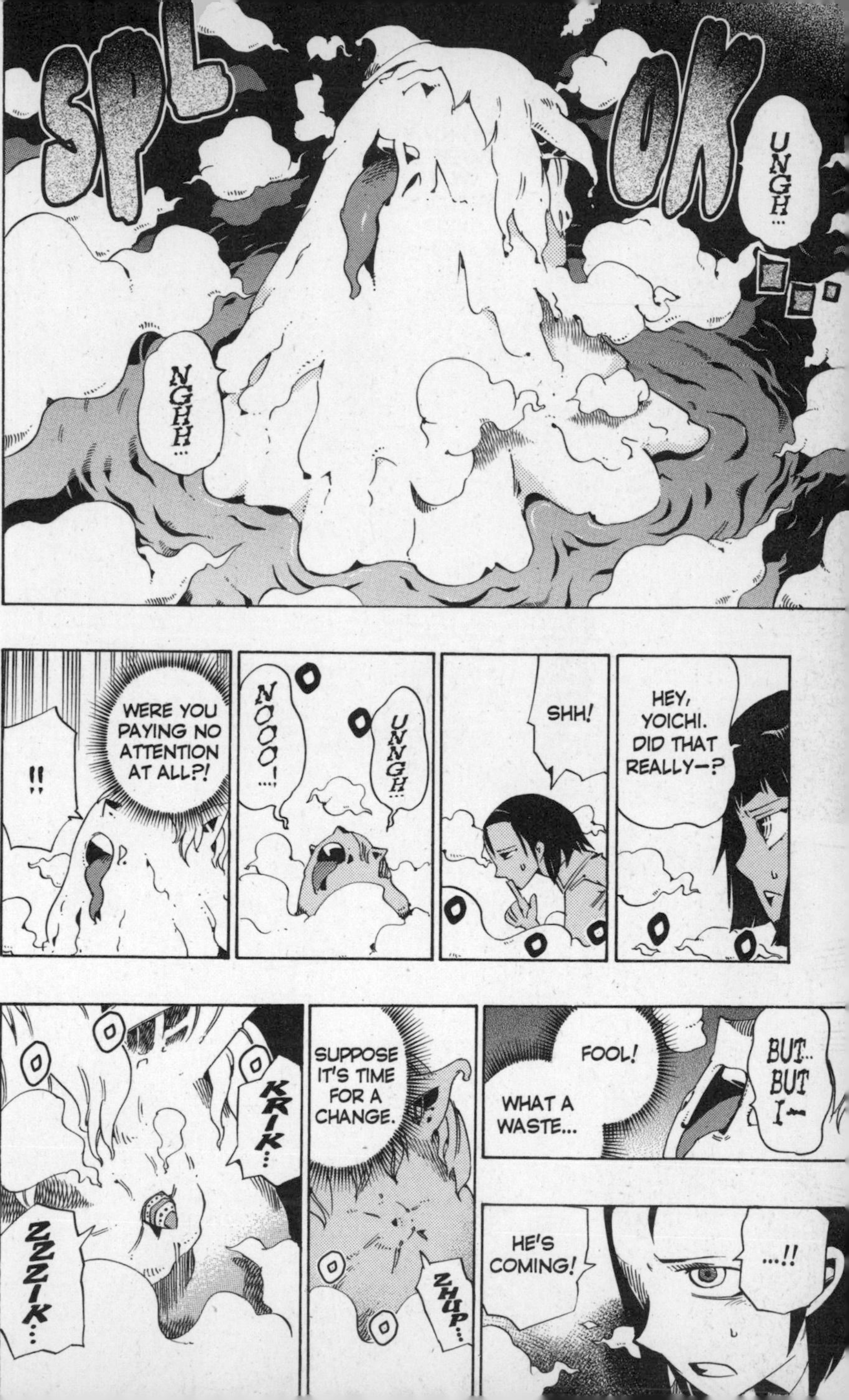
SPLOK
UNGH...
NGHH...
HEY, YOICHI. DID THAT REALLY—?
SHH!
UNNGH...
NOOOO...!
WERE YOU PAYING NO ATTENTION AT ALL?!
!!
BUT.. BUT I—
FOOL!
WHAT A WASTE...
...!!
HE'S COMING!
SUPPOSE IT'S TIME FOR A CHANGE.
ZHUP...
KRIK...
ZZZIK...

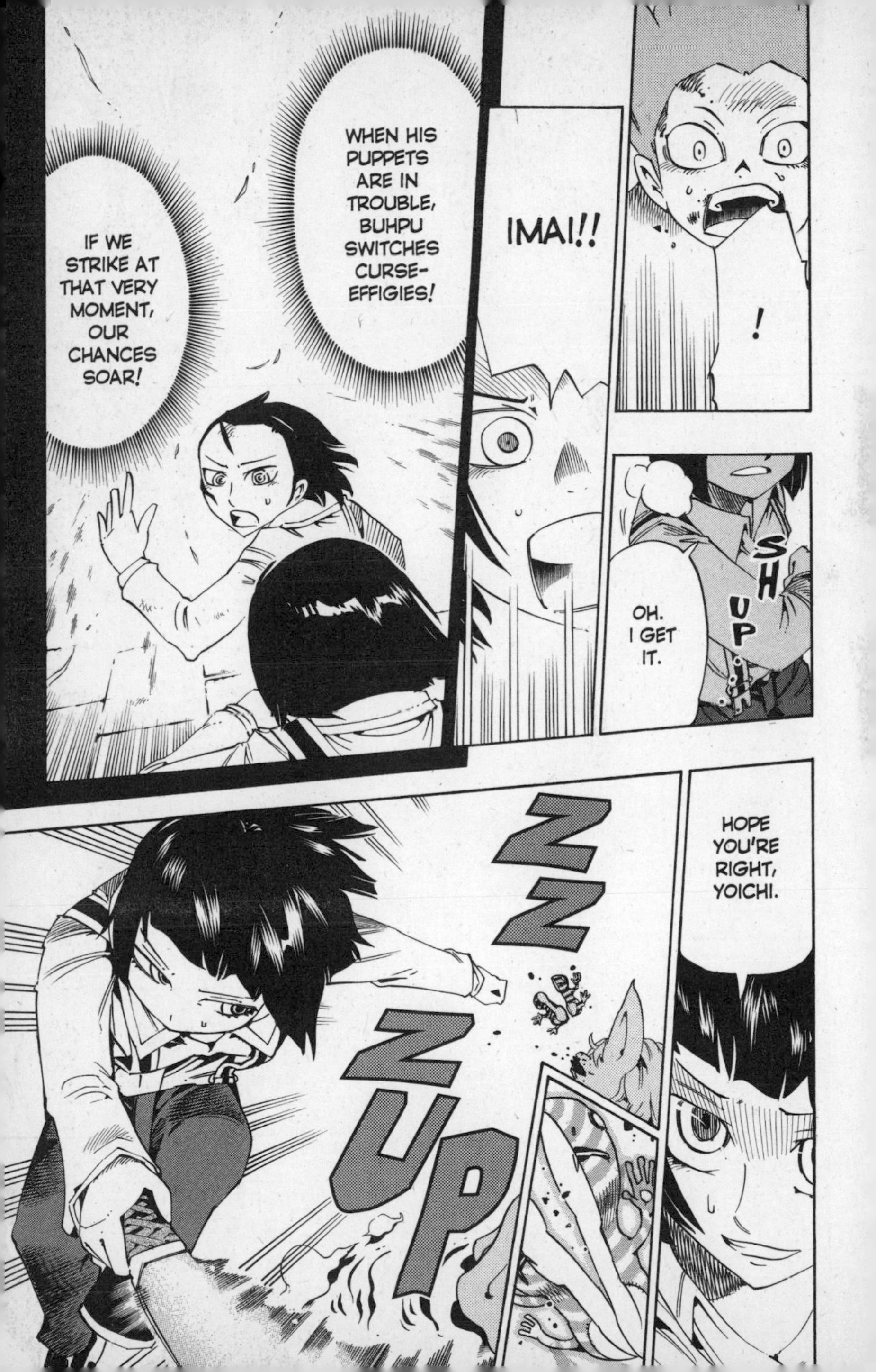
!
SHUP
OH. I GET IT.
IMAI!!
WHEN HIS PUPPETS ARE IN TROUBLE, BUHPU SWITCHES CURSE-EFFIGIES!
IF WE STRIKE AT THAT VERY MOMENT, OUR CHANCES SOAR!
HOPE YOU'RE RIGHT, YOICHI.
ZZZUP

Q: IF YOU'VE CONTRACTED WITH AN ENVOY ONCE, DO YOU HAVE TO CONTRACT WITH THEM AGAIN TO CALL THEM A SECOND TIME?

-Y.S., OSAKA

A: WELL, YES, BUT TO BE MORE PRECISE, NOT REALLY. (?) ERM... THIS NEVER REALLY COMES OUT IN THE STORY, BUT YOU START BY EXECUTING A REGISTRATION CONTRACT TO REGISTER AN ENVOY WITH A PARTICULAR BOOK OF MAGIC LAW. THAT'S WHAT YOU SEE IN THE FIGHT WITH MUHYO (YUURI) VS. PLUTO (SEE ILLUSTATION 1). ONCE THEY'RE REGISTERED, YOU CAN CALL THEM (SEE ILLUSTRATION 2).

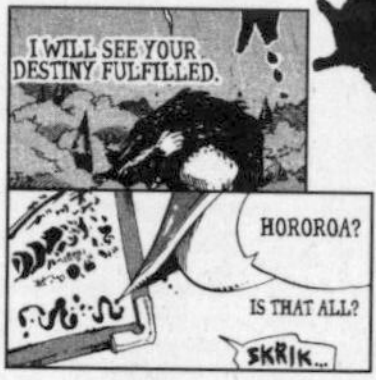
I WILL SEE YOUR DESTINY FULFILLED.
HOROROA?
IS THAT ALL?
SKRIK...

Illus. ②

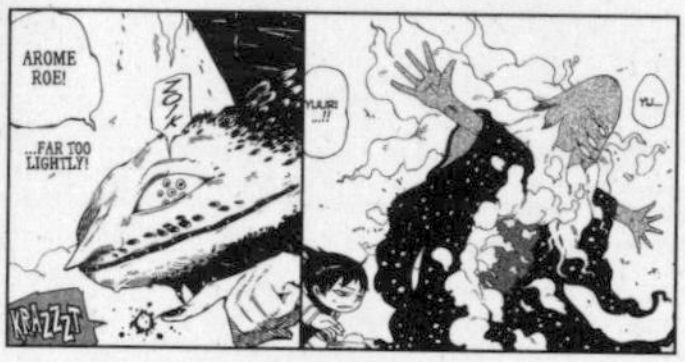
YU...
YUURI ...!!
AROME ROE!
...FAR TOO LIGHTLY!
KRAZZZT

Illus. ①

NOW WHEN YOU WANT TO CALL AN ENVOY, YOU NEED A SPELL OF SUMMONING. THAT'S WHAT THE MAGIC LAW PRACTITIONERS CALL AN "ENVOY CONTRACT." THAT'S WHAT THE WORDS THAT MUHYO WAS MUMBLING IN THE FIGHT AGAINST SOPHIE WERE. FOR YOUR TYPICAL EXECUTOR, GORYO INCLUDED, YOU NEED AN ENVOY CONTRACT FOR JUST ABOUT EVERY ENVOY YOU SUMMON. HOWEVER, MUHYO ONLY REALLY NEEDS A CONTRACT WHEN HE'S DEALING WITH SOMETHING OF ADMIRAL CLASS OR HIGHER.

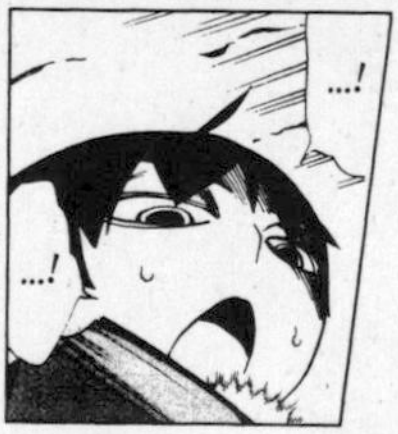
...!
...!

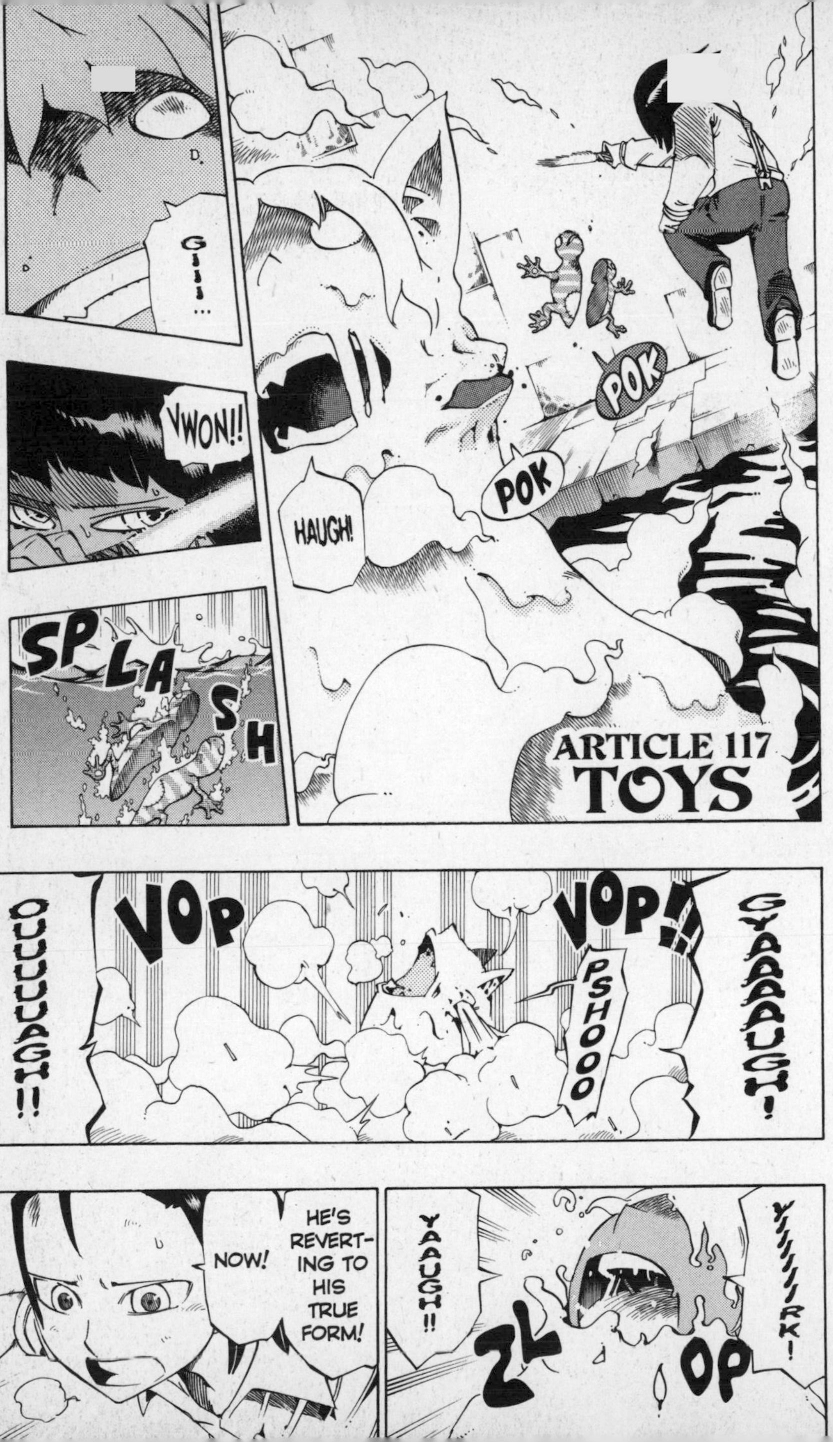
POK
POK
HAUGH!
ARTICLE 117
TOYS
GIII...
VWON!!
SPLASH
GYAAAAUGH!
VOP!!
PSHOOOO
VOP
OUUUUUAGH!!
YIIIIIIRK!
YAAUGH!!
HE'S REVERTING TO HIS TRUE FORM!
NOW!

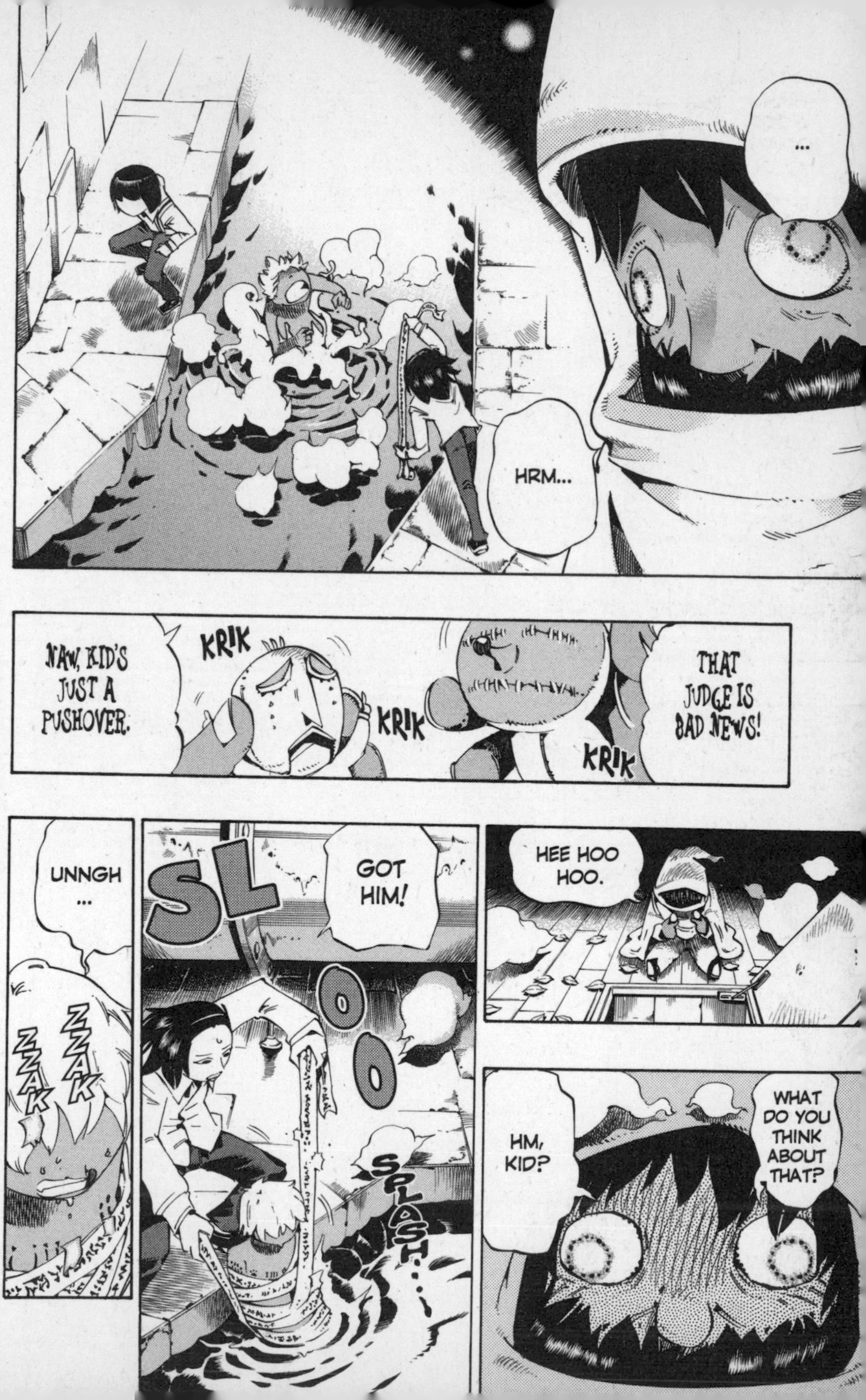
...
HRM...
THAT JUDGE IS BAD NEWS!
KRIK
KRIK
NAW, KID'S JUST A PUSHOVER.
KRIK
HEE HOO HOO.
WHAT DO YOU THINK ABOUT THAT?
HM, KID?
GOT HIM!
SLOOO
SPLASH...
UNNGH ...
ZZAK
ZZAK

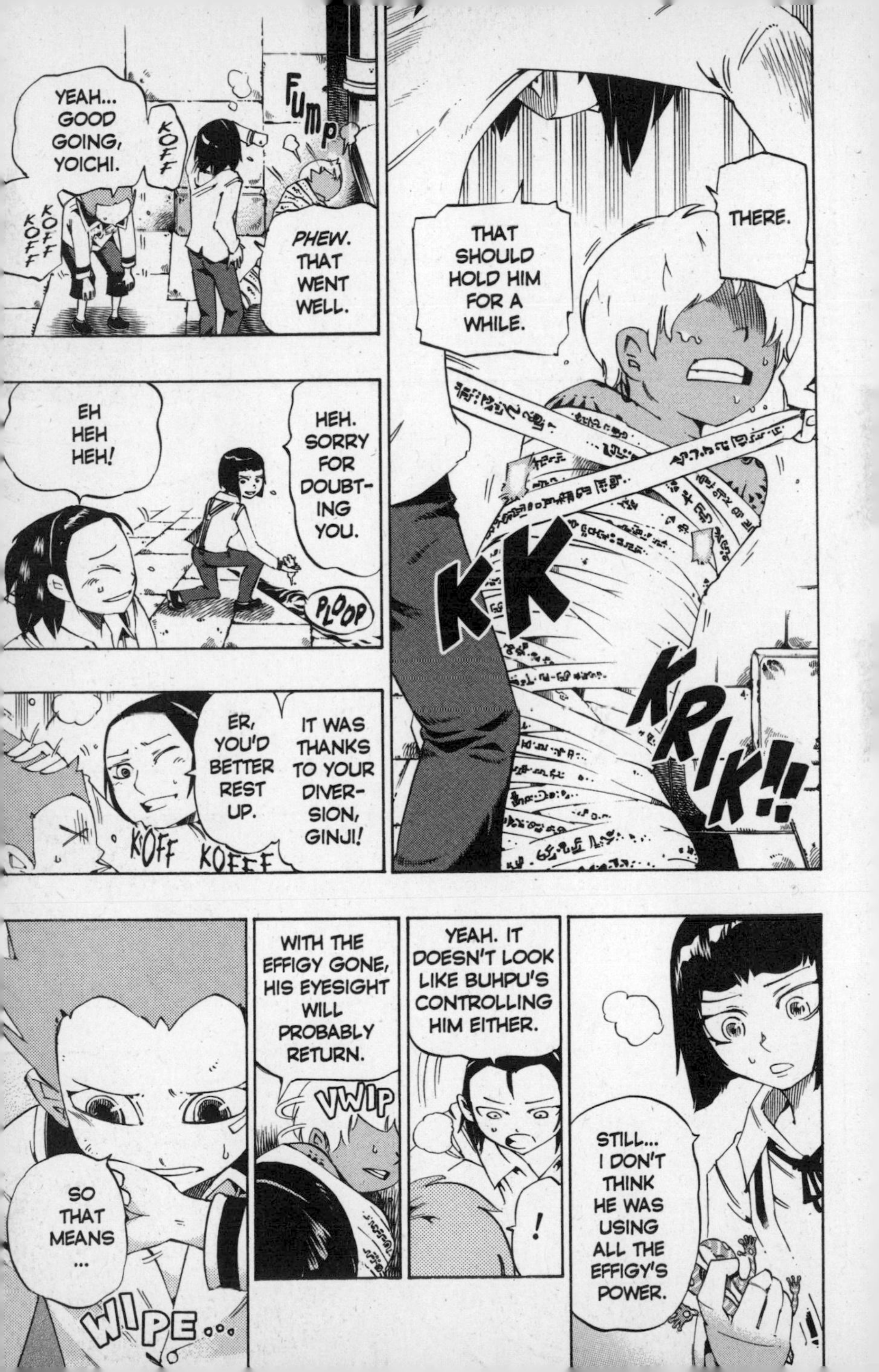
THERE.
THAT SHOULD HOLD HIM FOR A WHILE.
KK
KRIK!!
FUMP
PHEW. THAT WENT WELL.
KOFF
YEAH... GOOD GOING, YOICHI.
KOFF KOFF
HEH. SORRY FOR DOUBT-ING YOU.
PLOOP
EH HEH HEH!
IT WAS THANKS TO YOUR DIVER-SION, GINJI!
ER, YOU'D BETTER REST UP.
KOFF KOFFF
STILL... I DON'T THINK HE WAS USING ALL THE EFFIGY'S POWER.
YEAH. IT DOESN'T LOOK LIKE BUHPU'S CONTROLLING HIM EITHER.
!
WITH THE EFFIGY GONE, HIS EYESIGHT WILL PROBABLY RETURN.
VWIP
SO THAT MEANS ...
WIPE...

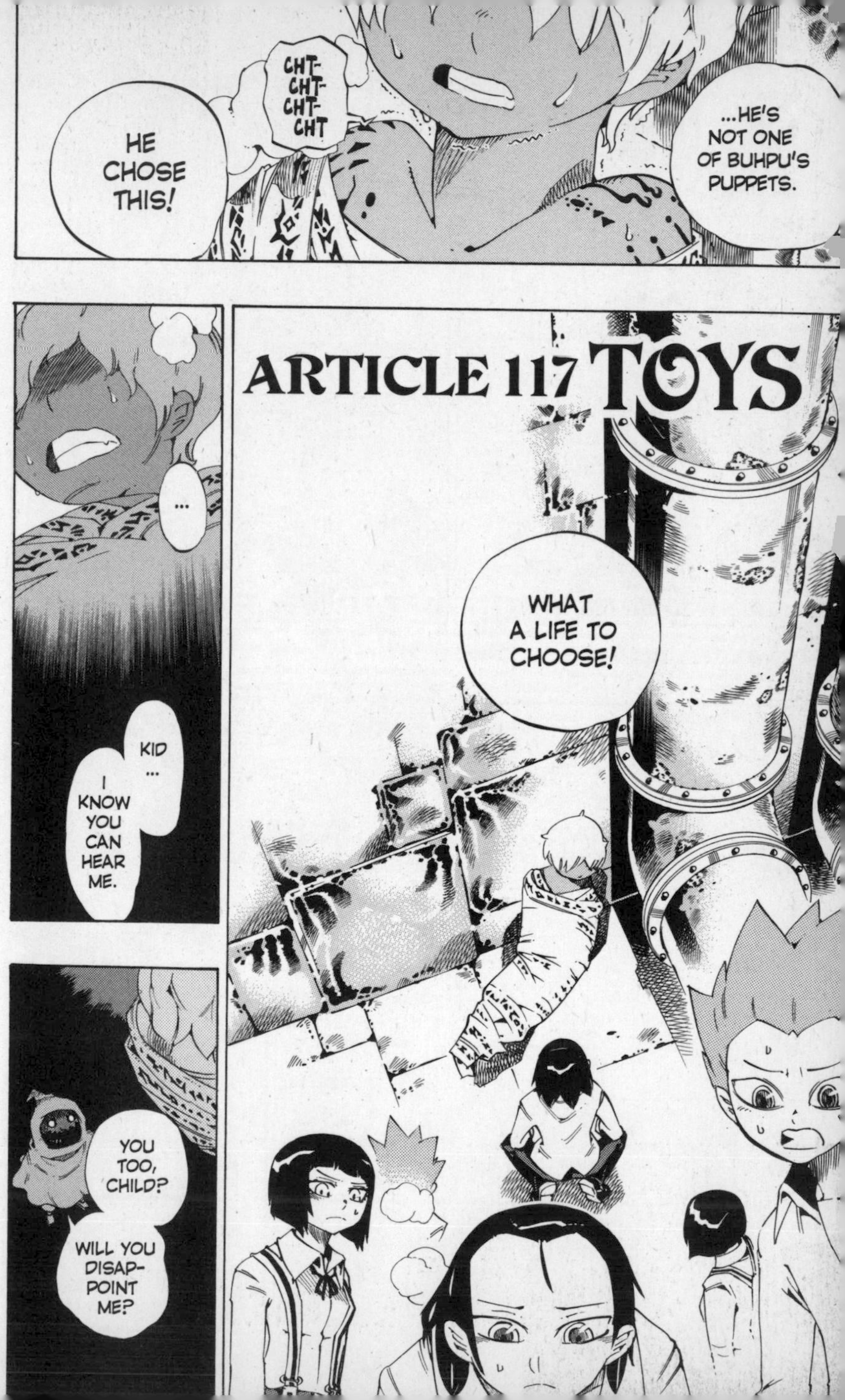
...HE'S NOT ONE OF BUHPU'S PUPPETS.
CHT-CHT-CHT-CHT
HE CHOSE THIS!
ARTICLE 117 TOYS
WHAT A LIFE TO CHOOSE!
...
KID ...
I KNOW YOU CAN HEAR ME.
YOU TOO, CHILD?
WILL YOU DISAP-POINT ME?

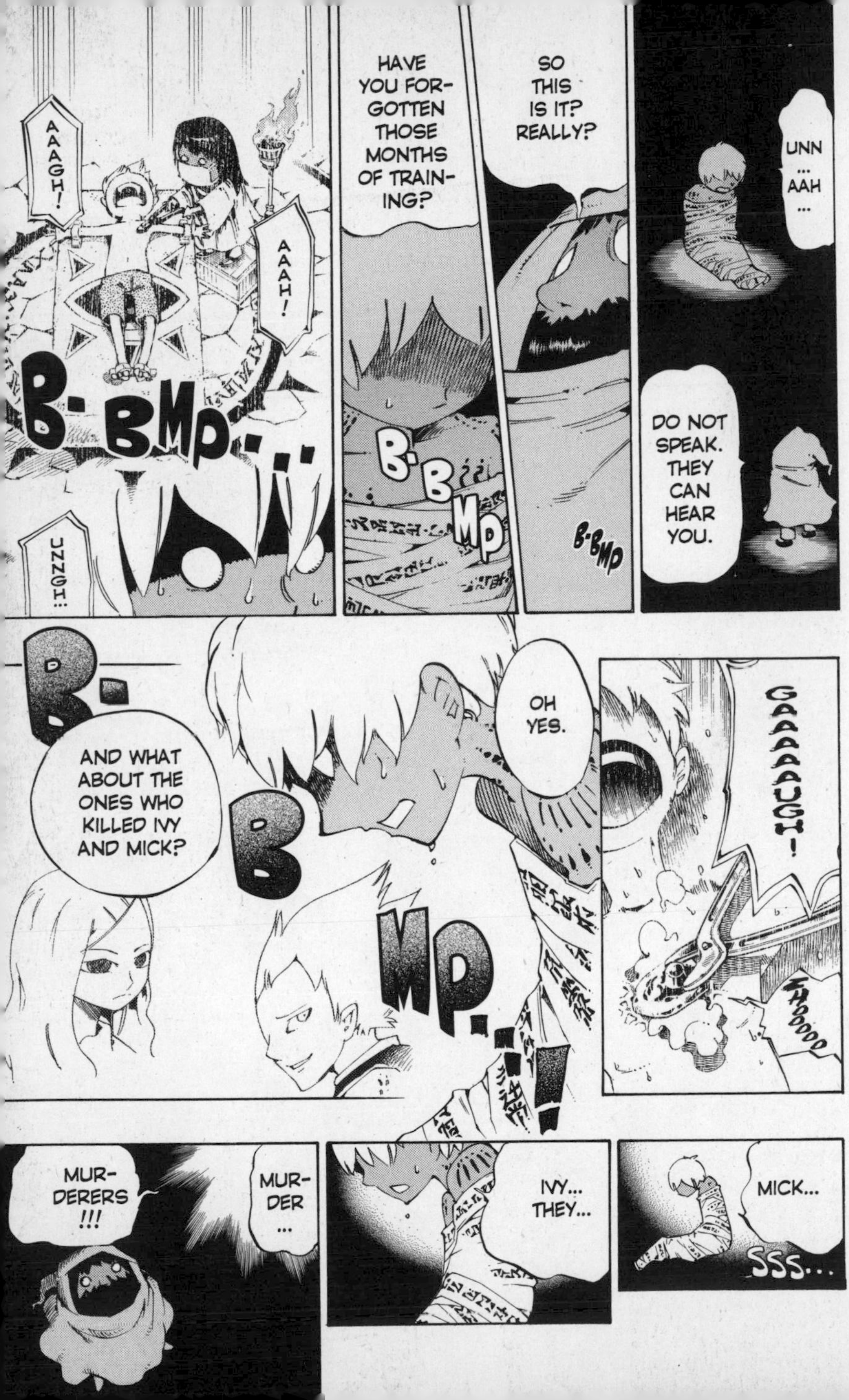
UNN ... AAH ...
DO NOT SPEAK. THEY CAN HEAR YOU.
SO THIS IS IT? REALLY?
B-BMP
HAVE YOU FOR-GOTTEN THOSE MONTHS OF TRAIN-ING?
B-BMP
AAAH!
AAAGH!
B-BMP...
UNNGH...
GAAAAAAUGH!
THOOOOOO
OH YES.
AND WHAT ABOUT THE ONES WHO KILLED IVY AND MICK?
B-BMP..!
MICK...
SSS...
IVY... THEY...
MUR-DER ...
MUR-DERERS !!!

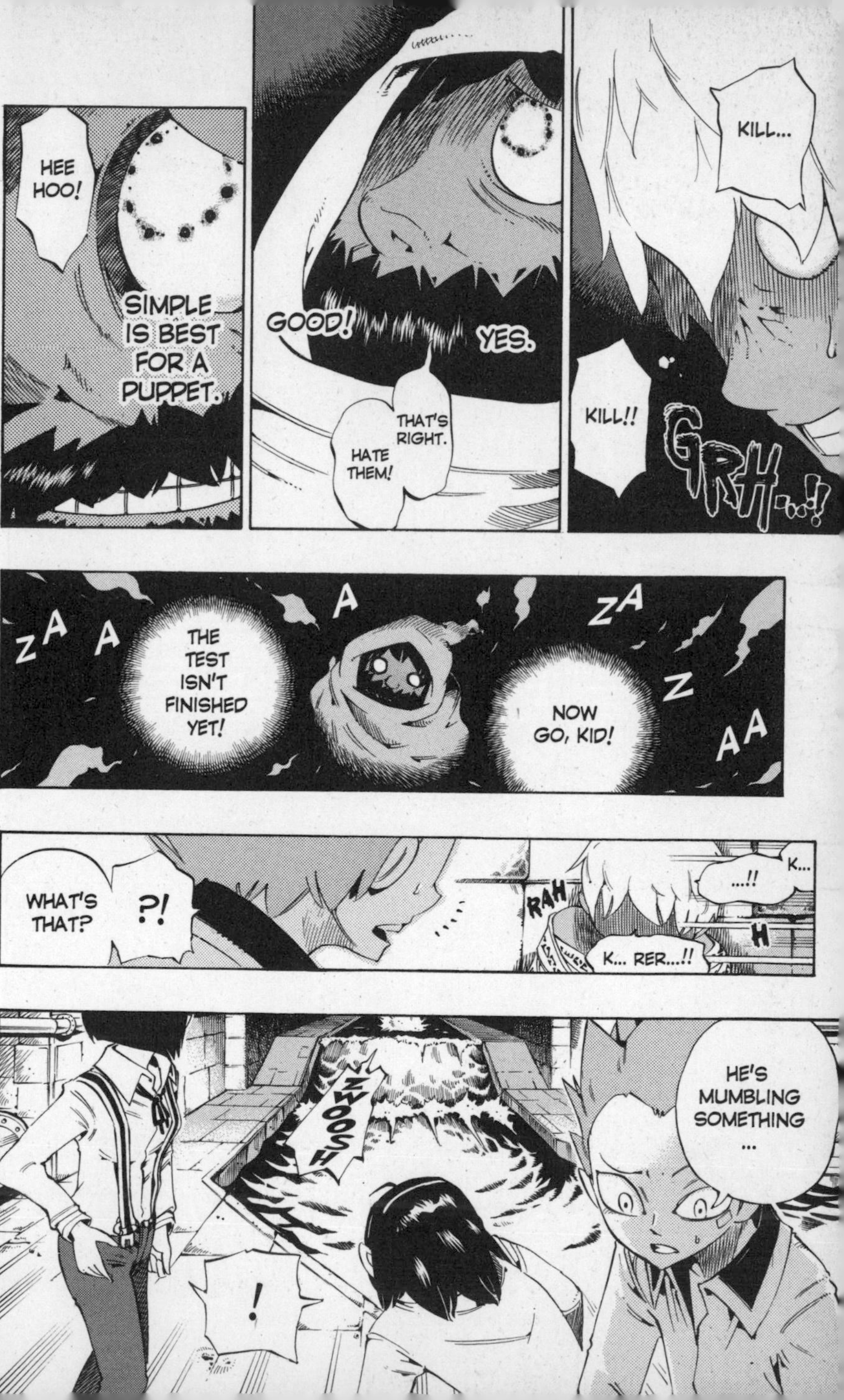
KILL...
KILL!!
GRH...!
YES.
GOOD!
THAT'S RIGHT.
HATE THEM!
HEE HOO!
SIMPLE IS BEST FOR A PUPPET.
ZA A
AA
Z
NOW GO, KID!
A
THE TEST ISN'T FINISHED YET!
ZA A
K... ...!!
H
K... RER...!!
RAH
?!
WHAT'S THAT?
HE'S MUMBLING SOMETHING ...
ZWOOSH
!

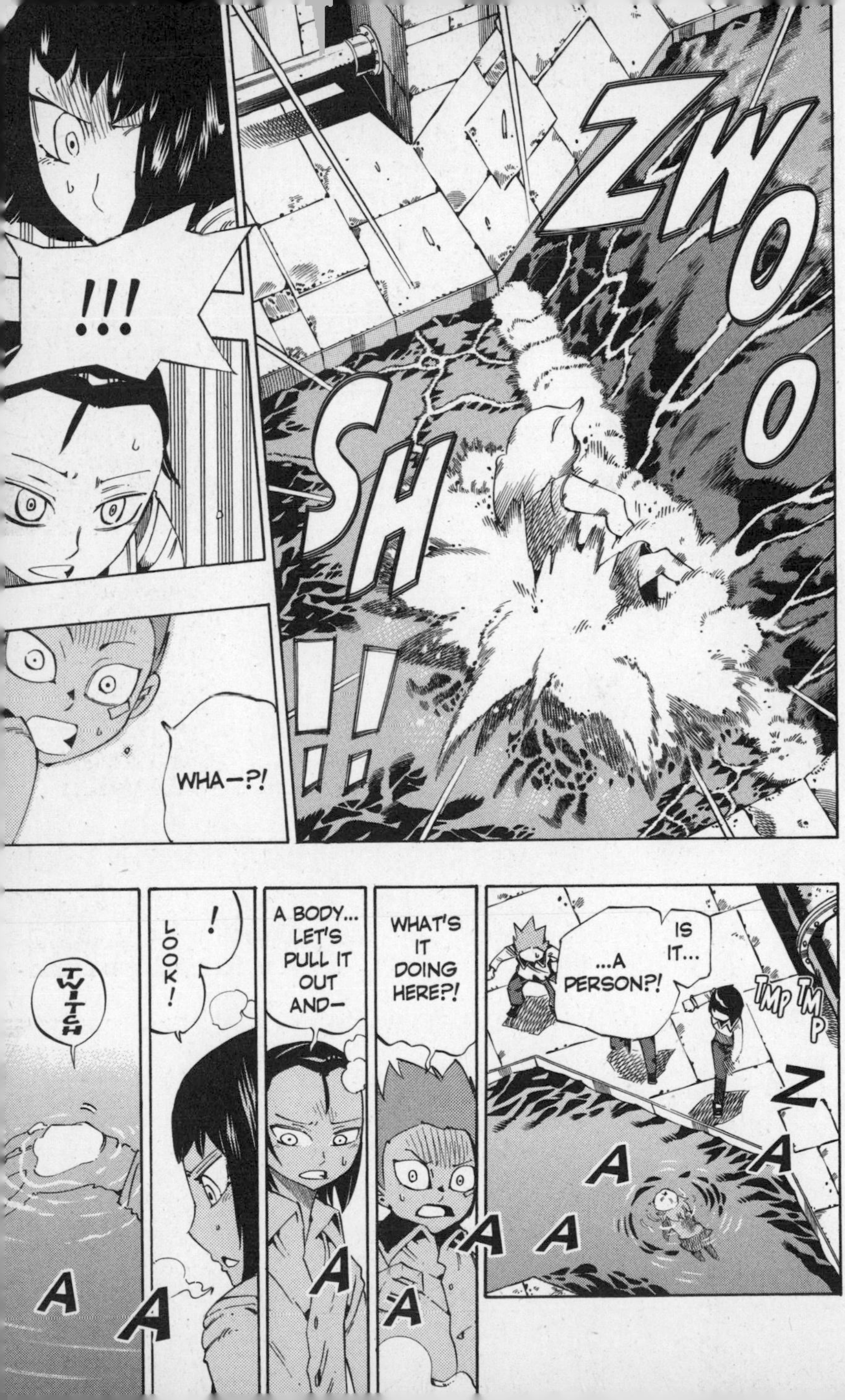
ZWOOOSH!!
!!!
WHA—?!
IS IT... ...A PERSON?!
TMP TMP
ZAAAAAAAA
WHAT'S IT DOING HERE?!
A BODY... LET'S PULL IT OUT AND—
!
LOOK!
TWITCH

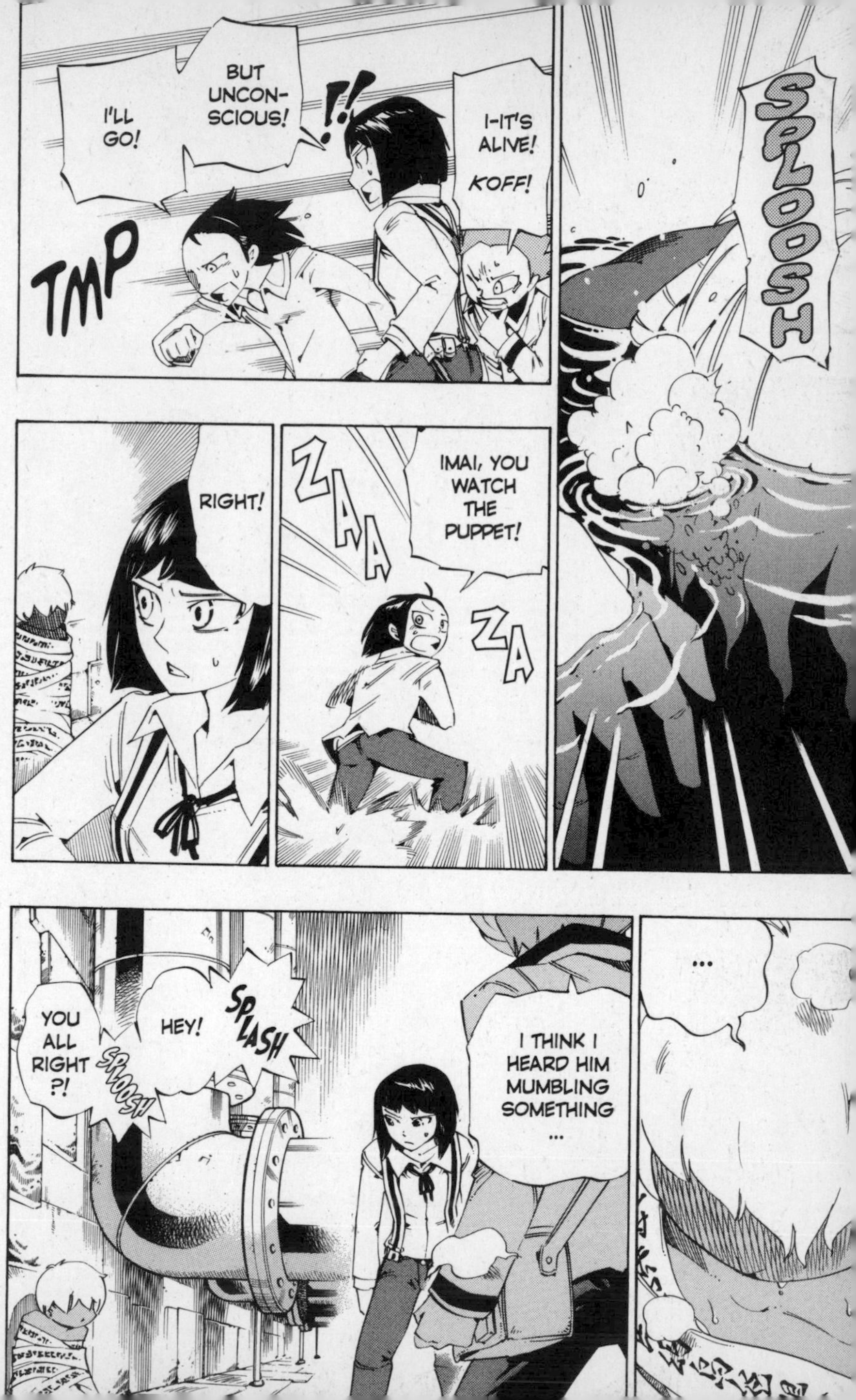
SPLOOSH
I-IT'S ALIVE!
KOFF!
!!
BUT UNCON-SCIOUS!
I'LL GO!
TMP
IMAI, YOU WATCH THE PUPPET!
ZAA
ZA
RIGHT!
...
I THINK I HEARD HIM MUMBLING SOMETHING ...
SPLASH
HEY!
SPLOOSH
YOU ALL RIGHT ?!

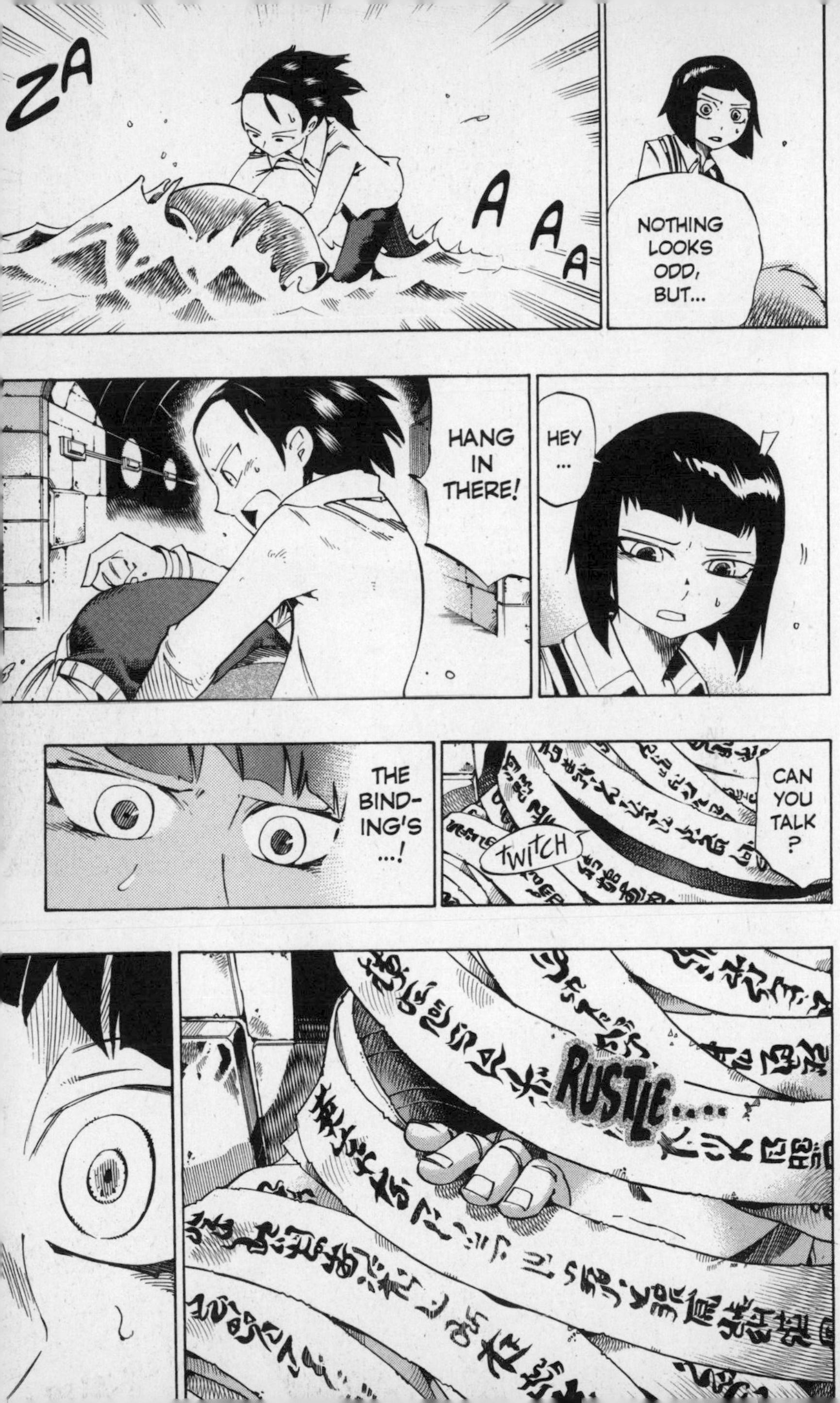
NOTHING LOOKS ODD, BUT...
ZA
A A A
HEY ...
HANG IN THERE!
CAN YOU TALK?
TWITCH
THE BINDING'S ...!
RUSTLE....

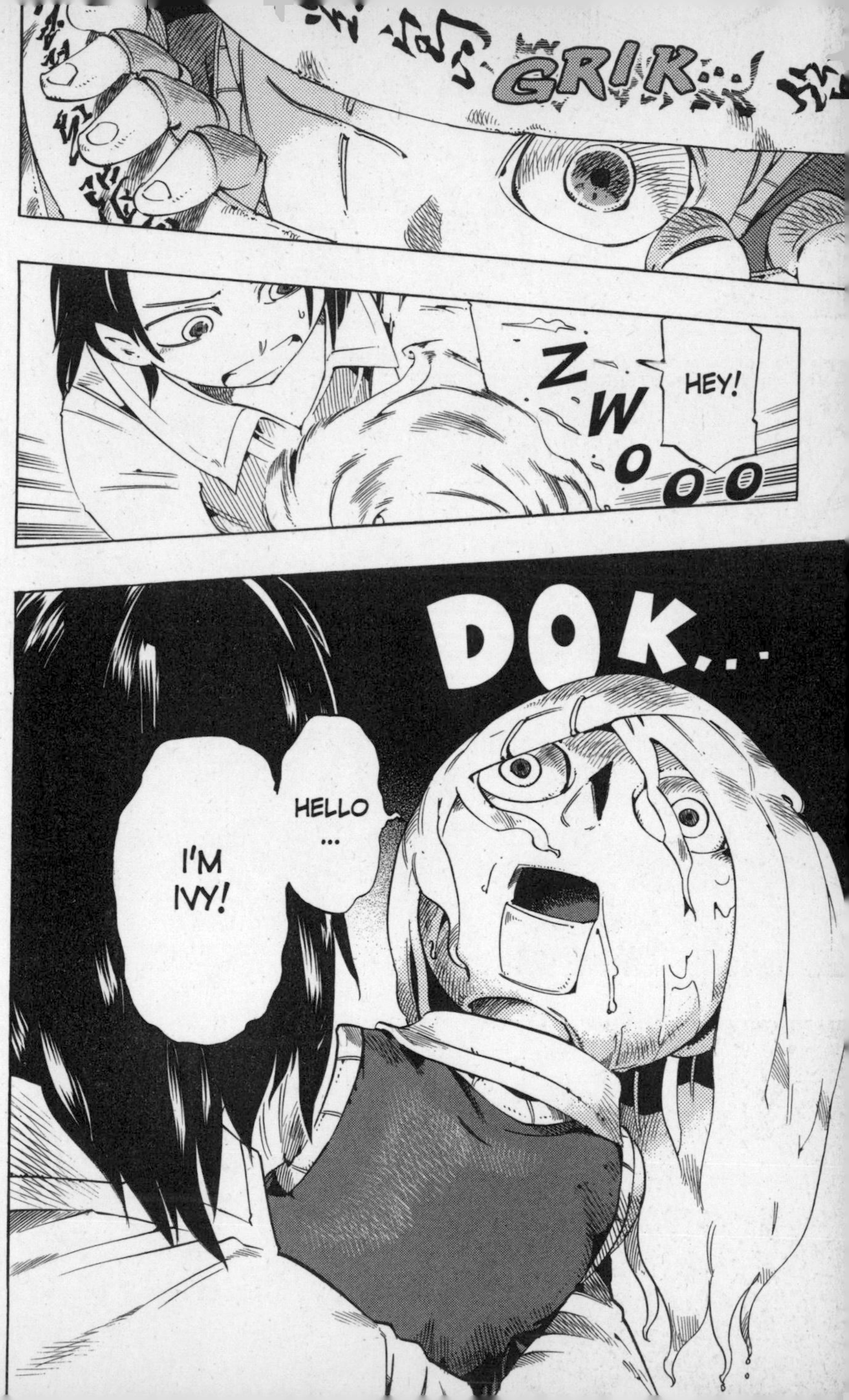
GRIK...
ZWOOO
HEY!
DOK...
HELLO ...
I'M IVY!

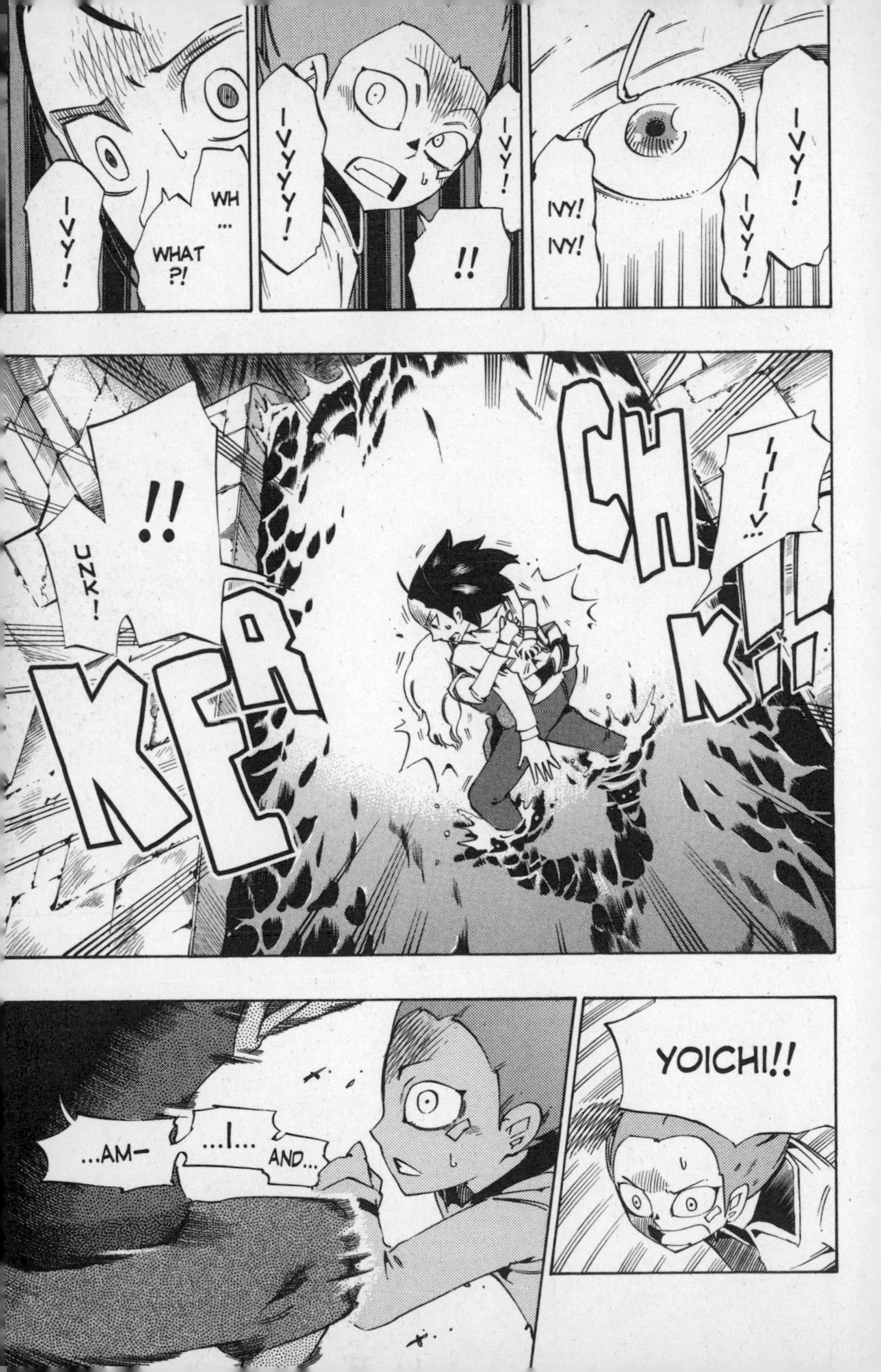
IVY!
IVY!
IVY!
IVY!
IVY!
!!
IVYYY!
WH... WHAT?!
IVY!
...!!
CHK!!
KER
UNK!
!!
YOICHI!!
AND...
...I...
...AM–

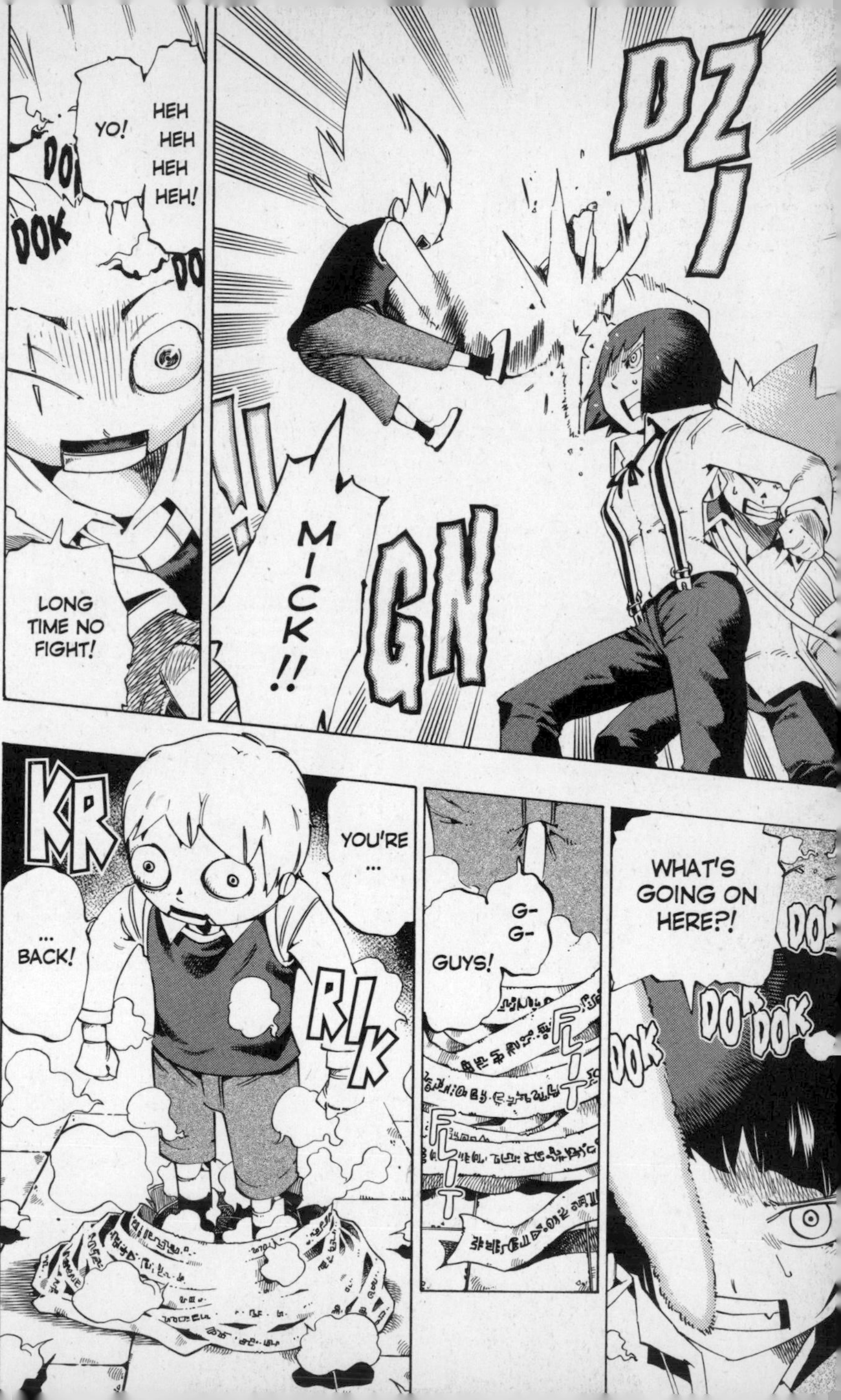
DZI
MICK!!
GN
HEH HEH HEH HEH!
YO!
DOK
LONG TIME NO FIGHT!
WHAT'S GOING ON HERE?!
DOK DOK DOK
G- G- GUYS!
FLIT
FLIT
YOU'RE ...
... BACK!
KR
RIK

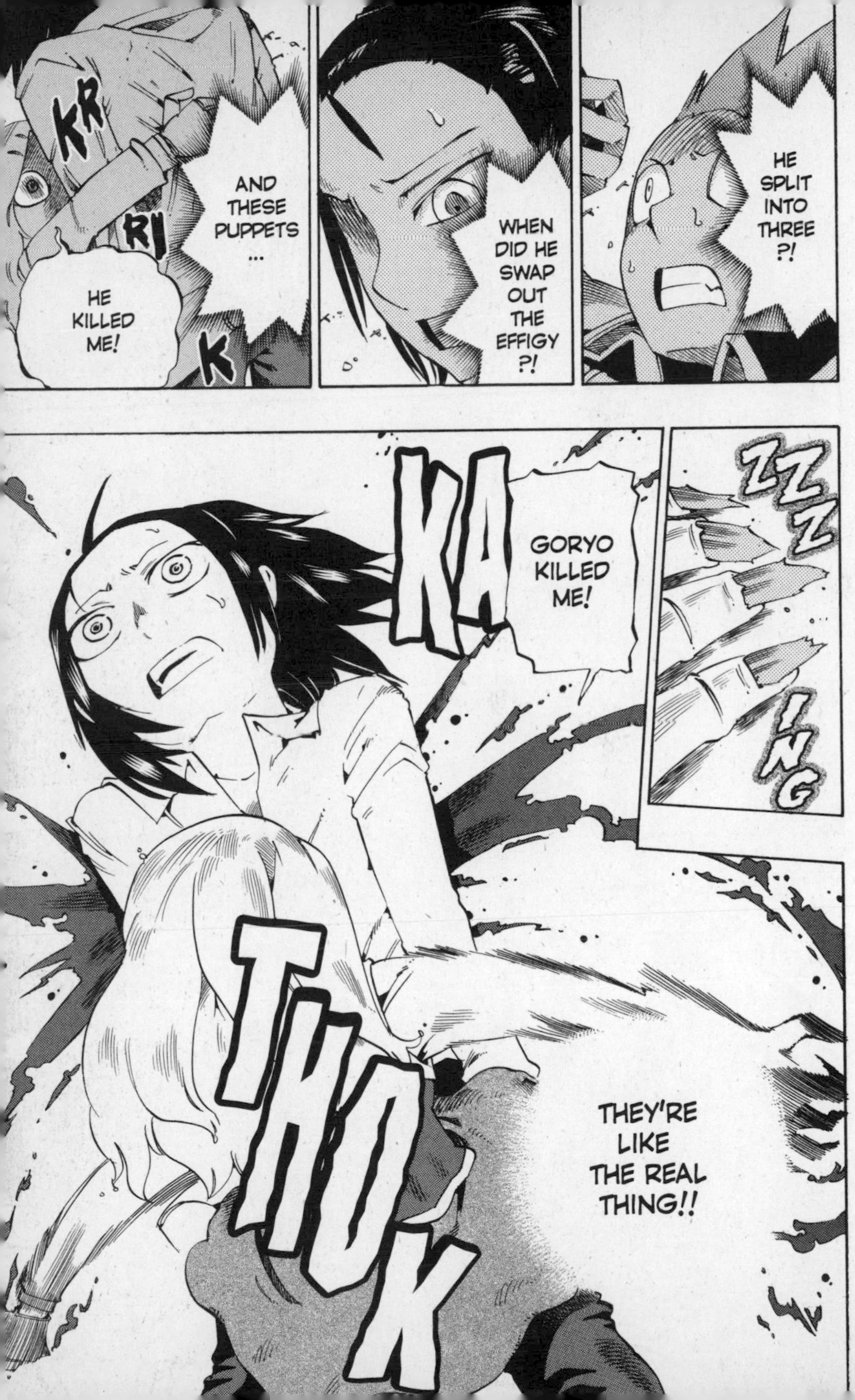
HE SPLIT INTO THREE ?!
WHEN DID HE SWAP OUT THE EFFIGY ?!
AND THESE PUPPETS ...
KRRIK
HE KILLED ME!
ZZZING
GORYO KILLED ME!
KA
THOK
THEY'RE LIKE THE REAL THING!!

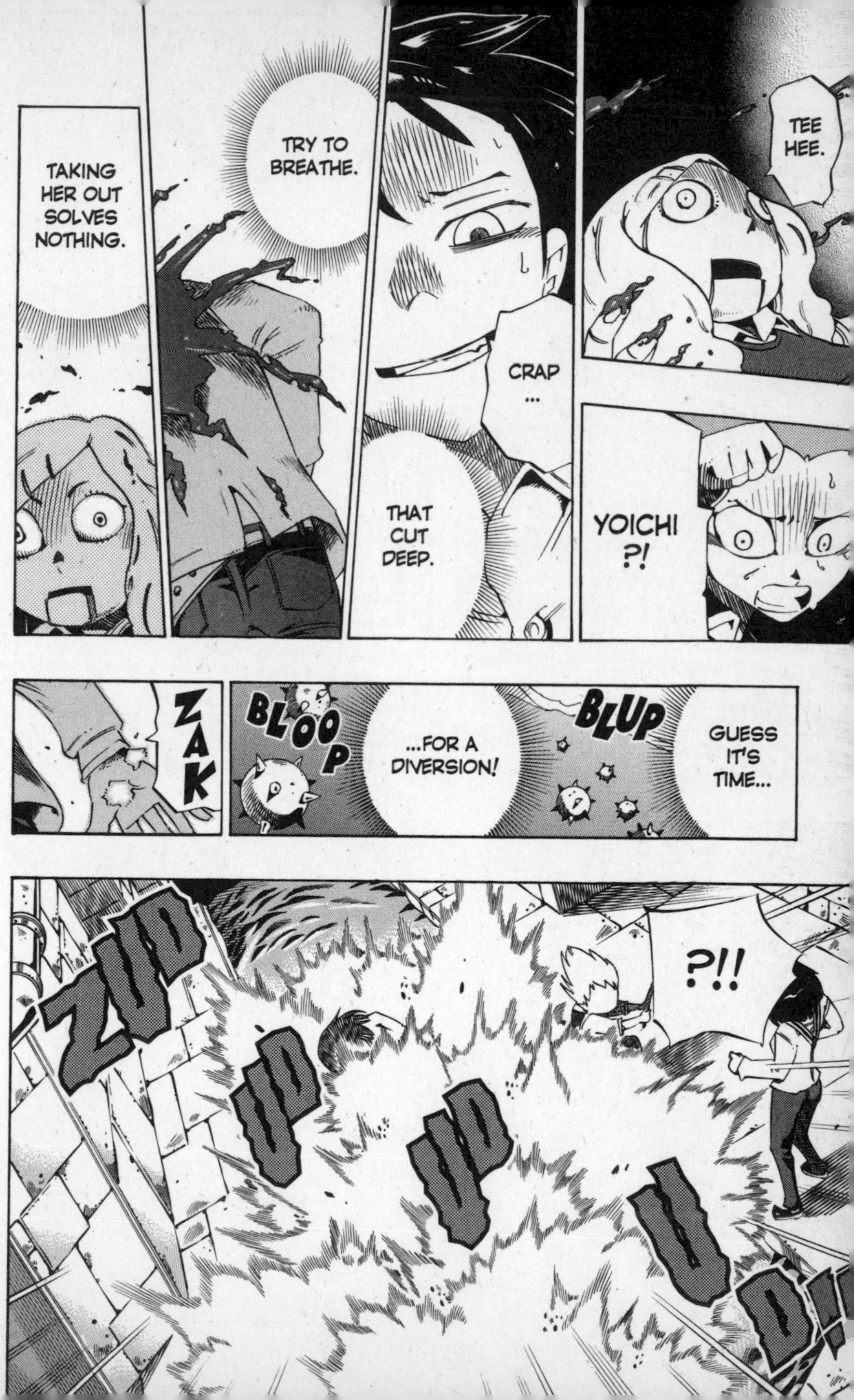
TEE HEE.
YOICHI ?!
CRAP ...
THAT CUT DEEP.
TRY TO BREATHE.
TAKING HER OUT SOLVES NOTHING.
GUESS IT'S TIME...
BLUP
...FOR A DIVERSION!
BLOOP
ZAK
?!!
ZUD UD UD UD D!

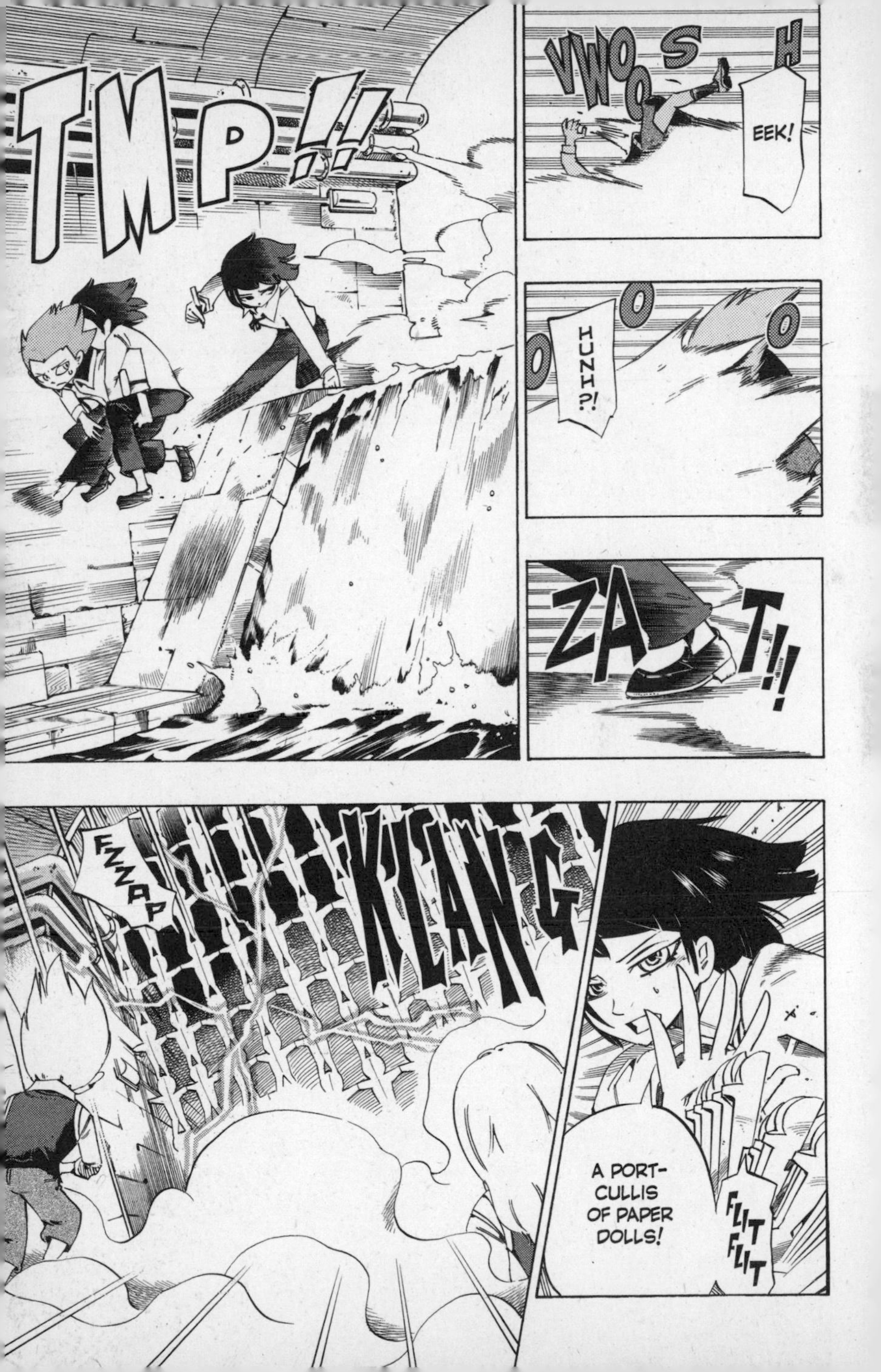
VWOOSH
EEK!
HUNH?!
OOOO
ZAT!!
TMP!!
A PORT-CULLIS OF PAPER DOLLS!
FLIT FLIT
KLANG
FZZAP

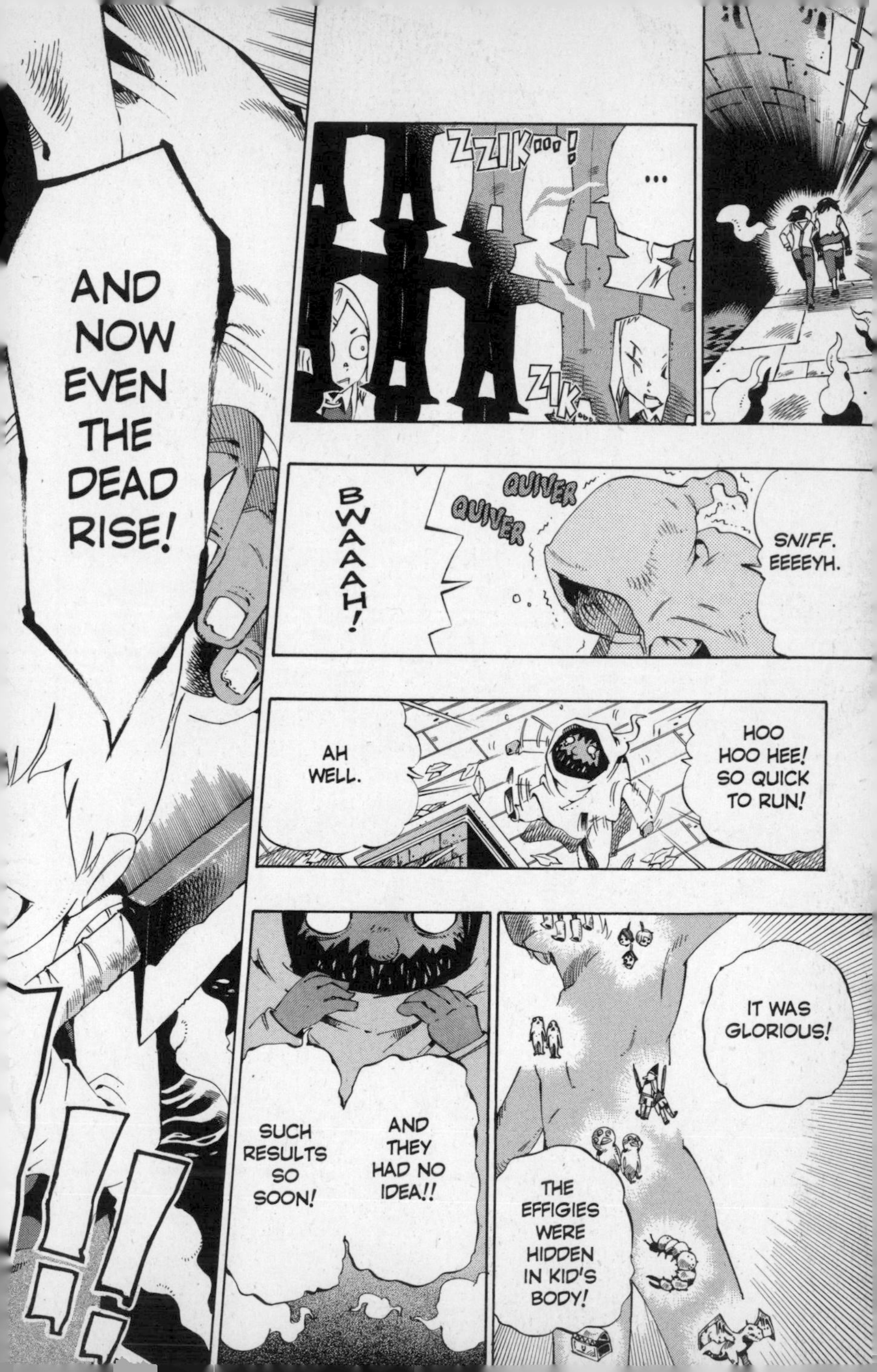
...
ZZIK...!
ZIK...
SNIFF. EEEEYH.
QUIVER
QUIVER
BWAAAAH!
HOO HOO HEE! SO QUICK TO RUN!
AH WELL.
IT WAS GLORIOUS!
THE EFFIGIES WERE HIDDEN IN KID'S BODY!
AND THEY HAD NO IDEA!!
SUCH RESULTS SO SOON!
AND NOW EVEN THE DEAD RISE!
!!

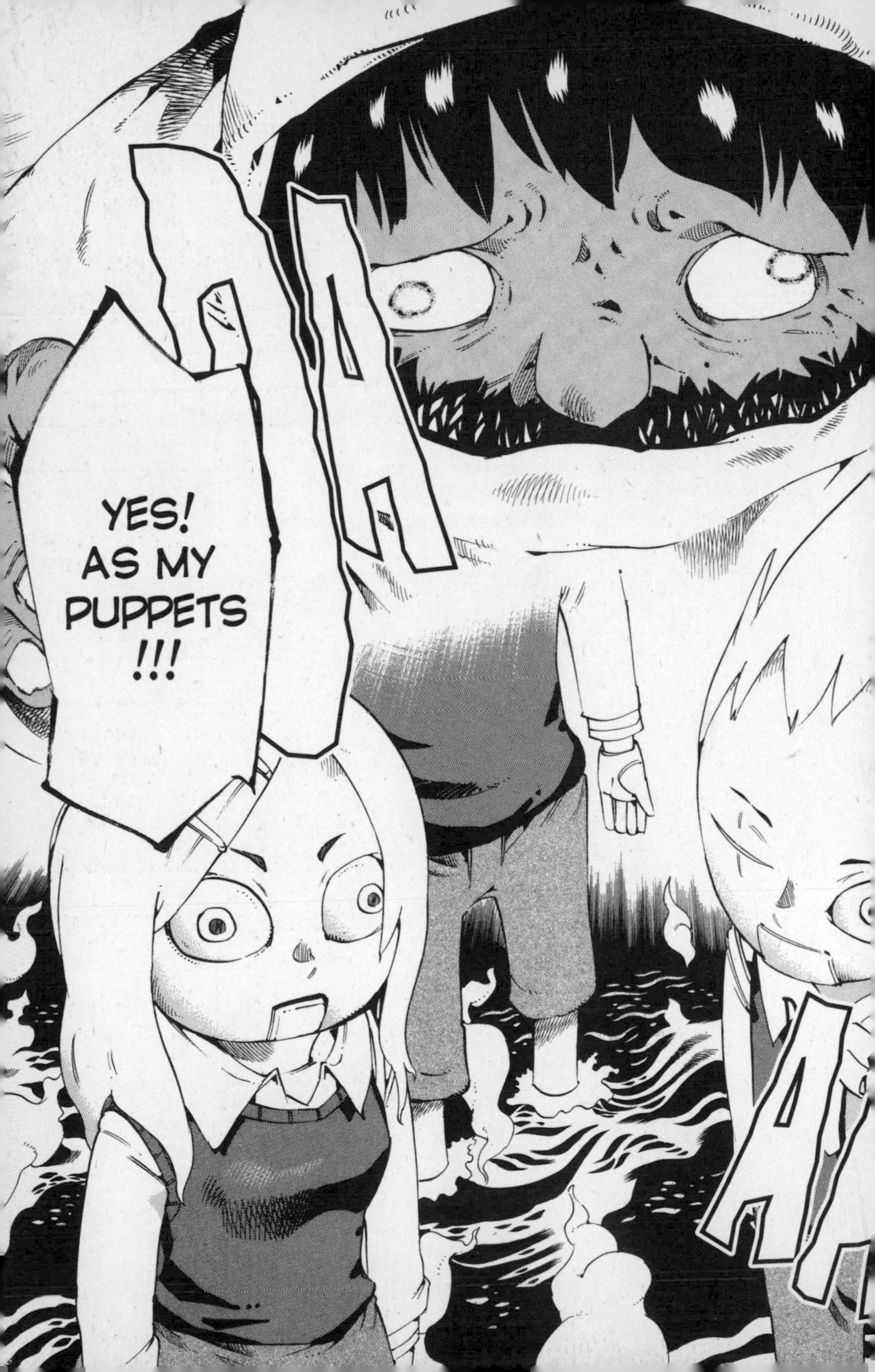
YES! AS MY PUPPETS !!!

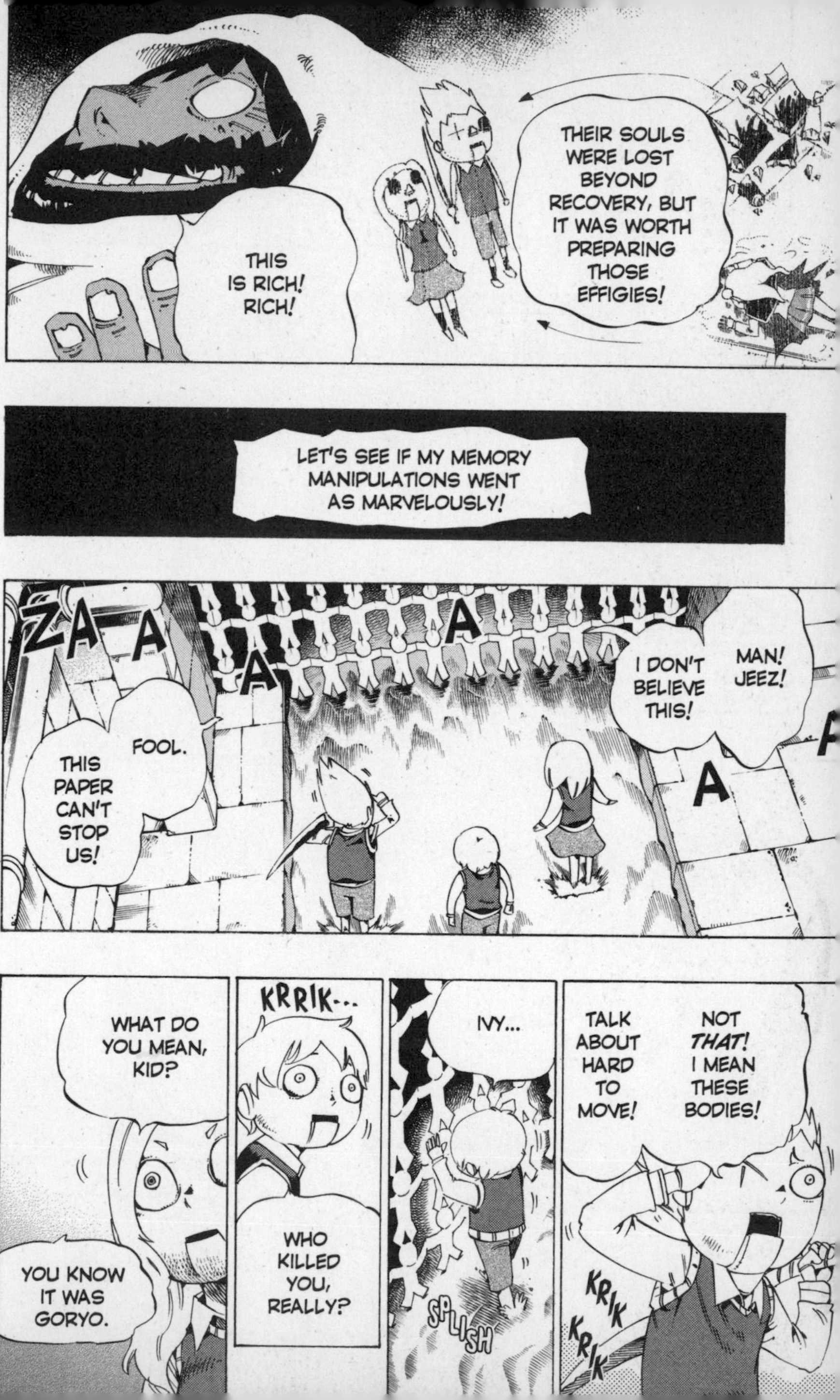
THEIR SOULS WERE LOST BEYOND RECOVERY, BUT IT WAS WORTH PREPARING THOSE EFFIGIES!
THIS IS RICH! RICH!
LET'S SEE IF MY MEMORY MANIPULATIONS WENT AS MARVELOUSLY!
MAN! JEEZ!
I DON'T BELIEVE THIS!
ZA A A A A A
FOOL.
THIS PAPER CAN'T STOP US!
NOT *THAT*! I MEAN THESE BODIES!
TALK ABOUT HARD TO MOVE!
KRIK KRIK
IVY...
SPLISH
KRRIK...
WHO KILLED YOU, REALLY?
WHAT DO YOU MEAN, KID?
YOU KNOW IT WAS GORYO.

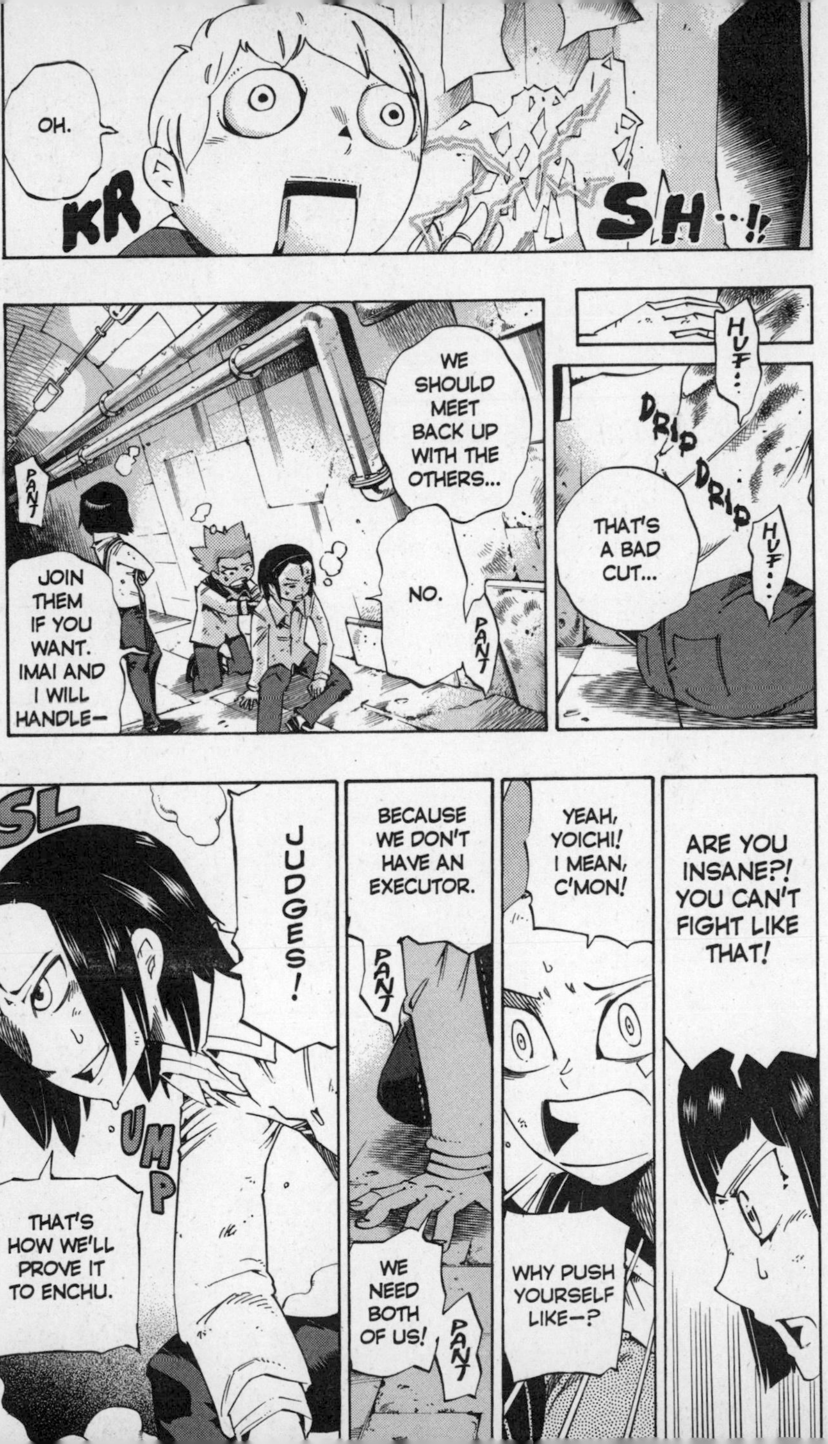
SH…!!
OH.
KR
HUF…
DRIP DRIP
HUF…
THAT'S A BAD CUT…
WE SHOULD MEET BACK UP WITH THE OTHERS…
NO.
PANT
PANT
JOIN THEM IF YOU WANT. IMAI AND I WILL HANDLE—
ARE YOU INSANE?! YOU CAN'T FIGHT LIKE THAT!
YEAH, YOICHI! I MEAN, C'MON!
WHY PUSH YOURSELF LIKE—?
BECAUSE WE DON'T HAVE AN EXECUTOR.
PANT
WE NEED BOTH OF US!
PANT
JUDGES!
SL
UMP
THAT'S HOW WE'LL PROVE IT TO ENCHU.

Q1: WHICH OF BIKO'S BAKED BREADS DOES RIO LIKE THE MOST?
Q2: WHICH OF RIO'S GRATINS DOES BIKO LIKE THE MOST?
Q3: WHICH MAGIC LAW DOES MUHYO LIKE THE MOST?

-Y.S., OSAKA

A1:

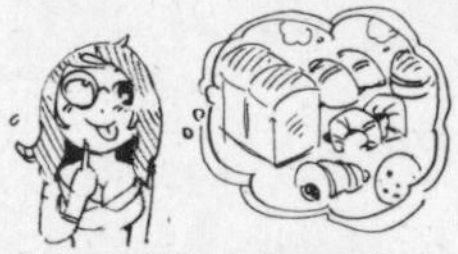

SHE SAYS SHE LIKES THEM ALL, BUT I HAVE IT ON GOOD AUTHORITY THAT THE RARE AND HIGHLY PRIZED CHOCOLATE TWISTS ARE A FAVORITE.

A2:

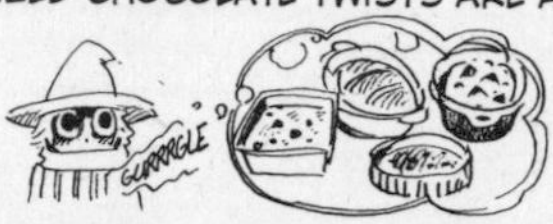
GURRRGLE

SHE WOULD EAT THEM ALL RIGHT NOW IF SHE COULD, BUT IF SHE HAD TO PICK JUST ONE, IT'D BE THE "RIO SPECIAL." I ASKED WHAT FLAVOR THAT WAS, AND ALL I HEARD WAS BIKO'S STOMACH GROWLING. MUST BE GOOD!

A3:

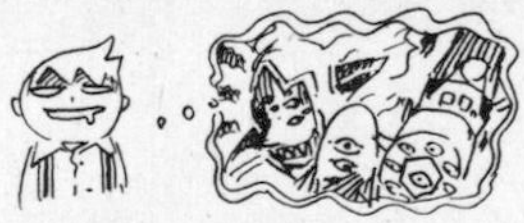

I DON'T KNOW IF "LIKE" IS THE RIGHT WORD, BUT MUHYO DOES SEEM FOND OF THE NIGHT TRAIN, ADMIRAL BELOW AND YUURI. HIS REASON? "IT'S A RUSH..." NOW I WISH I HADN'T ASKED...

ARTICLE 118
BACKUP PLAN

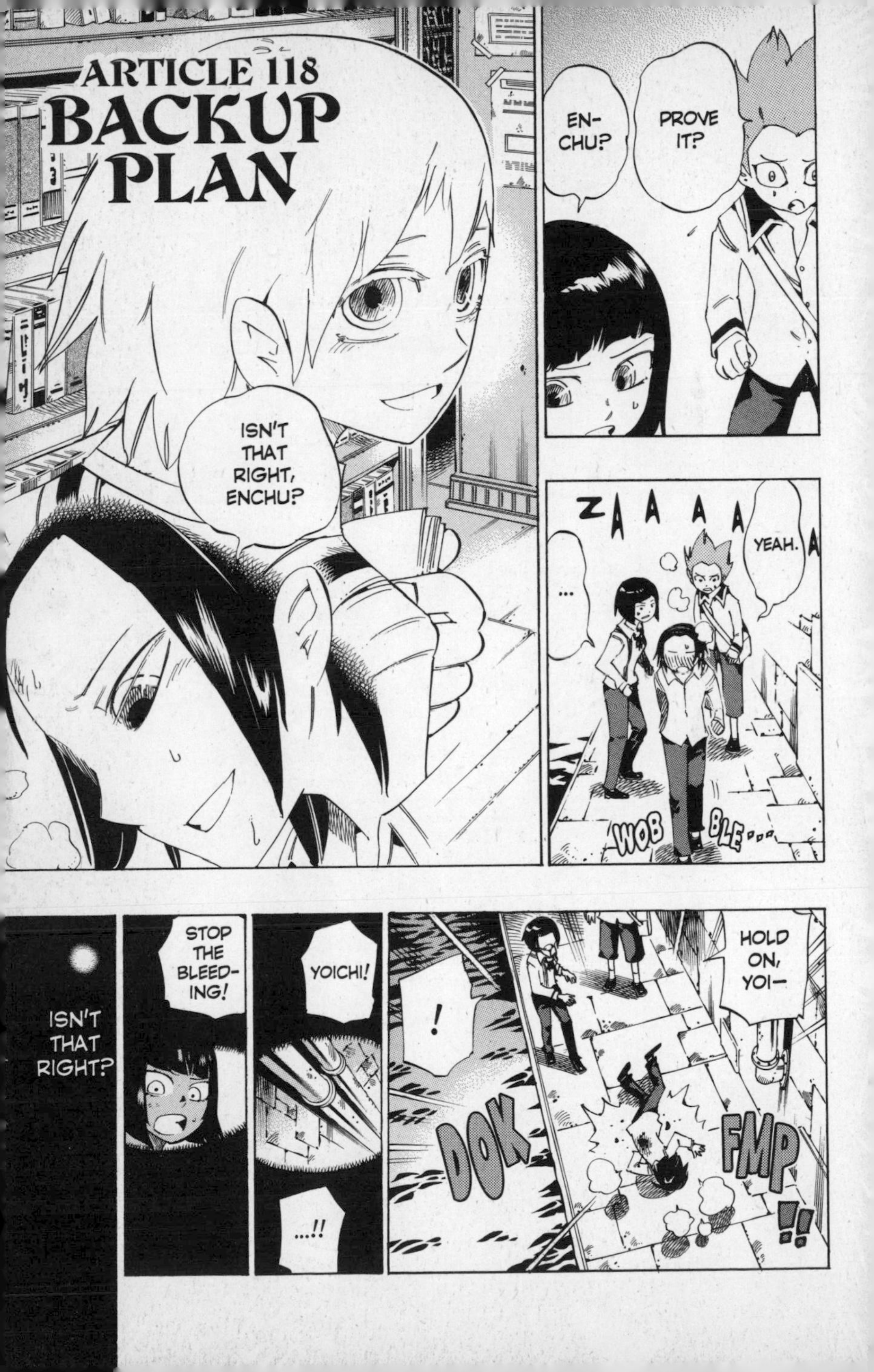
PROVE IT?
EN-CHU?
YEAH.
ZAAAAAA
...
WOBBLE...
ISN'T THAT RIGHT, ENCHU?
HOLD ON, YOI—
!
DOK
FMP!!
YOICHI!
...!!
STOP THE BLEED-ING!
ISN'T THAT RIGHT?

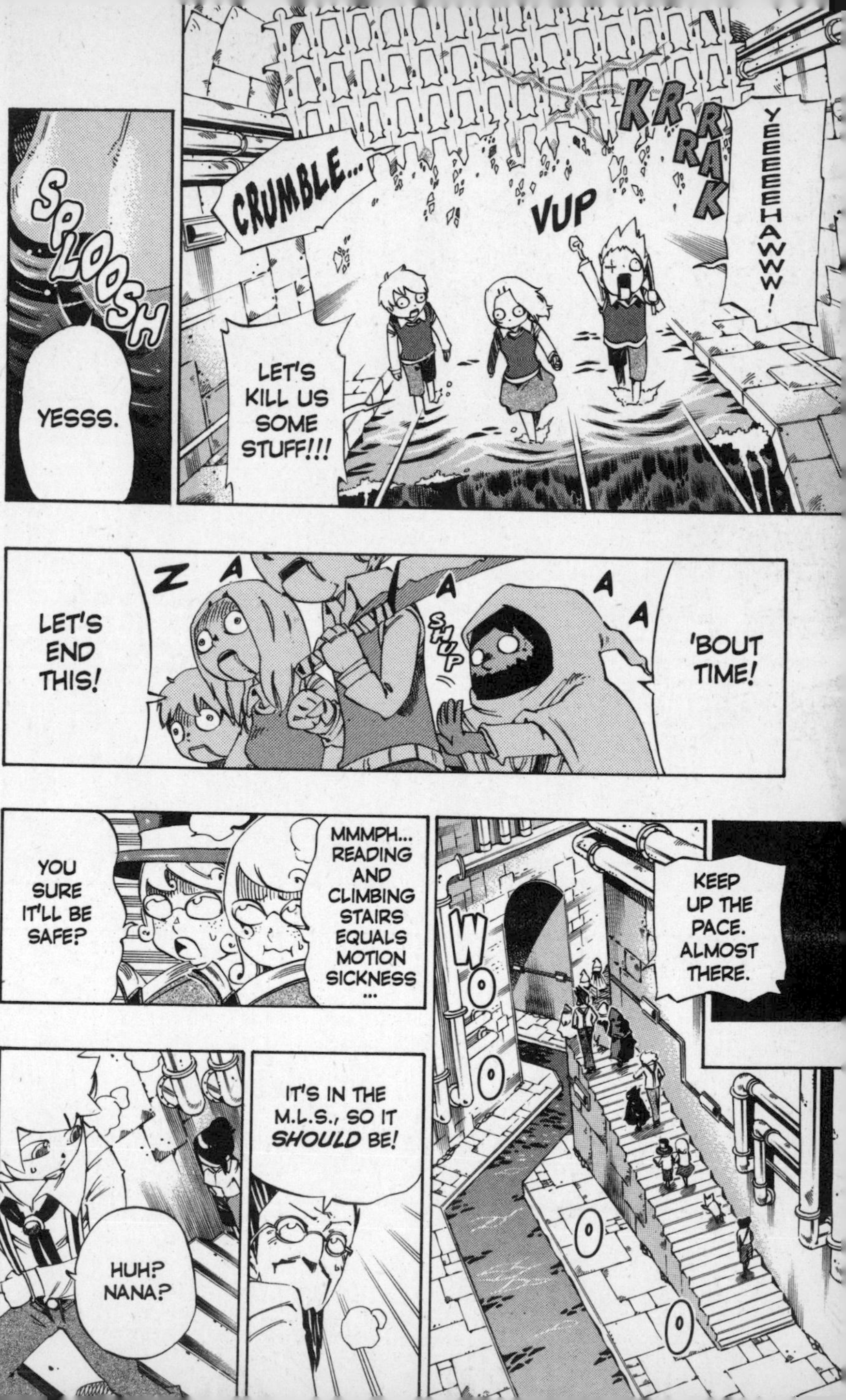
YEEEEHAWWW!
KRRRAK
VUP
CRUMBLE...
LET'S KILL US SOME STUFF!!!
SPLOOSH
YESSS.
'BOUT TIME!
ZAAAA
SHUP
LET'S END THIS!
KEEP UP THE PACE. ALMOST THERE.
WOOOOO
MMMPH... READING AND CLIMBING STAIRS EQUALS MOTION SICKNESS...
YOU SURE IT'LL BE SAFE?
IT'S IN THE M.L.S., SO IT *SHOULD* BE!
HUH? NANA?

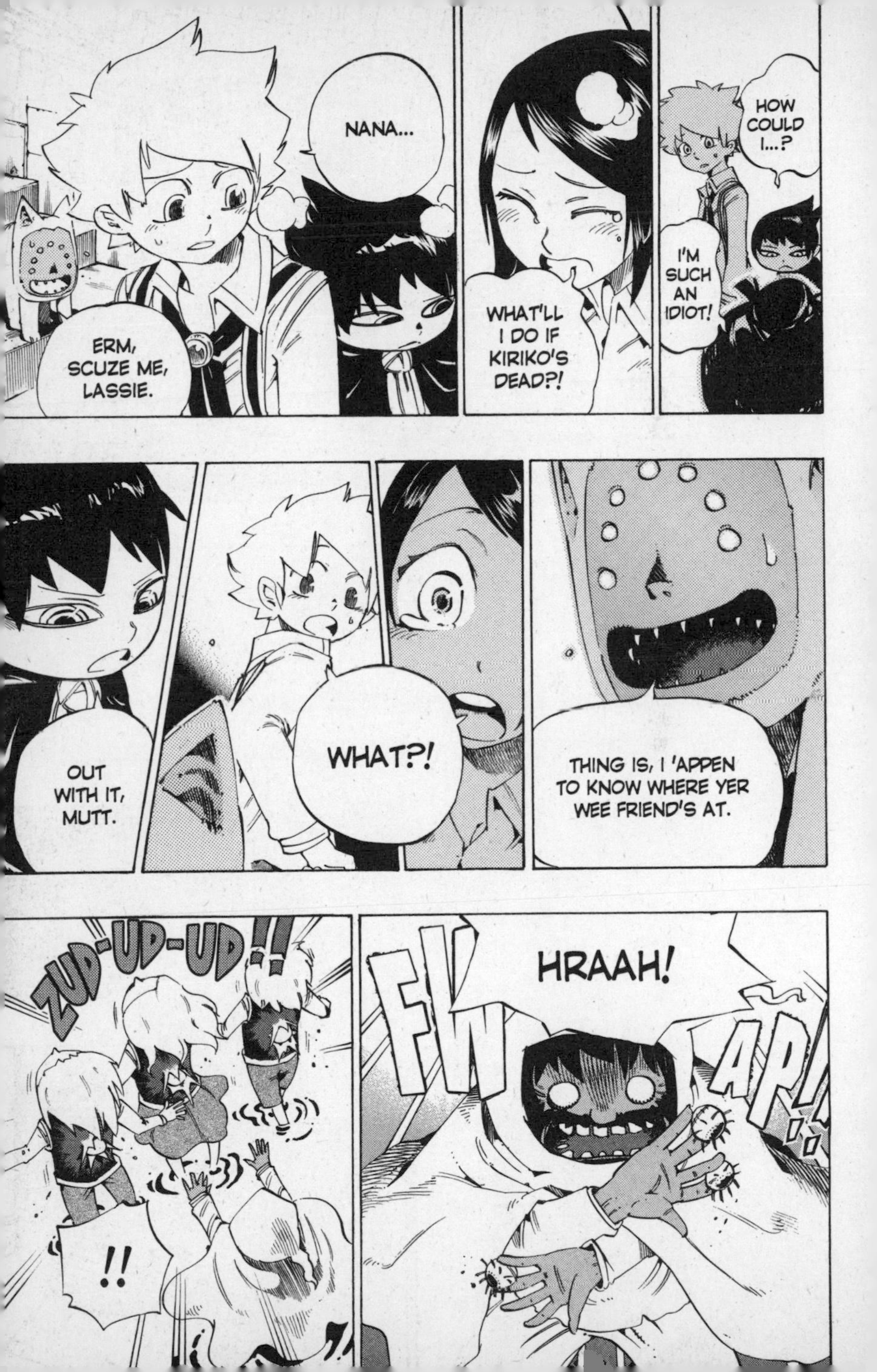
HOW COULD I...?
I'M SUCH AN IDIOT!
WHAT'LL I DO IF KIRIKO'S DEAD?!
NANA...
ERM, SCUZE ME, LASSIE.
THING IS, I 'APPEN TO KNOW WHERE YER WEE FRIEND'S AT.
WHAT?!
OUT WITH IT, MUTT.
HRAAH!
FW
AP!
ZUD-UD-UD!!
!!

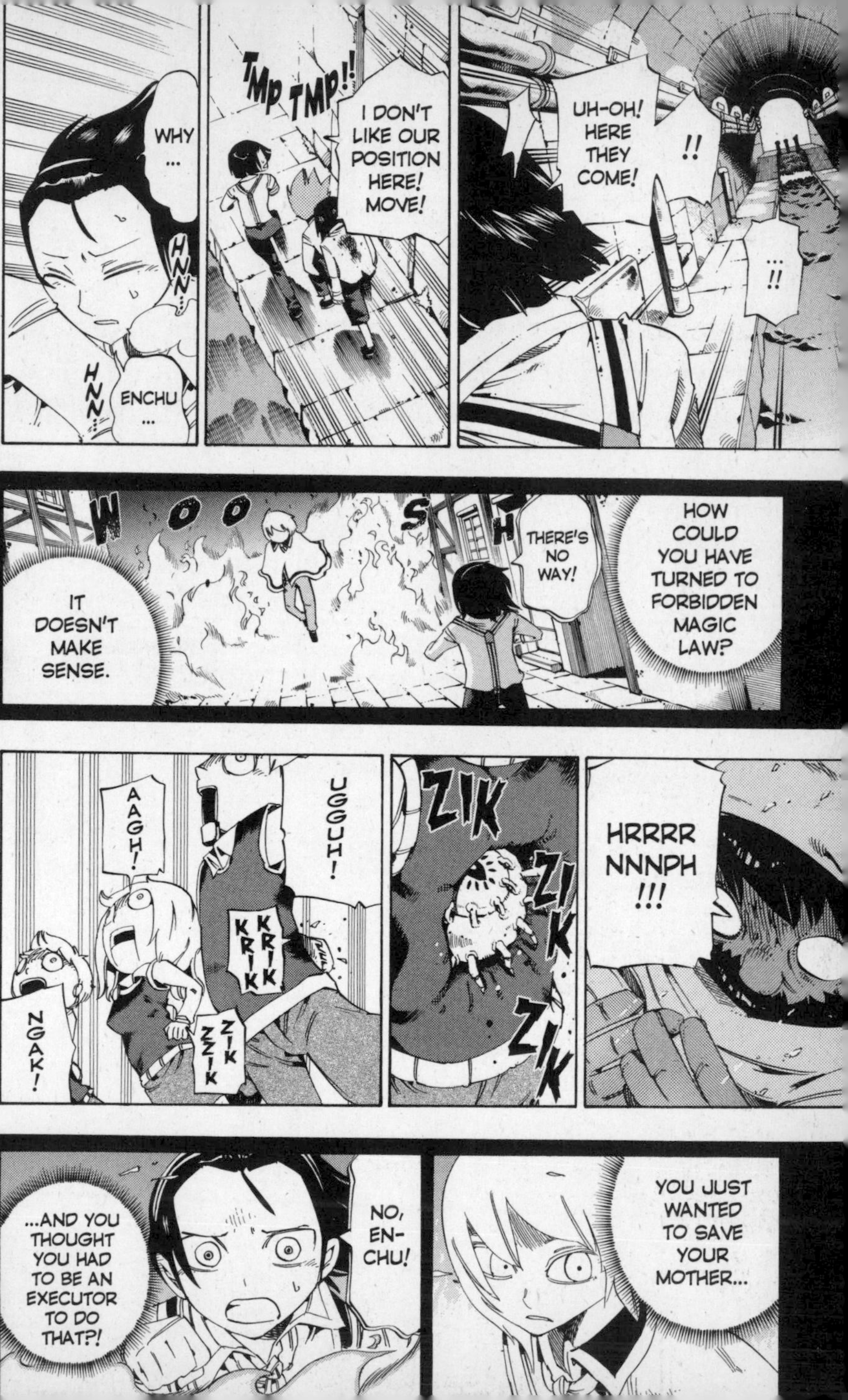
UH-OH! HERE THEY COME!
!!
... !!
TMP TMP!!
I DON'T LIKE OUR POSITION HERE! MOVE!
WHY ...
HNN...
HNN...
ENCHU ...
HOW COULD YOU HAVE TURNED TO FORBIDDEN MAGIC LAW?
THERE'S NO WAY!
WOOOSH
IT DOESN'T MAKE SENSE.
HRRRR NNNPH !!!
ZIK
ZIK ZIK
UGGUH!
AAGH!
KRIK KRIK
ZZIK ZIK
NGAK!
YOU JUST WANTED TO SAVE YOUR MOTHER...
NO, EN-CHU!
...AND YOU THOUGHT YOU HAD TO BE AN EXECUTOR TO DO THAT?!

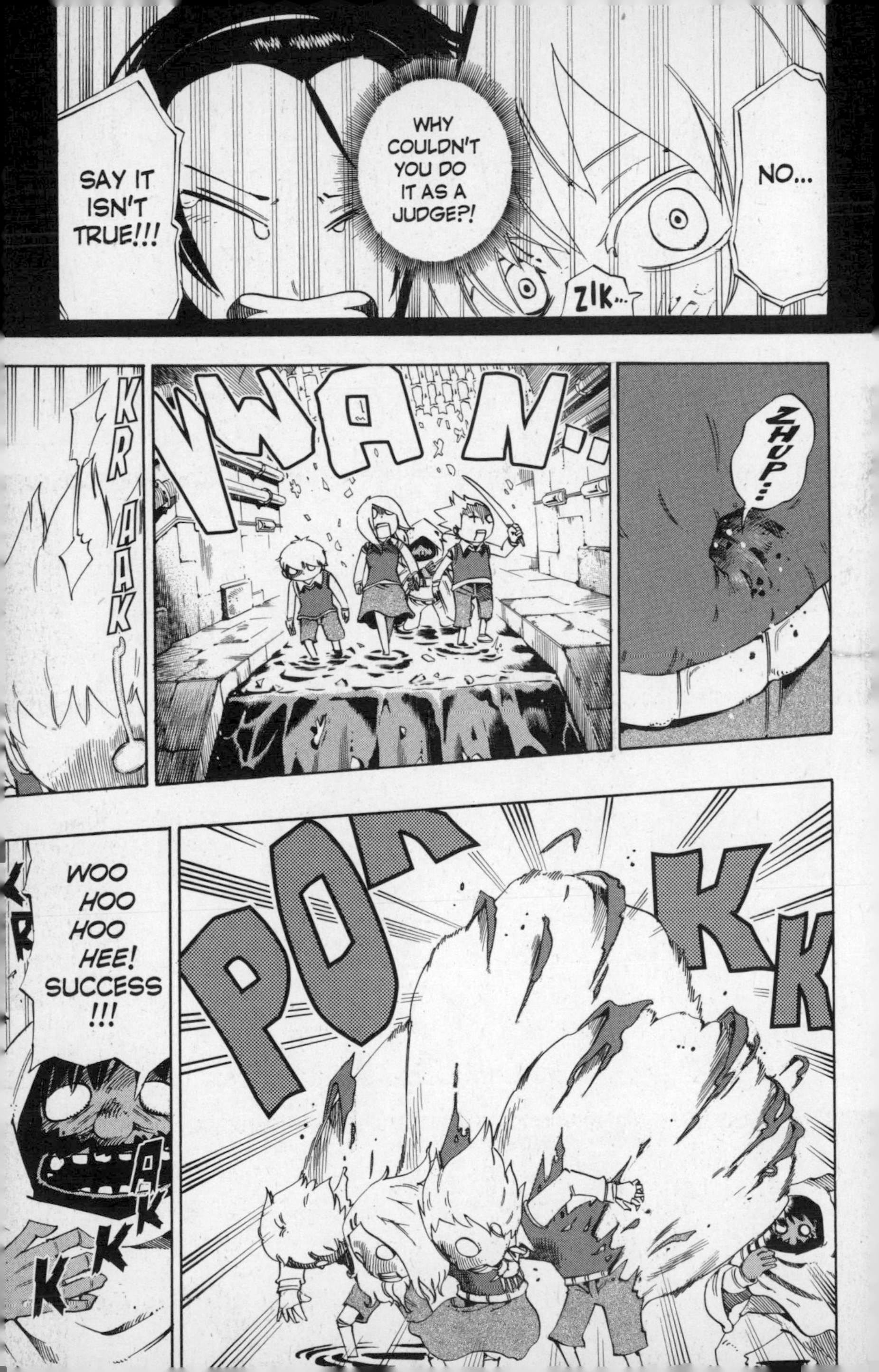
NO...
WHY COULDN'T YOU DO IT AS A JUDGE?!
ZIK...
SAY IT ISN'T TRUE!!!
ZHUP..
WAAN..
KRRAAK
POKKK
WOO HOO HOO HEE! SUCCESS!!!

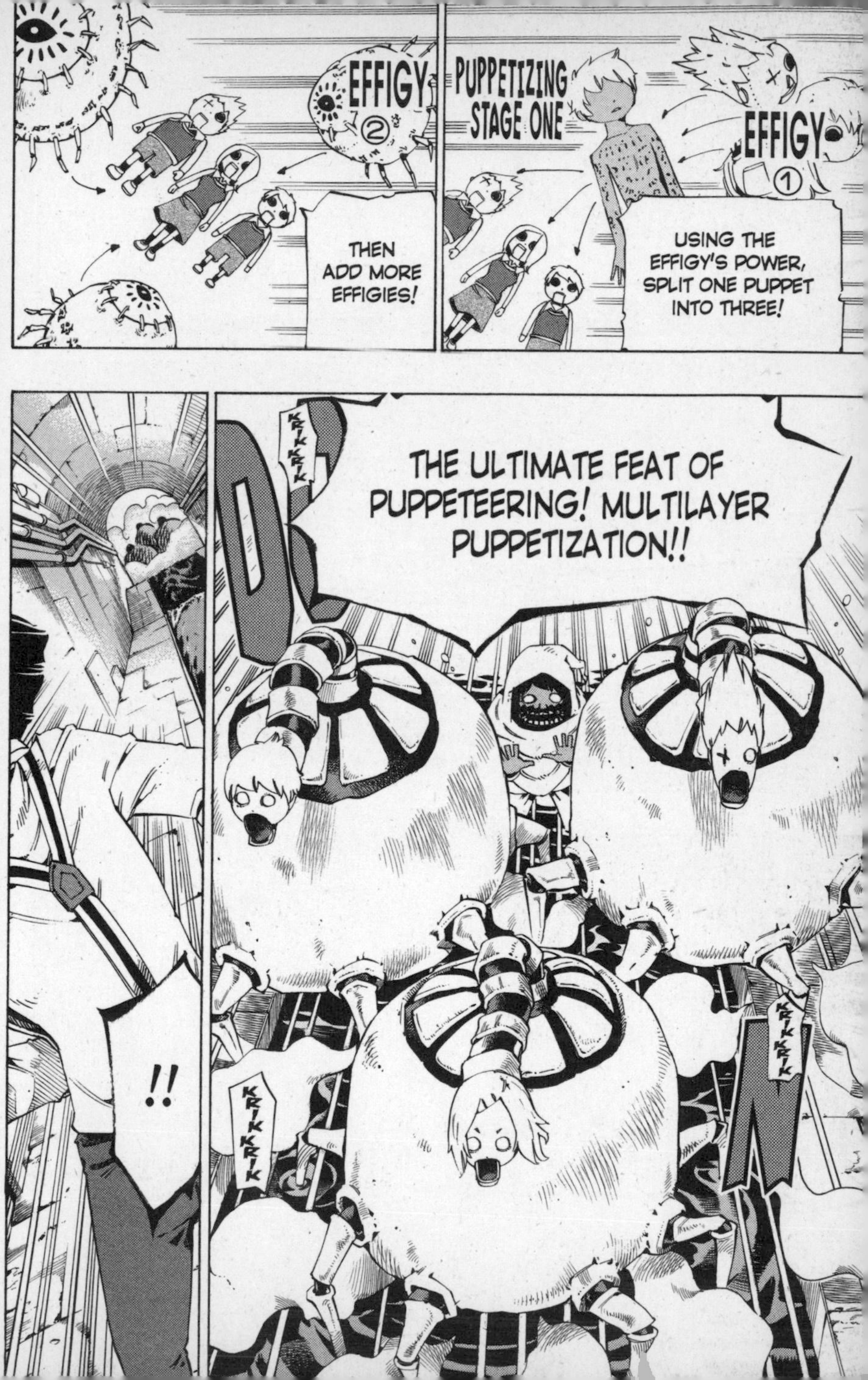
EFFIGY ①
PUPPETIZING STAGE ONE
USING THE EFFIGY'S POWER, SPLIT ONE PUPPET INTO THREE!
EFFIGY ②
THEN ADD MORE EFFIGIES!
KRIK KRIK
THE ULTIMATE FEAT OF PUPPETEERING! MULTILAYER PUPPETIZATION!!
KRIK KRIK
KRIK KRIK
!!

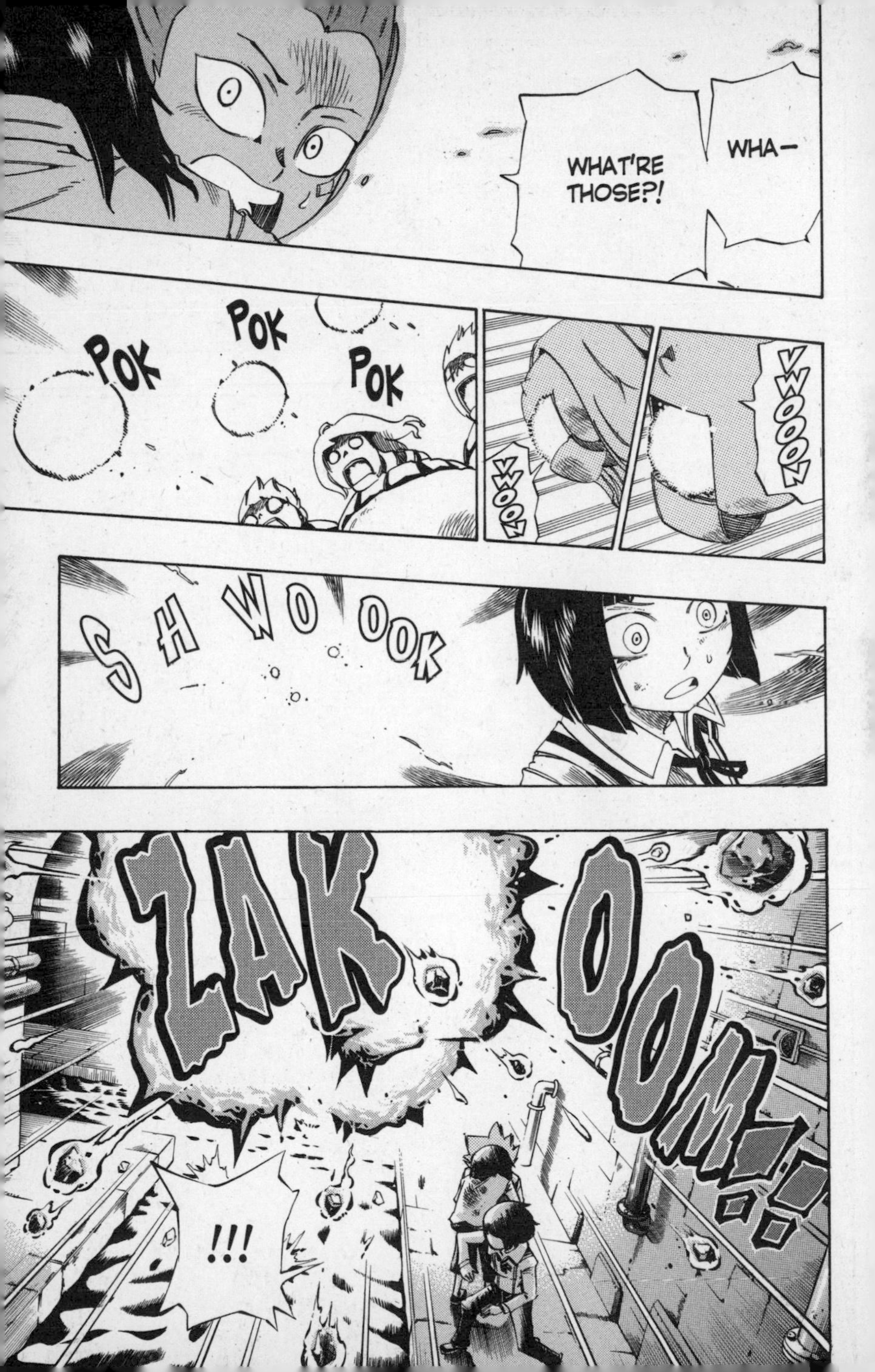
WHA—
WHAT'RE THOSE?!
VWOOOON
VWOON
POK
POK
POK
SHWOOOK
ZAKOOOM!!
!!!

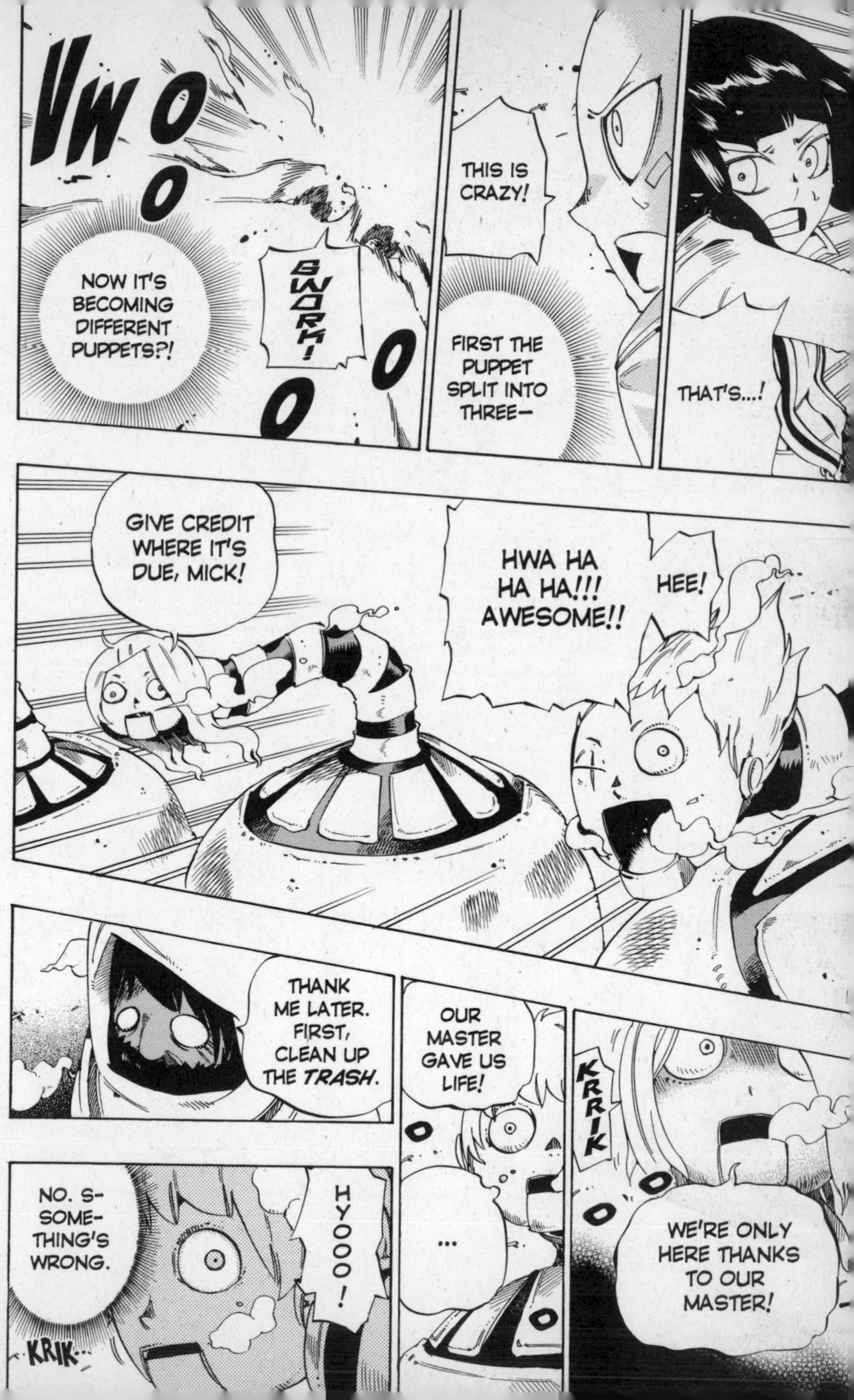
THAT'S...!
THIS IS CRAZY!
FIRST THE PUPPET SPLIT INTO THREE—
VWOOO
GWORK!
OO
NOW IT'S BECOMING DIFFERENT PUPPETS?!
HEE!
HWA HA HA HA!!! AWESOME!!
GIVE CREDIT WHERE IT'S DUE, MICK!
KRRIK
WE'RE ONLY HERE THANKS TO OUR MASTER!
OUR MASTER GAVE US LIFE!
...
THANK ME LATER. FIRST, CLEAN UP THE TRASH.
HYOOO!
NO. S-SOME-THING'S WRONG.
KRIK...

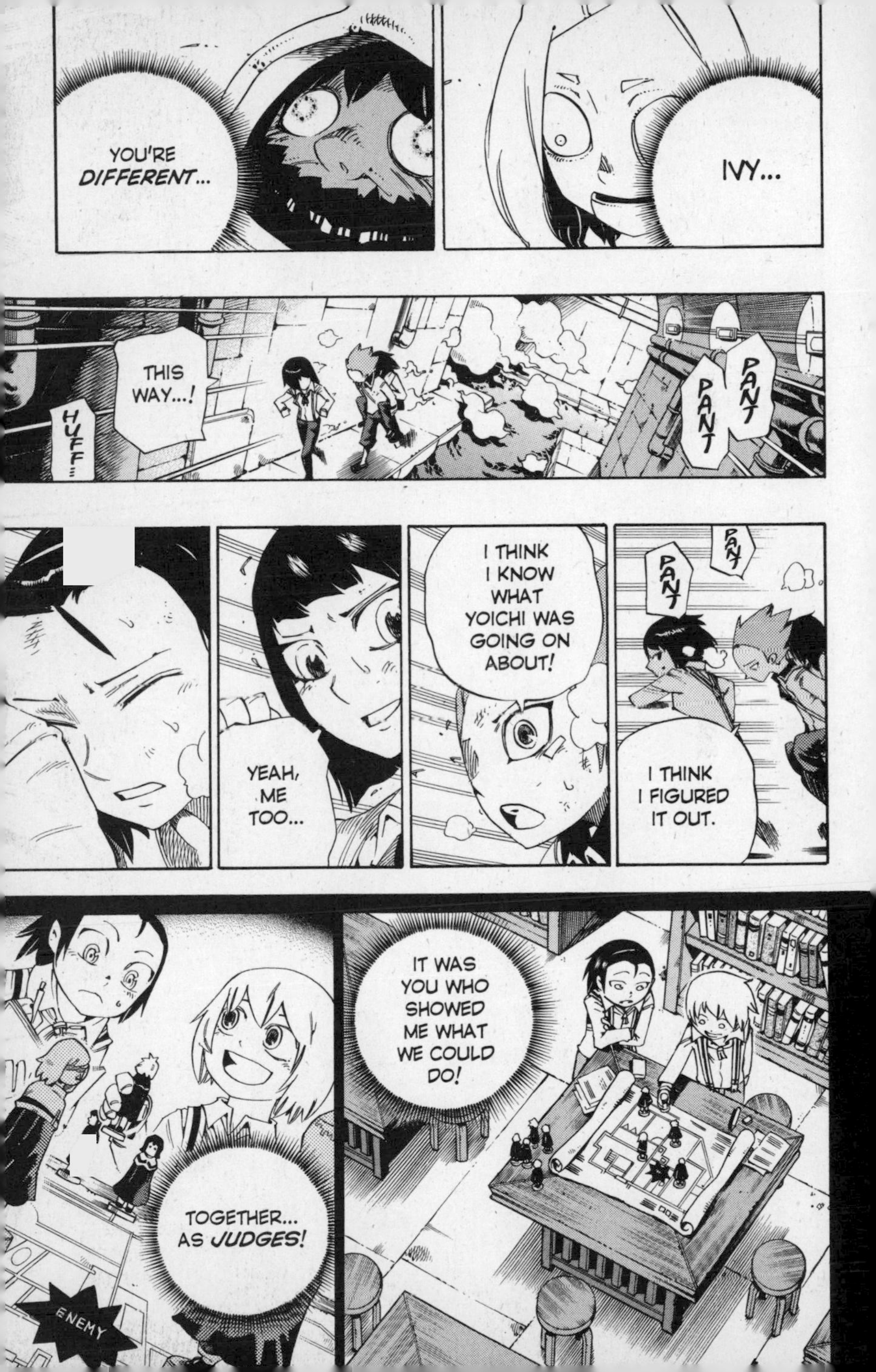
IVY...
YOU'RE *DIFFERENT*...
PANT PANT
THIS WAY...!
HUFF...
PANT PANT
I THINK I FIGURED IT OUT.
I THINK I KNOW WHAT YOICHI WAS GOING ON ABOUT!
YEAH, ME TOO...
IT WAS YOU WHO SHOWED ME WHAT WE COULD DO!
TOGETHER... AS *JUDGES*!
ENEMY

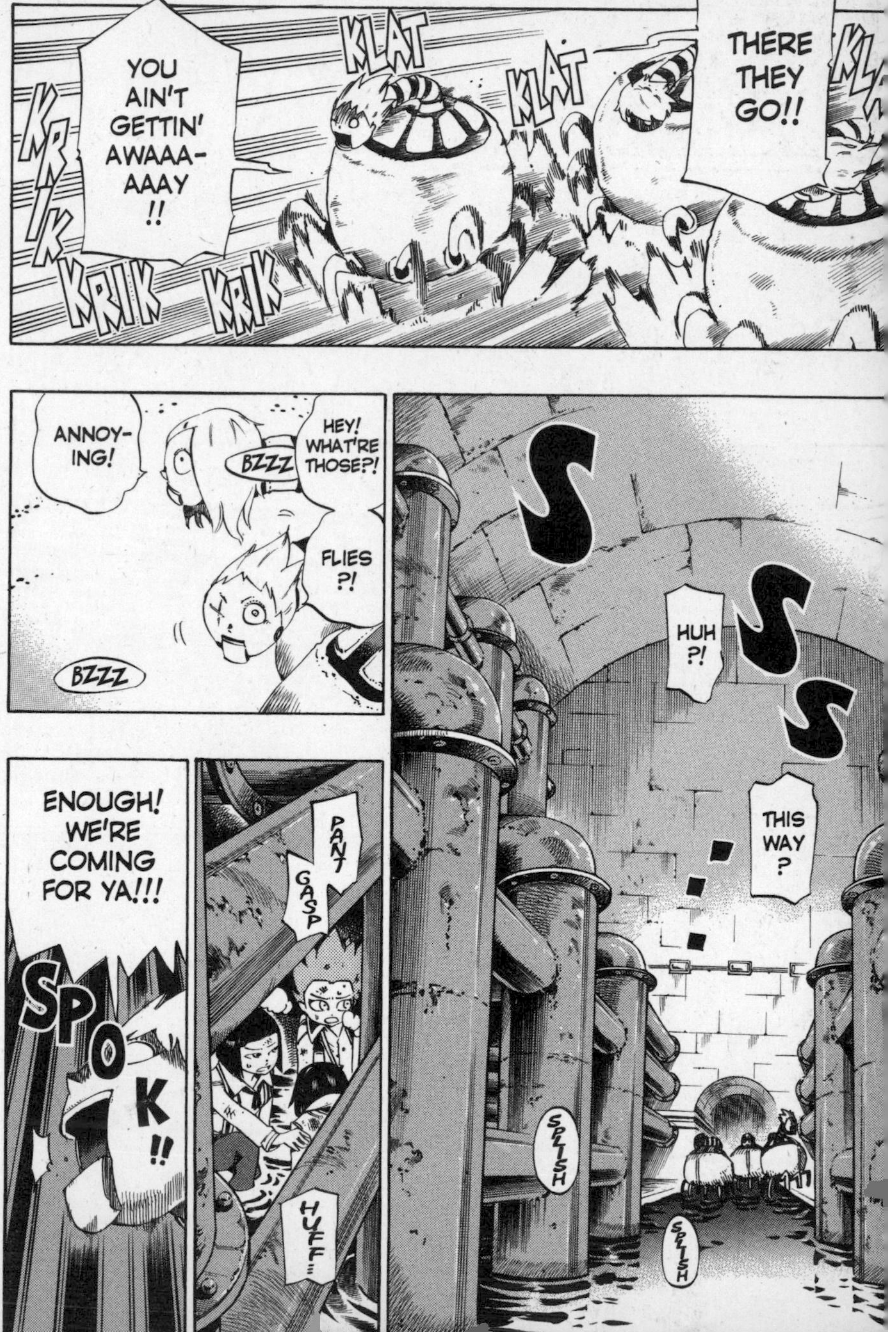
THERE THEY GO!!
KLA
KLAT
KLAT
YOU AIN'T GETTIN' AWAAAA-AAAY!!
KRIK
KRIK
KRIK
HUH?!
SSS
THIS WAY?
SPLISH
SPLISH
HEY! WHAT'RE THOSE?!
BZZZ
ANNOY-ING!
FLIES?!
BZZZ
PANT
GASP
HUFF...
ENOUGH! WE'RE COMING FOR YA!!!
SPOK!!

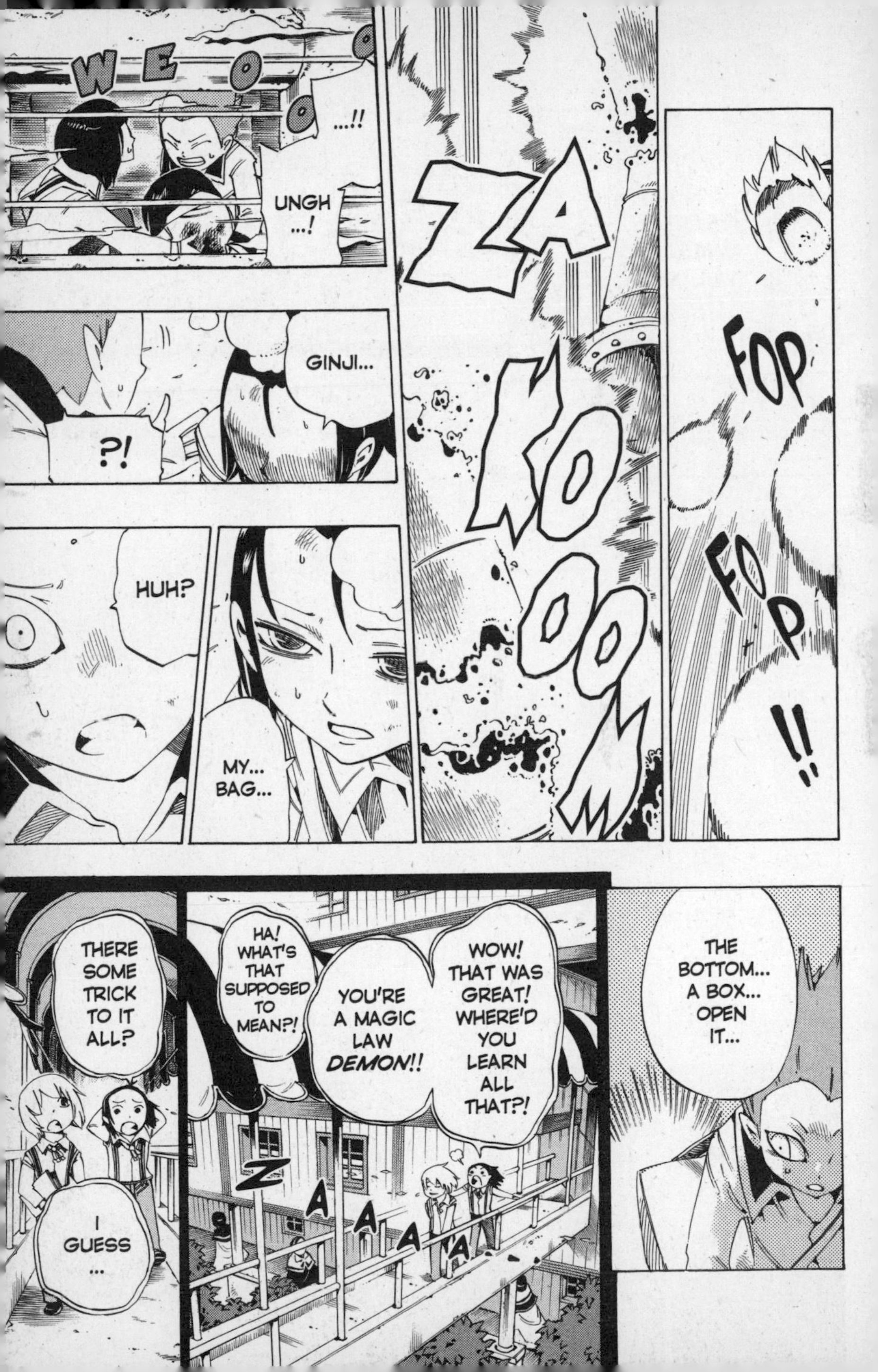
FOP
FOP
!!
ZAKOOOM
WEOOO
...!!
UNGH ...!
GINJI...
?!
MY... BAG...
HUH?
THE BOTTOM... A BOX... OPEN IT...
WOW! THAT WAS GREAT! WHERE'D YOU LEARN ALL THAT?!
YOU'RE A MAGIC LAW *DEMON*!!
HA! WHAT'S THAT SUPPOSED TO MEAN?!
ZAAAAA
THERE SOME TRICK TO IT ALL?
I GUESS ...

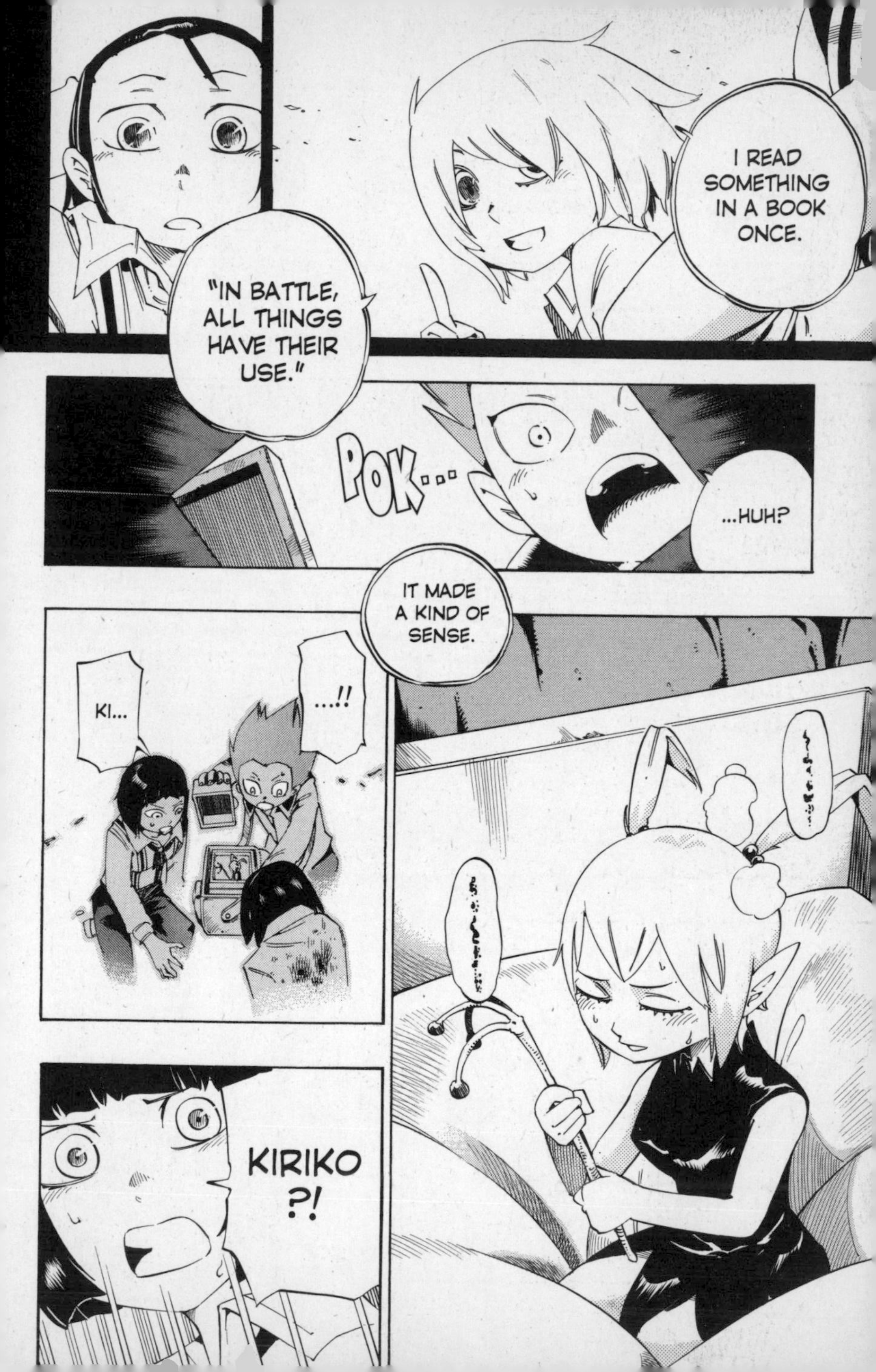
I READ SOMETHING IN A BOOK ONCE.
"IN BATTLE, ALL THINGS HAVE THEIR USE."
...HUH?
POK...
IT MADE A KIND OF SENSE.
...!!
KI...
KIRIKO ?!

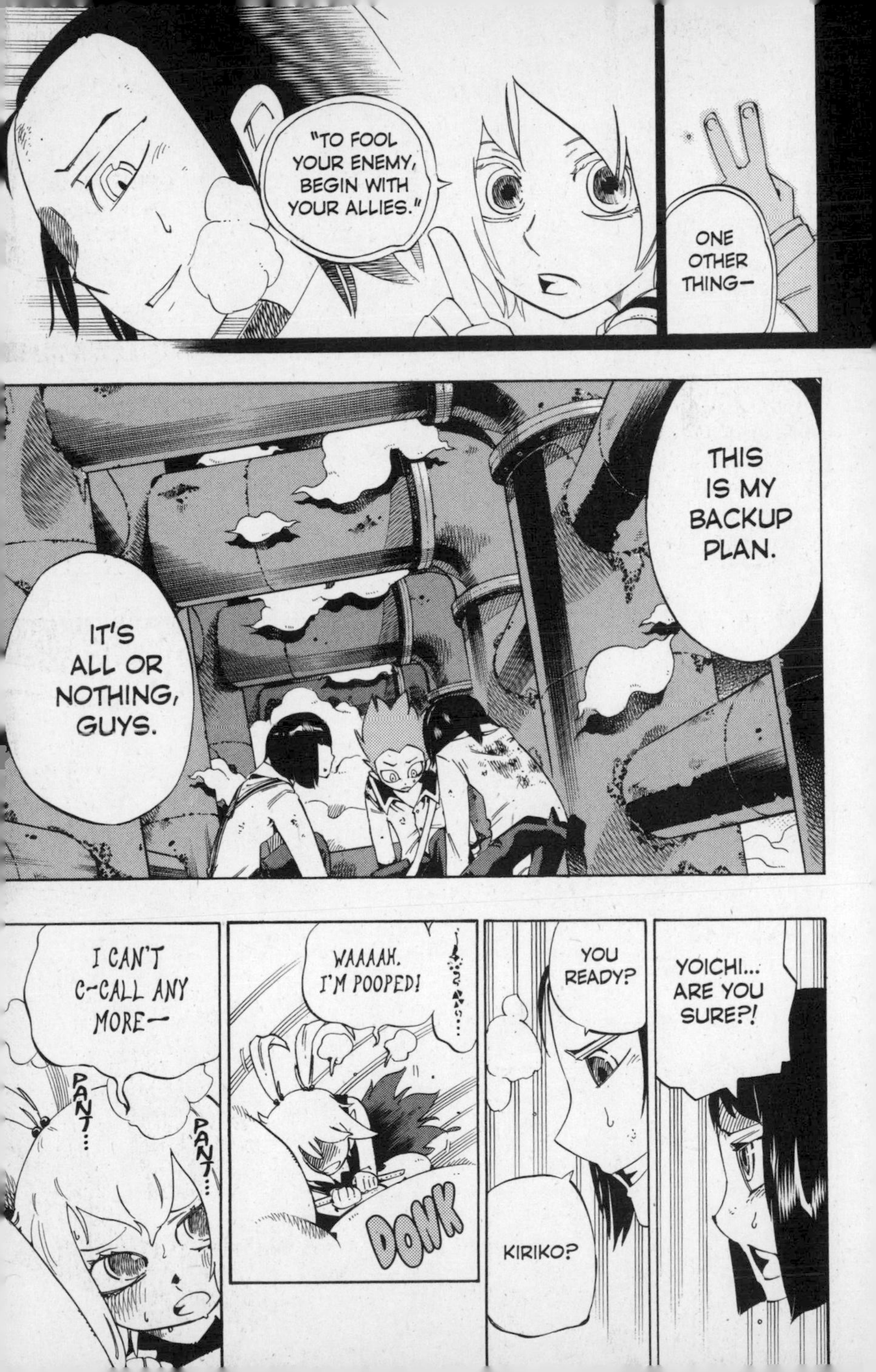
ONE OTHER THING—
"TO FOOL YOUR ENEMY, BEGIN WITH YOUR ALLIES."
THIS IS MY BACKUP PLAN.
IT'S ALL OR NOTHING, GUYS.
YOICHI... ARE YOU SURE?!
YOU READY?
KIRIKO?
WAAAAH. I'M POOPED!
DONK
I CAN'T C-CALL ANY MORE—
PANT...
PANT...

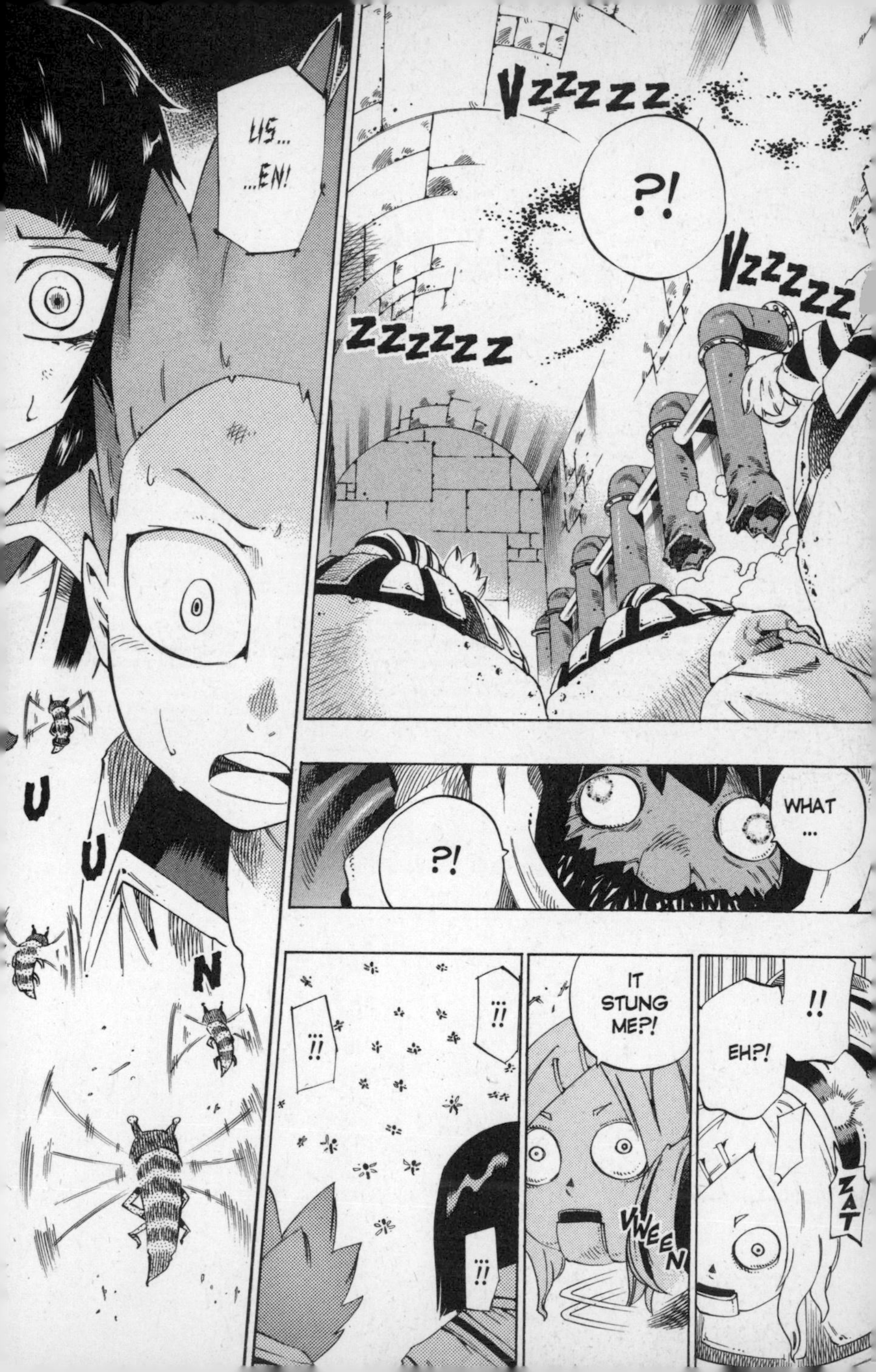

VZZZZZZ
?!
VZZZZZZ
ZZZZZZZ
WHAT ...
?!
!!
EH?!
ZAT
IT STUNG ME?!
VWEEN
...!!
...!!
...!!
US...
...EN!
U
U
N

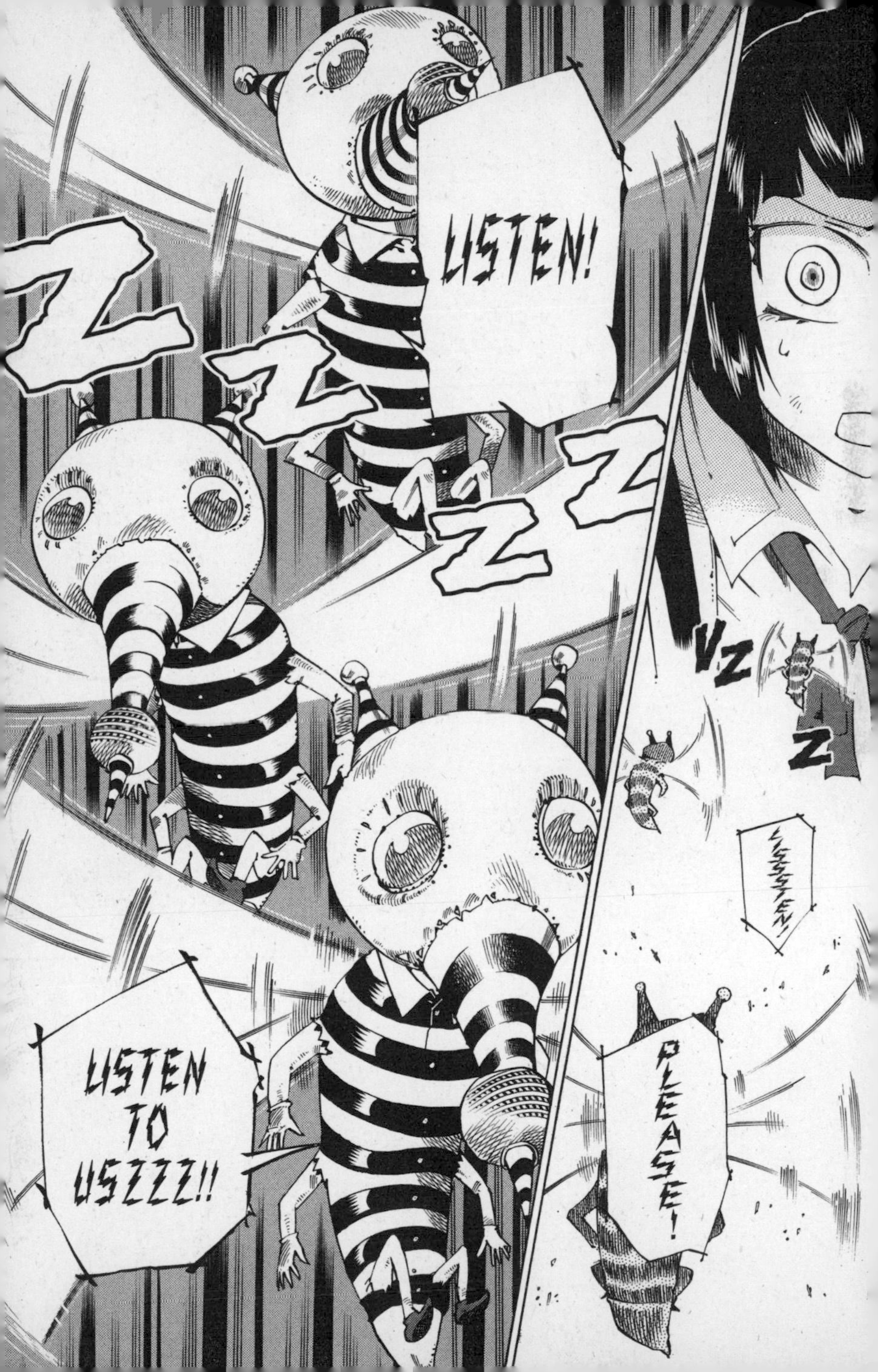
VZ Z
LISSSTEN!
PLEASE!
LISTEN!
ZZ
ZZ
LISTEN TO USZZZ!!

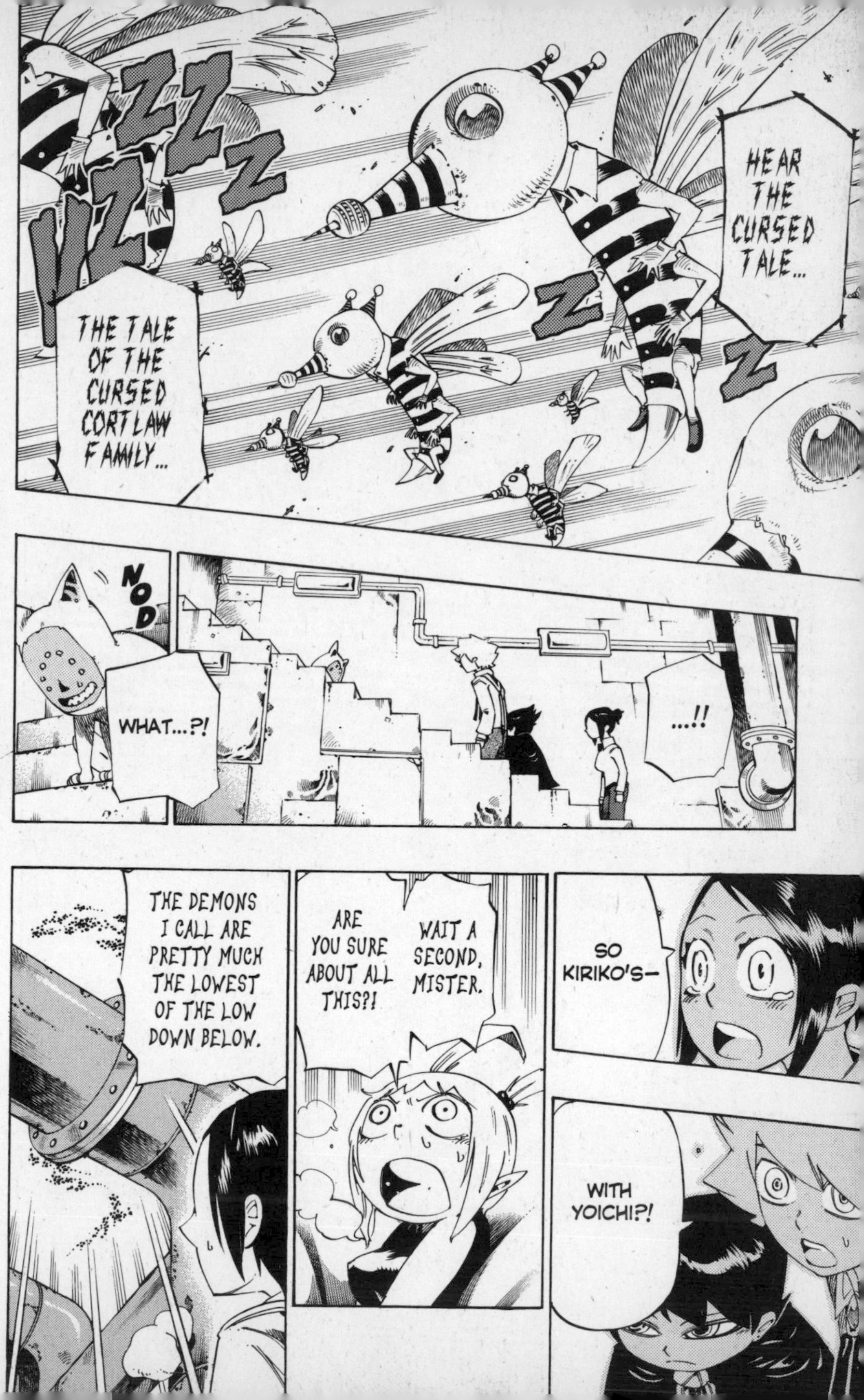
HEAR THE CURSED TALE...
THE TALE OF THE CURSED CORTLAW FAMILY...
VZZZZ
Z
Z
...!!
NOD
WHAT...?!
SO KIRIKO'S—
WITH YOICHI?!
WAIT A SECOND, MISTER.
ARE YOU SURE ABOUT ALL THIS?!
THE DEMONS I CALL ARE PRETTY MUCH THE LOWEST OF THE LOW DOWN BELOW.

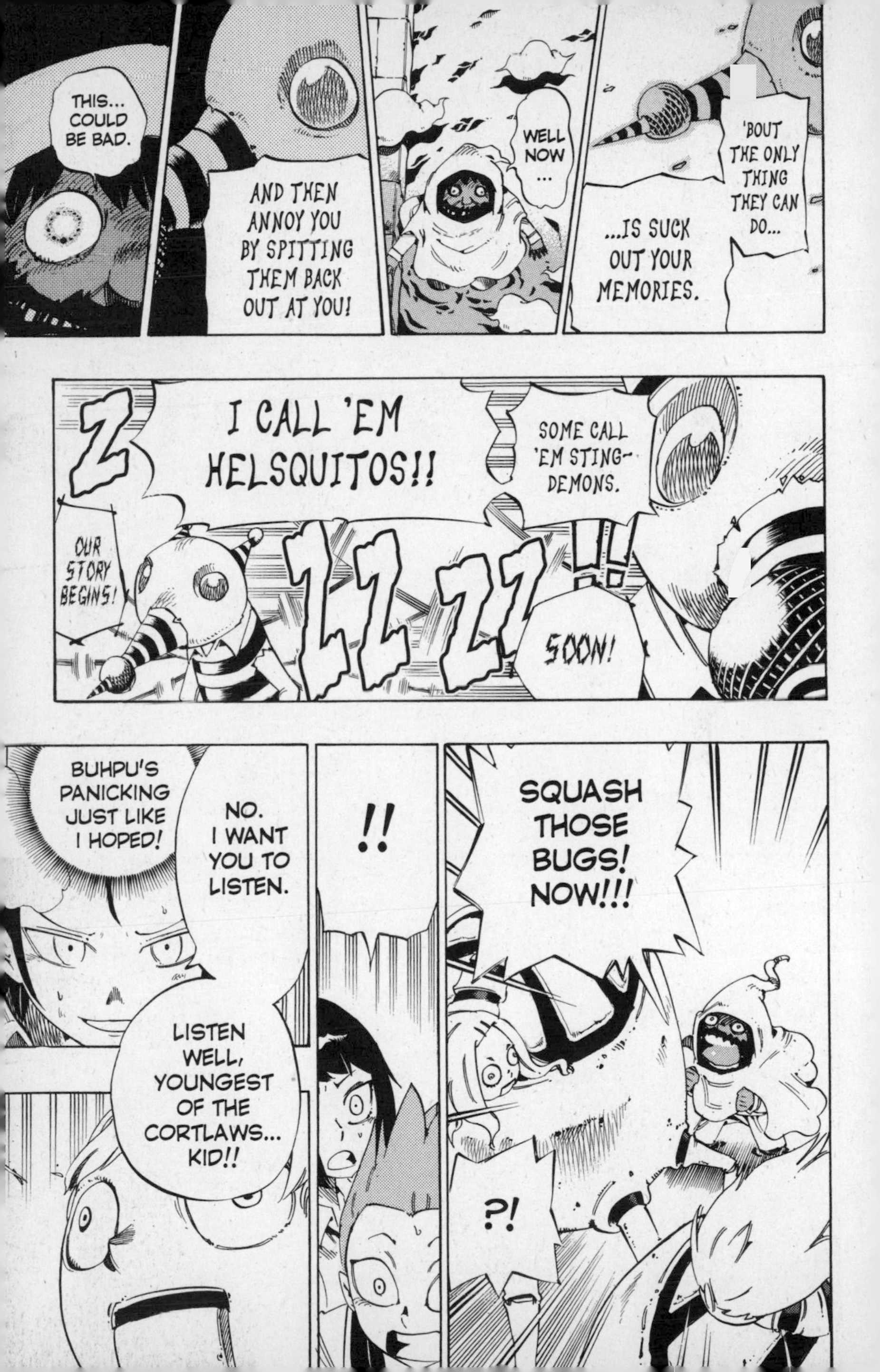
'BOUT THE ONLY THING THEY CAN DO...
...IS SUCK OUT YOUR MEMORIES.
WELL NOW ...
AND THEN ANNOY YOU BY SPITTING THEM BACK OUT AT YOU!
THIS... COULD BE BAD.
SOME CALL 'EM STING-DEMONS.
I CALL 'EM HELSQUITOS!!
SOON!
ZZZZ
OUR STORY BEGINS!
Z
SQUASH THOSE BUGS! NOW!!!
?!
!!
NO. I WANT YOU TO LISTEN.
BUHPU'S PANICKING JUST LIKE I HOPED!
LISTEN WELL, YOUNGEST OF THE CORTLAWS... KID!!

WHAT, FOOL YOUR FRIENDS? YOU MEAN YOU'D FOOL ME?!

NO, DON'T TAKE IT SO LITERALLY! I JUST READ IT IN A BOOK!

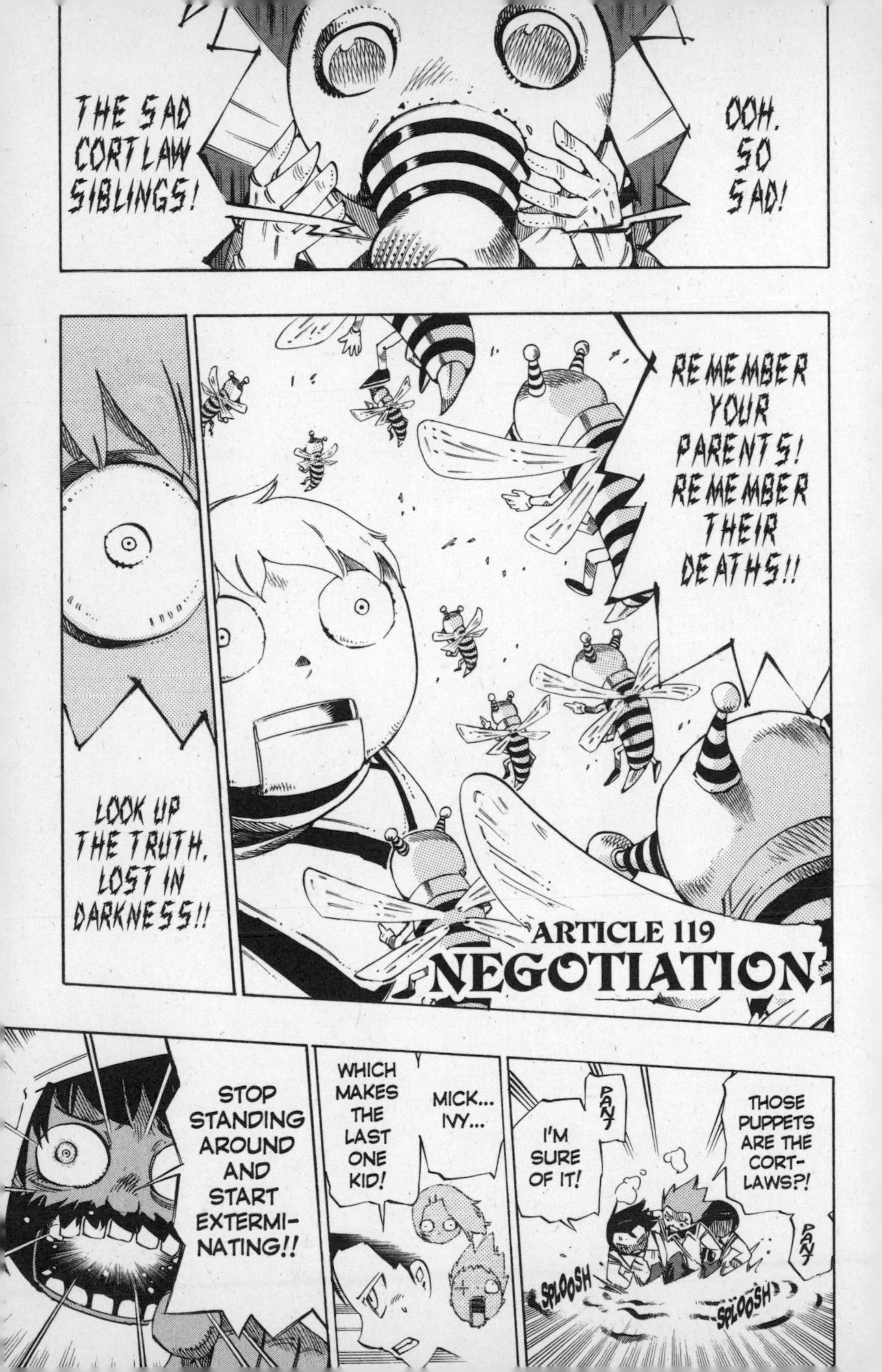
OOH. SO SAD!
THE SAD CORTLAW SIBLINGS!
REMEMBER YOUR PARENTS! REMEMBER THEIR DEATHS!!
ARTICLE 119
NEGOTIATION
LOOK UP THE TRUTH, LOST IN DARKNESS!!
THOSE PUPPETS ARE THE CORT-LAWS?!
PANT
I'M SURE OF IT!
PANT
SPLOOSH
SPLOOSH
MICK... IVY...
WHICH MAKES THE LAST ONE KID!
STOP STANDING AROUND AND START EXTERMI-NATING!!

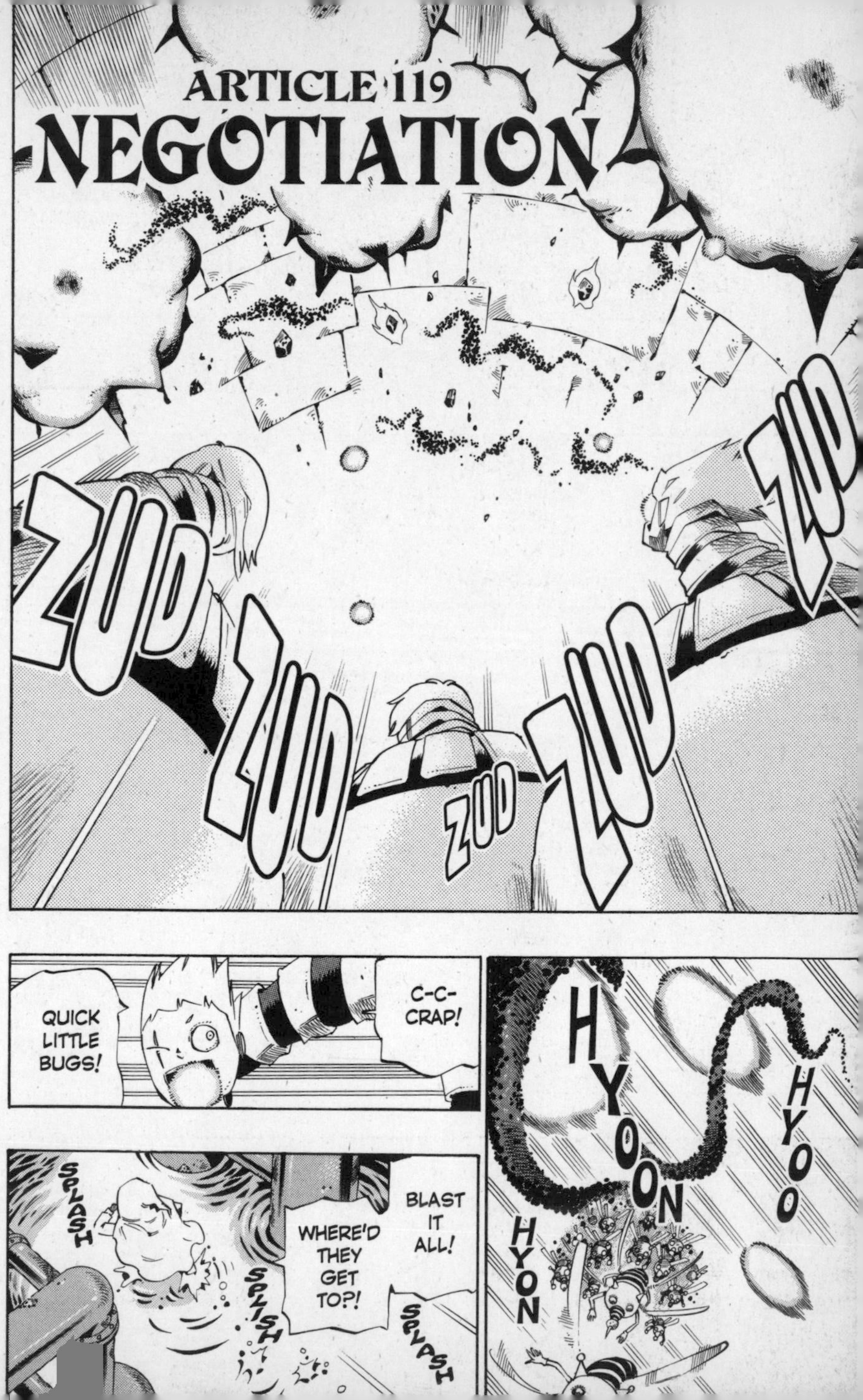
ARTICLE 119
NEGOTIATION
ZUD
ZUD
ZUD
ZUD
ZUD
ZUD
HYOON
HYOO
HYON
C-C-CRAP!
QUICK LITTLE BUGS!
SPLASH
SPLASH
BLAST IT ALL!
WHERE'D THEY GET TO?!
SPLASH
SPLASH

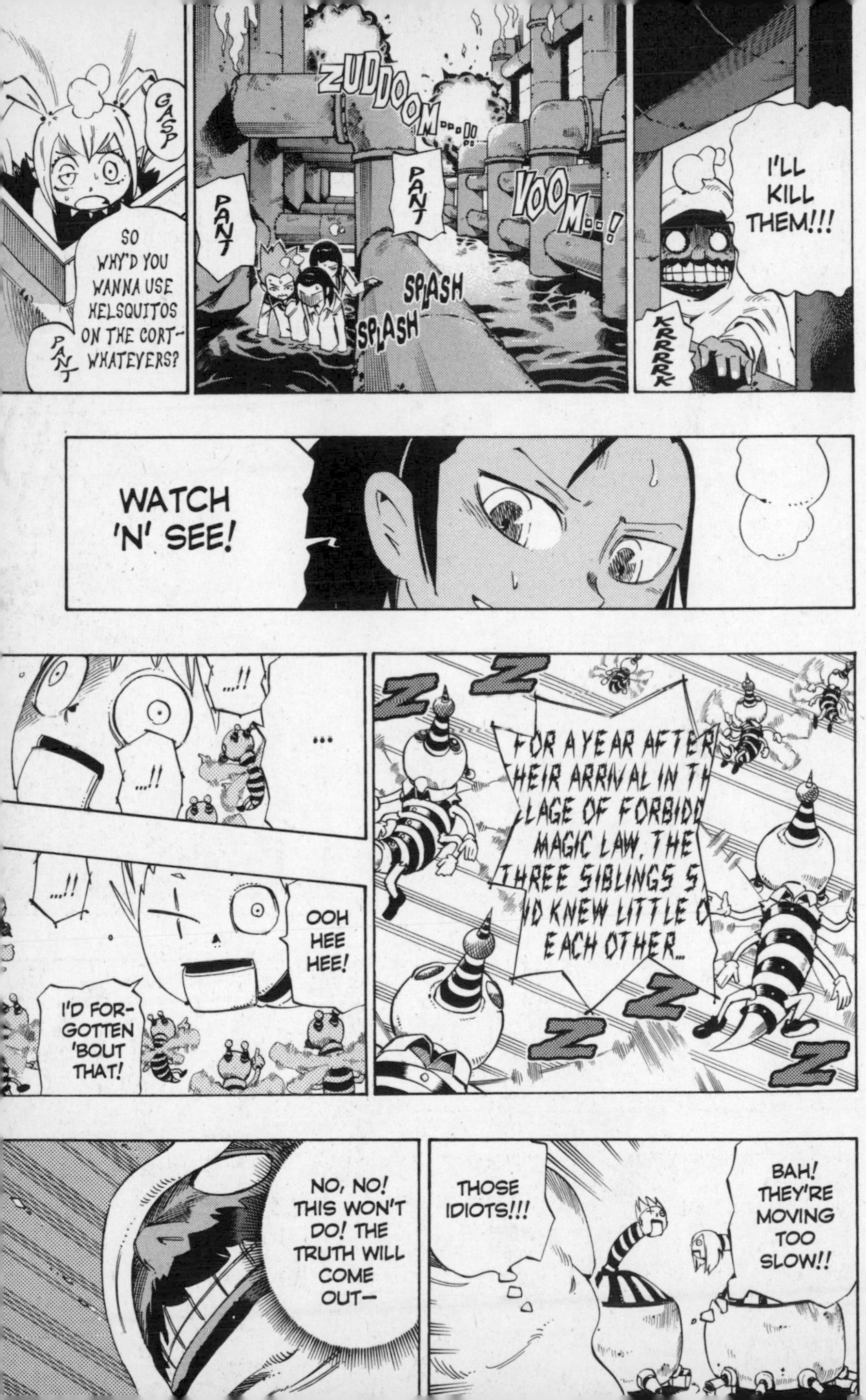
I'LL KILL THEM!!!
KRRRRK
ZUDDOOM...!!
PANT
PANT
VOOM..!
SPLASH
SPLASH
GASP
SO WHY'D YOU WANNA USE HELSQUITOS ON THE CORT-WHATEVERS?
PANT
WATCH 'N' SEE!
FOR A YEAR AFTER
HEIR ARRIVAL IN TH
LAGE OF FORBIDD
MAGIC LAW, THE
THREE SIBLINGS S
ND KNEW LITTLE O
EACH OTHER...
...!!
...
...!!
...!!
OOH HEE HEE!
I'D FOR-GOTTEN 'BOUT THAT!
BAH! THEY'RE MOVING TOO SLOW!!
THOSE IDIOTS!!!
NO, NO! THIS WON'T DO! THE TRUTH WILL COME OUT—

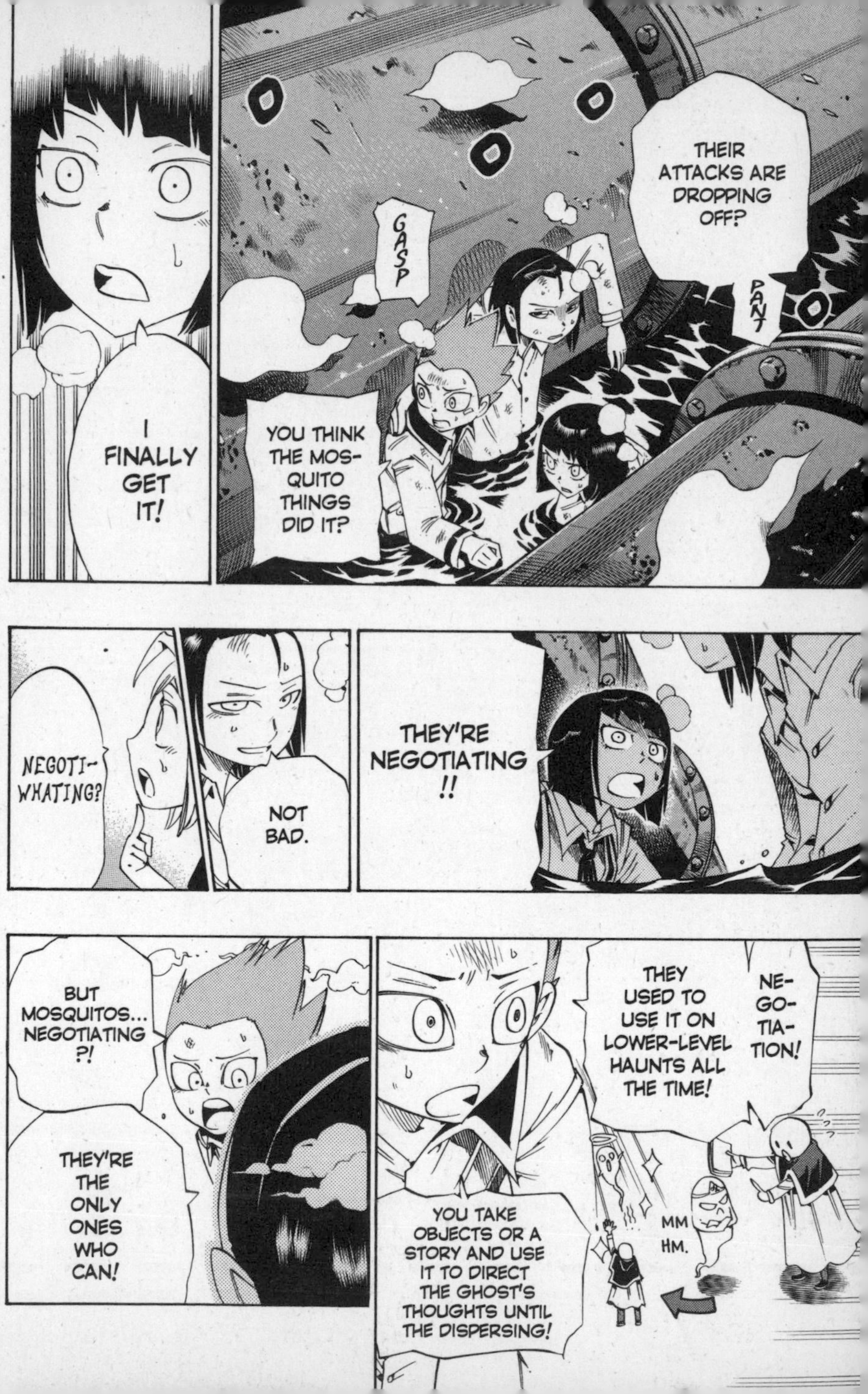
THEIR ATTACKS ARE DROPPING OFF?
PANT
GASP
YOU THINK THE MOS-QUITO THINGS DID IT?
I FINALLY GET IT!
THEY'RE NEGOTIATING !!
NOT BAD.
NEGOTI-WHATING?
NE-GO-TIA-TION!
THEY USED TO USE IT ON LOWER-LEVEL HAUNTS ALL THE TIME!
MM HM.
YOU TAKE OBJECTS OR A STORY AND USE IT TO DIRECT THE GHOST'S THOUGHTS UNTIL THE DISPERSING!
BUT MOSQUITOS... NEGOTIATING ?!
THEY'RE THE ONLY ONES WHO CAN!

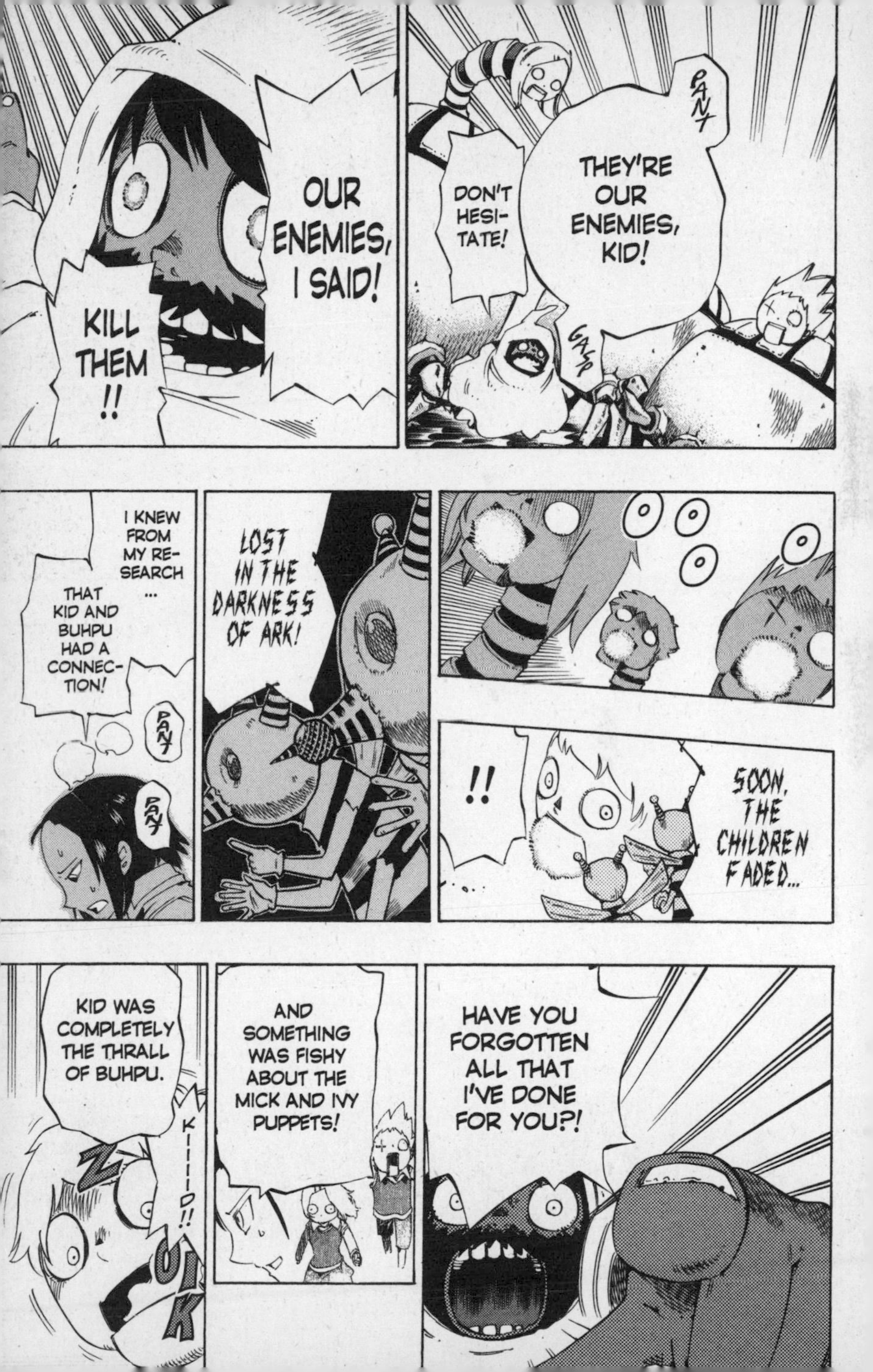
PANT
THEY'RE OUR ENEMIES, KID!
DON'T HESI-TATE!
GASP
OUR ENEMIES, I SAID!
KILL THEM !!
!!
SOON, THE CHILDREN FADED...
...
LOST IN THE DARKNESS OF ARK!
I KNEW FROM MY RE-SEARCH ...
THAT KID AND BUHPU HAD A CONNEC-TION!
PANT
PANT
HAVE YOU FORGOTTEN ALL THAT I'VE DONE FOR YOU?!
AND SOMETHING WAS FISHY ABOUT THE MICK AND IVY PUPPETS!
KID WAS COMPLETELY THE THRALL OF BUHPU.
KIIIID!!
ZUK

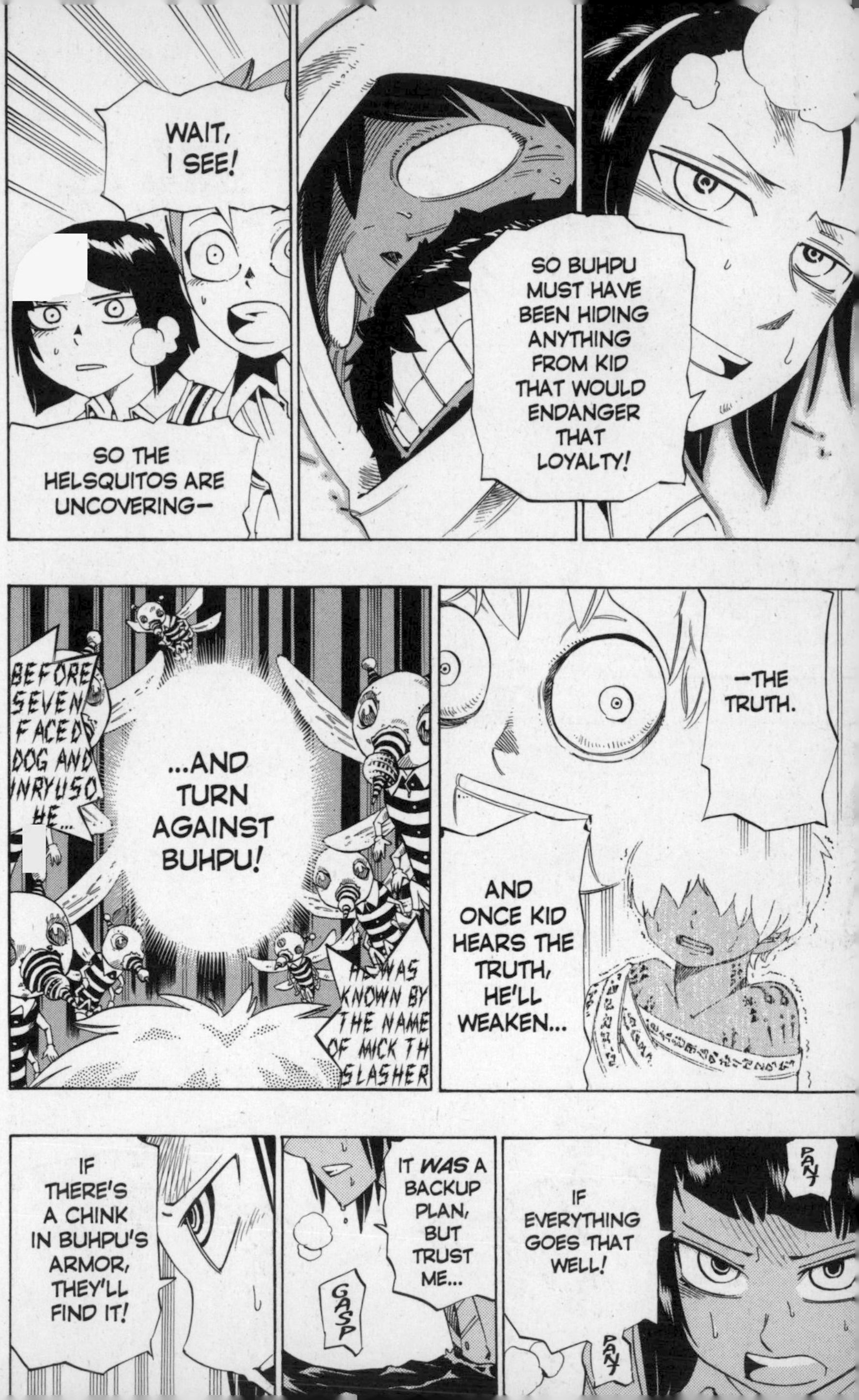
SO BUHPU MUST HAVE BEEN HIDING ANYTHING FROM KID THAT WOULD ENDANGER THAT LOYALTY!
WAIT, I SEE!
SO THE HELSQUITOS ARE UNCOVERING—
—THE TRUTH.
AND ONCE KID HEARS THE TRUTH, HE'LL WEAKEN...
...AND TURN AGAINST BUHPU!
BEFORE SEVEN FACED DOG AND NRYUSO HE...
WAS KNOWN BY THE NAME OF MICK TH SLASHER
PANT
IF EVERYTHING GOES THAT WELL!
PANT
IT *WAS* A BACKUP PLAN, BUT TRUST ME...
GASP
IF THERE'S A CHINK IN BUHPU'S ARMOR, THEY'LL FIND IT!

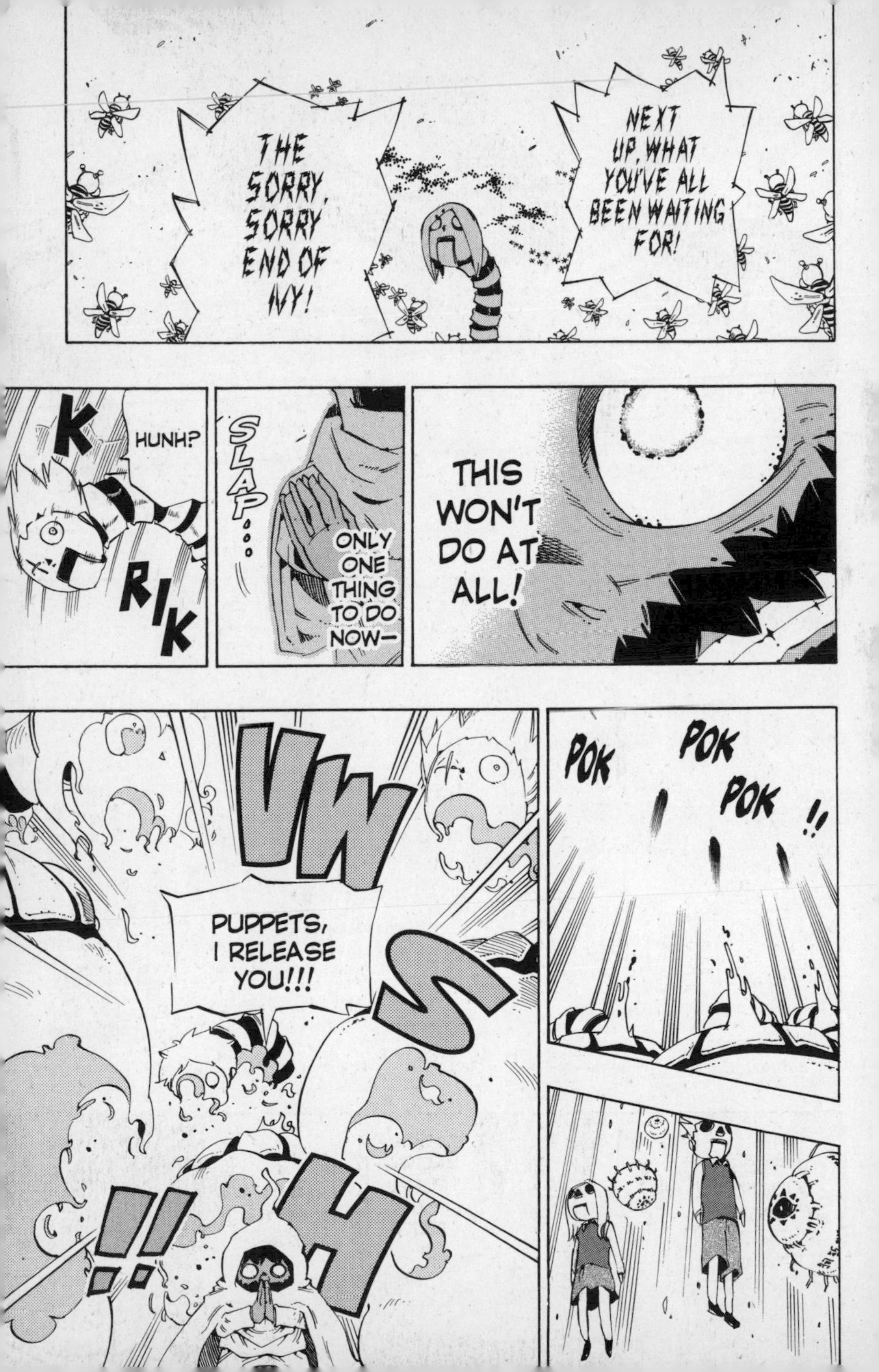
NEXT UP, WHAT YOU'VE ALL BEEN WAITING FOR!
THE SORRY, SORRY END OF IVY!
THIS WON'T DO AT ALL!
SLAP...
ONLY ONE THING TO DO NOW—
HUNH?
KRIK
POK POK POK !!
PUPPETS, I RELEASE YOU!!!
VWSH!!

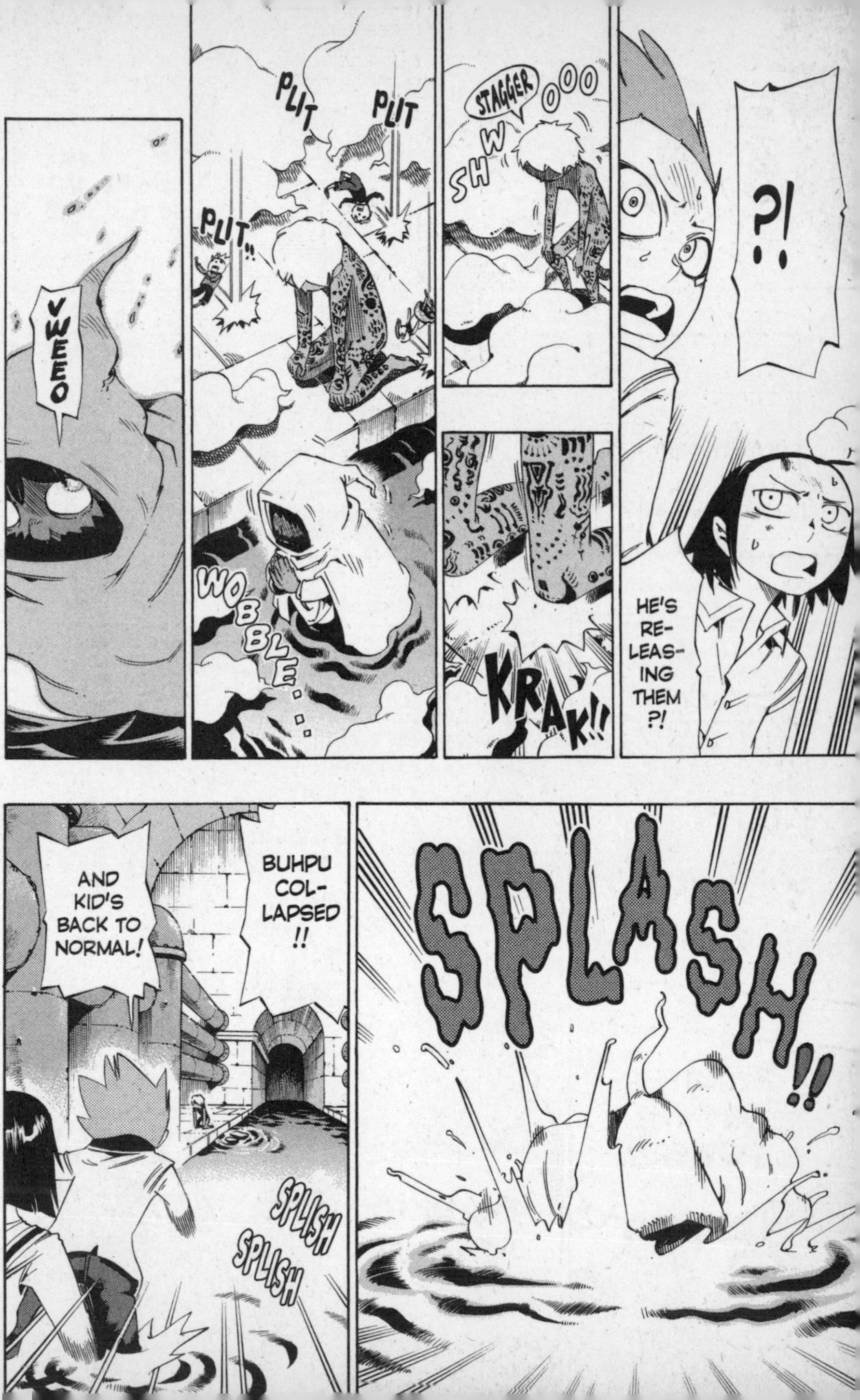
?!
HE'S RE-LEASING THEM ?!
STAGGER
SHWOOO
KRAK!!
PLIT
PLIT
PLIT!!
WOBBLE...
VWEEO
SPLASH!!
BUHPU COL-LAPSED !!
AND KID'S BACK TO NORMAL!
SPLISH
SPLISH

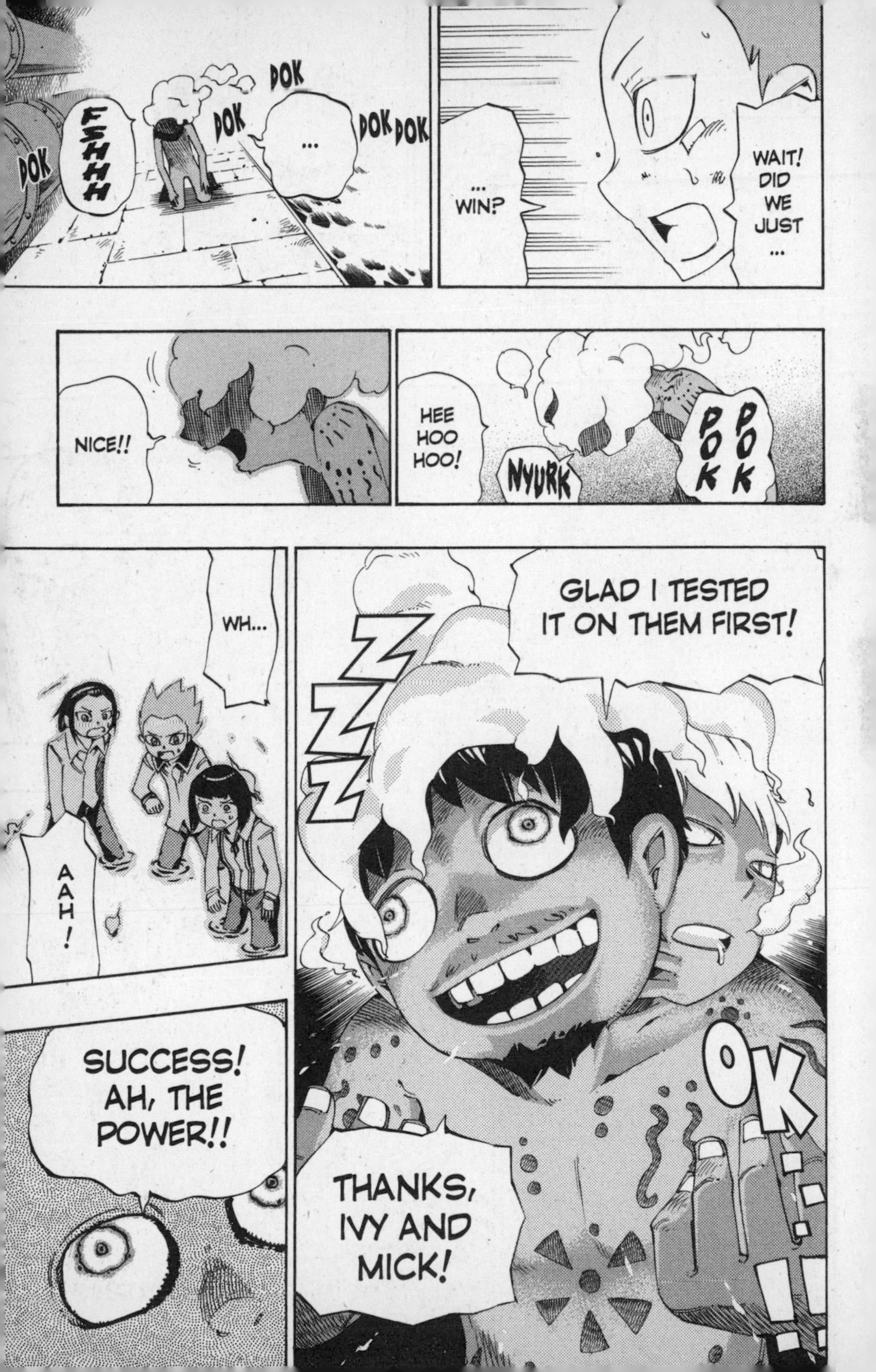
WAIT! DID WE JUST ...
... WIN?
DOK DOK
DOK
DOK
...
FSHHH
DOK
POK POK
HEE HOO HOO!
NYURK
NICE!!
GLAD I TESTED IT ON THEM FIRST!
ZZZ
OK
THANKS, IVY AND MICK!
!!
WH...
AAH!
SUCCESS! AH, THE POWER!!

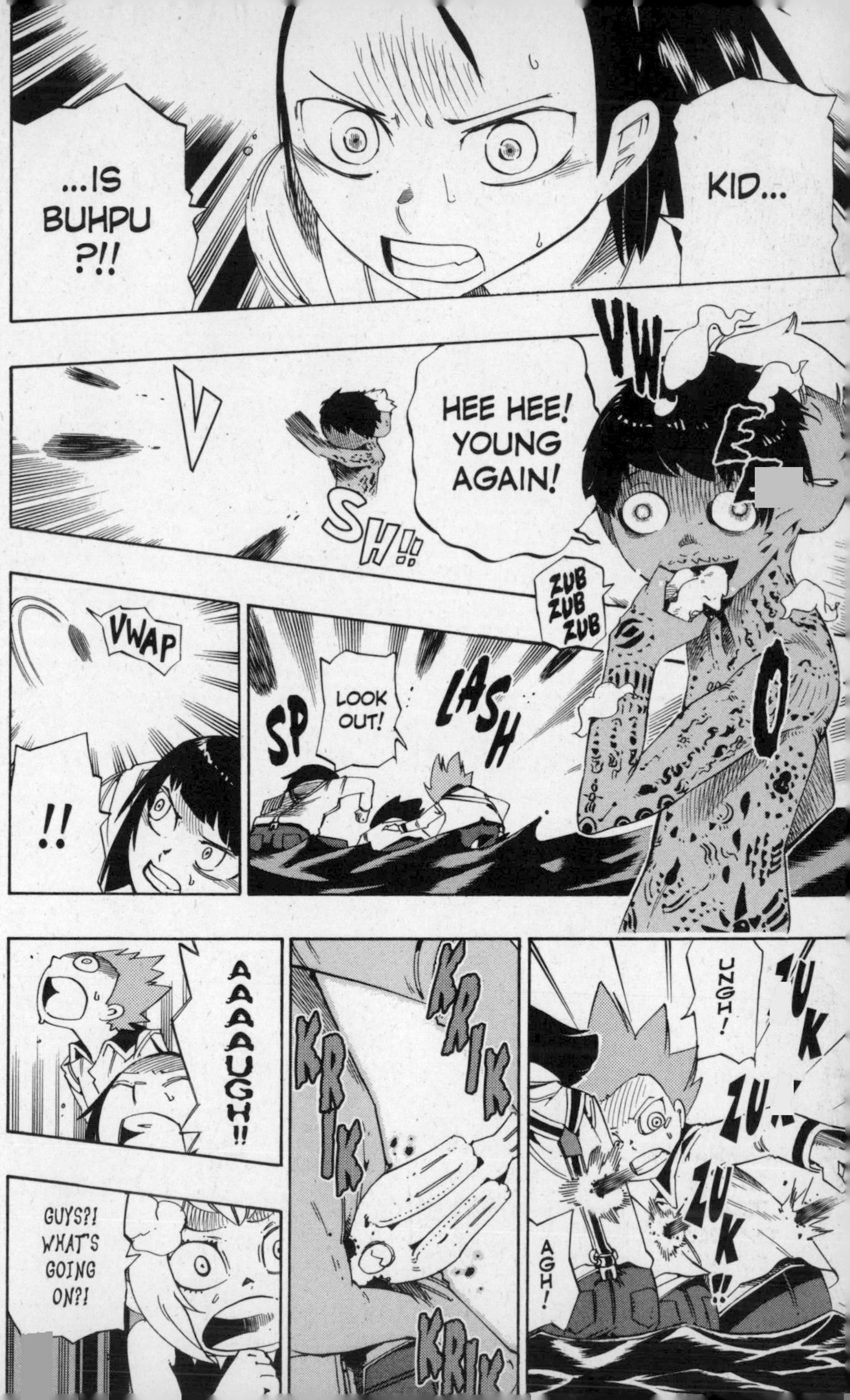
KID...
...IS BUHPU ?!!
VWEO
HEE HEE! YOUNG AGAIN!
SH!!
ZUB ZUB ZUB
SPLASH
LOOK OUT!
VWAP
!!
UNGH!
ZUK
ZUK
ZUK!!
AGH!
KRIK
KRIK
KRIK
AAAAUGH!!
GUYS?! WHAT'S GOING ON?!

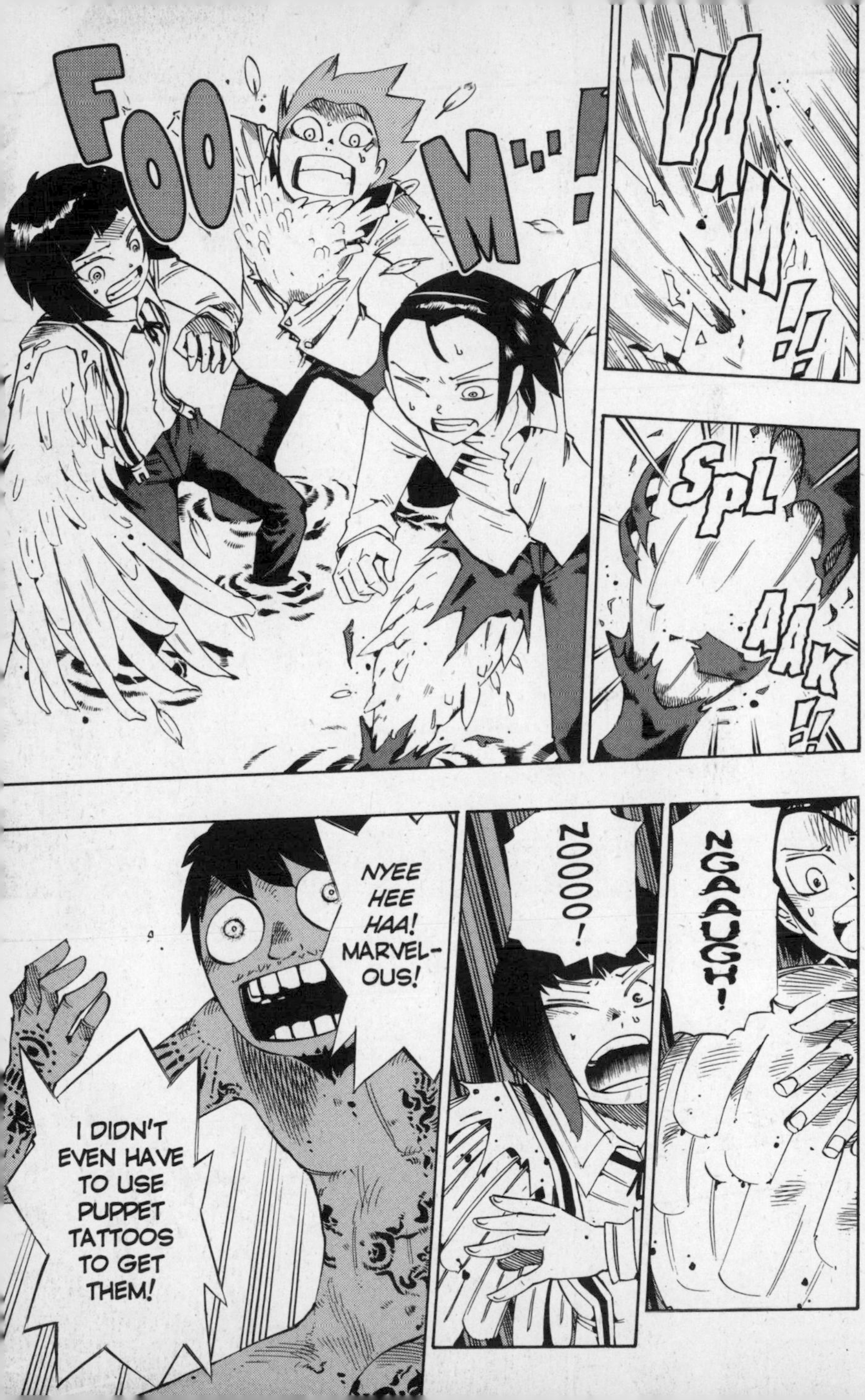
VAM!!
SPLAAK!!
FOOOM...!
NGAAUGH!
NOOOO!
NYEE HEE HAA! MARVEL-OUS!
I DIDN'T EVEN HAVE TO USE PUPPET TATTOOS TO GET THEM!

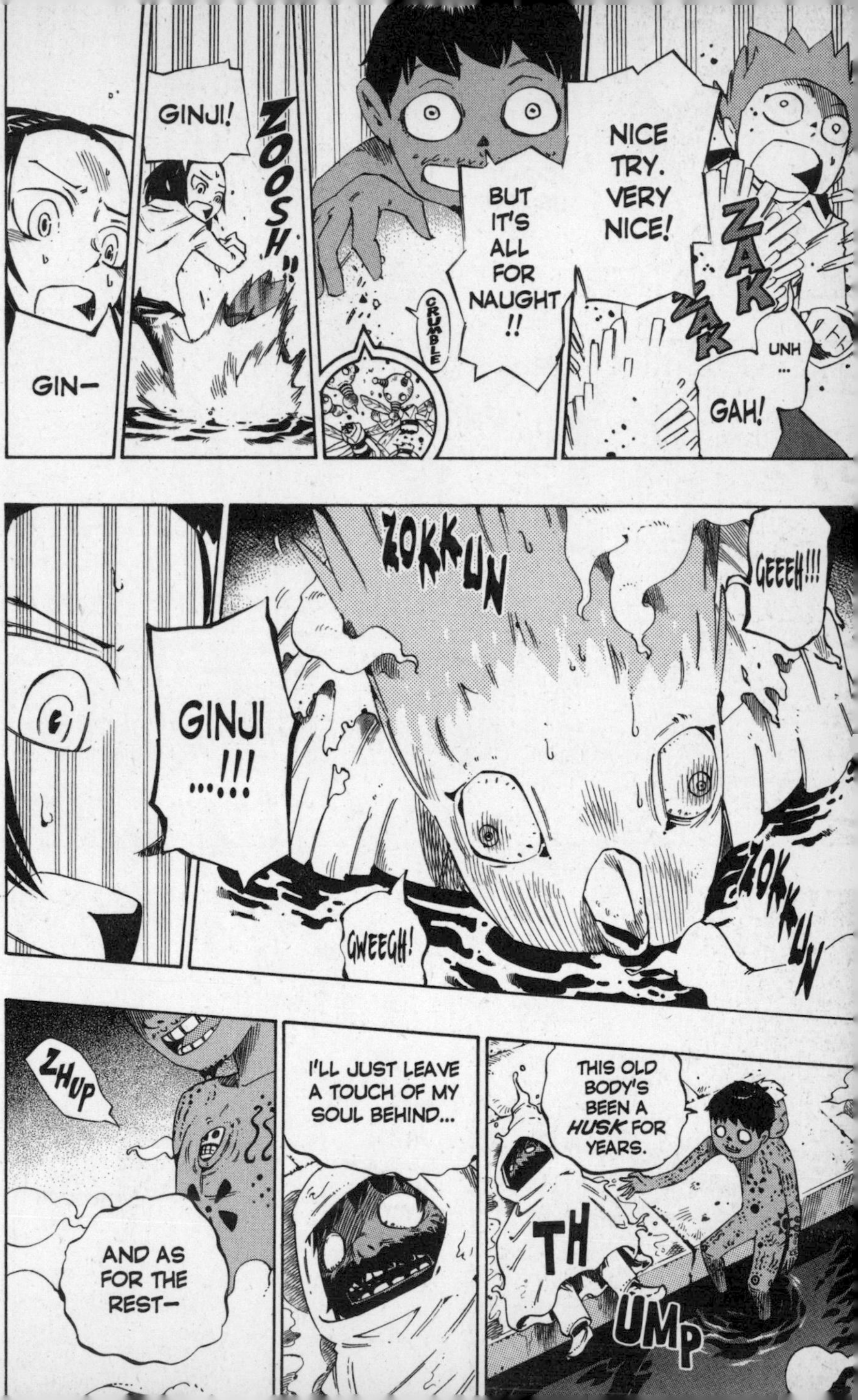
NICE TRY. VERY NICE!
ZAK ZAK
UNH...
GAH!
BUT IT'S ALL FOR NAUGHT!!
CRUMBLE
ZOOSH!!
GINJI!
GIN-
GEEEH!!!
ZOKKUN
ZOKKUN
GWEEGH!
GINJI ...!!!
THIS OLD BODY'S BEEN A *HUSK* FOR YEARS.
THUMP
I'LL JUST LEAVE A TOUCH OF MY SOUL BEHIND...
ZHUP
AND AS FOR THE REST-

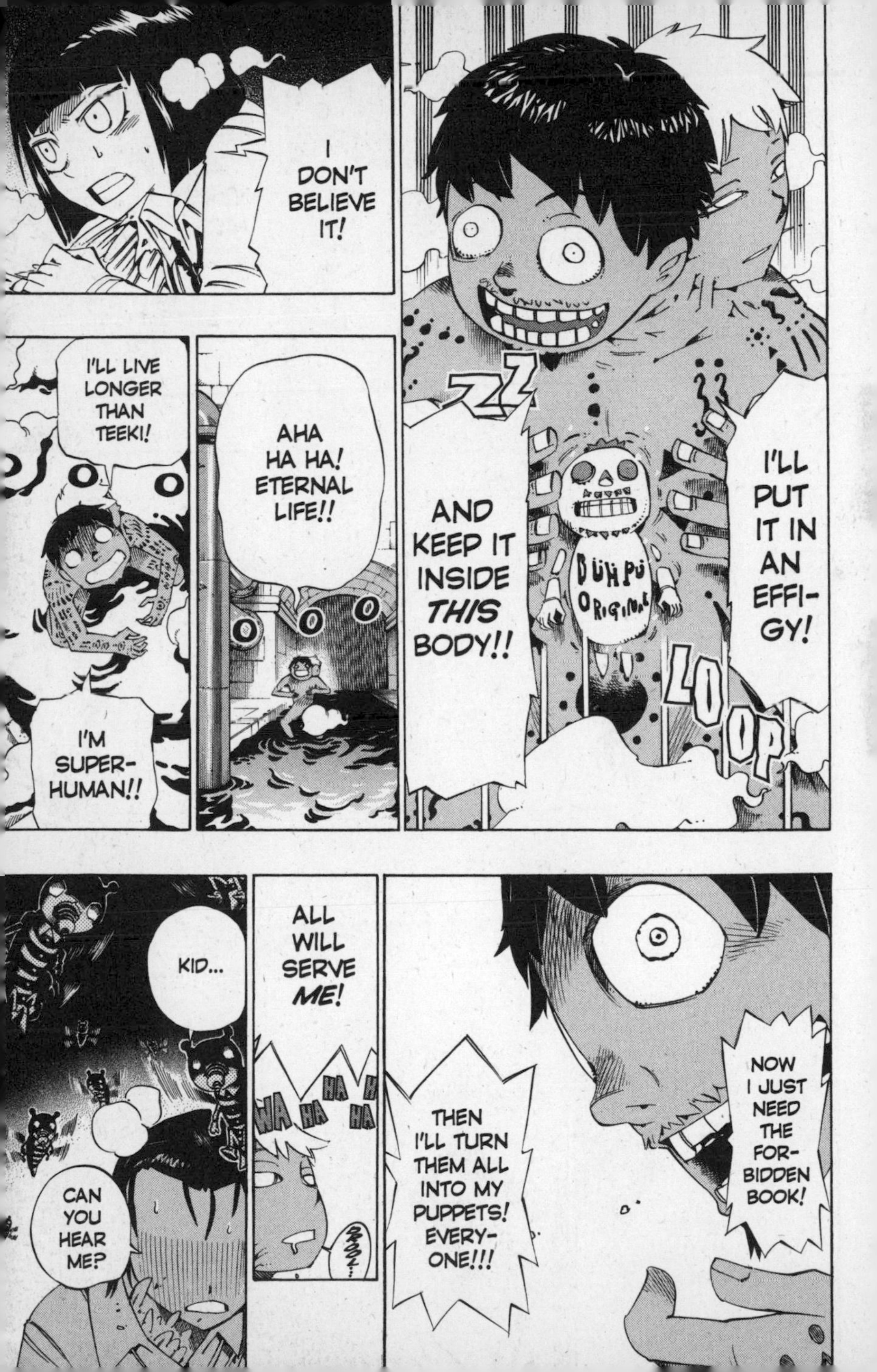
I'LL PUT IT IN AN EFFIGY!
AND KEEP IT INSIDE *THIS* BODY!!
ZZ
BUHPU ORIGINAL
LOOP
I DON'T BELIEVE IT!
AHA HA HA! ETERNAL LIFE!!
I'LL LIVE LONGER THAN TEEKI!
I'M SUPER-HUMAN!!
NOW I JUST NEED THE FOR-BIDDEN BOOK!
THEN I'LL TURN THEM ALL INTO MY PUPPETS! EVERY-ONE!!!
ALL WILL SERVE *ME*!
HA HA HA HA
KID...
CAN YOU HEAR ME?

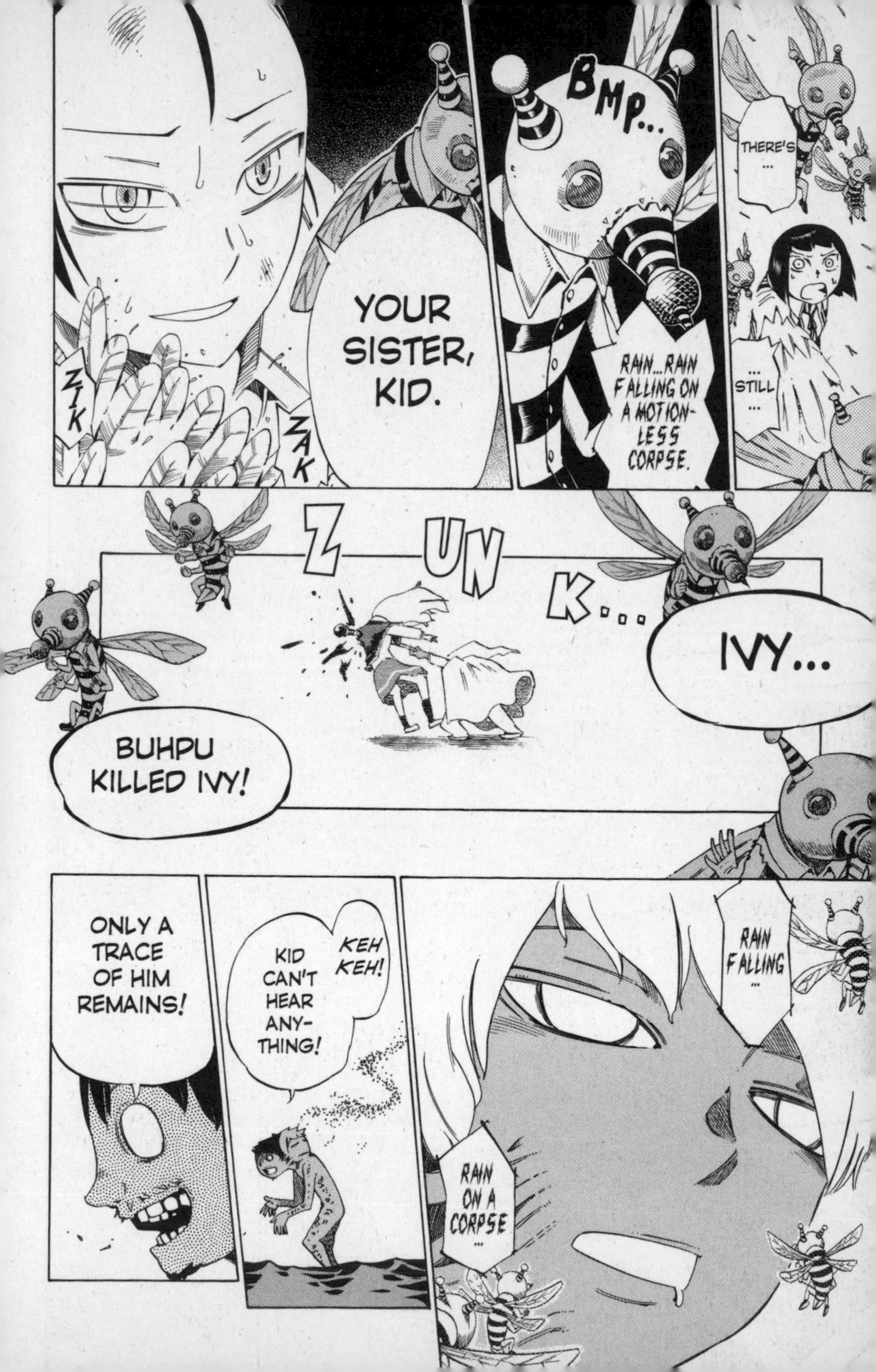
THERE'S ...
... STILL ...
BMP...
RAIN...RAIN FALLING ON A MOTION-LESS CORPSE.
YOUR SISTER, KID.
ZIK
ZAK
ZUNK...
IVY...
BUHPU KILLED IVY!
RAIN FALLING ...
RAIN ON A CORPSE ...
KEH KEH!
KID CAN'T HEAR ANY-THING!
ONLY A TRACE OF HIM REMAINS!

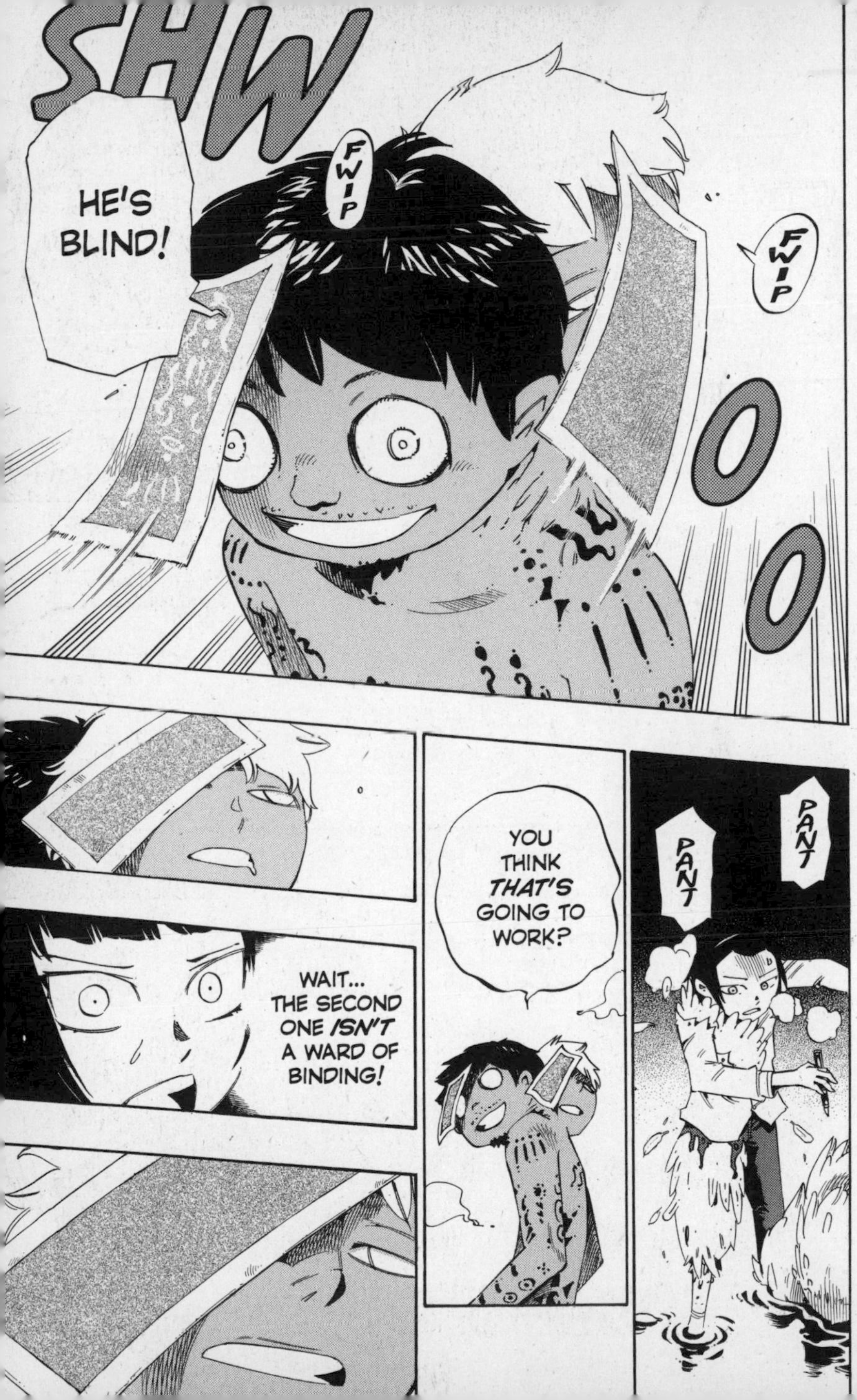
FWIP
OO
SHW
FWIP
HE'S BLIND!
PANT PANT
YOU THINK *THAT'S* GOING TO WORK?
WAIT... THE SECOND ONE *ISN'T* A WARD OF BINDING!

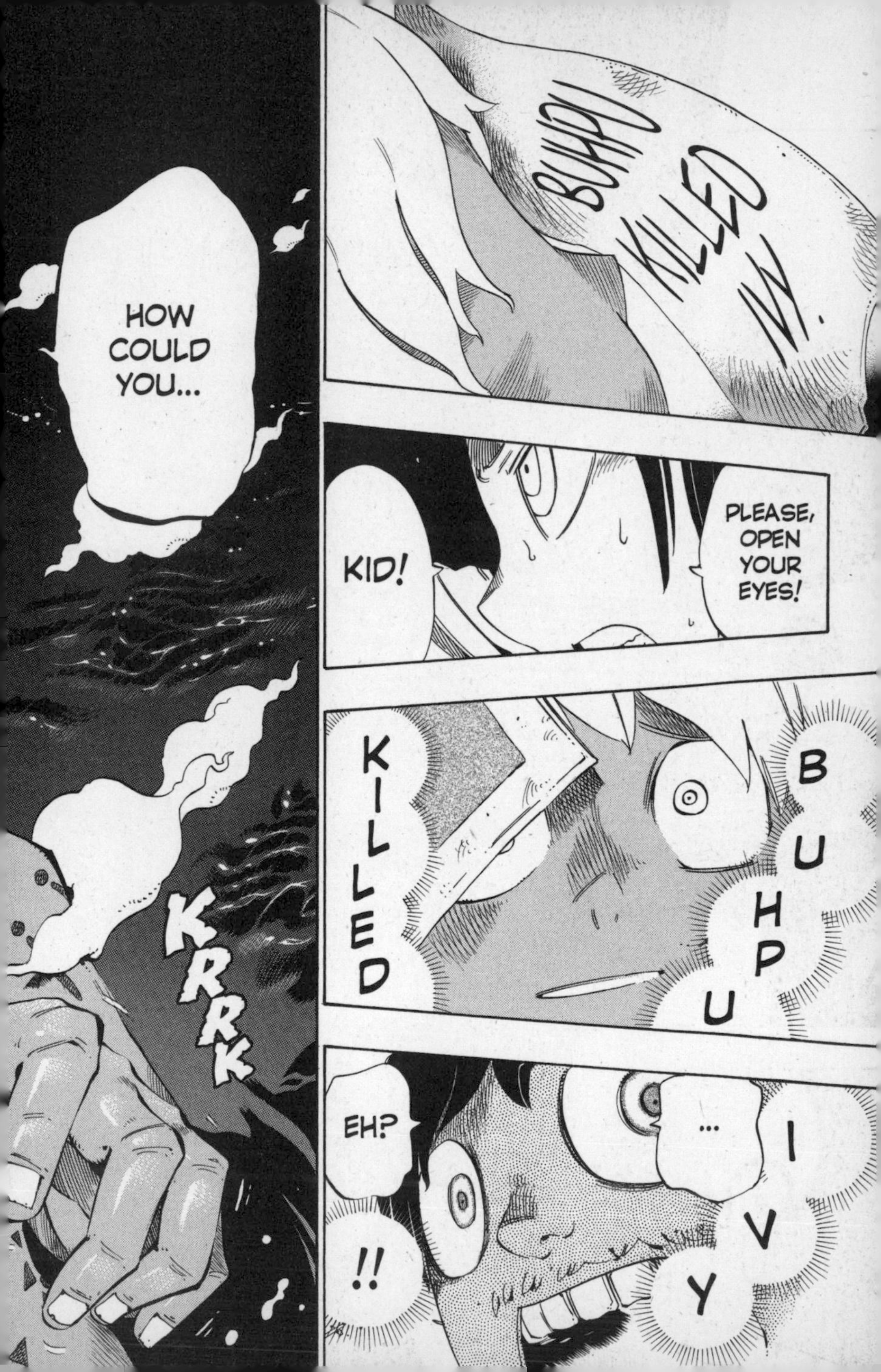
BUHP!
KILLED
AA.
PLEASE, OPEN YOUR EYES!
KID!
BUHPU
KILLED
...
IVY
EH?
!!
HOW COULD YOU...
KRRK

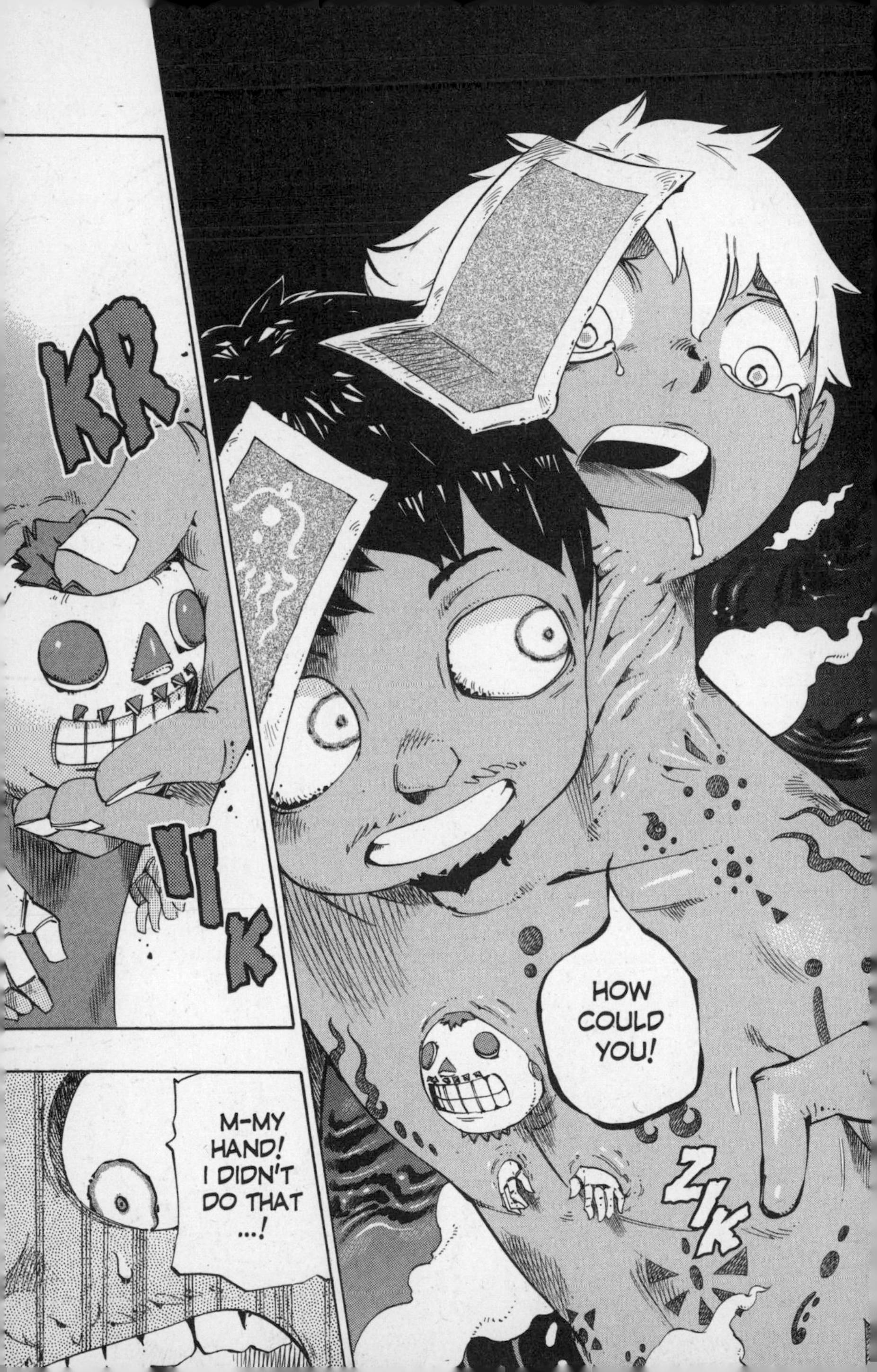
HOW COULD YOU!
ZIK
KRIIK
M-MY HAND! I DIDN'T DO THAT ...!

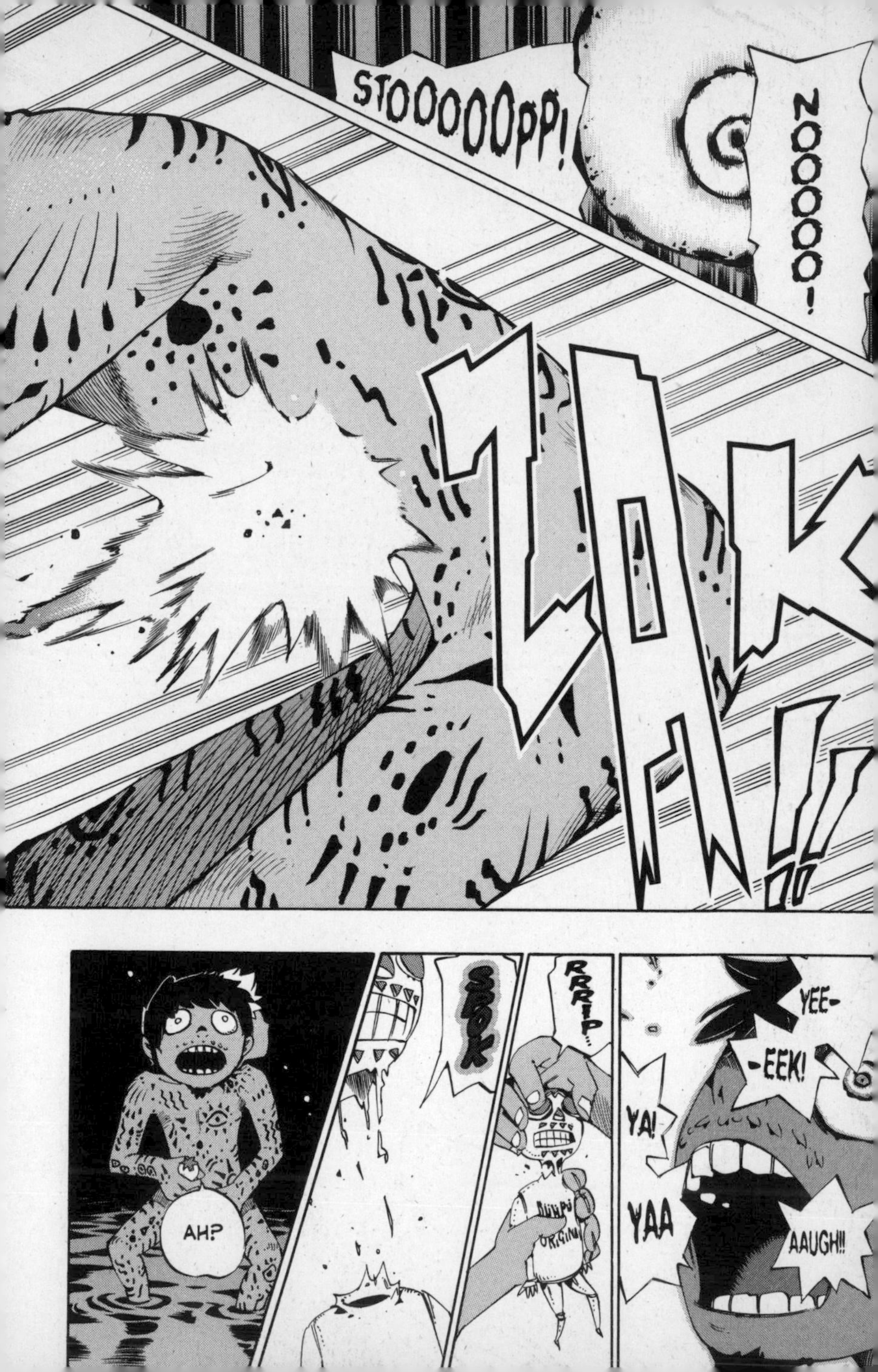
NOOOOOO!
STOOOOOOPP!
ZAK!!
YEE-
-EEK!
YA!
YAA
AAUGH!!
RRRIP...
SPOK
AH?

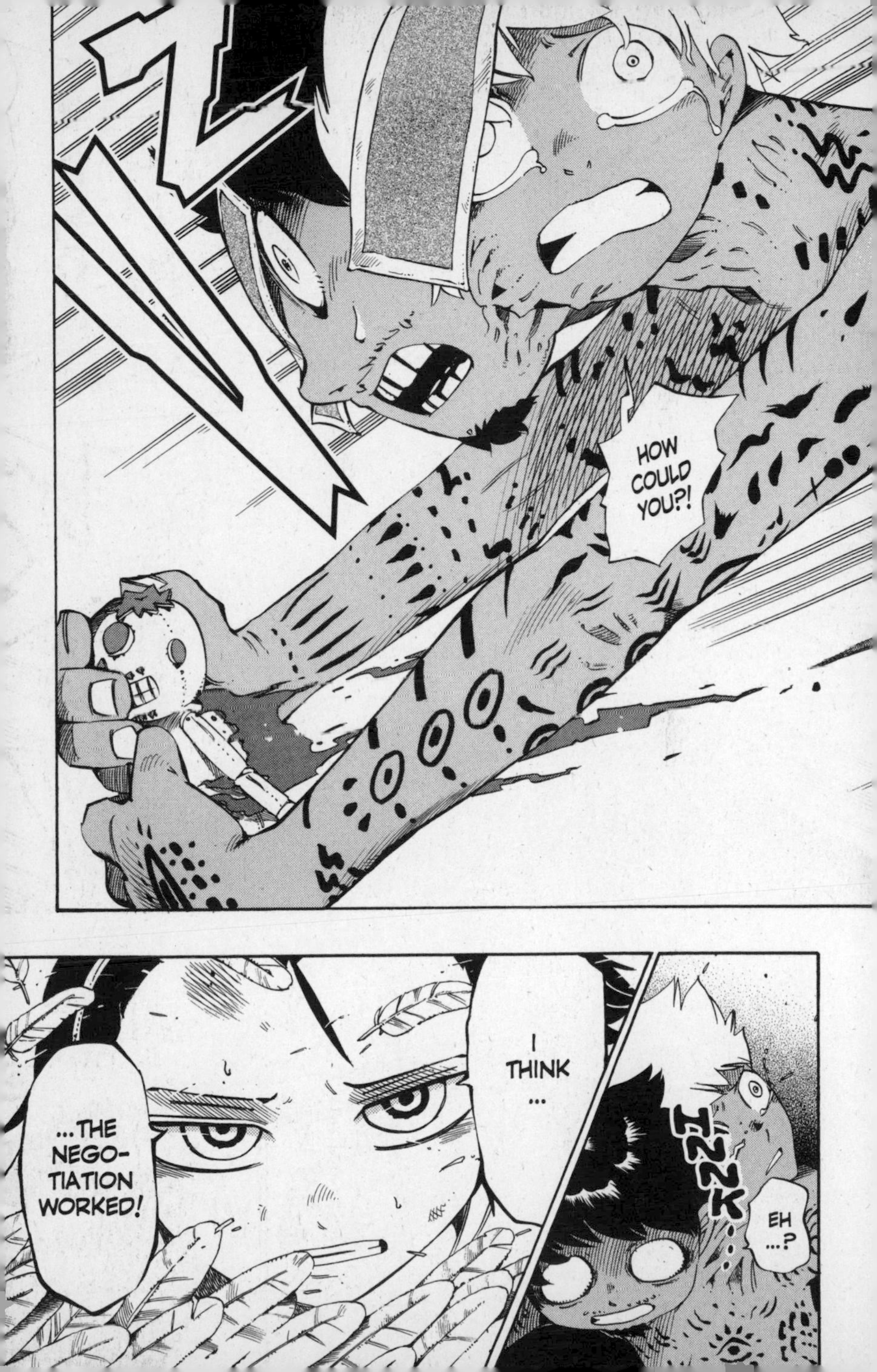
HOW COULD YOU?!
HNNK...
EH ...?
I THINK ...
...THE NEGO-TIATION WORKED!

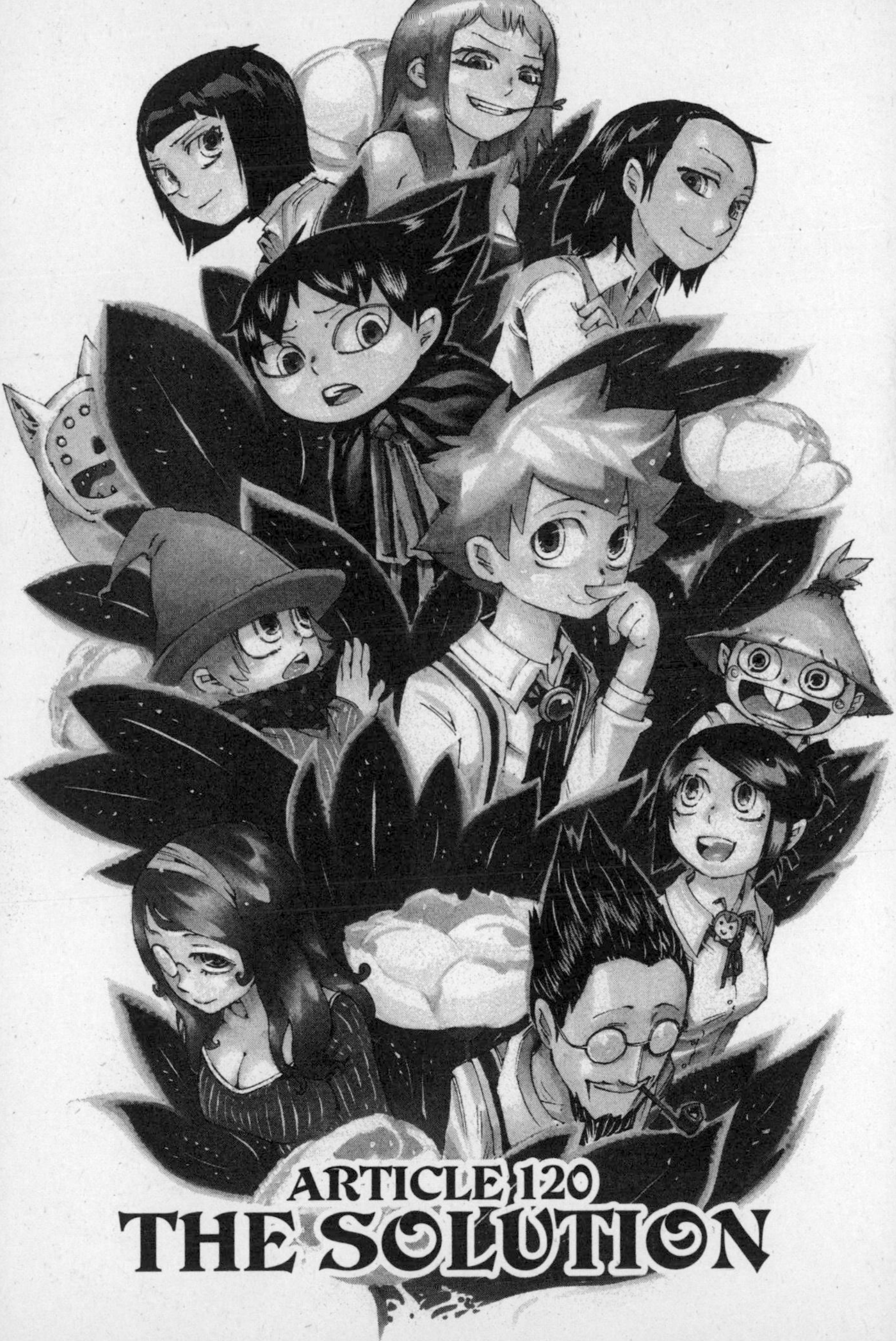

ARTICLE 120
THE SOLUTION

Q: IF MUHYO'S SUCH A GENIUS, WHY IS HE SO POOR? HOW DOES HE GET PAID FOR JOBS? OR DOES HE GET A SALARY? HOW DOES HE GET MONEY FOR LIVING EXPENSES?

-O.Y., NARA PREFECTURE

A: I WONDER!

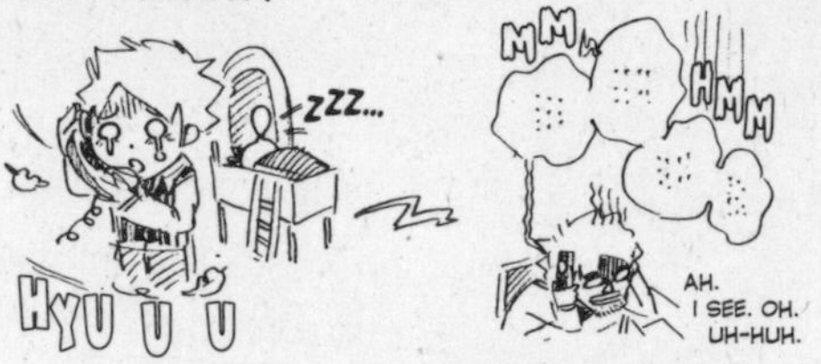
MMM
HMMM
AH.
I SEE. OH.
UH-HUH.
ZZZ...
HYUUU

YEEEESH! THAT TOOK FOREVER!!

LOOKS LIKE RUNNING THAT OFFICE ISN'T ALL IT'S CRACKED UP TO BE! NOT ONLY IS THERE A COMPLETE LACK OF STRUCTURE, BUT THERE ARE HARDLY ANY CUSTOMERS. IT'S BECAUSE OF LOCATION PARTLY. THEY'RE IN A BIG CITY, SO A LOT OF THE WORK GETS SCOOPED UP BY THE BIG FIRMS. IT'S NOT JUST THE GORYO GROUP OUT THERE, YOU KNOW.

ALSO, MUHYO'S ONLY REALLY FAMOUS INSIDE THE ASSOCIATION. HIS NAME DOESN'T CARRY MUCH WEIGHT ON THE OPEN MARKET. ONE GOOD THING THOUGH—THEIR LANDLORD IS CUTTING THEM A DEAL ON RENT, SO THEY DON'T PAY MUCH FOR THEIR OFFICE SPACE AT LEAST. AS FOR FOOD MONEY, THEY HAVE ABOUT $3 ON A GOOD DAY AND $0.50 ON A BAD ONE...

WHICH MEANS FOR ONE MEAL, THAT'S... ON SECOND THOUGHT, LET'S NOT GO THERE. MUHYO MAY BE THE FAMOUS ONE, BUT ROJI IS A GENIUS WHEN IT COMES TO KEEPING THEM ALIVE!

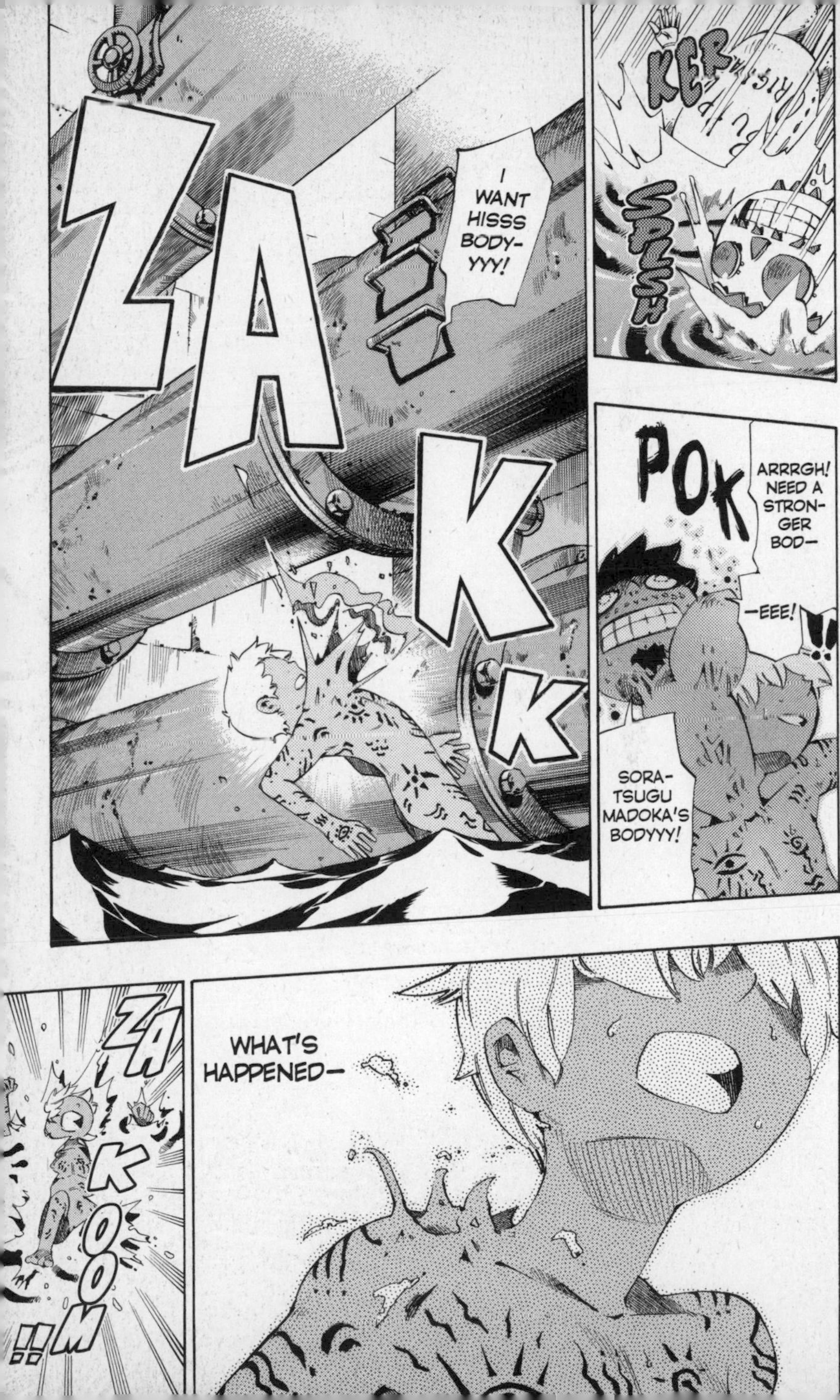
KER
SPLSH
POK
ARRRGH! NEED A STRONGER BOD—
—EEE!
!!
SORA-TSUGU MADOKA'S BODYYY!
ZAKK
I WANT HISSS BODY-YYY!
WHAT'S HAPPENED—
ZAKOOOM!!

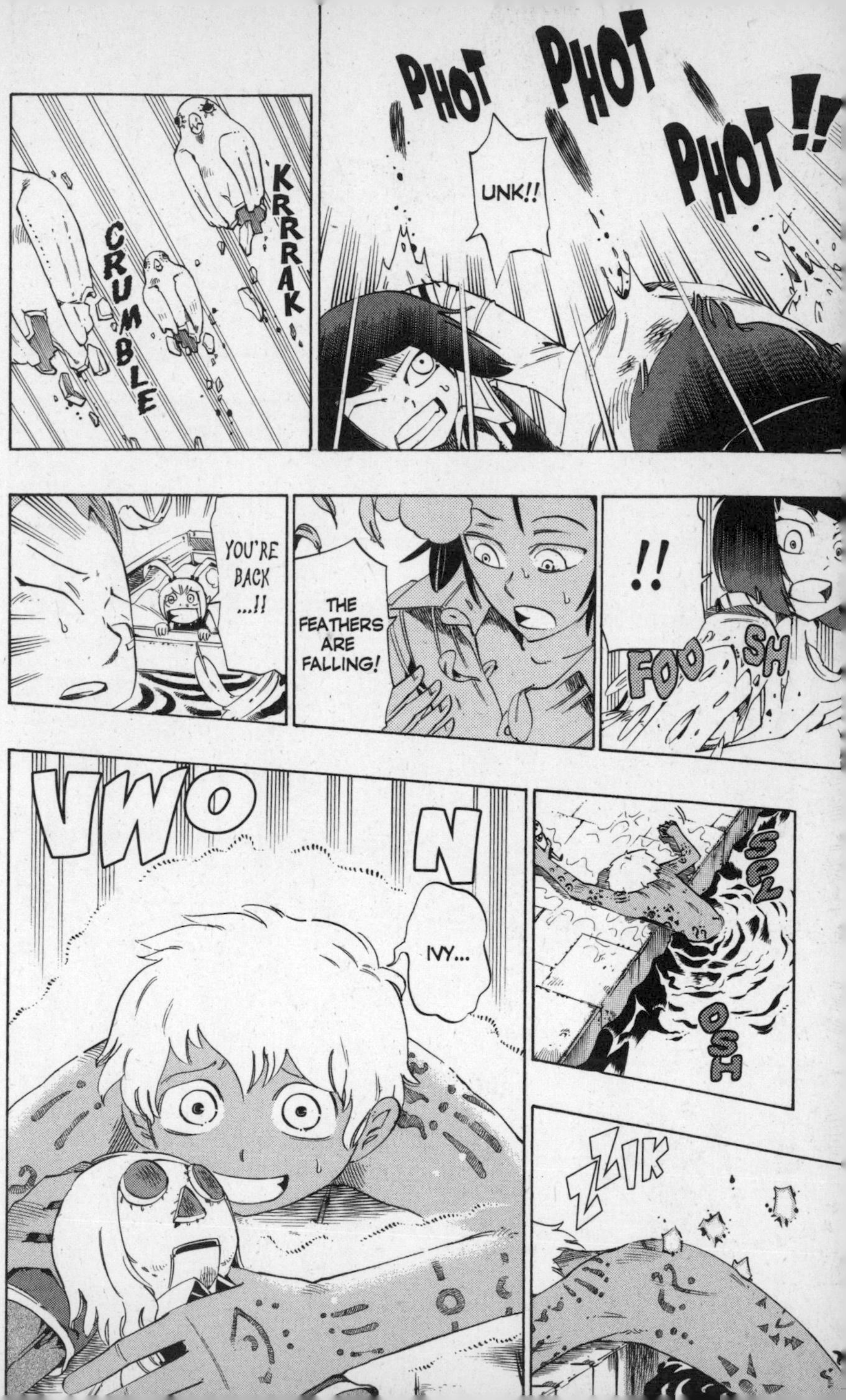
PHOT PHOT PHOT!!
UNK!!
KRRRAK
CRUMBLE
!!
FOOSH
THE FEATHERS ARE FALLING!
YOU'RE BACK ...!!
SPWOSH
ZZIK
VWON
IVY...

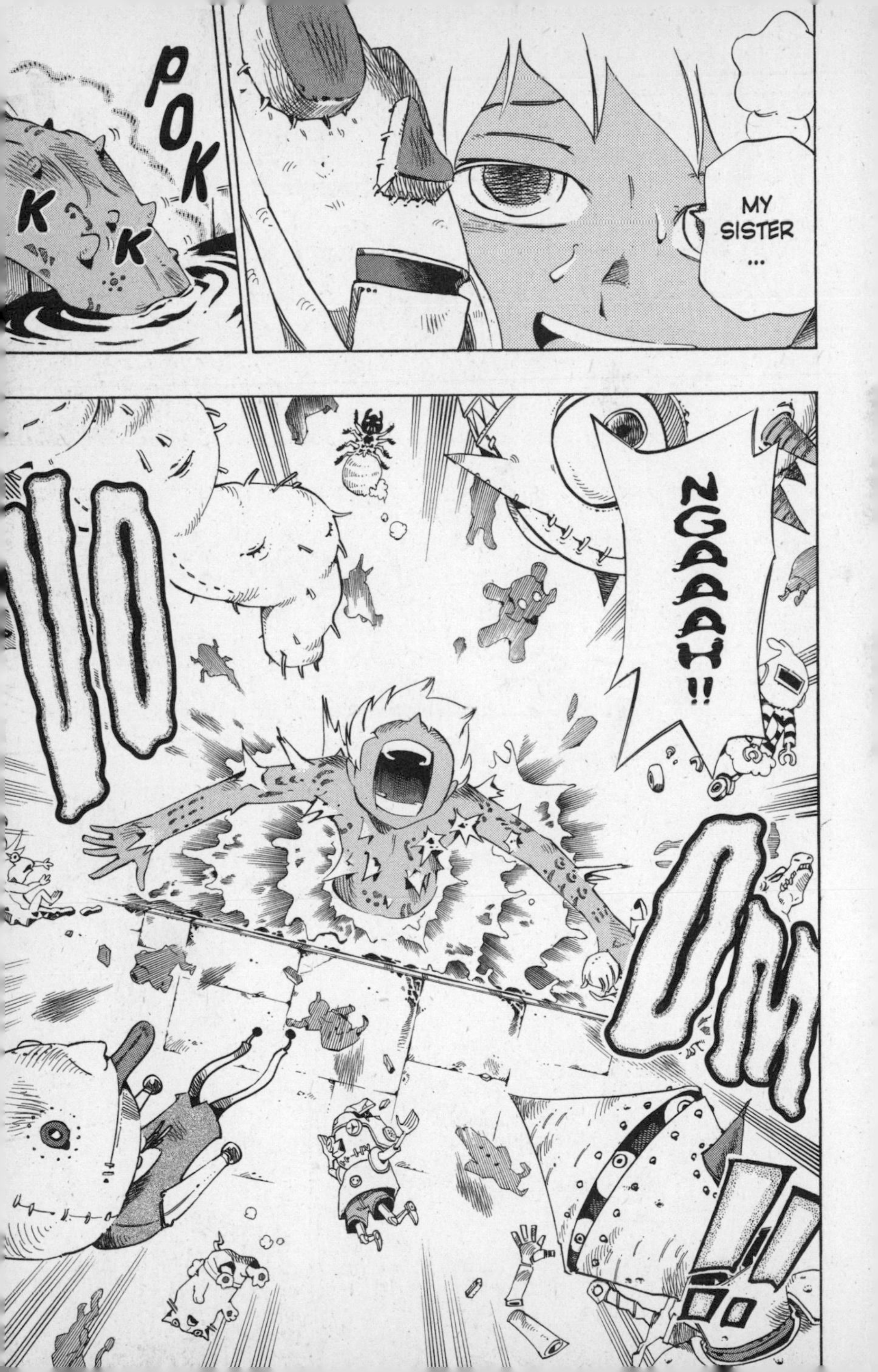
MY SISTER ...
POK
K K
NGAAAH!!

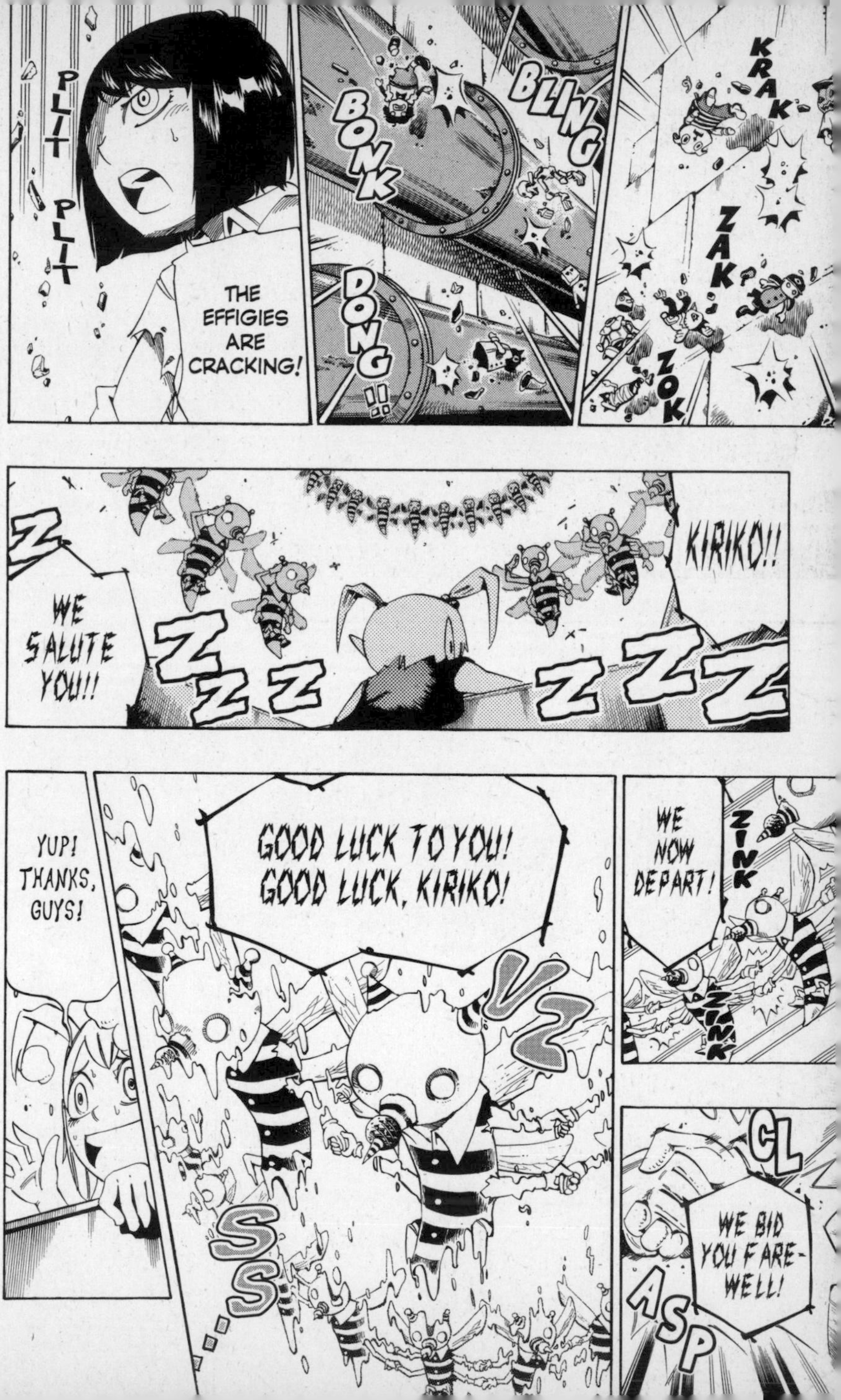
KRAK
ZAK
ZOK
BLING
BONK
DONG!!
PLIT
PLIT
PLIT
THE EFFIGIES ARE CRACKING!
KIRIKO!!
ZZZZZZZ
WE SALUTE YOU!!
WE NOW DEPART!
ZINK
ZINK
CL
WE BID YOU FARE-WELL!
ASP
GOOD LUCK TO YOU! GOOD LUCK, KIRIKO!
VZ
SS
YUP! THANKS, GUYS!

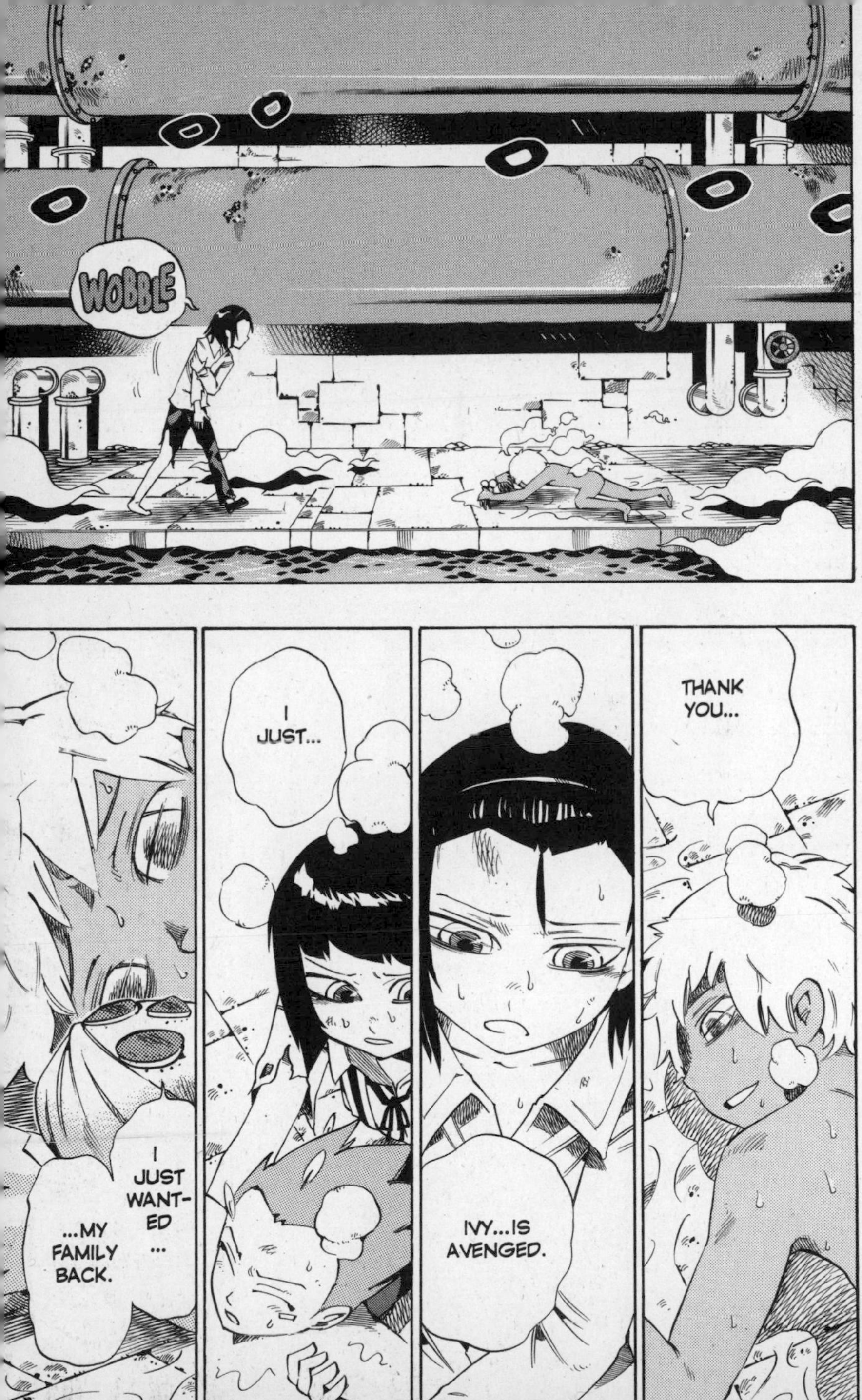
WOBBLE
THANK YOU...
IVY...IS AVENGED.
I JUST...
I JUST WANT-ED ...
...MY FAMILY BACK.

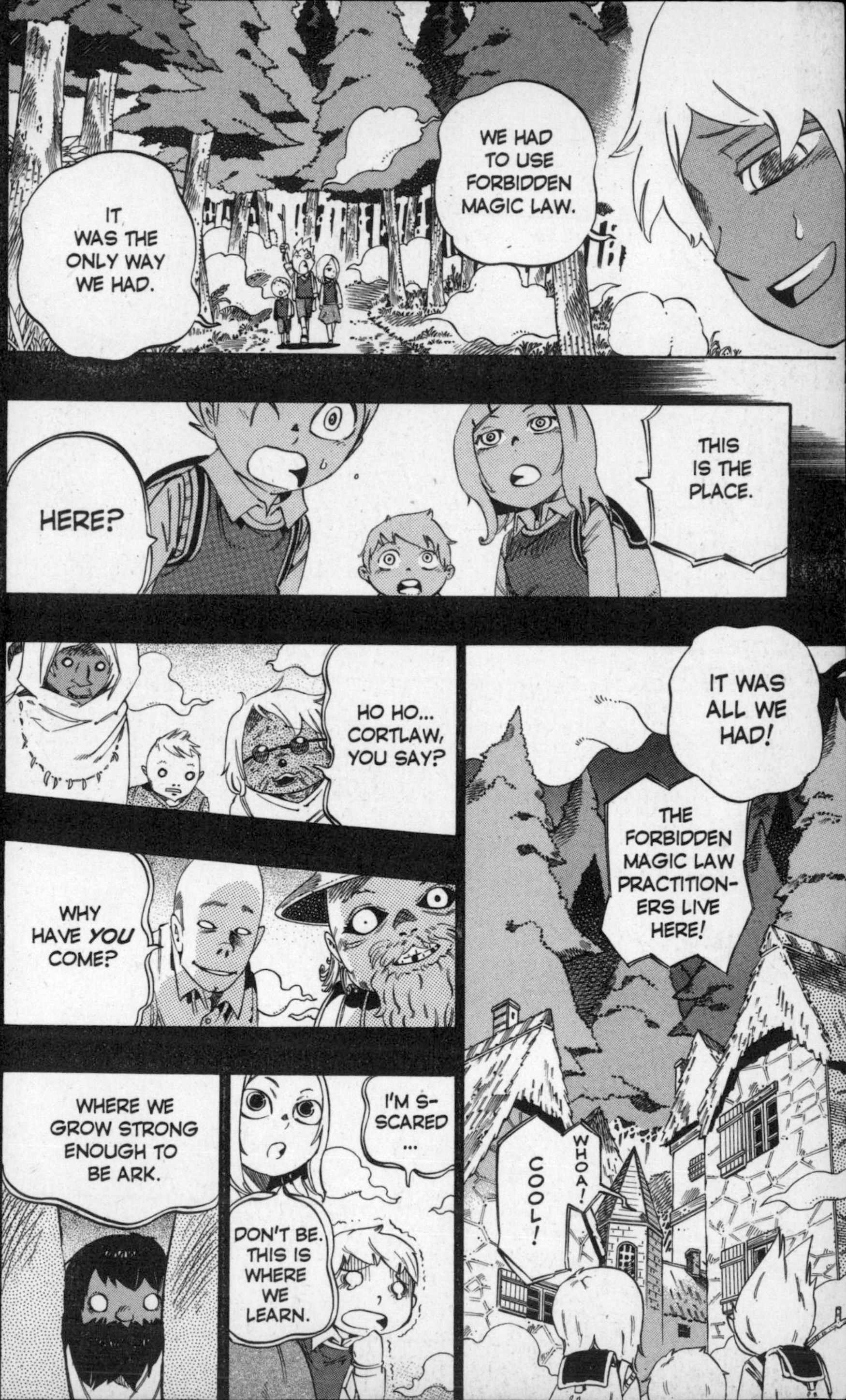
WE HAD TO USE FORBIDDEN MAGIC LAW.
IT WAS THE ONLY WAY WE HAD.
THIS IS THE PLACE.
HERE?
IT WAS ALL WE HAD!
THE FORBIDDEN MAGIC LAW PRACTITIONERS LIVE HERE!
WHOA!
COOL!
HO HO... CORTLAW, YOU SAY?
WHY HAVE *YOU* COME?
I'M S-SCARED ...
DON'T BE. THIS IS WHERE WE LEARN.
WHERE WE GROW STRONG ENOUGH TO BE ARK.

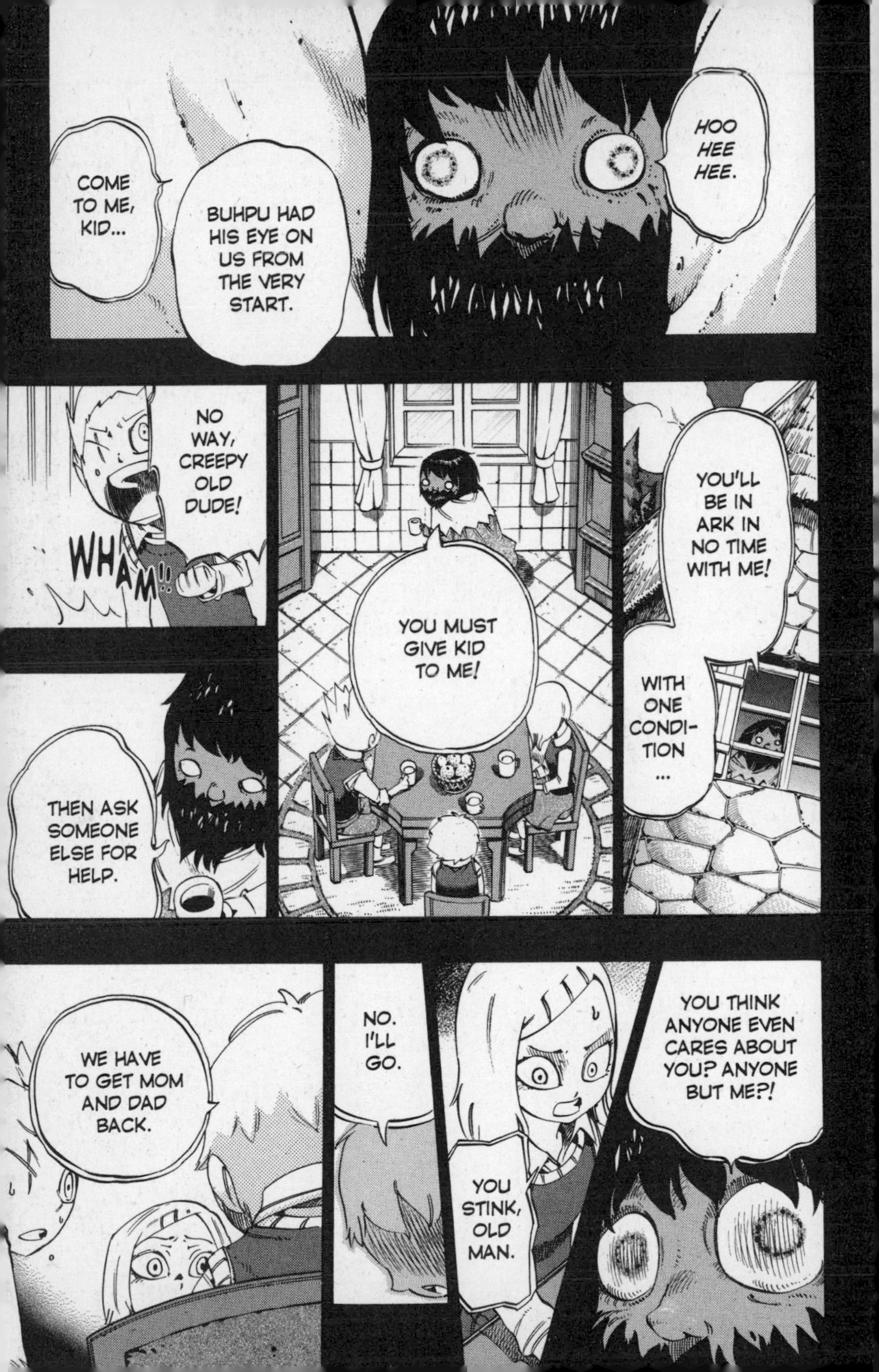
HOO HEE HEE.
BUHPU HAD HIS EYE ON US FROM THE VERY START.
COME TO ME, KID...
YOU'LL BE IN ARK IN NO TIME WITH ME!
WITH ONE CONDITION...
YOU MUST GIVE KID TO ME!
NO WAY, CREEPY OLD DUDE!
WHAM!!
THEN ASK SOMEONE ELSE FOR HELP.
YOU THINK ANYONE EVEN CARES ABOUT YOU? ANYONE BUT ME?!
YOU STINK, OLD MAN.
NO. I'LL GO.
WE HAVE TO GET MOM AND DAD BACK.

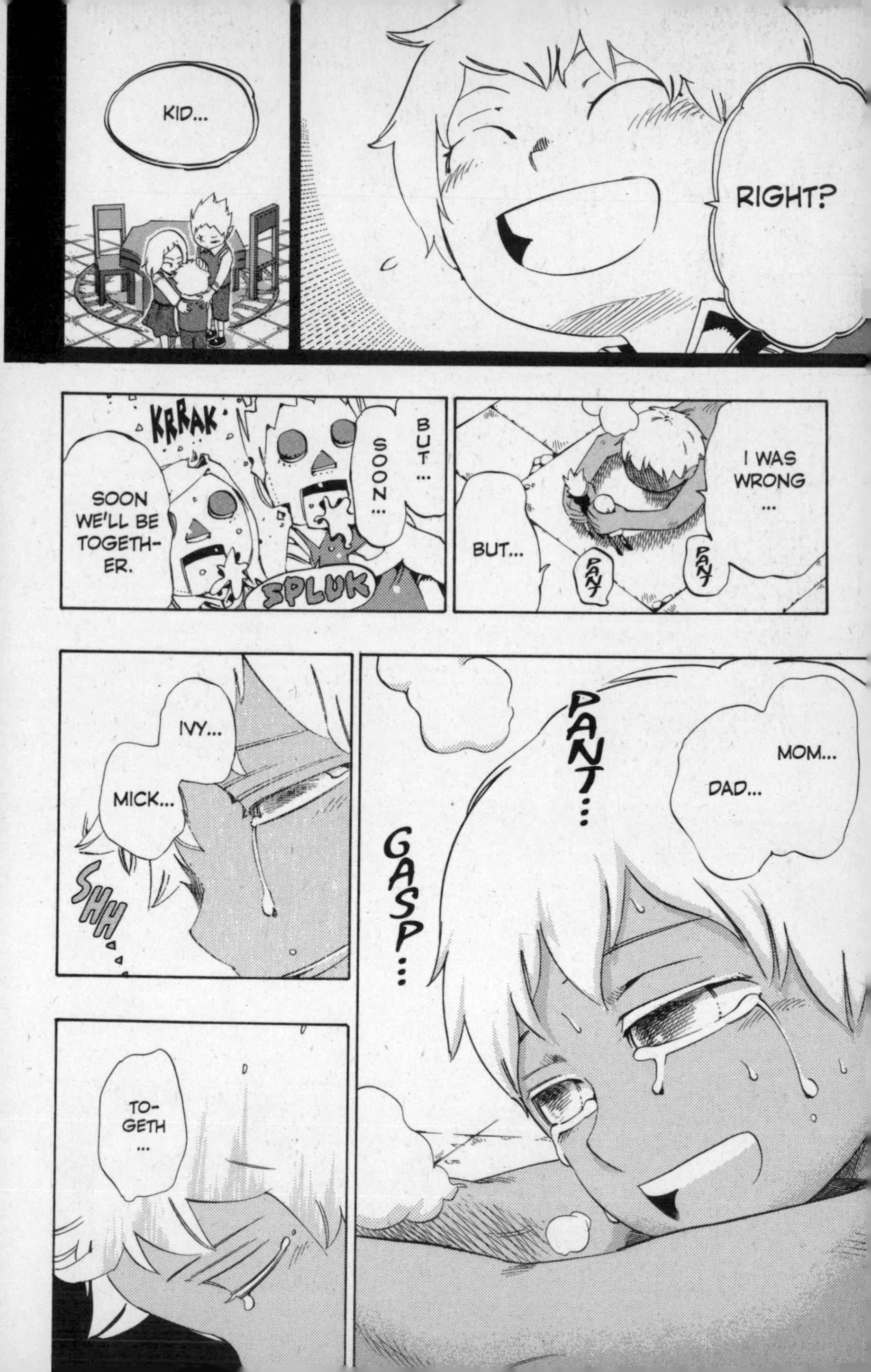
RIGHT?
KID...
I WAS WRONG ...
PANT
PANT
BUT...
BUT... SOON...
KRRAK
SOON WE'LL BE TOGETH-ER.
SPLUK
MOM...
DAD...
PANT...
GASP...
IVY...
MICK...
SHH
TO-GETH ...

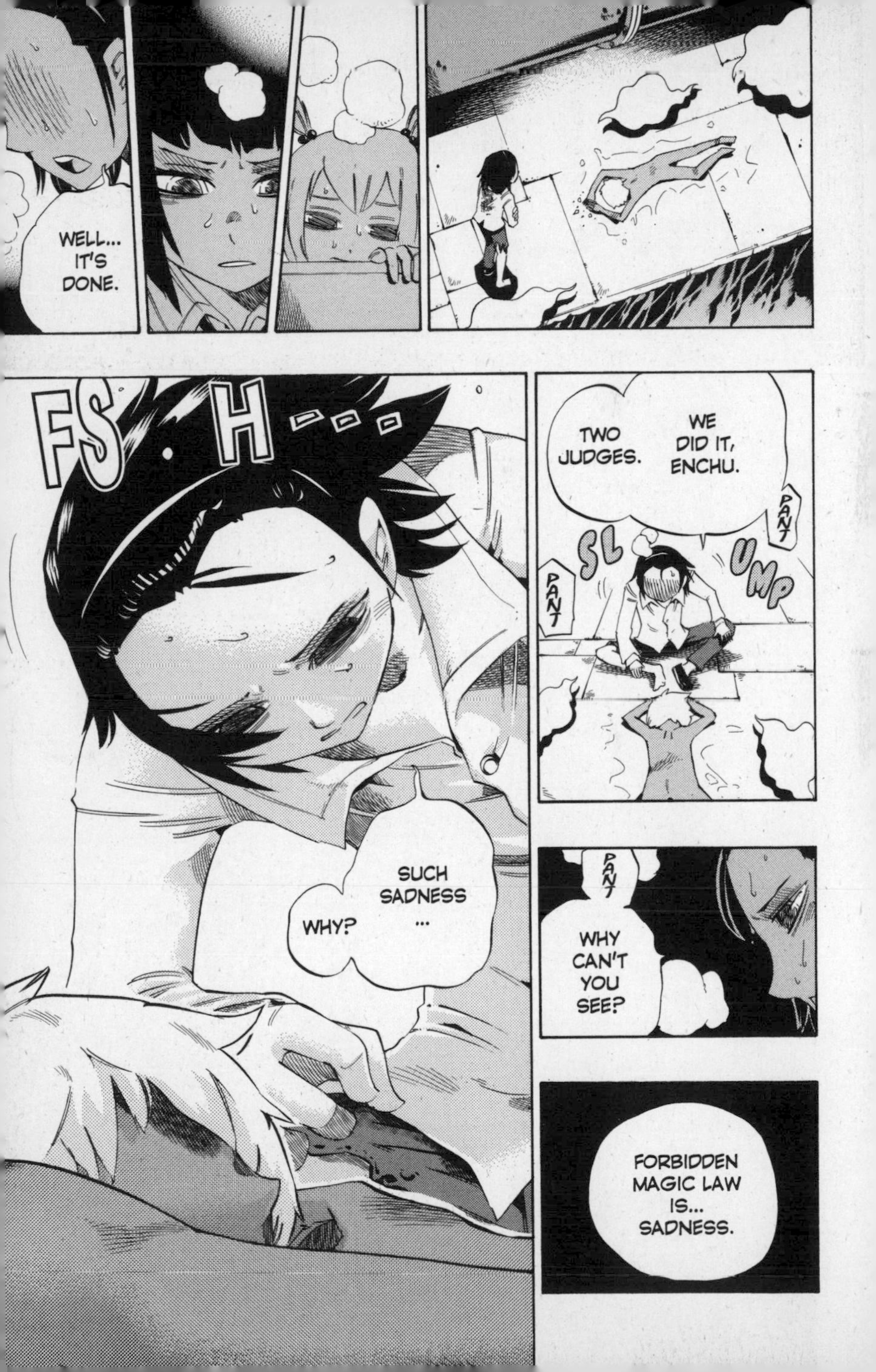
WELL... IT'S DONE.
WE DID IT, ENCHU.
TWO JUDGES.
PANT
SLUMP
PANT
PANT
WHY CAN'T YOU SEE?
FORBIDDEN MAGIC LAW IS... SADNESS.
FS...H...
SUCH SADNESS...
WHY?

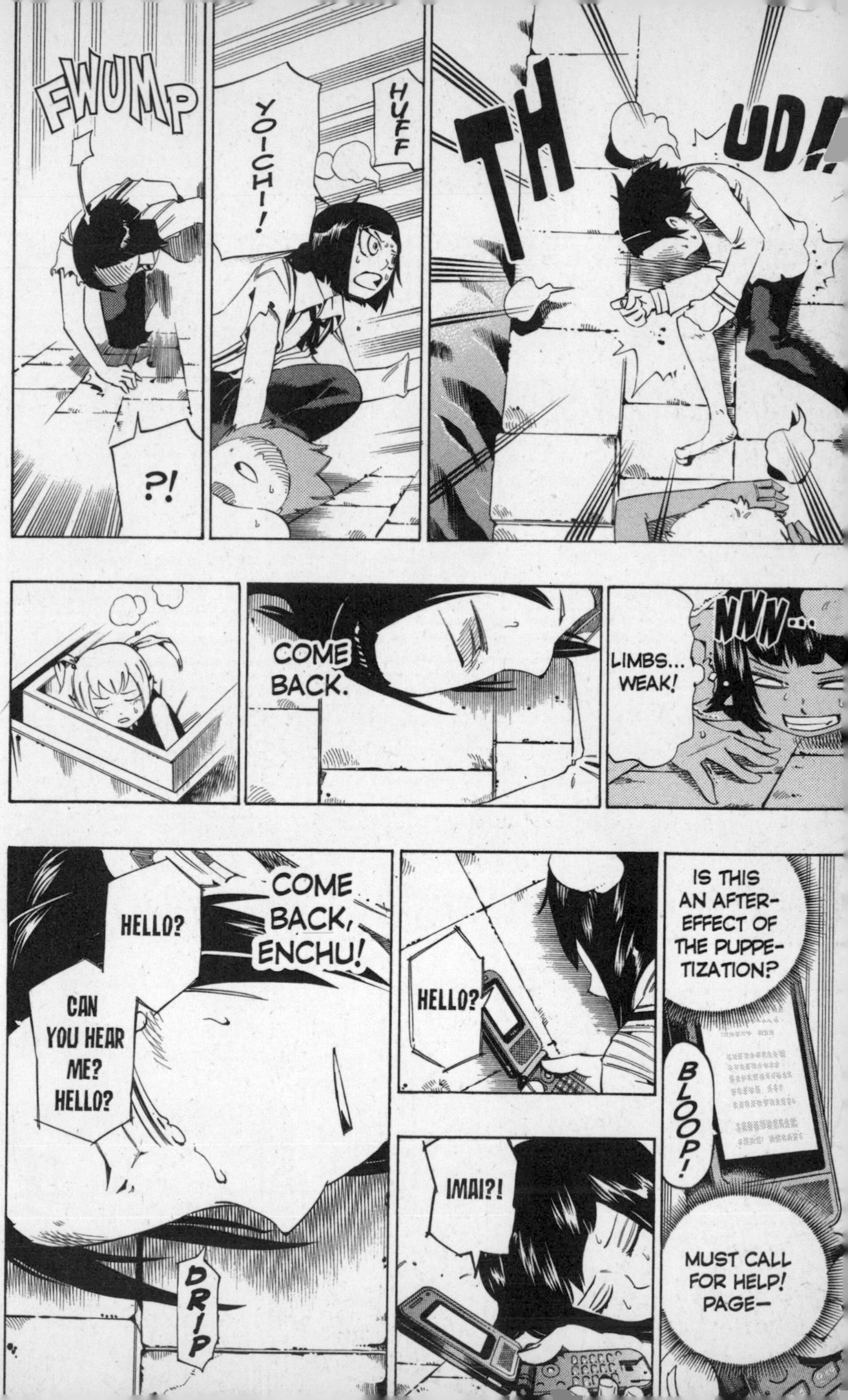
THUD!!
HUFF
YOICHI!
FWUMP
?!
NNN...
LIMBS... WEAK!
COME BACK.
IS THIS AN AFTER-EFFECT OF THE PUPPE-TIZATION?
BLOOP!
MUST CALL FOR HELP! PAGE—
HELLO?
IMAI?!
COME BACK, ENCHU!
HELLO?
CAN YOU HEAR ME? HELLO?
DRIP

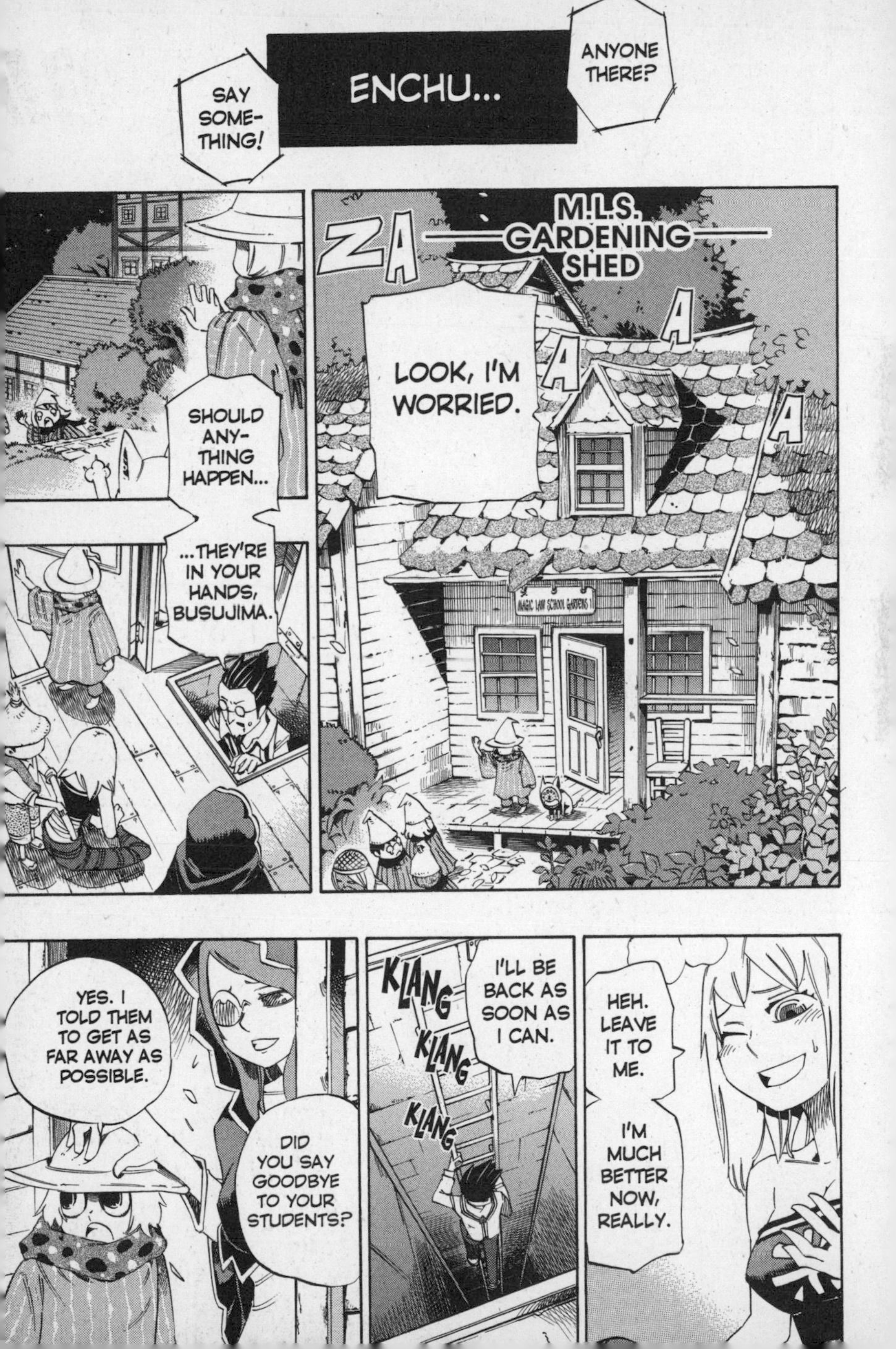
ANYONE THERE?
ENCHU...
SAY SOME-THING!
ZA-A-A-A
M.L.S. GARDENING SHED
LOOK, I'M WORRIED.
MAGIC LAW SCHOOL GARDENS 1
SHOULD ANY-THING HAPPEN...
...THEY'RE IN YOUR HANDS, BUSUJIMA.
HEH. LEAVE IT TO ME.
I'M MUCH BETTER NOW, REALLY.
KLANG
KLANG
KLANG
I'LL BE BACK AS SOON AS I CAN.
DID YOU SAY GOODBYE TO YOUR STUDENTS?
YES. I TOLD THEM TO GET AS FAR AWAY AS POSSIBLE.

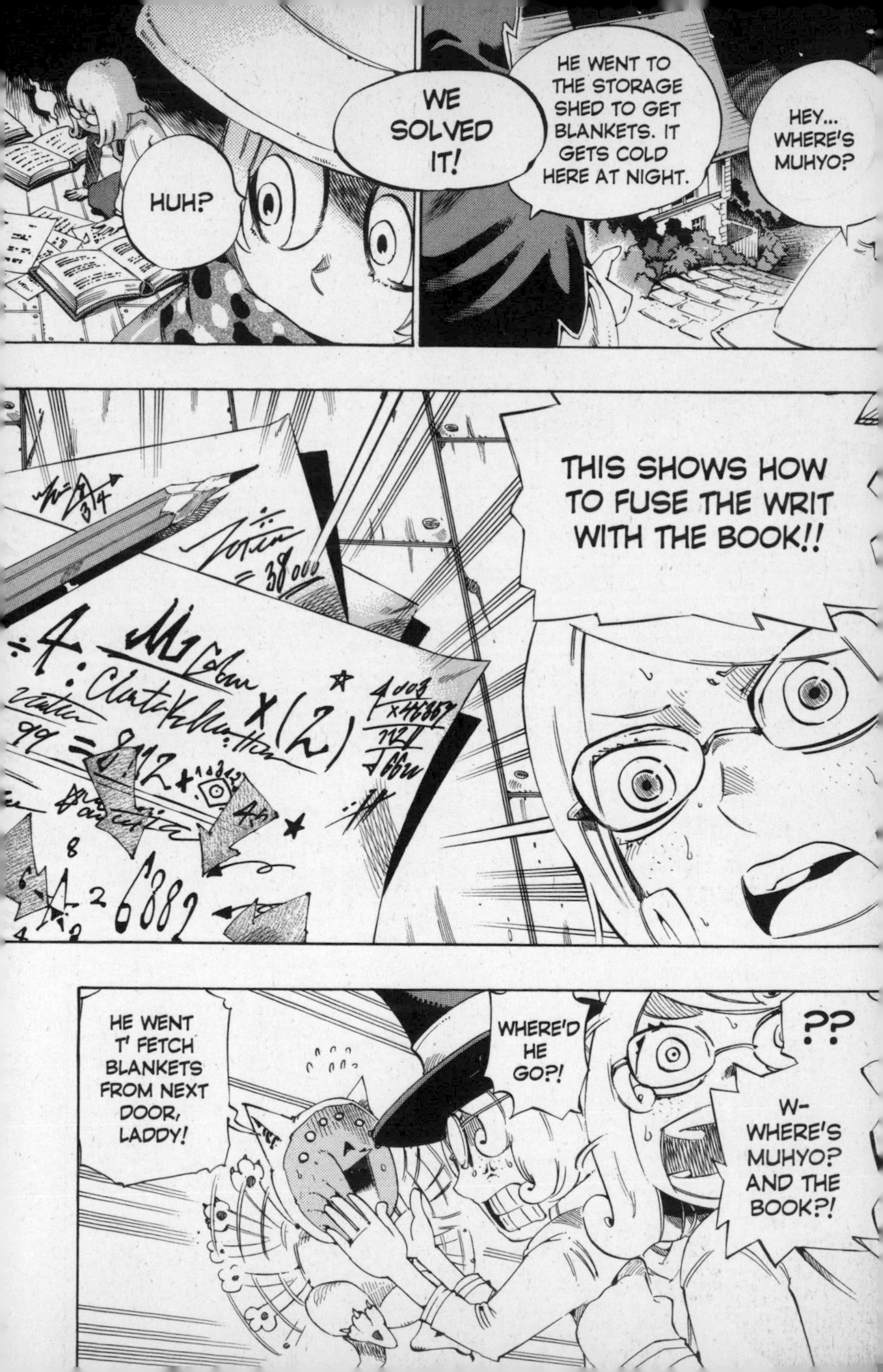
HEY... WHERE'S MUHYO?
HE WENT TO THE STORAGE SHED TO GET BLANKETS. IT GETS COLD HERE AT NIGHT.
WE SOLVED IT!
HUH?
THIS SHOWS HOW TO FUSE THE WRIT WITH THE BOOK!!
??
W-WHERE'S MUHYO? AND THE BOOK?!
WHERE'D HE GO?!
HE WENT T' FETCH BLANKETS FROM NEXT DOOR, LADDY!

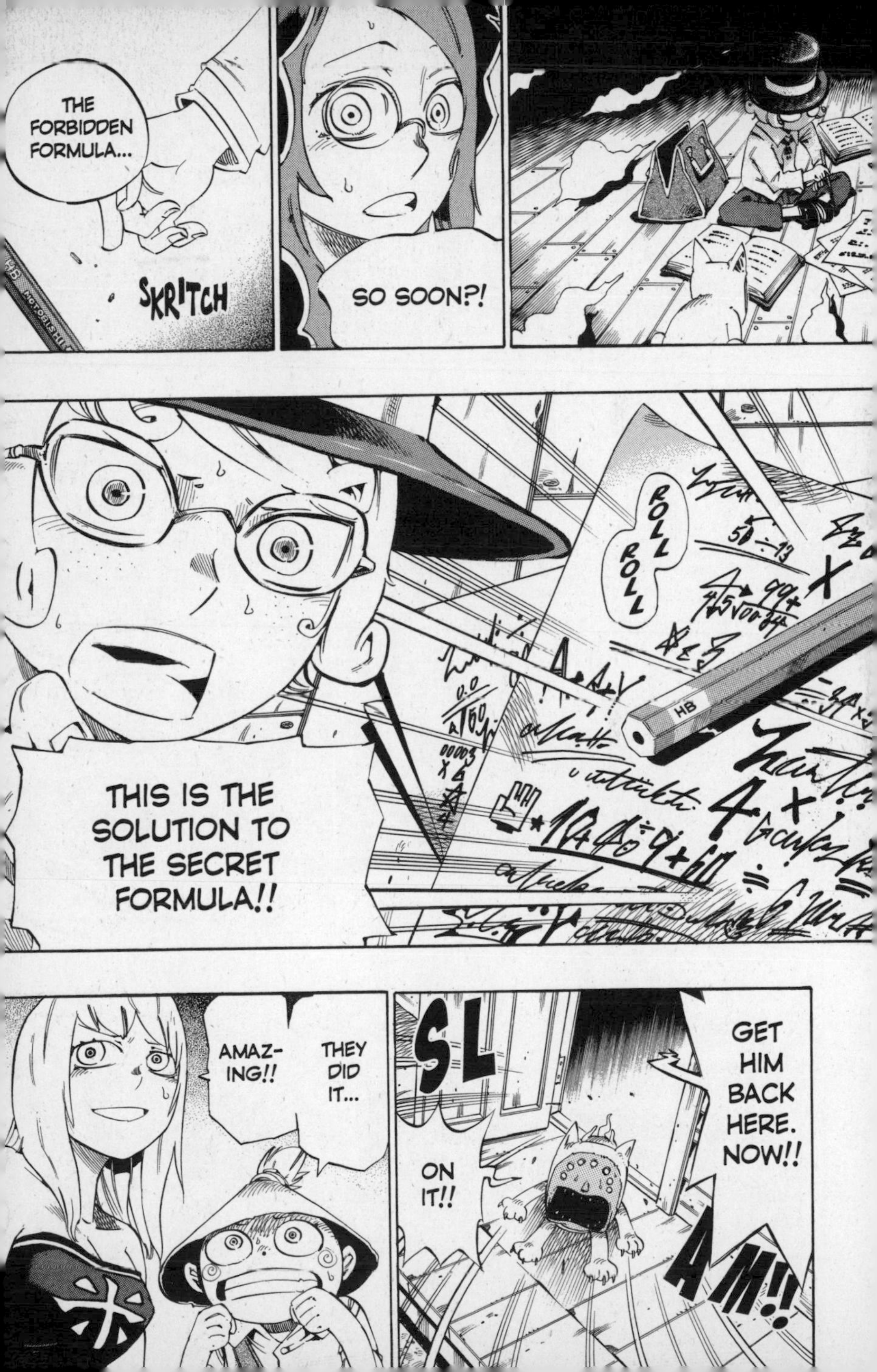
SO SOON?!
THE FORBIDDEN FORMULA...
SKRITCH
ROLL ROLL ROLL
THIS IS THE SOLUTION TO THE SECRET FORMULA!!
GET HIM BACK HERE. NOW!!
SL
ON IT!!
AM!!
THEY DID IT...
AMAZ-ING!!

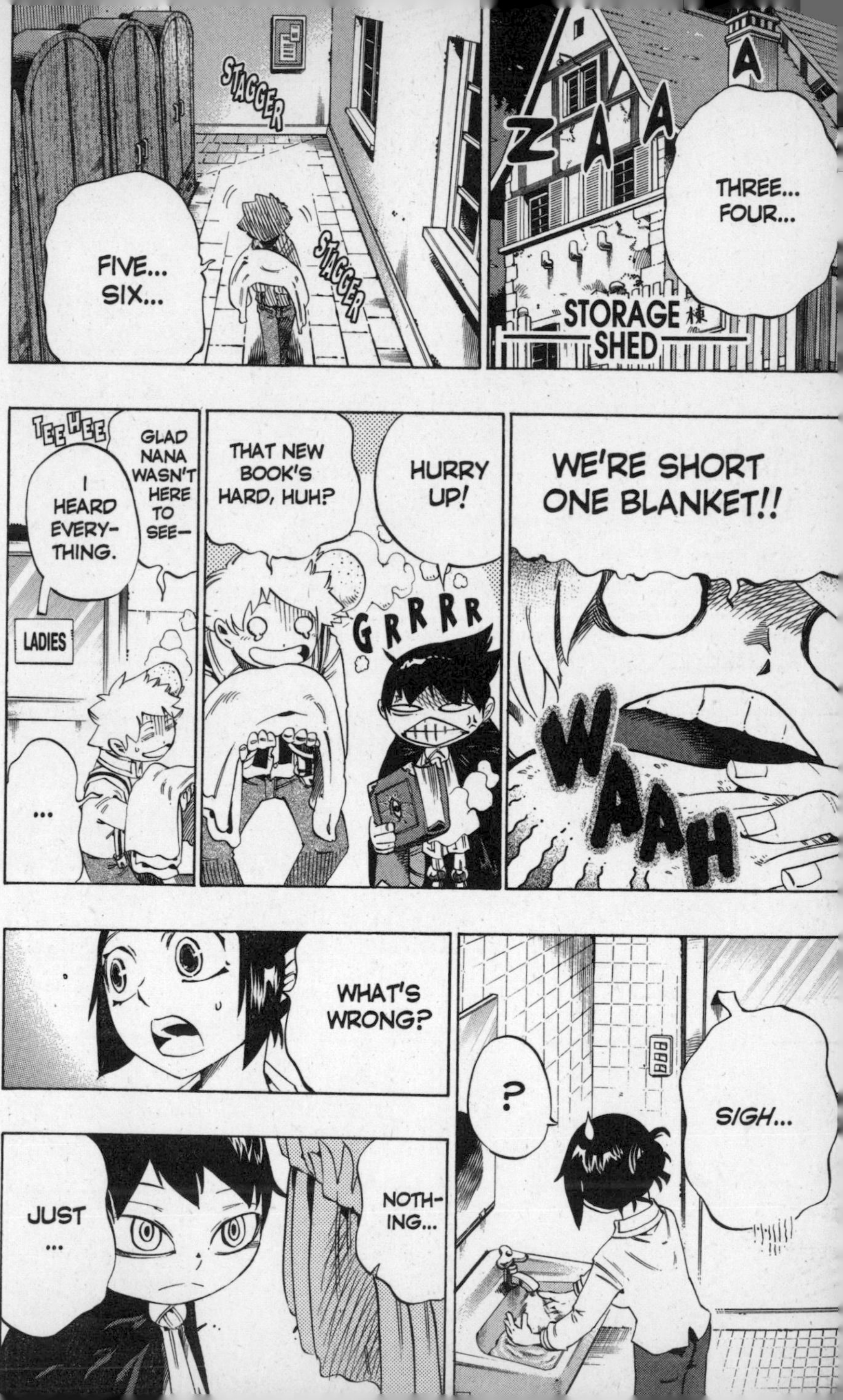
ZAAA
THREE... FOUR...
STORAGE 棟 SHED
STAGGER
STAGGER
FIVE... SIX...
WE'RE SHORT ONE BLANKET!!
WAAAH
HURRY UP!
GRRRR
THAT NEW BOOK'S HARD, HUH?
GLAD NANA WASN'T HERE TO SEE—
TEE HEE
I HEARD EVERY-THING.
LADIES
...
SIGH...
?
WHAT'S WRONG?
NOTH-ING...
JUST ...

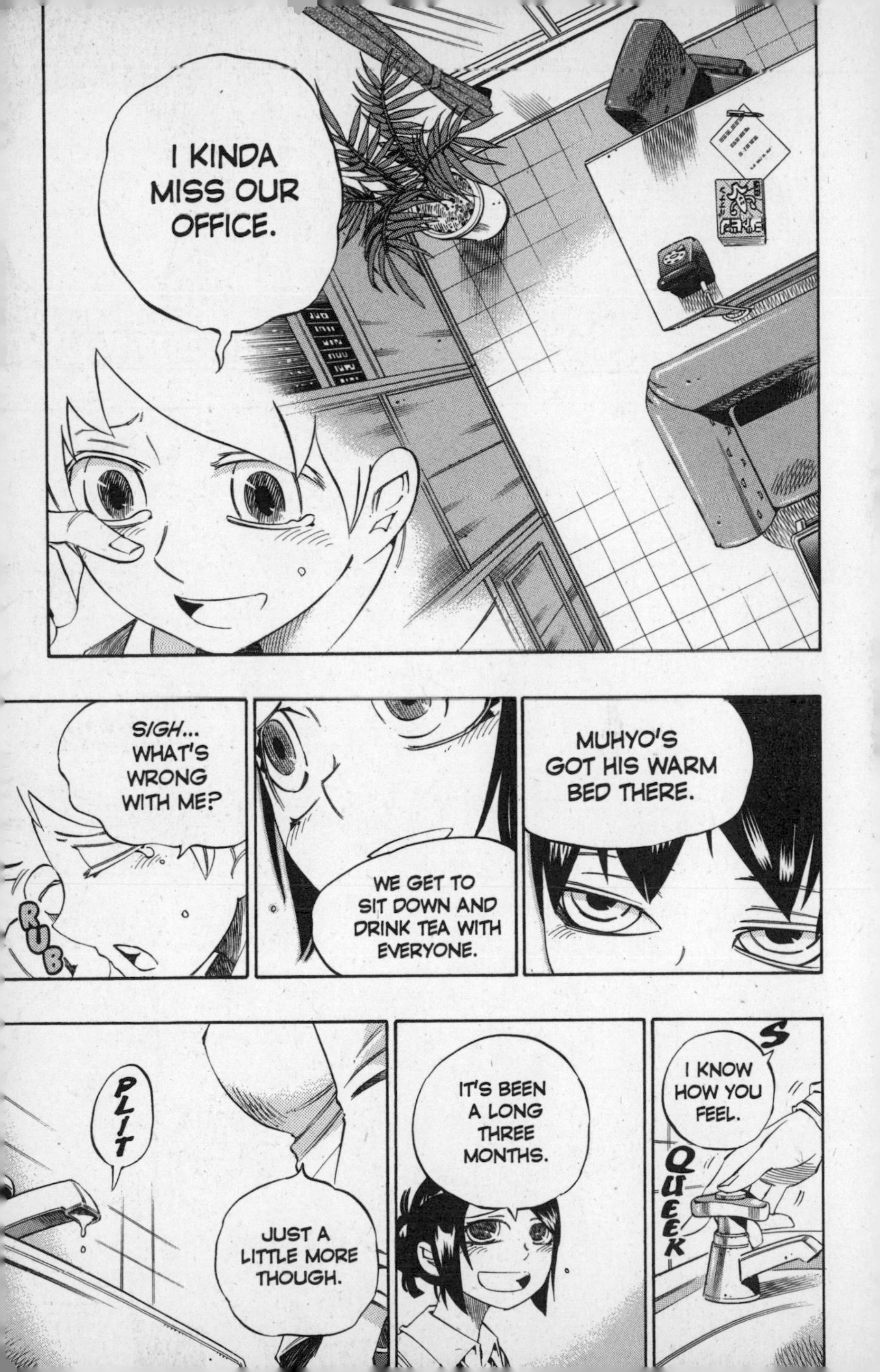
I KINDA MISS OUR OFFICE.
MUHYO'S GOT HIS WARM BED THERE.
WE GET TO SIT DOWN AND DRINK TEA WITH EVERYONE.
SIGH... WHAT'S WRONG WITH ME?
RUB
S
I KNOW HOW YOU FEEL.
QUEEK
IT'S BEEN A LONG THREE MONTHS.
JUST A LITTLE MORE THOUGH.
PLIT

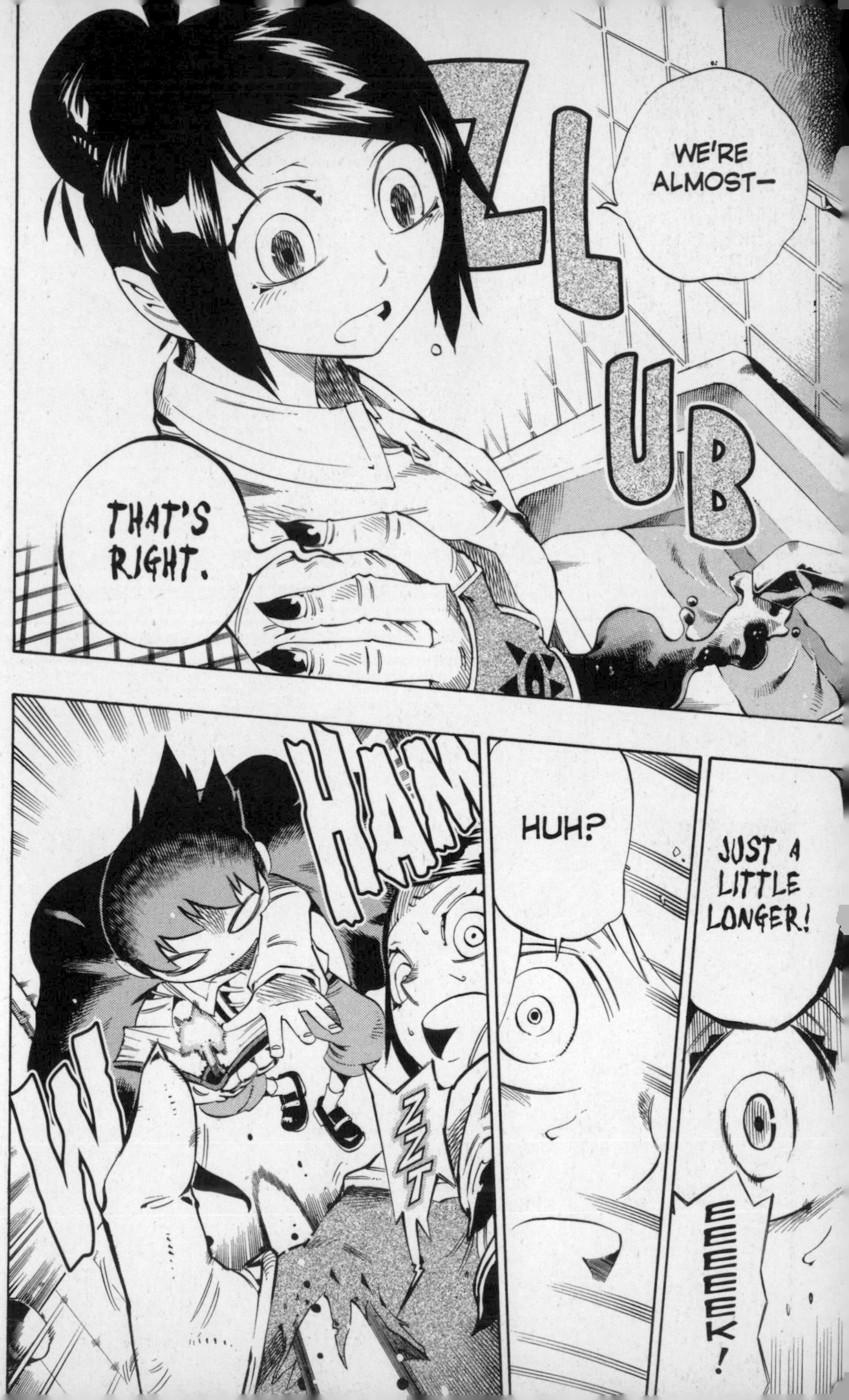
WE'RE ALMOST—
ZLLUB
THAT'S RIGHT.
JUST A LITTLE LONGER!
EEEEEK!
HUH?
HAM
ZZT

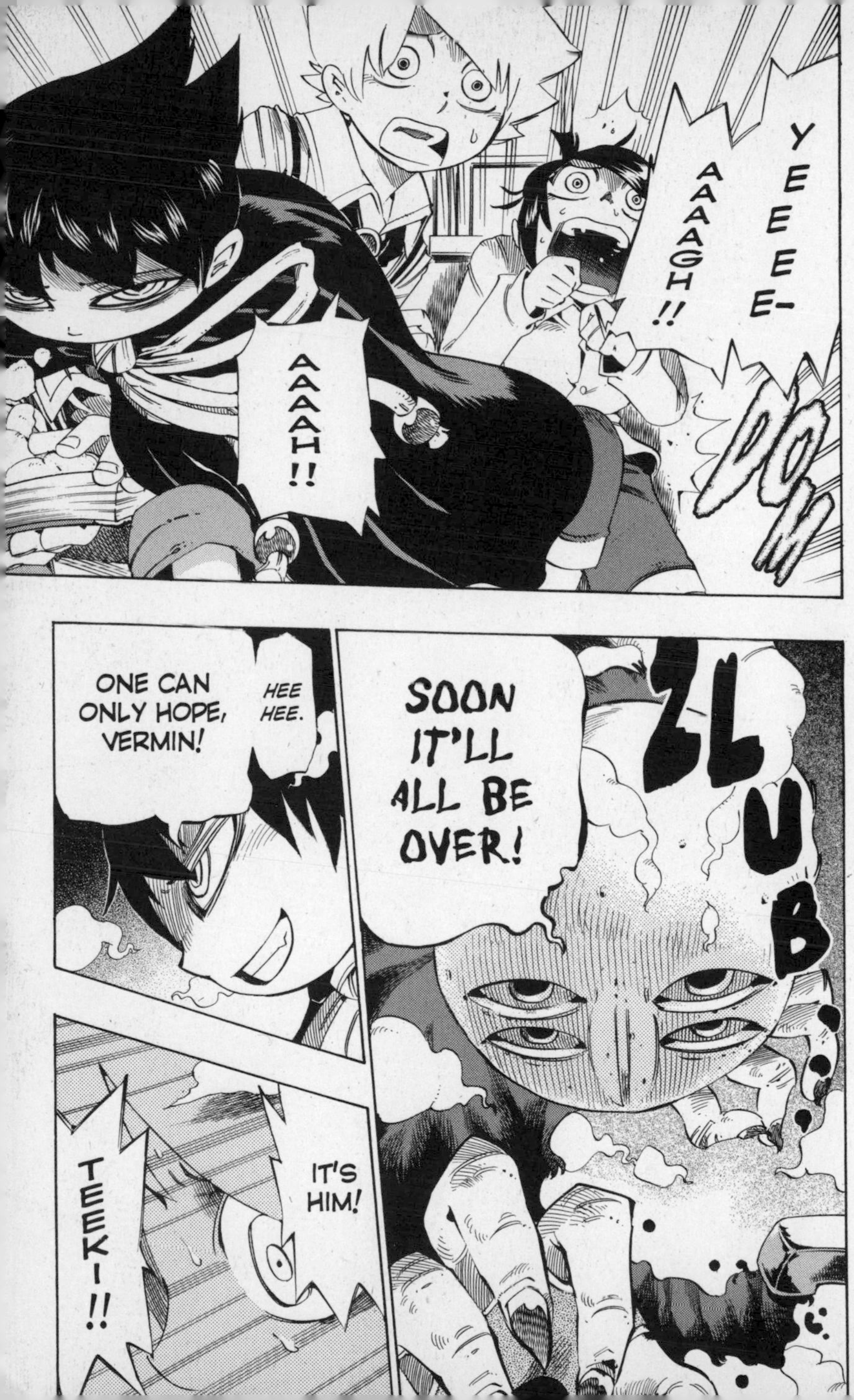
YEEEEE-
AAAAGH!!
DOM
AAAAH!!
SOON IT'LL ALL BE OVER!
ZLUB
HEE HEE.
ONE CAN ONLY HOPE, VERMIN!
IT'S HIM!
TEEKI!!

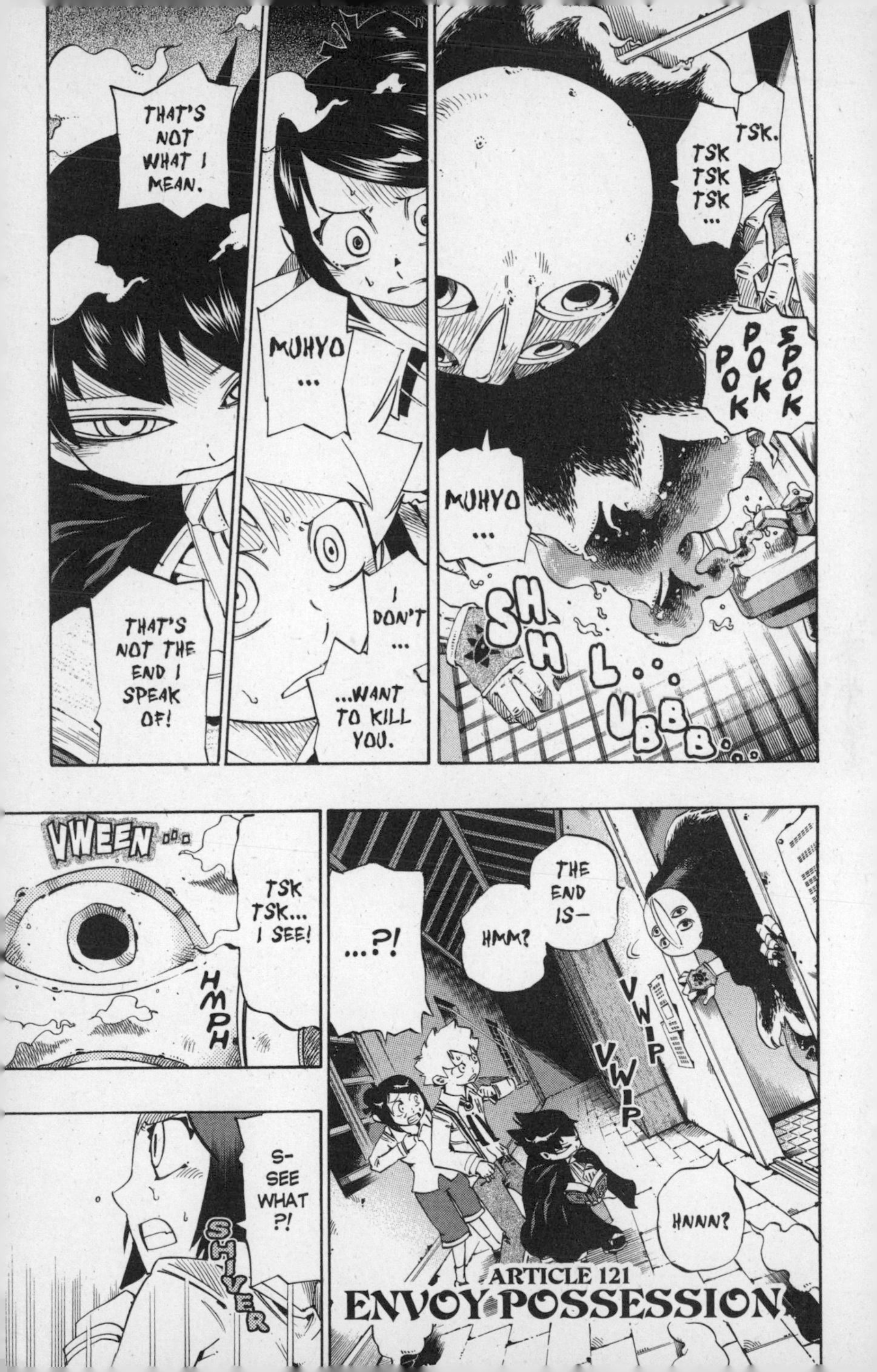
TSK. TSK TSK TSK ...
SPOK POK POK
MUHYO ...
SHHLUBBB...
MUHYO ...
I DON'T ...
...WANT TO KILL YOU.
THAT'S NOT WHAT I MEAN.
THAT'S NOT THE END I SPEAK OF!
THE END IS—
HMM?
...?!
VWIP VWIP
HNNN?
ARTICLE 121
ENVOY POSSESSION
VWEEN...
TSK TSK... I SEE!
HMPH
S- SEE WHAT?!
SHIVER

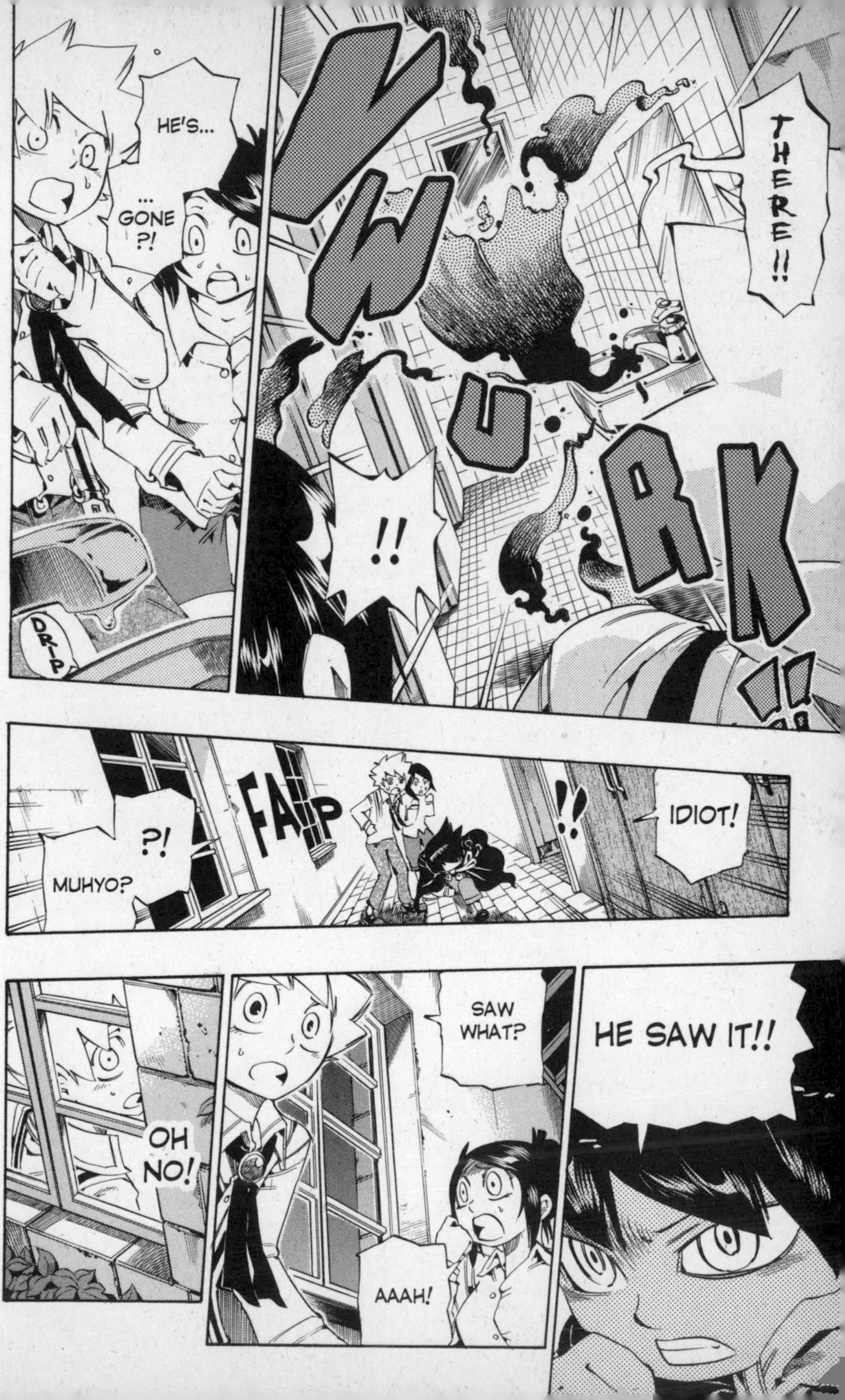
THERE!!
WWURK!!
!!
HE'S...
...GONE?!
DRIP
IDIOT!
!!
FAP
?!
MUHYO?
HE SAW IT!!
SAW WHAT?
AAAH!
OH NO!

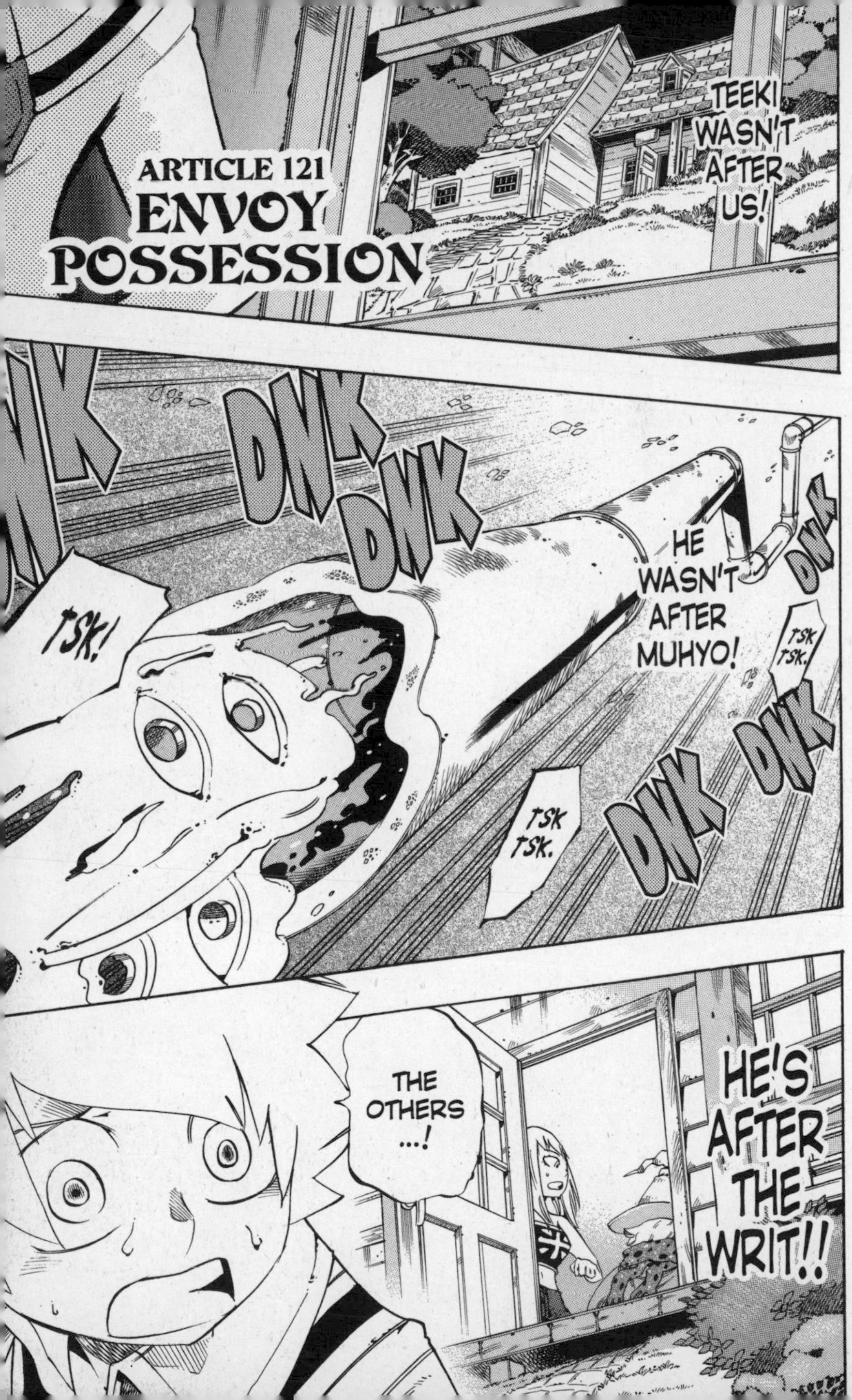
TEEKI WASN'T AFTER US!
ARTICLE 121
ENVOY POSSESSION
DNK
DNK DNK
HE WASN'T AFTER MUHYO!
TSK TSK.
DNK DNK
TSK TSK.
DNK DNK
TSK!
HE'S AFTER THE WRIT!!
THE OTHERS ...!

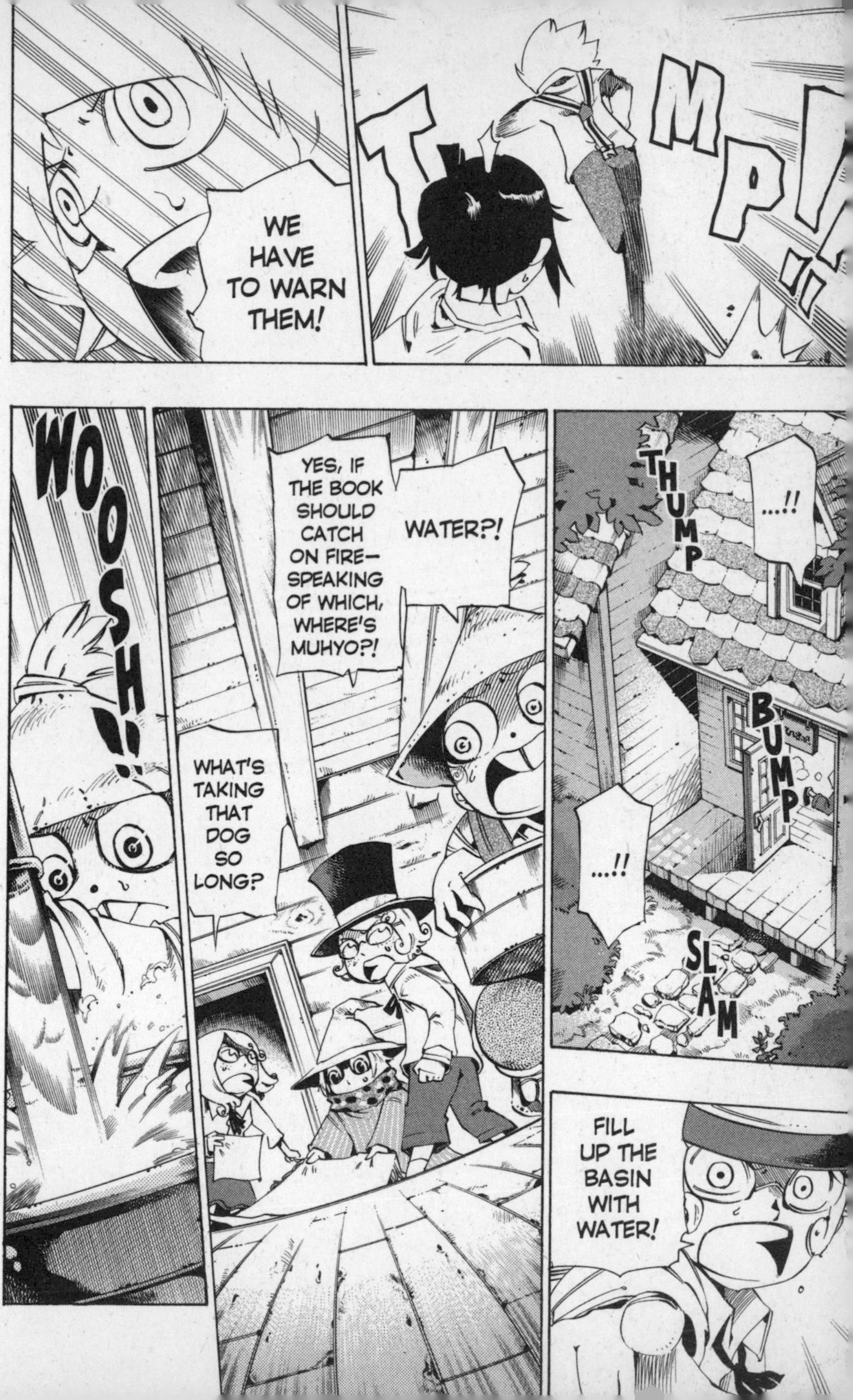
TMP!!
WE HAVE TO WARN THEM!
...!!
THUMP
BUMP
...!!
SLAM
FILL UP THE BASIN WITH WATER!
WATER?!
YES, IF THE BOOK SHOULD CATCH ON FIRE—SPEAKING OF WHICH, WHERE'S MUHYO?!
WHAT'S TAKING THAT DOG SO LONG?
WOOSH!!

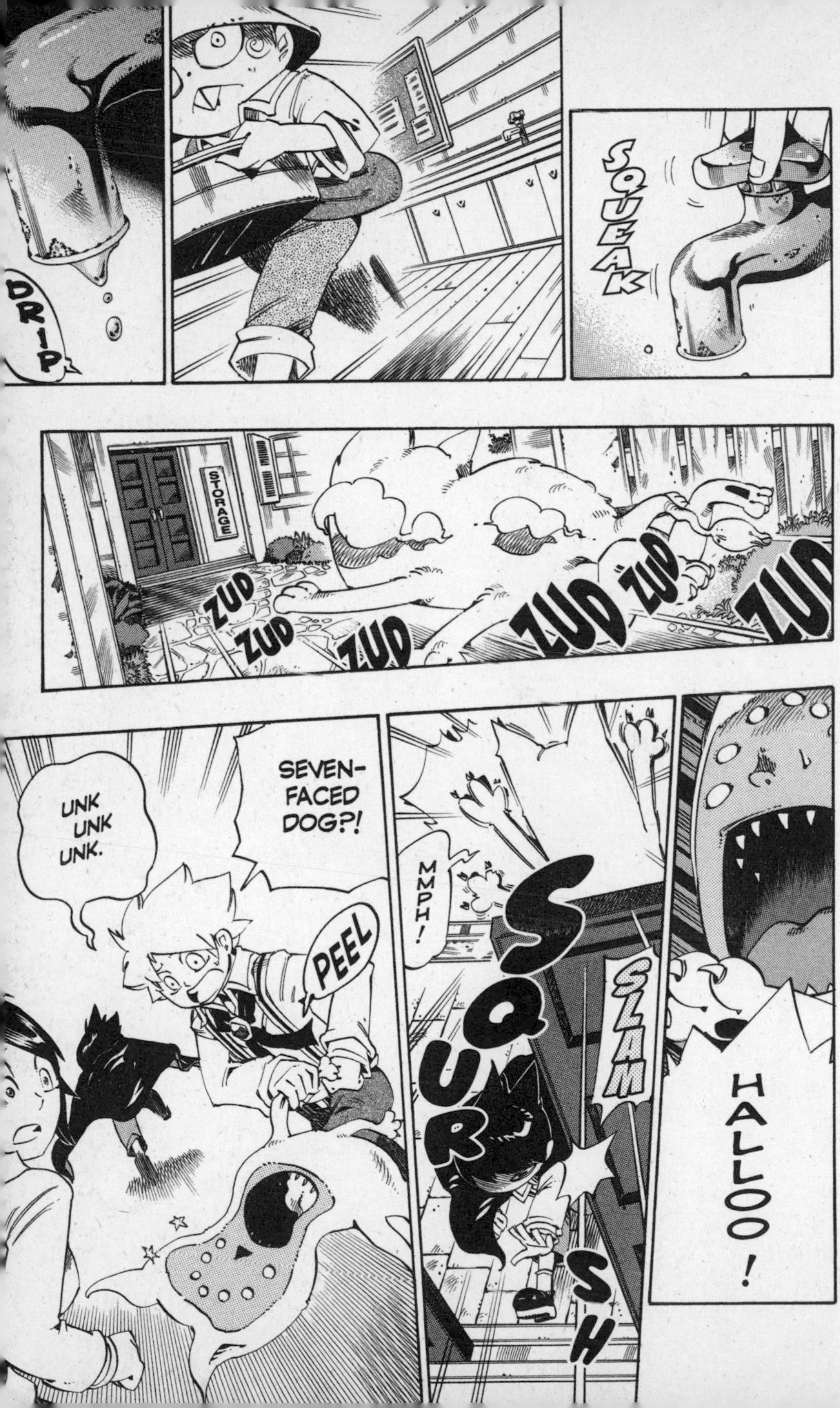
SQUEAK
DRIP
ZUD
ZUD
ZUD
ZUD
ZUD
ZUD
ZUD
HALLOO!
SLAM
SQURSH
MMPH!
SEVEN-FACED DOG?!
UNK UNK UNK.
PEEL

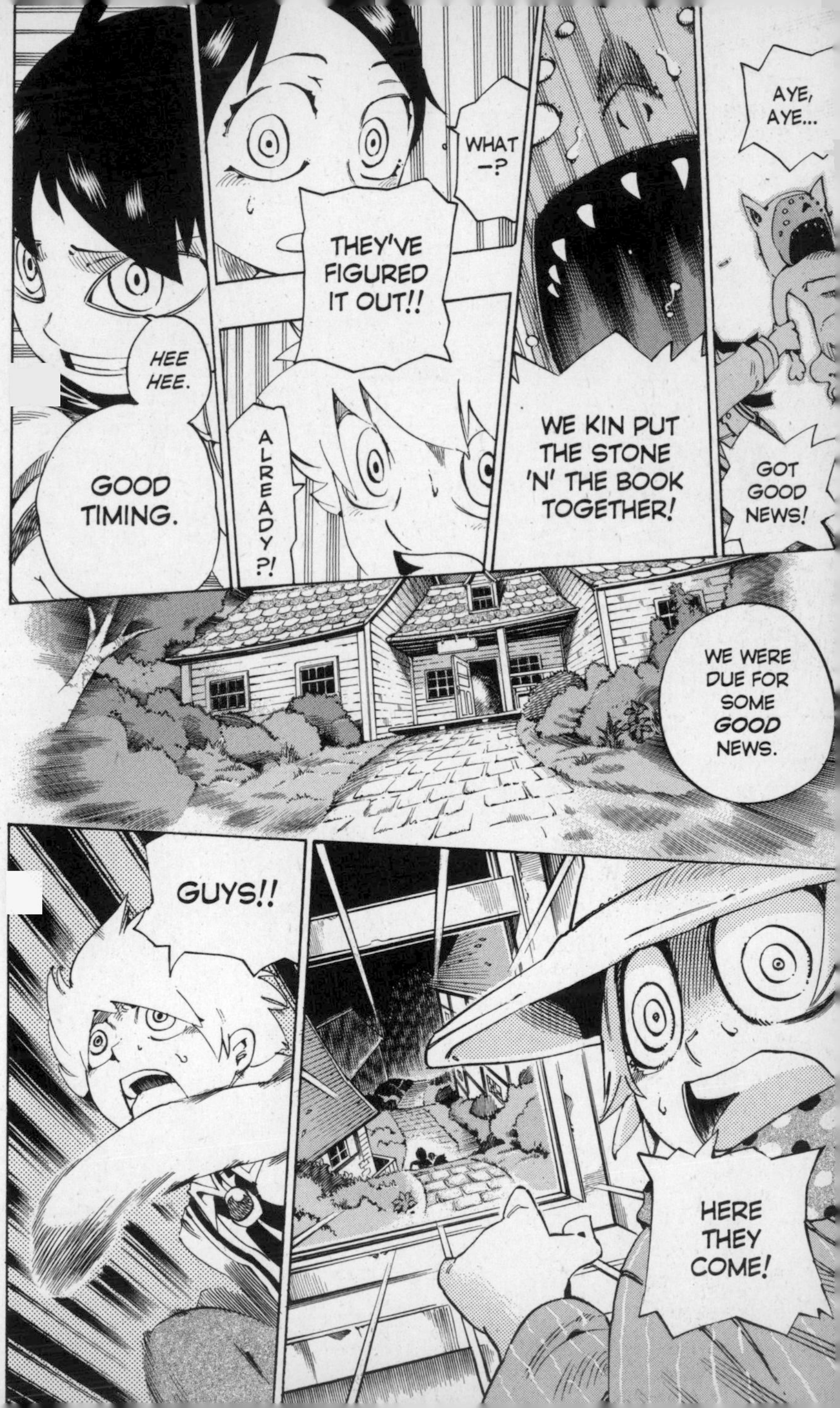
AYE, AYE...
GOT GOOD NEWS!
WE KIN PUT THE STONE 'N' THE BOOK TOGETHER!
WHAT—?
THEY'VE FIGURED IT OUT!!
ALREADY?!
HEE HEE.
GOOD TIMING.
WE WERE DUE FOR SOME GOOD NEWS.
HERE THEY COME!
GUYS!!

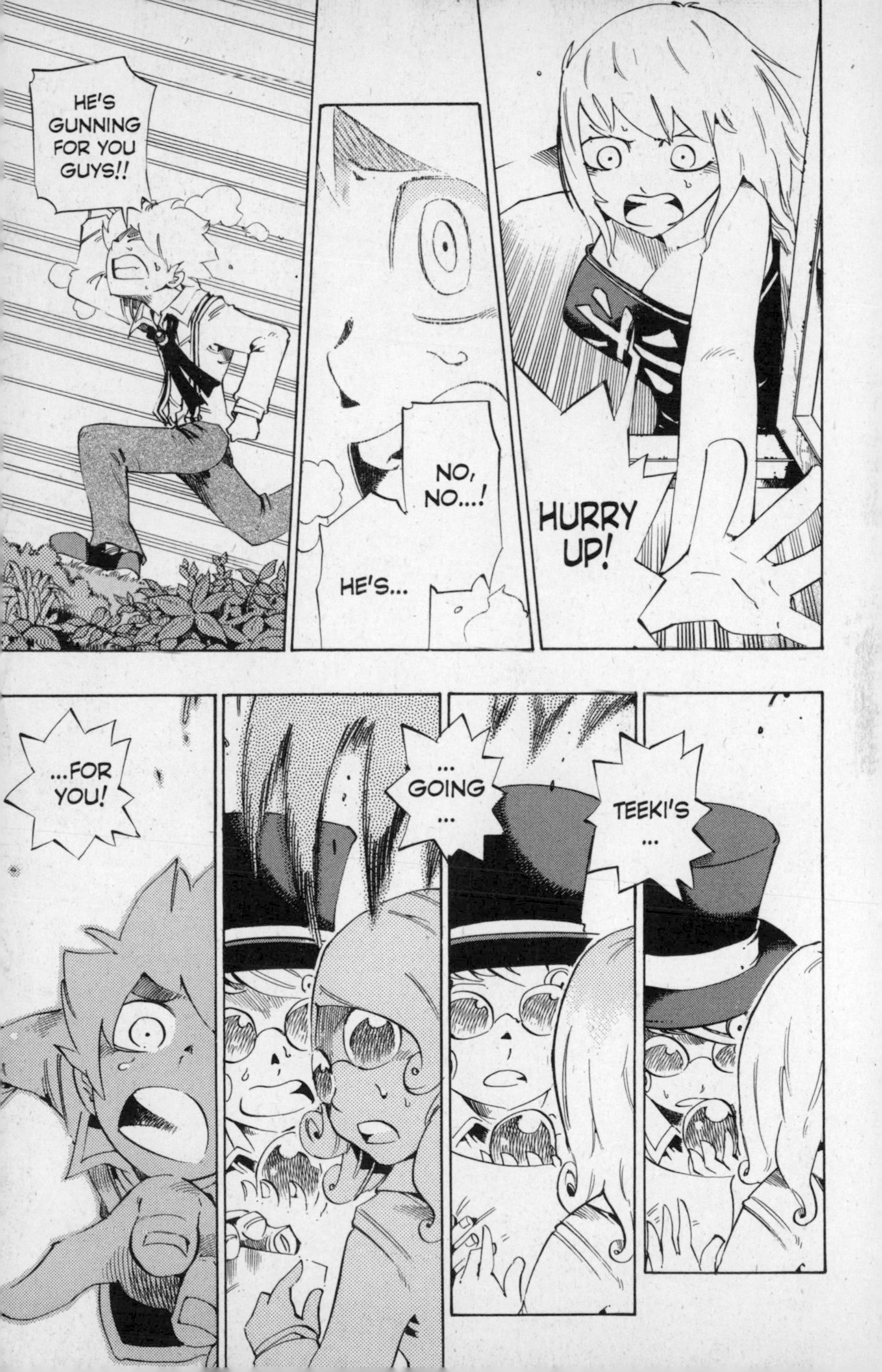
HURRY UP!
NO, NO...!
HE'S...
HE'S GUNNING FOR YOU GUYS!!
TEEKI'S ...
... GOING ...
...FOR YOU!

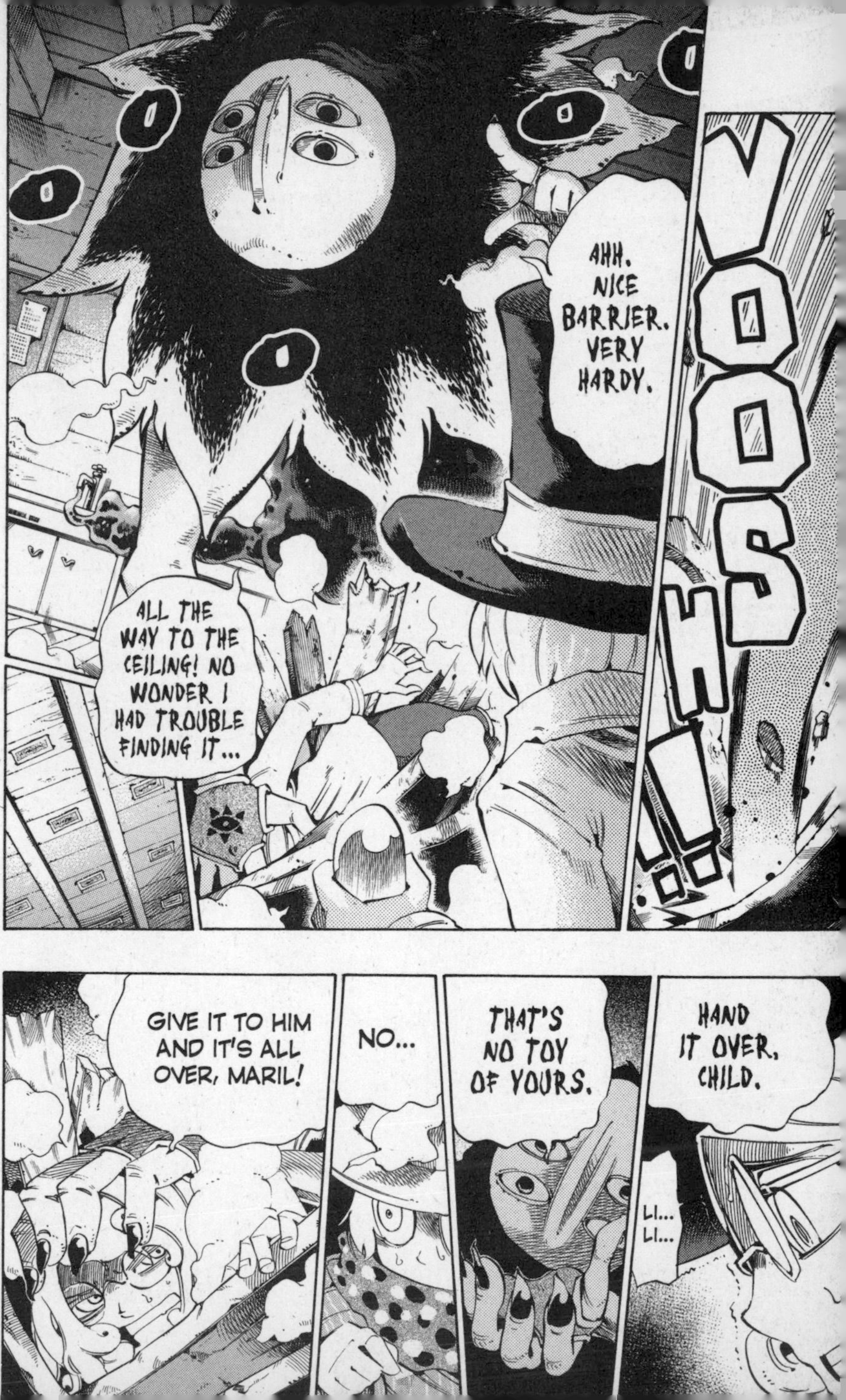
VOOSH!!
AHH. NICE BARRIER. VERY HARDY.
ALL THE WAY TO THE CEILING! NO WONDER I HAD TROUBLE FINDING IT...
HAND IT OVER, CHILD.
LI... LI...
THAT'S NO TOY OF YOURS.
NO...
GIVE IT TO HIM AND IT'S ALL OVER, MARIL!

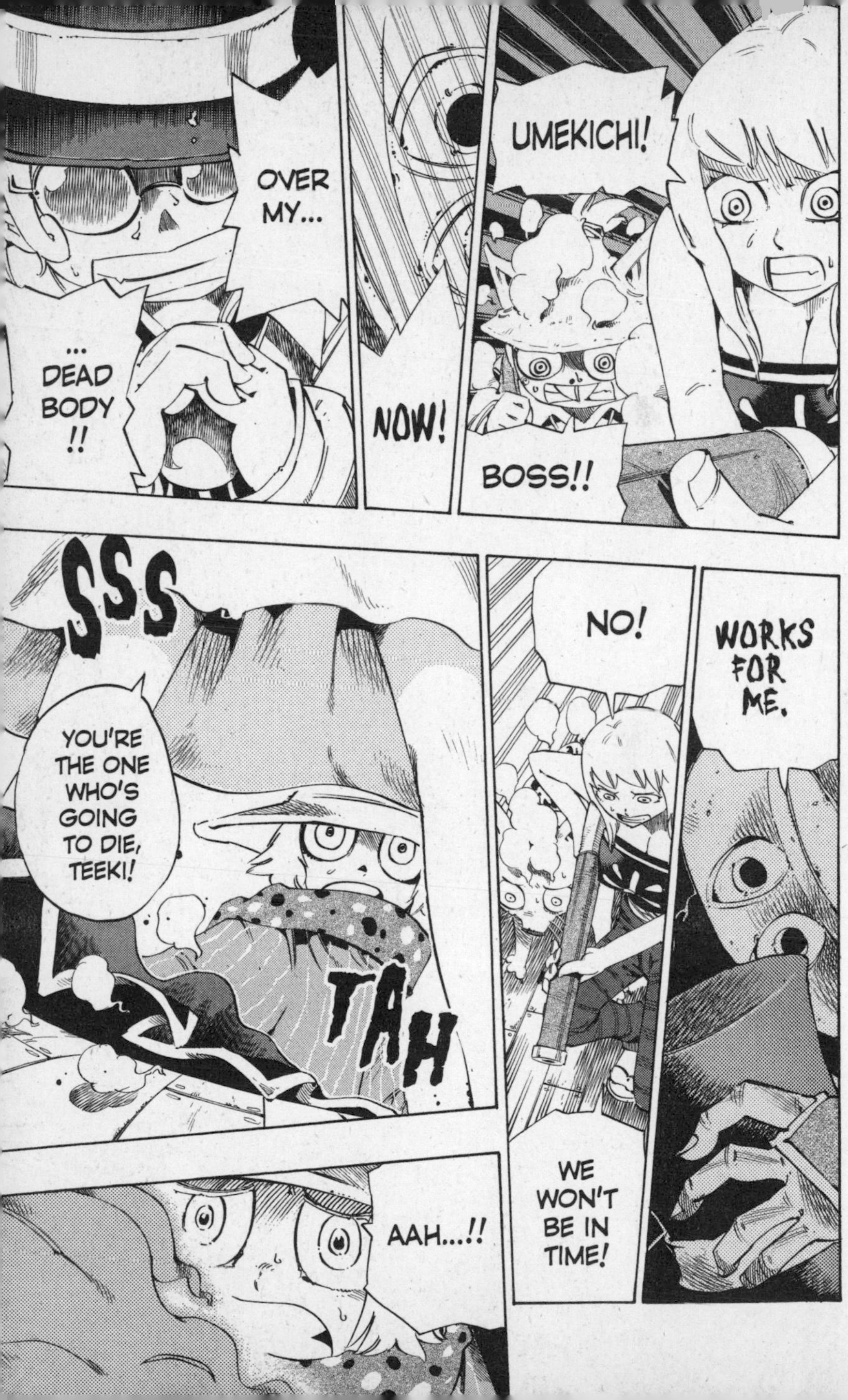
UMEKICHI!
BOSS!!
NOW!
OVER MY...
... DEAD BODY !!
WORKS FOR ME.
NO!
WE WON'T BE IN TIME!
SSS
YOU'RE THE ONE WHO'S GOING TO DIE, TEEKI!
TAH
AAH...!!

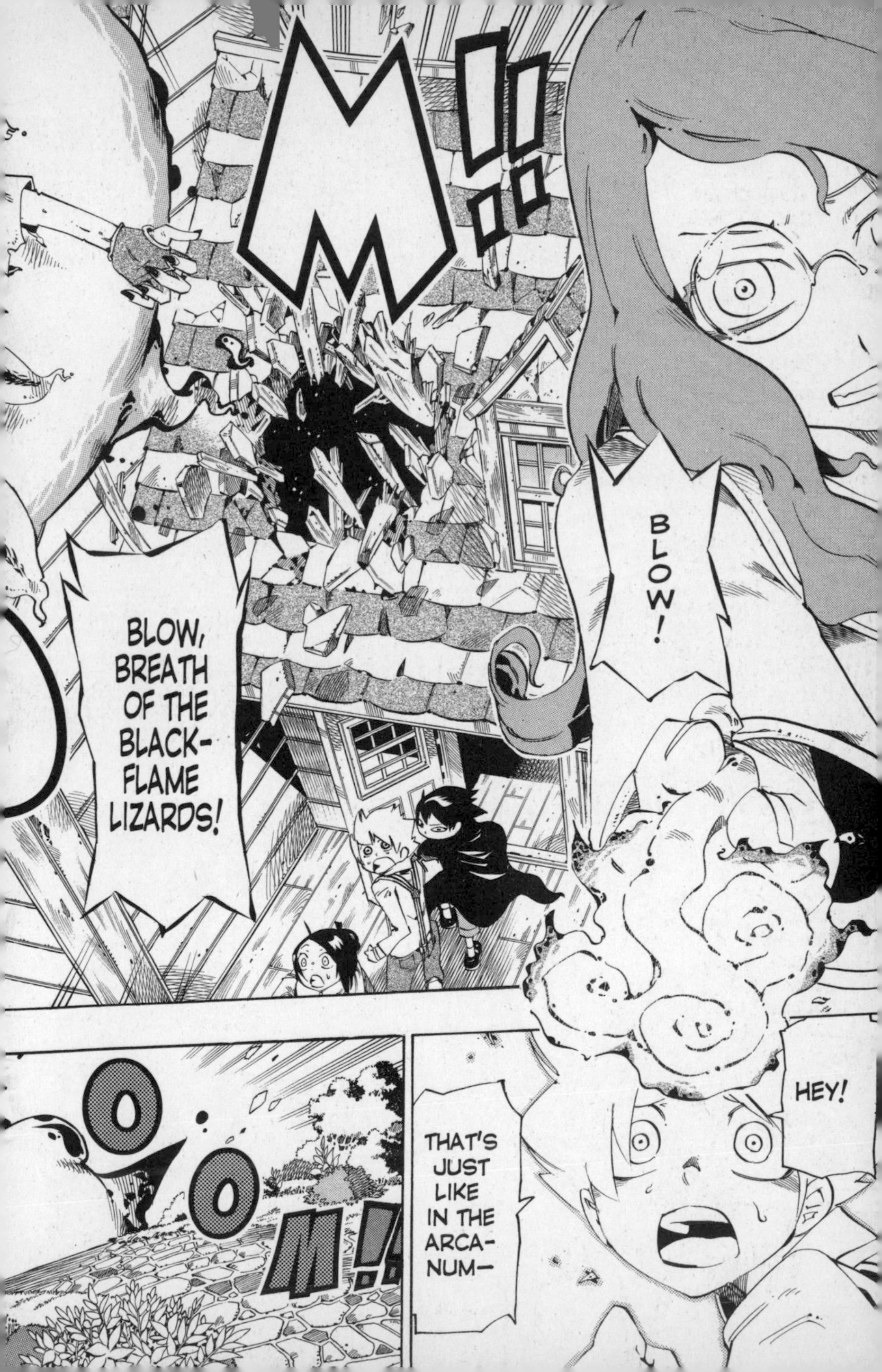
M!!
BLOW!
BLOW, BREATH OF THE BLACK-FLAME LIZARDS!
HEY!
THAT'S JUST LIKE IN THE ARCANUM—
OOM!!

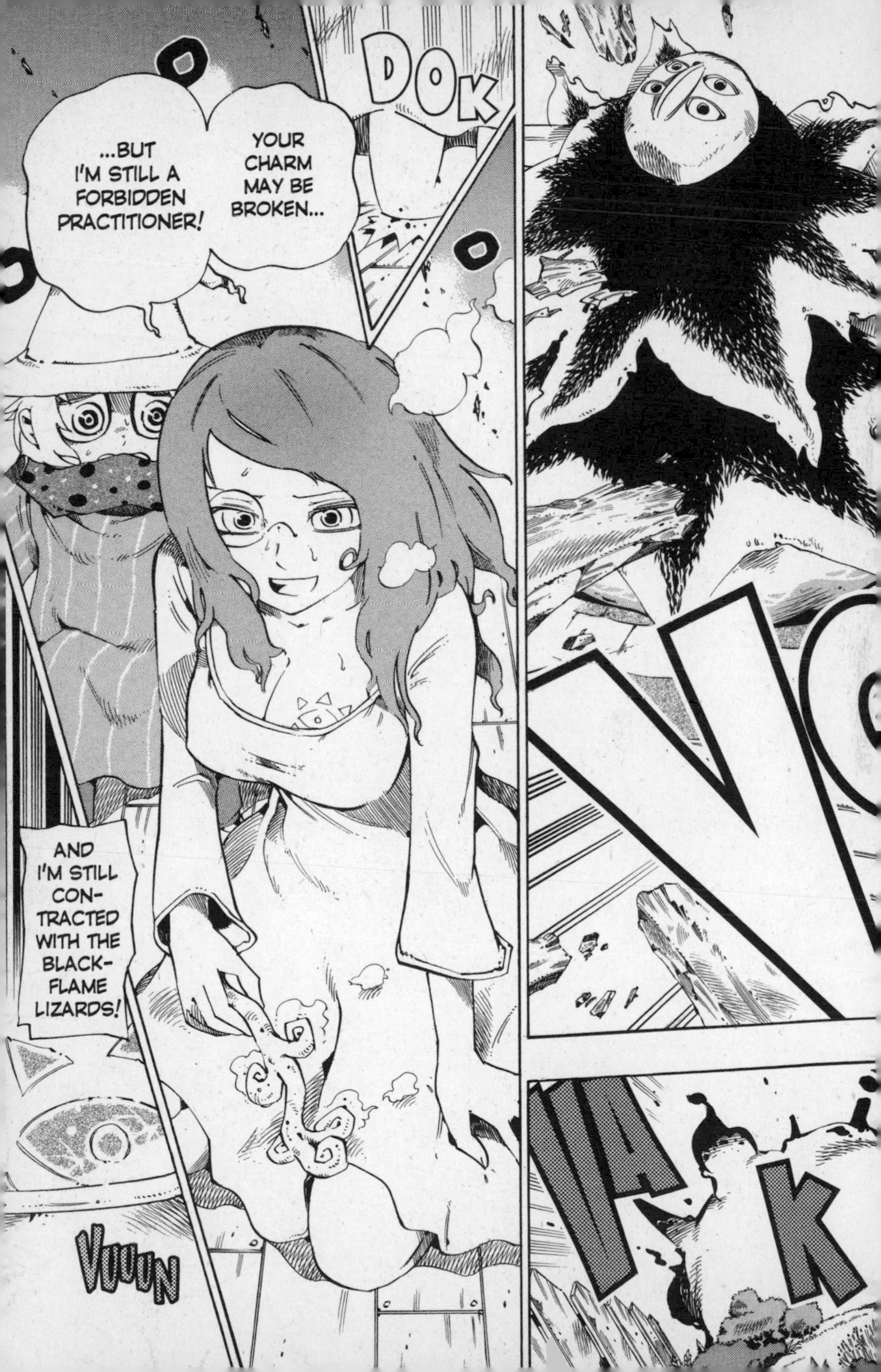
DOK
YOUR CHARM MAY BE BROKEN...
...BUT I'M STILL A FORBIDDEN PRACTITIONER!
AND I'M STILL CON-TRACTED WITH THE BLACK-FLAME LIZARDS!
VUUUN

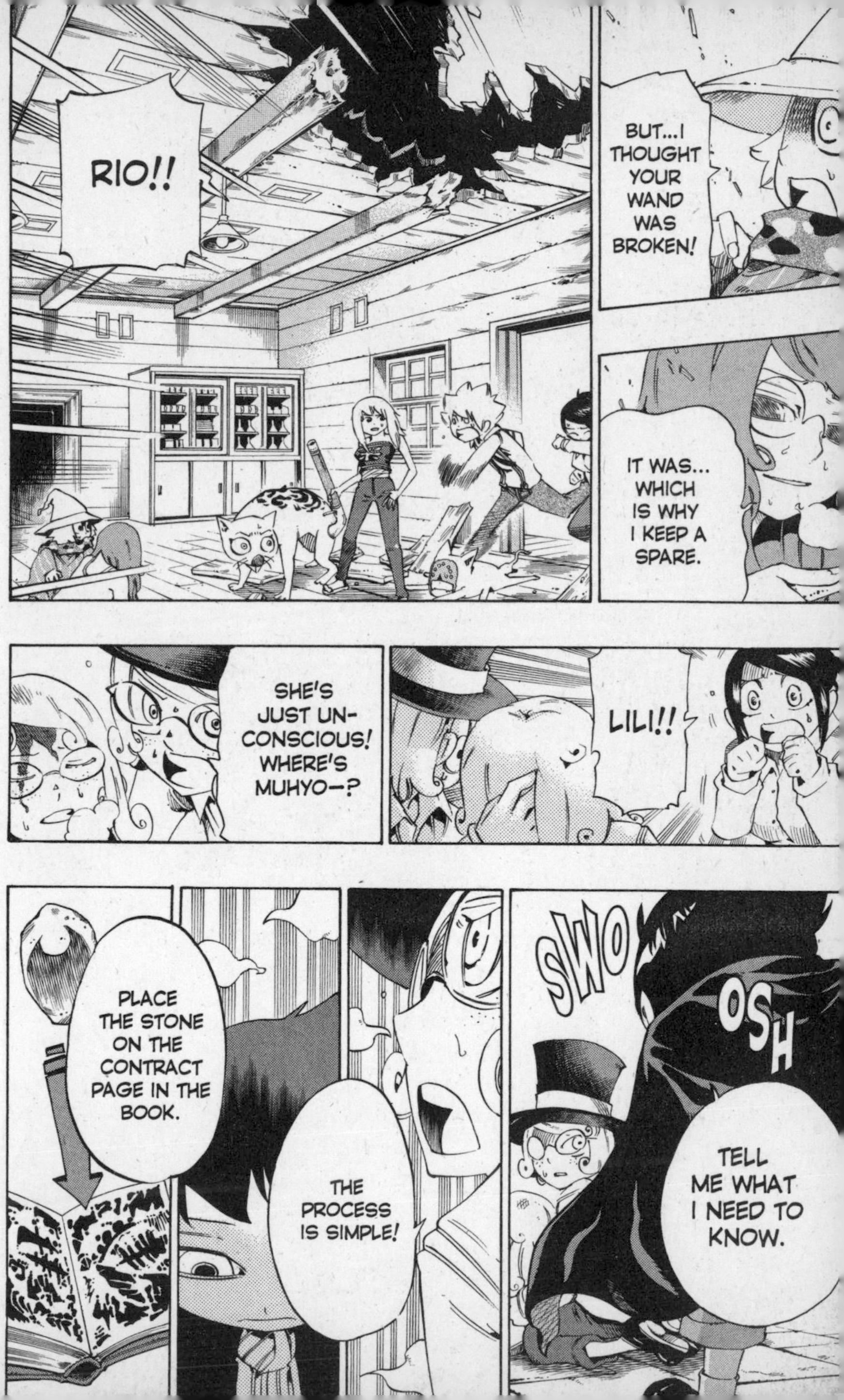
BUT...I THOUGHT YOUR WAND WAS BROKEN!
IT WAS... WHICH IS WHY I KEEP A SPARE.
RIO!!
LILI!!
SHE'S JUST UN-CONSCIOUS! WHERE'S MUHYO—?
SWOOSH
TELL ME WHAT I NEED TO KNOW.
THE PROCESS IS SIMPLE!
PLACE THE STONE ON THE CONTRACT PAGE IN THE BOOK.

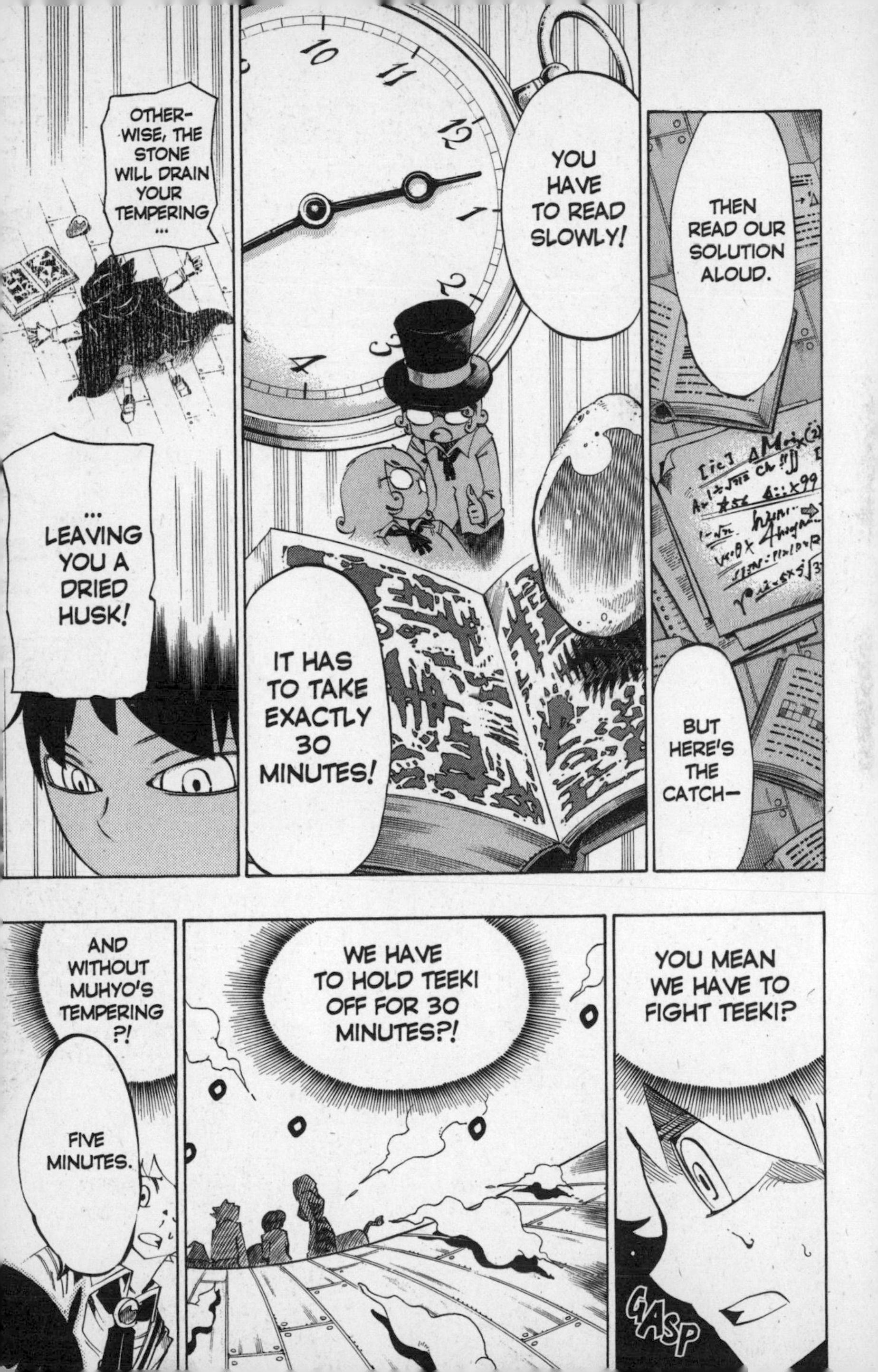
THEN READ OUR SOLUTION ALOUD.
BUT HERE'S THE CATCH—
YOU HAVE TO READ SLOWLY!
IT HAS TO TAKE EXACTLY 30 MINUTES!
OTHER-WISE, THE STONE WILL DRAIN YOUR TEMPERING ...
... LEAVING YOU A DRIED HUSK!
YOU MEAN WE HAVE TO FIGHT TEEKI?
GASP
WE HAVE TO HOLD TEEKI OFF FOR 30 MINUTES?!
AND WITHOUT MUHYO'S TEMPERING ?!
FIVE MINUTES.

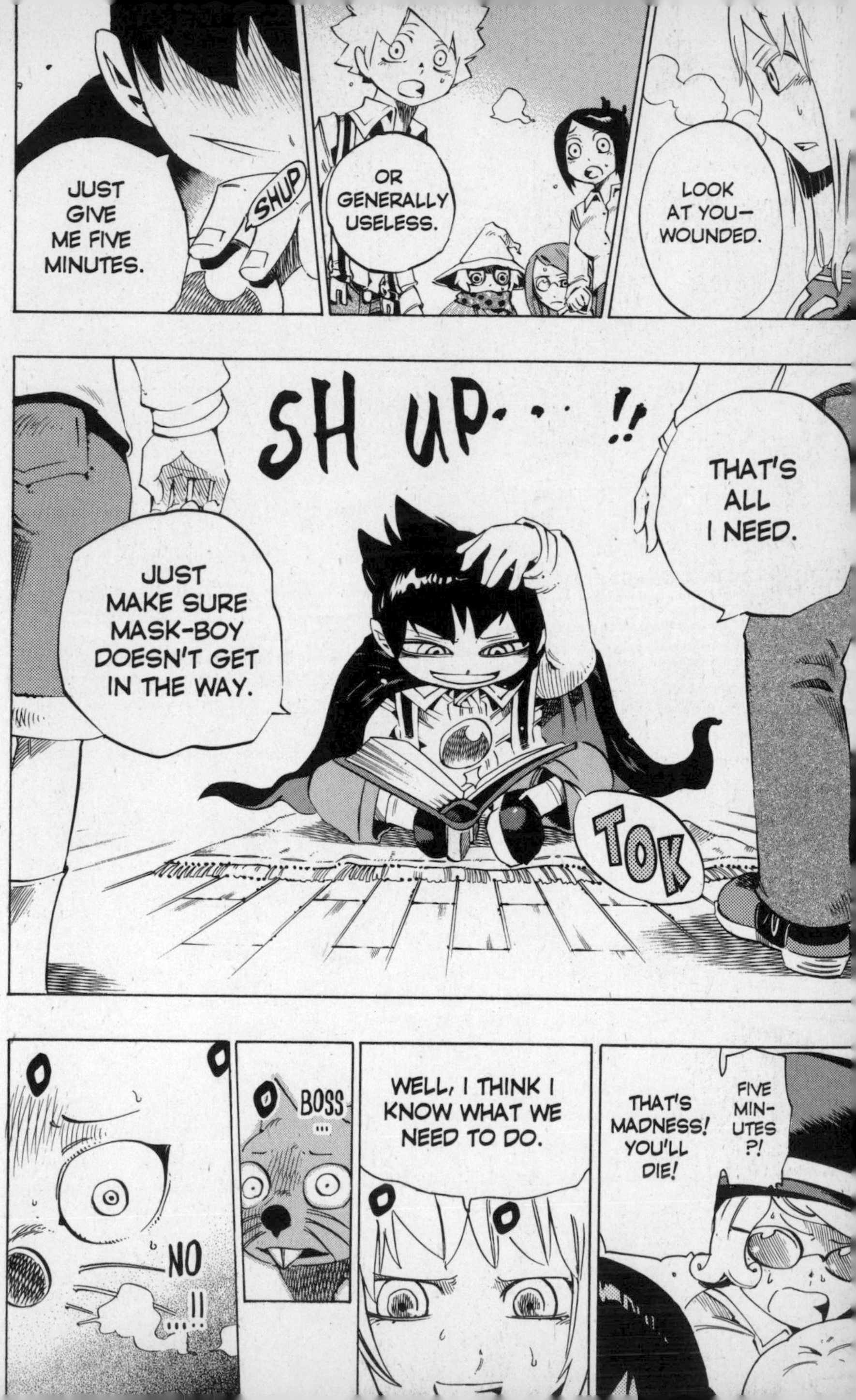
LOOK AT YOU— WOUNDED.
OR GENERALLY USELESS.
SHUP
JUST GIVE ME FIVE MINUTES.
THAT'S ALL I NEED.
SH UP...!!
JUST MAKE SURE MASK-BOY DOESN'T GET IN THE WAY.
TOK
FIVE MIN-UTES?!
THAT'S MADNESS! YOU'LL DIE!
WELL, I THINK I KNOW WHAT WE NEED TO DO.
BOSS...
NO...!!

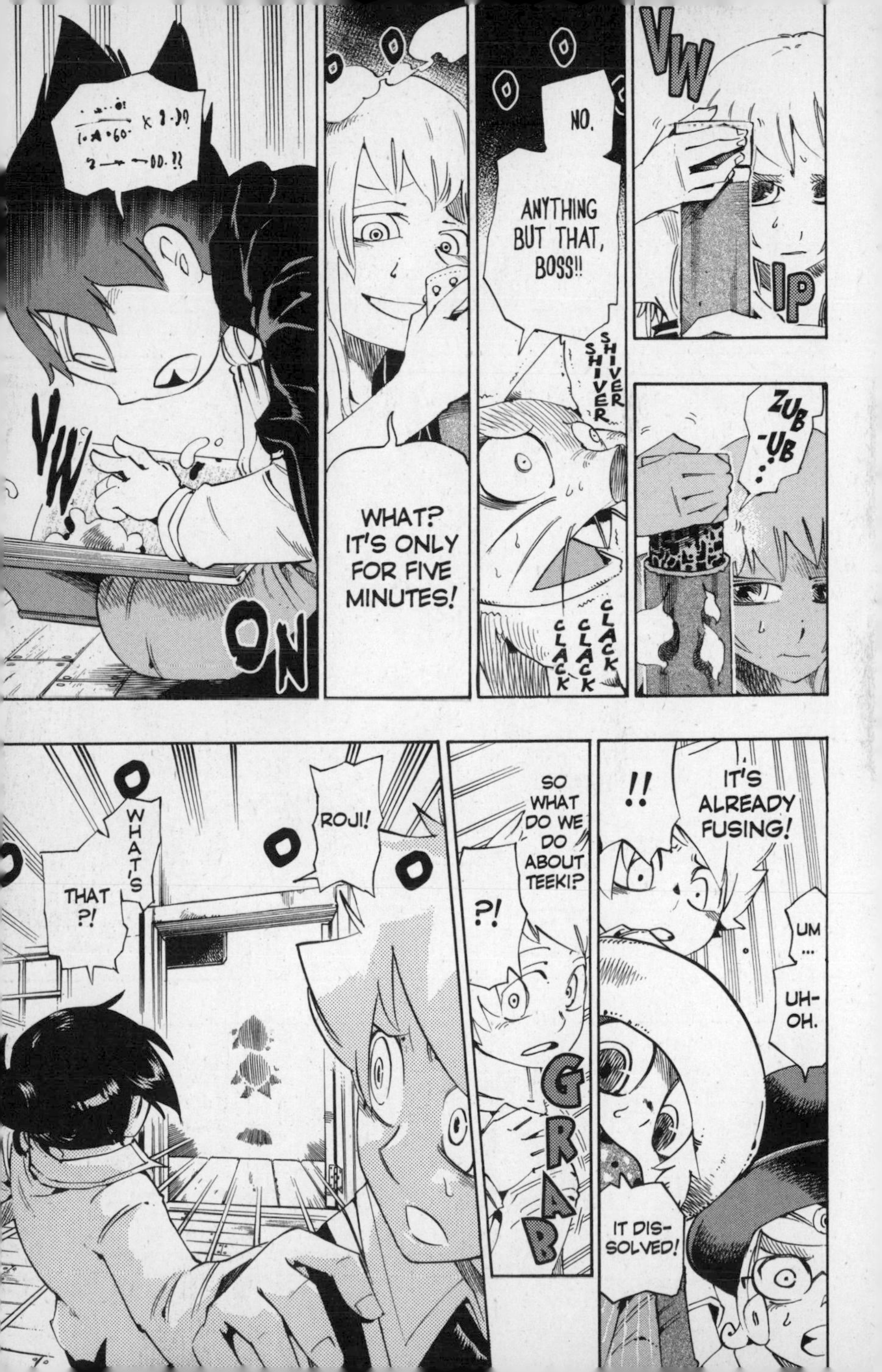
VW
IP
ZUB-UB...
NO.
ANYTHING BUT THAT, BOSS!!
SHIVER SHIVER
CLACK CLACK CLACK
WHAT? IT'S ONLY FOR FIVE MINUTES!
VW
ON
IT'S ALREADY FUSING!
!!
UM ... UH-OH.
IT DIS-SOLVED!
SO WHAT DO WE DO ABOUT TEEKI!?
?!
GRAB
ROJI!
WHAT'S THAT?!
OOOO

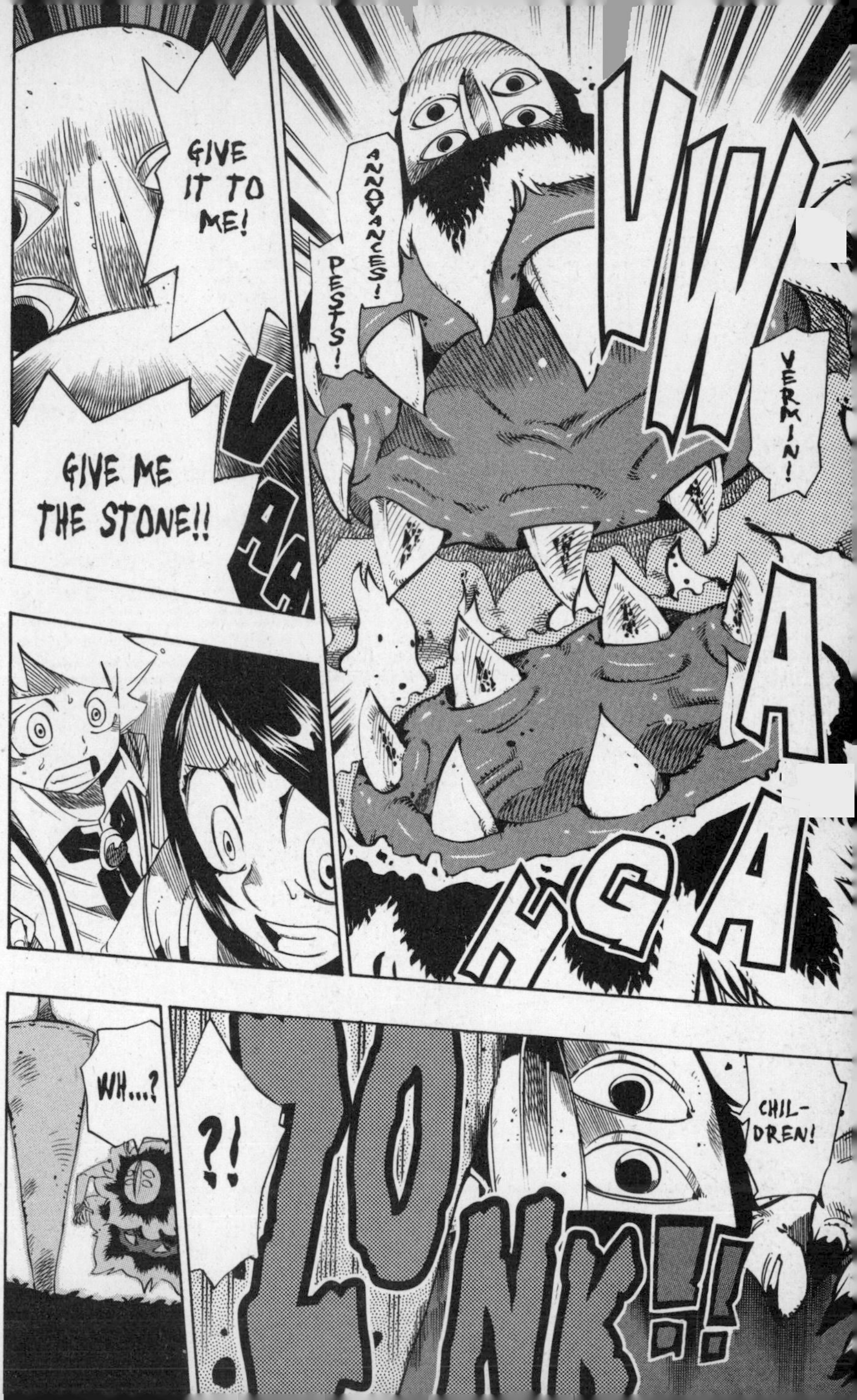
ANNOYANCES!
PESTS!
VERMIN!
VWAAGH
GIVE IT TO ME!
GIVE ME THE STONE!!
VAA
CHIL-DREN!
ZONK!!
?!
WH...?

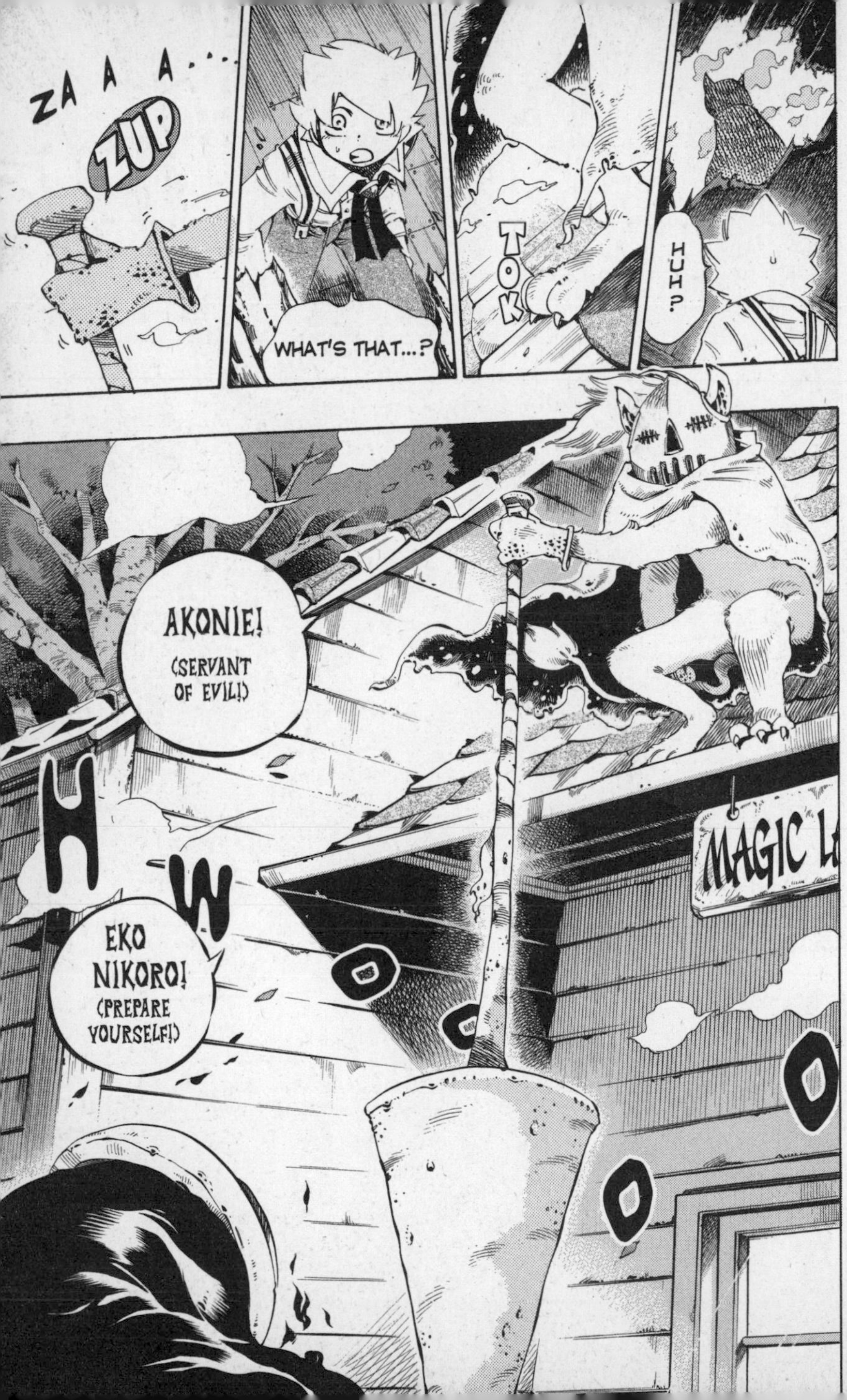
HUH?
TOK
WHAT'S THAT...?
ZA A A...
ZUP
AKONIE! (SERVANT OF EVIL!)
EKO NIKORO! (PREPARE YOURSELF!)
H W O O O O
MAGIC La

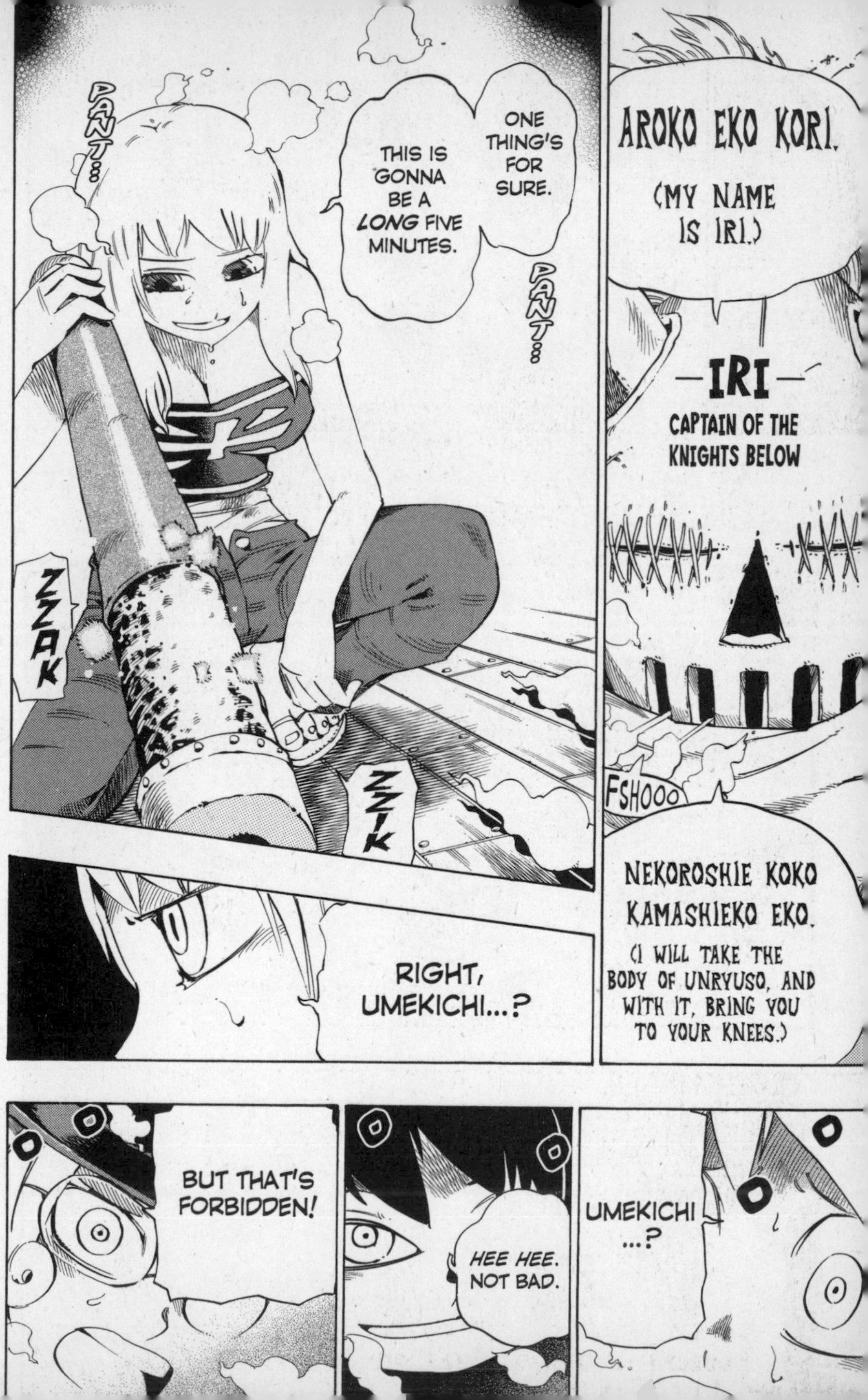
AROKO EKO KORI.
(MY NAME IS IRI.)
—IRI—
CAPTAIN OF THE KNIGHTS BELOW
FSHOOO
PANT...
ONE THING'S FOR SURE.
THIS IS GONNA BE A *LONG* FIVE MINUTES.
PANT...
ZZAK
ZZIK
NEKOROSHIE KOKO KAMASHIEKO EKO.
(I WILL TAKE THE BODY OF UNRYUSO, AND WITH IT, BRING YOU TO YOUR KNEES.)
RIGHT, UMEKICHI...?
UMEKICHI ...?
HEE HEE. NOT BAD.
BUT THAT'S FORBIDDEN!

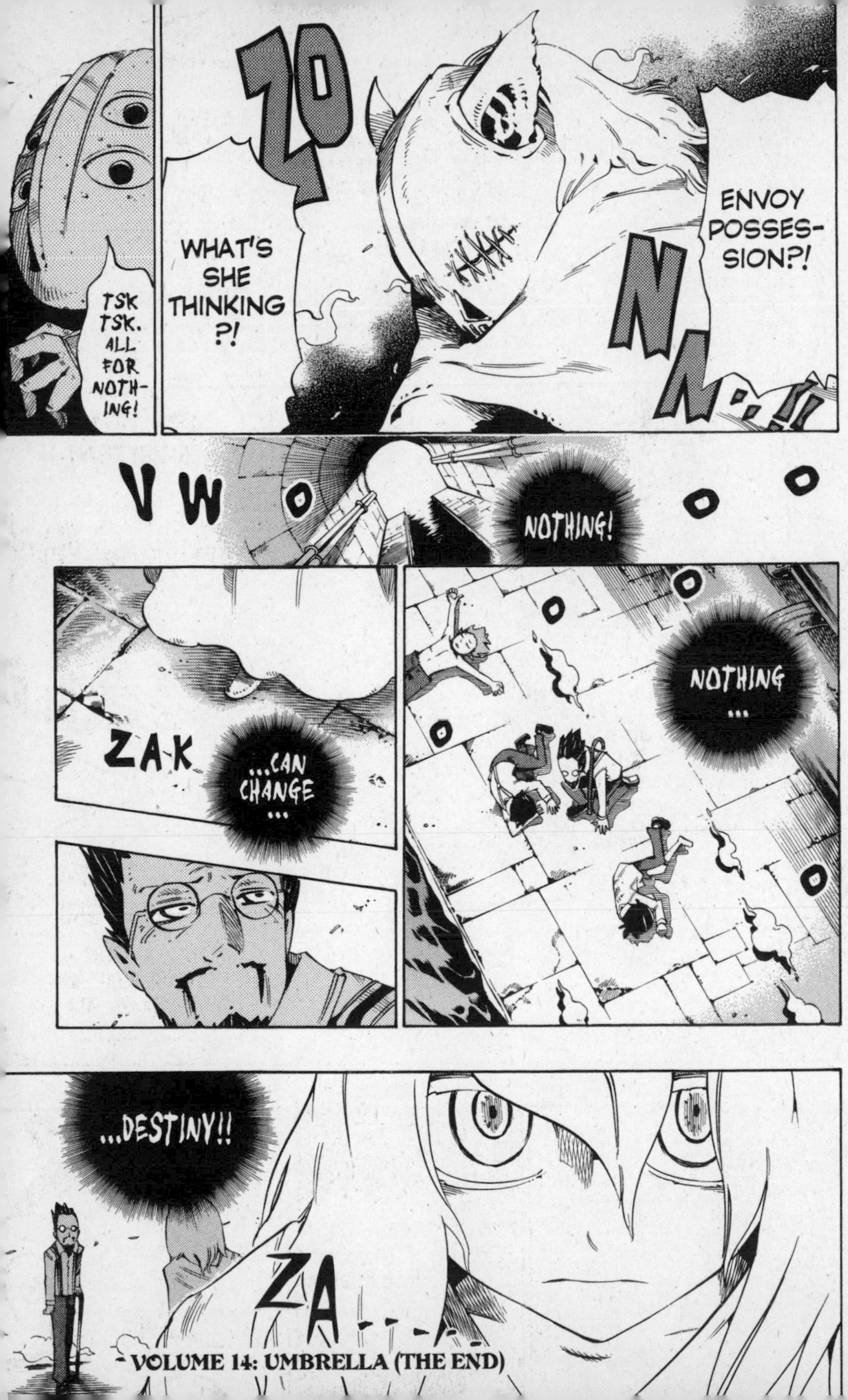
ENVOY POSSES-SION?!
ZO
NN...!!
WHAT'S SHE THINKING ?!
TSK TSK. ALL FOR NOTH-ING!
VWOOOO
NOTHING!
NOTHING ...
ZAK
...CAN CHANGE ...
...DESTINY!!
ZA...
- VOLUME 14: UMBRELLA (THE END)

In The Next Volume...

Page goes up against Enchu... so it's a good thing he's got some help!

Available February 2010!

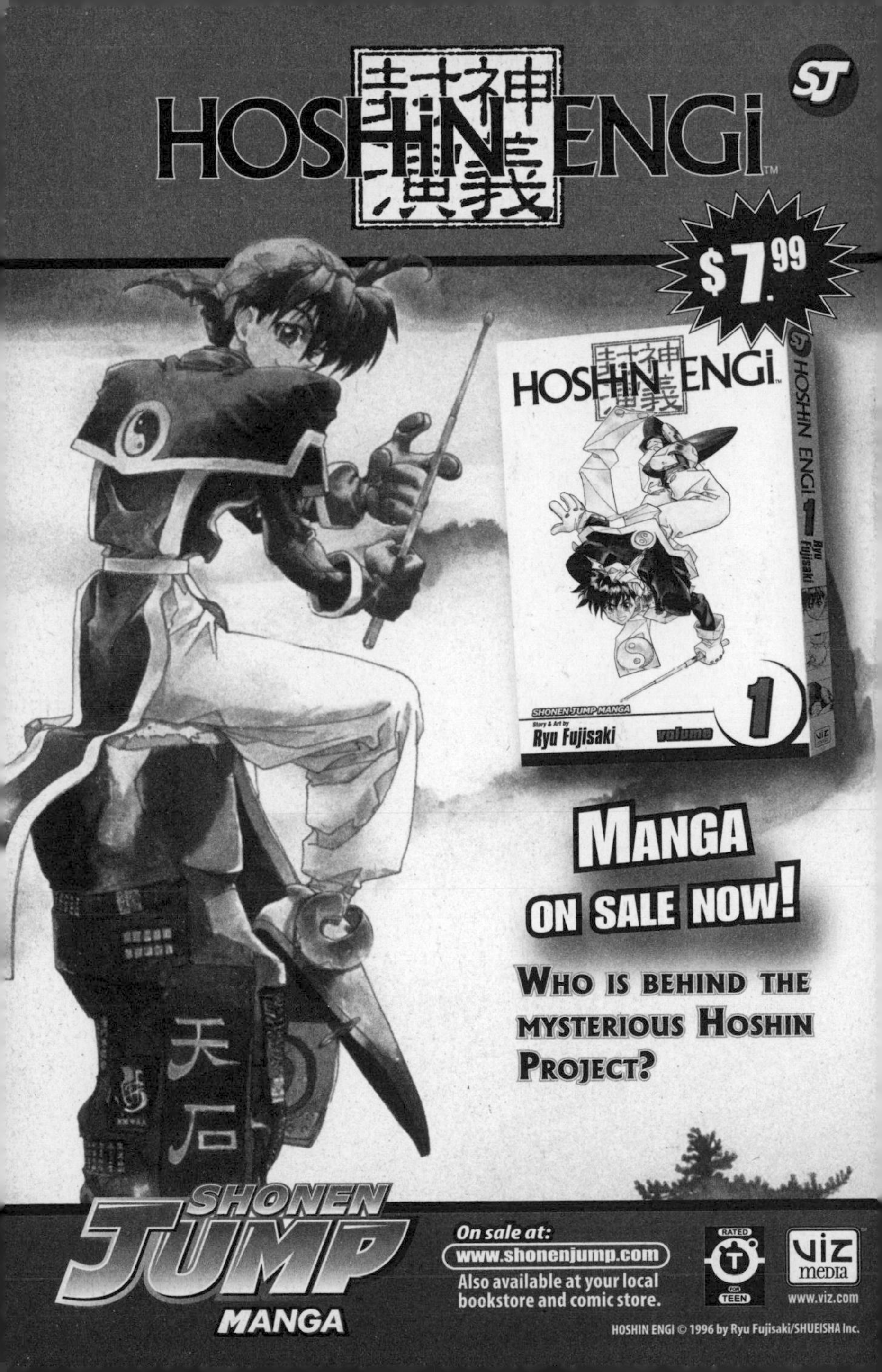

HOSHIN ENGI
封神演義
$7.99
HOSHIN ENGI
SHONEN JUMP MANGA
Story & Art by Ryu Fujisaki
volume 1
MANGA ON SALE NOW!
WHO IS BEHIND THE MYSTERIOUS HOSHIN PROJECT?
SHONEN JUMP MANGA
On sale at:
www.shonenjump.com
Also available at your local bookstore and comic store.
RATED T FOR TEEN
VIZ media
www.viz.com
HOSHIN ENGI © 1996 by Ryu Fujisaki/SHUEISHA Inc.

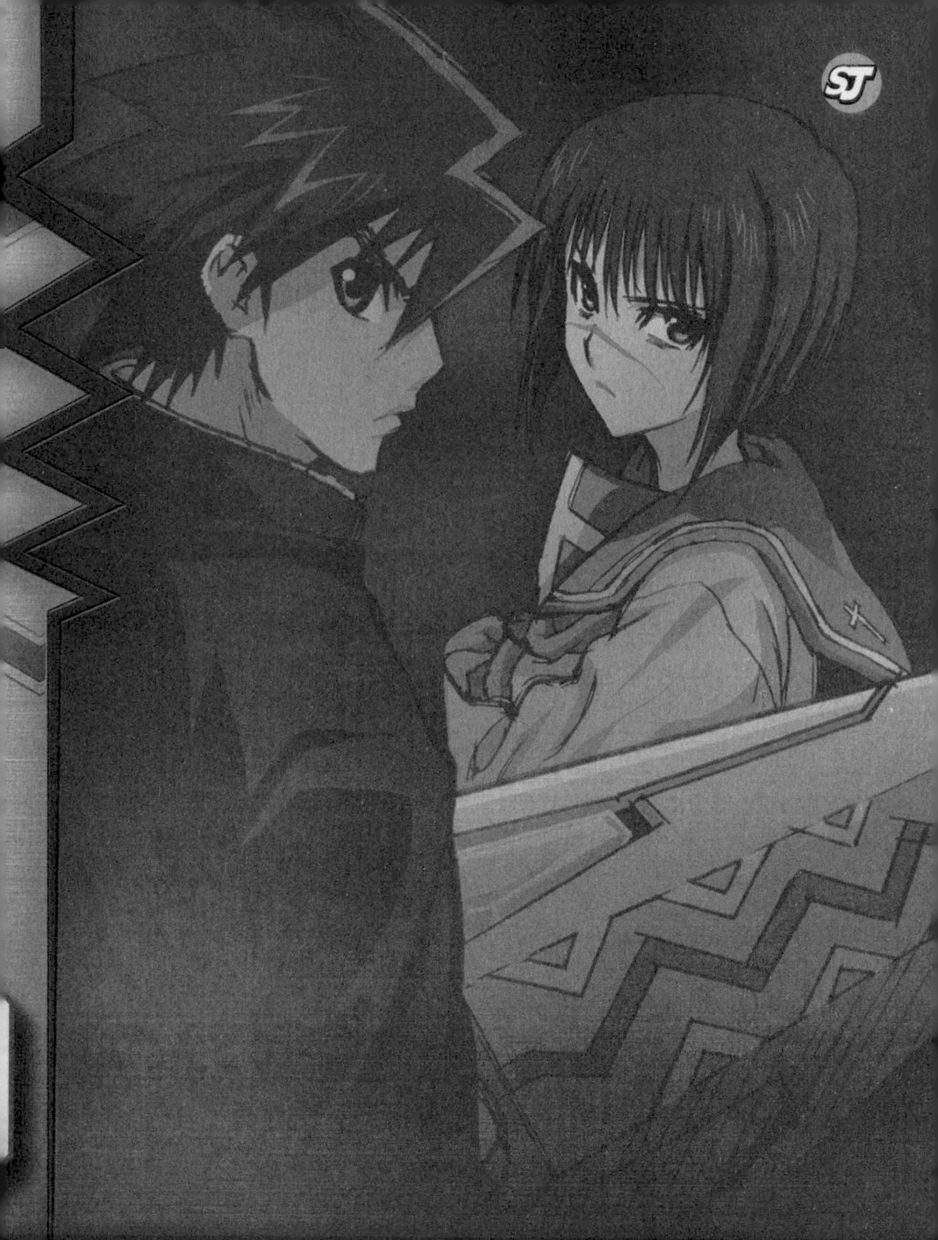

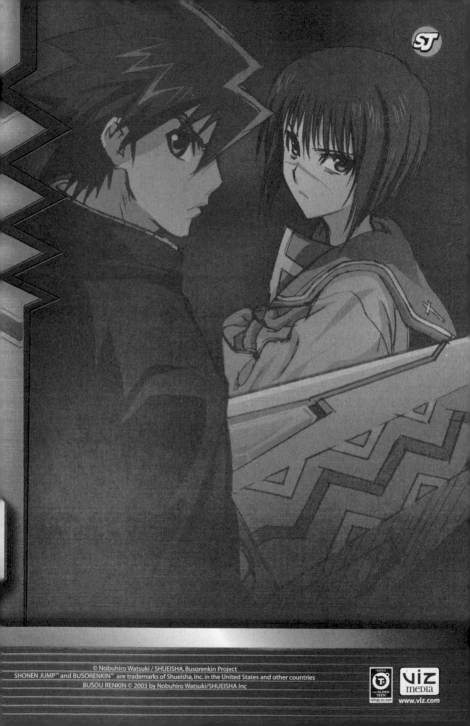

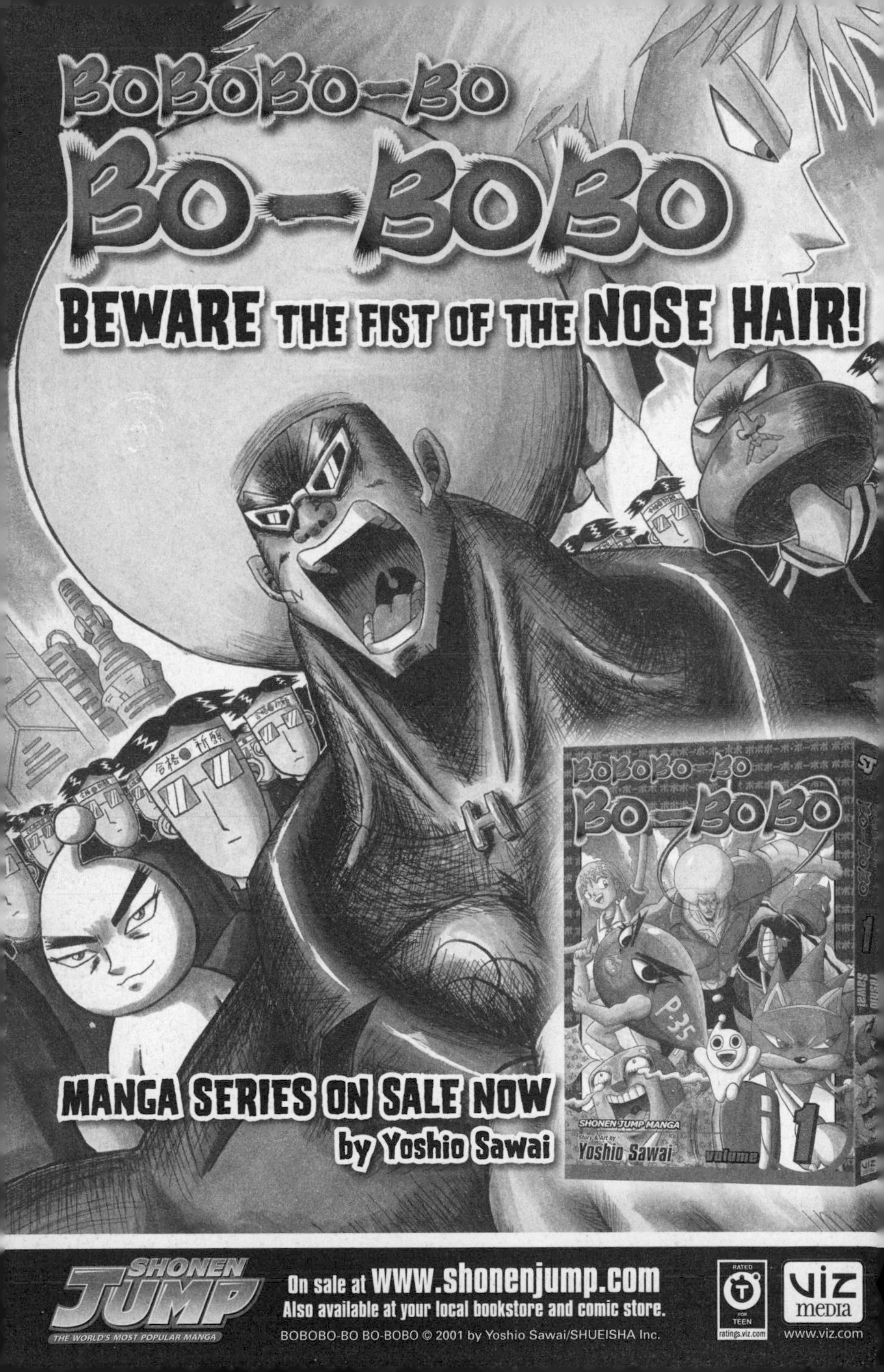
BOBOBO-BO
BO-BOBO
BEWARE THE FIST OF THE NOSE HAIR!
MANGA SERIES ON SALE NOW
by Yoshio Sawai
BOBOBO-BO BO-BOBO
SHONEN JUMP MANGA
Story & Art by Yoshio Sawai
volume 1
SHONEN JUMP
THE WORLD'S MOST POPULAR MANGA
On sale at www.shonenjump.com
Also available at your local bookstore and comic store.
BOBOBO-BO BO-BOBO © 2001 by Yoshio Sawai/SHUEISHA Inc.
RATED T FOR TEEN
ratings.viz.com
viz media
www.viz.com

Tell us what you think about SHONEN JUMP manga!

Our survey is now available online.
Go to: *www.SHONENJUMP.com/mangasurvey*

Help us make our product offering better!

THE REAL ACTION
STARTS IN...

www.shonenjump.com

HRYA

SAVE 50% OFF
THE COVER PRICE!

IT'S LIKE GETTING 6 ISSUES
FREE!

OVER 350+ PAGES PER ISSUE

THE WORLD'S MOST POPULAR MANGA

This monthly magazine contains 7 of the coolest manga available in the U.S., PLUS anime news, and info about video & card games, toys AND more!

❏ **I want 12 HUGE issues of SHONEN JUMP for only $29.95*!**

NAME

ADDRESS

CITY/STATE/ZIP

EMAIL ADDRESS   **DATE OF BIRTH**

❏ YES, send me via email information, advertising, offers, and promotions related to VIZ Media, SHONEN JUMP, and/or their business partners.

❏ **CHECK ENCLOSED** (payable to SHONEN JUMP)   ❏ **BILL ME LATER**

CREDIT CARD: ❏ **Visa** ❏ **Mastercard**

ACCOUNT NUMBER   **EXP. DATE**

SIGNATURE

CLIP&MAIL TO:
SHONEN JUMP Subscriptions Service Dept.
P.O. Box 515
Mount Morris, IL 61054-0515

P9GNC1

* Canada price: $41.95 USD, including GST, HST, and QST. US/CAN orders only. Allow 6-8 weeks for delivery.
ONE PIECE © 1997 by Eiichiro Oda/SHUEISHA Inc. BLEACH © 2001 by Tite Kubo/SHUEISHA Inc.
NARUTO © 1999 by Masashi Kishimoto/SHUEISHA Inc.

RATED
FOR
TEEN
ratings.viz.com

VIZ
MEDIA
www.viz.com